Labour Markets, Institutions and Inequality

Labour Markets, Institutions and Inequality

Building Just Societies in the 21st Century

Edited by

Janine Berg

International Labour Office, Geneva, Switzerland

Edward Elgar
PUBLISHING

Cheltenham, UK • Northampton, MA, USA

International Labour Office

Geneva, Switzerland

Published by
Edward Elgar Publishing Limited
The Lypiatts
15 Lansdown Road
Cheltenham
Glos GL50 2JA
UK

Edward Elgar Publishing, Inc.
William Pratt House
9 Dewey Court
Northampton
Massachusetts 01060
USA

In association with:

International Labour Office
4 route des Morillons
CH-1211 Geneva 22
Switzerland
ISBN 978-92-2-128657-8 (paperback)

A catalogue record for this book
is available from the British Library

Library of Congress Control Number: 2014950918

This book is available electronically in the **Elgar**online
Economics subject collection
DOI 10.4337/9781784712105

ISBN 978 1 78471 209 9 (cased)
ISBN 978 1 78471 210 5 (eBook)

MIX
Paper from
responsible sources
FSC
www.fsc.org
FSC® C013056

Typeset by Servis Filmsetting Ltd, Stockport, Cheshire
Printed and bound in Great Britain by T.J. International Ltd, Padstow

Contents

PART III SOCIAL TRANSFERS AND INCOME REDISTRIBUTION

PART IV THE IMPACT OF LABOUR MARKET INSTITUTIONS ON DIFFERENT GROUPS

Contributors

Christina Behrendt is Senior Social Protection Policy Specialist in the Social Protection Department of the International Labour Office in Geneva. She holds a Master's degree in Politics and Public Administration and a PhD in Social Policy from the University of Konstanz, Germany.

Patrick Belser is Senior Economist with the Inclusive Labour Markets, Labour Relations and Working Conditions Branch of the International Labour Office in Geneva. He holds a PhD in Economics from the Institute of Development Studies at the University of Sussex, UK.

Janine Berg is Senior Economist in the Inclusive Labour Markets, Labour Relations and Working Conditions Branch of the International Labour Office in Geneva. She received her PhD in Economics from the New School for Social Research, USA.

Sandrine Cazes is a Senior Economist at the Organisation for Economic Co-operation and Development and was previously Head of the Employment Analysis and Research Unit at the International Labour Office in Geneva.

Juliana Martínez Franzoni is Associate Professor in the Institute of Social Research and the Center of Research and Political Studies at the University of Costa Rica, Costa Rica.

Sarah Gammage is an Economist and Policy Advisor on Economic Institutions working with UN WOMEN. She previously worked at the ILO Office for the Southern Cone Region in Santiago as a specialist in social protection and development.

Megan Gerecke is a Technical Officer with the Social Determinants of Health unit of the World Health Organization in Geneva. Prior to joining the WHO, she worked as a research officer with the ILO, the UN Research Institute for Social Development and the McGill Institute for Health and Social Policy. She received her Master's in Political Science from McGill University, Canada.

Damian Grimshaw is Professor of Employment Studies at the University of Manchester, UK and Director of the European Work and Employment Research Centre (EWERC).

Susan Hayter is Senior Industrial Relations and Collective Bargaining Specialist with the Inclusive Labour Markets, Labour Relations and Working Conditions Branch of the International Labour Office in Geneva.

Martina Hengge is currently studying International Economics at the Graduate Institute of International and Development Studies, Geneva. She previously worked on macroeconomic and labour market policies for the Country Employment Policy Unit at the International Labour Office in Geneva.

Iyanatul ('Yan') Islam received a PhD in Economics from the University of Cambridge, UK. He is Chief of the Employment and Labour Markets Branch of the International Labour Office in Geneva.

Christiane Kuptsch works as a Senior Specialist in Migration Policy at the International Labour Office in Geneva. She is a political scientist specializing in International Relations (Graduate Institute of International and Development Studies, Geneva), and has a background in law (University of Hamburg, Germany).

Juan Ramón de Laiglesia is an Economist in the Multi-dimensional Country Reviews Unit of the OECD Development Centre. He previously worked in the Inclusive Labour Markets, Labour Relations and Working Conditions Branch of the International Labour Office in Geneva. He is an Engineer of the Ecole Polytechnique and holds a PhD and an MSc in Economics from the London School of Economics, UK.

Sangheon Lee is the Special Advisor to the Deputy Director-General for Policy of the International Labour Office in Geneva. He received his PhD in Economics from the University of Cambridge, UK.

Malte Luebker is Senior Wage Specialist at the ILO Regional Office for Asia and the Pacific in Bangkok. Prior to joining the ILO, he was a lecturer in Political Science at the Martin Luther University Halle-Wittenberg, Germany.

Jon C. Messenger is Senior Research Officer with the Inclusive Labour Markets, Labour Relations and Working Conditions Branch at the International Labour Office in Geneva.

Uma Rani is a Senior Development Economist with the Research Department of the International Labour Office in Geneva and an IZA (Institut zur Zukunft der Arbeit) Policy Fellow.

Nikhil Ray is a Project Officer with the Inter-Parliamentary Union in Geneva. He holds an MA in Economics and Finance from the University of St. Gallen, Switzerland.

Gerhard Reinecke is a Specialist for Employment Policy with the ILO Office for the Southern Cone Region in Santiago. He received his PhD in Political Science at the University of Hamburg, Germany.

Diego Sánchez-Ancochea is Associate Professor in the Political Economy of Latin America at the University of Oxford, UK and Governing Body Fellow of St Antony's College, University of Oxford.

John Woodall is a Fellow of the UK Institute of Actuaries. Before his retirement in 2013, he was Social Security Specialist with the ILO, first based in New Delhi and then in the Social Security (now Social Protection) Department in Geneva.

Foreword

The premise of this fine collection of essays has become unfashionable in recent decades. The rise of the neoliberal order, the Washington Consensus, 'there is no alternative' and *la pensée unique*, entailed a decline of professional interest, among economists, in social institutions and the structures of economic life.

As part of this, trade unions, wage norms, workplace standards and social insurance programs have come to be seen by many economists and political leaders as obstacles to rather than instruments of progress. We are told – even by the King of the Netherlands – that the 'welfare state has ended'. It is to be replaced by something called the 'participation society'. The irony of hearing this from the lips of a monarch, whose family activities cost the Dutch taxpayer some 100 000 000 euros per year, was perhaps not entirely lost on his subjects.[1]

Janine Berg and her colleagues at the International Labour Office present a different view. They argue that participation occurs through, and is mediated by, organizations, institutions and governments. Workers organize into unions to contest for rights in the workplace, for decent wages and social protections. Institutions consolidate gains, creating structures of precedent on which more gains can be based. In principle – if not always in practice – governments represent the expression of democratic will. Democratic politics and its consequence – the welfare state – are therefore the essence of participation and not some contradiction to it.

Moreover, though battered, besieged and often declared dead, the welfare state survives. It survives because it has to. It survives because in the modern world the alternative is chaos. There is a libertarian fantasy that economies can be re-based on individual saving, self-reliance, de-unionization, privatized health, education and retirement, and deregulation and de-supervision of markets. It is a fantasy with powerful backing, to be sure, but lobbies cannot turn fantasies into functional economics.

In the modern world, private markets depend on the assurance of quality that only effective regulation and supervision can provide. Without that, they have a strong tendency to collapse; people will not patronize markets or industries that they cannot trust. In the modern world, private markets also depend on the purchasing power of their customers, stable and consistent through time, which only effective social insurance and good wages can assure. Without that, they have a strong tendency to decay. People will not spend if they have no incomes they can rely on.

There are strong efforts to destroy the welfare state, and they have taken their toll. We see the consequences in the ongoing dysfunction of American banks. We see it in the ongoing crisis of the European periphery – a crisis of insolvent governments, failing institutions and declining demand. We see the consequence of a failure to construct the welfare state in the first place in the social stresses of India, of rural China, and many other regions. On the other hand, we also see the benefits of building a welfare state, even at this late date, in the recent progress of Brazil, Argentina and Ecuador.

The purpose of this book is to survey the major labour market and social welfare institutions around the world. This volume therefore brings together papers on trade unions, wage standards, pension protections, fixed contracts and part-time work, redistribution and social insurance, and public goods. It concludes with consideration of the specific effects on women, migrants, and youth.

In my view and that of these scholars, the essence of economic development lies in the defense, consolidation, and gradual expansion of social institutions, of social norms and standards and of social insurance. As shown here, the extent of these institutions varies greatly across the world. And the variations coincide closely with the common distinction between developed and developing countries: the stronger the institutions, the higher the state of development. This is not accidental.

Good governance, social stabilization and economic justice are not luxuries that weigh down and impede the process of development. They are the essence of development itself. They are what distinguish the successful countries from everyone else. At some level, we all know this. This book provides the documentation required to carry the point.

For this reason, those who would replace the great economic institutions of the past century with fanciful phrases about 'self-reliance' and 'participation' are not in the vanguard of some new form of progress. They are merely the wrecking crew. Much will depend on whether they can be stopped. In this book, Janine Berg and her ILO colleagues make a valuable and timely contribution to that end – and therefore to the cause of economic justice.

James K. Galbraith
Lloyd M. Bentsen Jr. Chair in Government/Business Relations and Professor of Government
Lyndon B. Johnson School of Public Affairs
The University of Texas at Austin,
Austin, Texas, USA

NOTE

1. *The Independent* (17 September 2013), 'Dutch King Willem-Alexander declares the end of the welfare state', accessed 24 August 2014 at http://www.independent.co.uk/news/world/europe/dutch-king-willemalexander-declares-the-end-of-the-welfare-state-8822421.html.

Acknowledgements

This book is the outcome of an ILO research project on labour market institutions and inequality. I would like to thank the contributors of this volume, for taking the time out of their busy schedules to be part of the project, for the high quality of their work, and for their commitment to social justice. Many of them are my colleagues at the ILO; it is a pleasure and honour to work with them.

The initial drafts of the chapter were presented at a two-day technical workshop held in ILO headquarters in February 2013. I would like to thank the participants of the seminar, particularly Sukti Dasgupta, Marzia Fontana, Hansjörg Herr, Frank Hoffer, David Howell, Rolph van der Hoeven, David Kucera, Robert Kyloh, Massimiliano La Marca, Roxana Maurizio and Kirsten Sehnbruch, for providing helpful feedback and for contributing to an engaging and lively discussion.

I would like to thank Stephen Pursey, Director of the ILO Multilaterals Department, who gave me the time to work on the project and arranged financial resources to support it, as well as Philippe Marcadent, Director of the Inclusive Labour Markets, Labour Relations and Working Conditions (INWORK) branch of the ILO, for his support.

The completed manuscript benefitted from the detailed and extremely helpful comments of four anonymous reviewers. We hope that our revised drafts assuage any concerns they may have had.

Finally, I would like to thank ILO Publications, particularly Chris Edgar, for the helpful advice and support provided during the course of the project.

Janine Berg
International Labour Office
Geneva, Switzerland

1. Labour market institutions: the building blocks of just societies

Janine Berg*

1.1 INTRODUCTION

Equitable societies with large middle classes are not the natural outcome of market forces. Equity, rather, is created by society, by the institutions – the laws, policies and practices – that govern the society, its economy and, in particular, its labour market. Building just societies means designing institutions that support the creation of quality jobs with decent wages and working conditions, as well as enacting policies to support those who cannot work or who are unable to find work.

This book argues that the lack of, or erosion of certain institutions that govern the labour market has contributed to rising inequality in many countries across the world, jeopardizing individual as well as societal well-being. Thus, if a country wants to improve equity it will need to strengthen its labour market institutions. The book employs a broad definition of labour market institutions that includes the more familiar institutions that regulate the workplace – collective bargaining, minimum wages, the type of employment contract, and working time regulations – as well as those institutions that redistribute income, including pensions, income support for the unemployed and the poor, as well as public social services. Because work is by far the most important source of household income among non-retired households, the book also considers full employment policies in its analysis. A commitment to full employment implies not treating employment as a residual outcome of economic growth, but designing and implementing policies that make job creation an explicit goal.

As the book is concerned with overall equity in a society, it considers not just wage and income inequality, but also inequality between groups. When labour markets are well regulated, when there are encompassing welfare states and when public social services are offered broadly to the population, there is greater equality between groups – as well as greater overall equality in wage and household income. Thus, achieving inclusiveness and equity requires constructing institutions that support people both in and out of the labour market. Too often, debates on labour market institutions have pitted workers against each other – as the privileges of 'insiders' gained at the expense of the 'outsiders' – resulting in calls to deregulate the labour market in the false hope of achieving greater equity. But the dismantling of labour protections and the retrenchment of social policies only leads to greater inequality, in society as a whole and between groups.

Institutions do not work independently, but are part of overarching systems that govern the labour market and the economy. Thus, in societies where wages are decent and more equitable, there is less need for redistribution through taxes and transfers. Moreover, social policies are not ex post interventions, but are part of these larger systems as they can influence access to the labour market as well as wage levels. For this reason, the policy focus on 'equality of opportunity' risks being short-sighted, unless there are policies that are also directed at 'equality of outcomes'. Indeed, where income is distributed more evenly, there is greater intergenerational mobility (Corak, 2013; Piketty, 2014). As the former Finnish president and 2008 Nobel Peace Prize laureate, Martti Ahtisaari, quipped, 'to live the American dream, you have to go to Sweden' (*Le Temps*, 2013).

Since its founding in 1919, the International Labour Organization (ILO) has sought to help its member States build just societies by adopting conventions and recommendations that govern the labour market. These international labour standards help shape national labour laws and policies and provide guidance on improving labour market governance. They address issues of employment, working conditions and social policies, but also freedom of association and collective bargaining, tripartite consultation and labour inspection. For this reason, many of the chapters in the book relate the policies discussed to the relevant international standards.

This introductory chapter sets forth the rationale for a new policy effort based on labour market institutions that can help build (or re-build) equitable societies. The rest of the book is divided into four parts. Part I on macroeconomic policies, development and inequality begins with an analysis of the relationship between economic development and income inequality and the role of political forces in shaping the distribution of income. This is followed by a chapter on the need for macroeconomic policies to promote full employment. Part II addresses some of the labour market institutions that affect income from work, including chapters on unions and collective bargaining, minimum wages, and the regulation of employment contracts (temporary and part-time work). Part III analyses social transfers and income redistribution and their contribution to fostering greater equality, including the design of tax and transfer policies, pensions, income support for the unemployed and the poor and public social services. Part IV addresses how labour market institutions affect the inequality of women, migrants and youth.

1.2 IN MOST REGIONS OF THE WORLD INEQUALITY HAS BEEN INCREASING

Since the 1980s, there has been an increase in income inequality in most regions of the world, including most industrialized as well as many developing countries. The growing income gaps have affected both the functional distribution – the distribution of the national income between profits and wages – as well as the personal income distribution, which is the distribution of income among households or individuals. Personal income distribution includes income from work (including self-employment), from investments, but also from private and public transfers, including remittances, as well as social security and social assistance transfers.

Most discussions of increased income inequality have been divorced from trends in the labour share, reflecting a bias in the economics professions towards the study of individual labour market earnings. This bias is due, in part, to the influence of human capital theory, which emphasizes how a person's education, experience and characteristics affect their earnings, but also as a result of the widespread availability of micro-datasets that have allowed researchers to estimate these returns, disassociated from larger movements in the macroeconomy. But workers' well-being is dictated by their relative gains from national economic growth, or how the growth in output is shared between capital and labour. When overall productivity growth surpasses total wage growth, then labour shares fall (and vice versa). Falling wage shares translate into the personal distribution as stagnant or slow average wage growth. And, to the extent that highly skilled workers command earnings that are tied to profits or are more favoured relative to low-skilled workers, then there will be divergences in the personal income distribution.

In the decades following World War II, both capital and labour benefitted from the rise in national income, and in some instances, labour's share increased in proportion as employment growth and wage gains led to rising wage shares in many countries. But beginning in the 1980s, in many countries of the world, the trend reversed and the share of national income accruing to capital began to widen, with profits commanding a greater share. Numerous reports from international organizations (IMF, 2007; ILO, 2008, 2010; IILS, 2011; OECD, 2011; UNCTAD, 2012) have documented this divergence for industrialized countries and some developing countries. The ILO (2013a) found, for example, that the labour share declined from 75 per cent of national income in the mid-1970s to 65 per cent in the years before the financial crisis for 16 advanced economies, calculated as a simple average. For developing countries, the picture has been more mixed. In Asia, the wage share declined by roughly 20 percentage points between 1994 and 2007; in China, between 2000 and 2007 the wage share fell by 10 percentage points, despite significant average wage increases (IILS, 2011). In Brazil, labour's share in the national income dropped by five percentage points during the difficult decade of the 1990s, but then recovered in the 2000s (IPEA, 2010).

The growing divide between profit shares and wage shares has, in many countries, been driven by a disconnect between productivity growth and wage growth. Between 1999 and 2011, average labour productivity growth outpaced average wage growth by a two-to-one ratio in 36 developed countries for which there were data (ILO, 2013a). But these trends have not been uniform across workers. Workers in less-skilled and semi-skilled occupations have had little, if any, real wage growth, whereas the wages of highly skilled workers and particularly those whose earnings are in the top 1 per cent of the income distribution have gained the most (ILO/IILS, 2011). Moreover, the concentration of wealth among the top 1 per cent of the income distribution has intensified in many industrialized countries, and will likely continue to do so unless significant reforms are implemented (Piketty, 2014). The trends in income concentration have been coupled with a retrenchment of the welfare state in many advanced economies. According to the OECD (2011), of 27 countries for which it has data, the growth of incomes in the bottom decile exceeded that of the national average in only eight countries[1] between the mid-1980s and the late 2000s, whereas the growth in incomes of the top decile exceeded the national average in 18 countries.

Figure 1.1 is a map of changes in household income inequality between the early 1990s and late 2000s.[2] In most industrialized countries – Canada, the United States, most of Europe and Australia and New Zealand – inequality, as measured by the Gini coefficient, increased. Inequality also increased in Asia, including India and China, and parts of Africa, particularly Southern Africa. In Latin America, inequality increased slightly in a few countries in the region, but fell in most of the region. Inequality also fell in a handful of African countries. Nevertheless, Latin America remains the most unequal region of the world, slightly below Southern Africa.

The increase in inequality in developing countries has not always been a concern of policy-makers, many of whom have subscribed to the view that rising inequality is part of the development process. The structural transformation of shifting production and workers from low-productivity agriculture to high-productivity manufacturing was believed to go hand in hand with widening urban–rural wage differentials, which would only cease

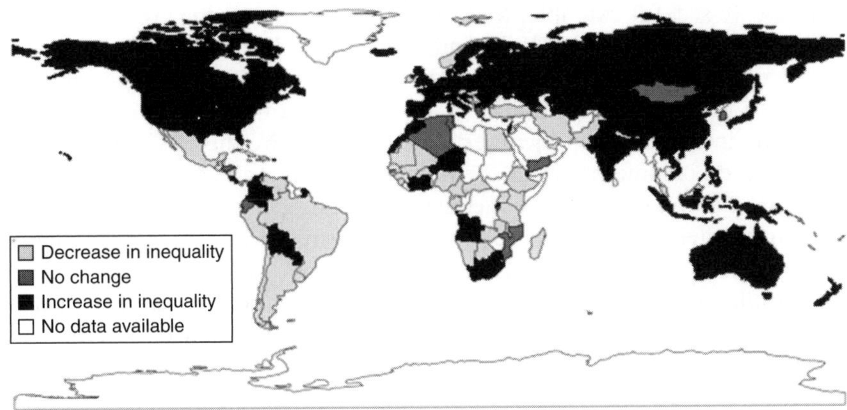

Notes:
The measure used is the comparison of Gini coefficients for the first year between 1990 and 1995 for which data is available and the last year between 2005 and 2010 for which data is available.
Due to data constraints for African countries, we employed a less strict definition and used data for the following countries and years: Burkina Faso: 1994 and 2003; Cameroon: 1990 and 2002; Central African Republic: 1992 and 2003; Gambia: 1992 and 2003; Ivory Coast: 1990 and 2002; Mauritania: 1990 and 2000; Mozambique: 1996 and 2005; Nigeria: 1990 and 2004; United Republic of Tanzania: 1990 and 2001.

Source: Standardized World Income Inequality Database (SWIID).

Figure 1.1 Changes in income inequality, early 1990s vs late 2000s

when the pool of surplus labour was exhausted and structural transformation completed (Lewis, 1954; Kuznets, 1955). The widening of inequality would be followed by a narrowing of the distribution as incomes reached a higher level, resulting in Kuznets's inverted-U curve. But as Sangheon Lee and Megan Gerecke (Chapter 2 of this volume) remind us, Kuznets 'never intended to offer an immutable law of inequality and development' (p. 41); nonetheless, the curve has been interpreted as a 'natural law' of inequality with little role given for policy interventions. Furthermore, as Lee and Gerecke point out, Kuznets argued that inequality would narrow as a result of growing political pressure from lower-income groups, facilitated by the spread of democracy. Thus, the distribution of income – whether it will narrow or continue to expand – is largely determined by political power and its influence on shaping distributive and redistributive policies (Chapter 2). Financialization, globalization and technological change have, however, eroded the bargaining power of the lower-income classes at the workplace as well as their ability to mobilize collectively for political change, affecting the distribution of income in many parts of the world.

Thus, we see, for example, that in the United States, the growth in real after-tax income between 1979 and 2007 was 278 per cent for the top 1 per cent of the income distribution, whereas for the bottom quintile it rose by a mere 18 per cent, and by just 35 per cent for the middle quintile.[3] The increase in top incomes was facilitated by the 1987 tax reform that lowered income tax rates for high earners as well as capital income, whereas the weakening of collective bargaining and low value of the minimum wage, along with the retrenchment in the welfare state, explain the stagnant income growth of the poorer classes.

Overall, income inequality has increased in Europe, though the experience among countries has been mixed as a result of country-specific tax policies, the extent that labour institutions support workers at the bottom of the income distribution, and the relative strength of the welfare state. Germany has seen an important rise in inequality, mainly due to a decline in earnings of those at the bottom of the wage distribution. There has been a divergence between productivity and wage growth, with labour productivity increasing by 23 per cent in the 1990s and 2000s, whereas real average monthly wage growth was flat, and even declined in the 2000s. The rise of 'mini-jobs' partly explains these trends, though on an hourly basis the same pattern holds (productivity growth of 12.8 per cent and wage growth of 0.4 per cent) (ILO, 2013a). In the Nordic countries, incomes of highly skilled workers have increased, but a strong welfare state has propped up incomes of the bottom deciles, thereby avoiding a polarization in incomes. In Sweden, however, inequality did increase – although it still remains low – as a result of widening gaps in market income and declines in redistribution. France had only a slight increase in inequality in the 2000s, which is attributable to the expansion of self-employment income (OECD, 2011). Wages of the lower-income groups continue to be supported by the minimum wage and extension mechanisms of collective bargaining.

Asia, which was known for its rapid growth with low levels of inequality during the 1980s and 1990s, has, in the first decades of the 21st century, given way to a pattern of exclusive growth. This is true of the more advanced economies of Japan and the Republic of Korea, where inequality has widened since the late 1990s, but is also the case with new giants such as China, Indonesia and India (ADB, 2012). Throughout the region, employment growth has been tepid and many of the jobs that have been created have been of poor quality. Informal self-employment has continued to expand and waged employment has been characterized by growing precarization and limited social protection coverage (ILO, 2010). Moreover, both China and India have witnessed speculative booms in real estate coupled with rising incomes in the banking, finance and information technology sectors (Galbraith, 2012). As a result, there has been both a decrease in the share of national income going to wages, as well as widening dispersion of income among workers.

Latin America, despite having the dubious distinction of being the most unequal region in the world, reduced inequality in the 2000s. The decline stems from a compression in wage earnings, with government transfers playing a supportive secondary role. The compression in incomes is partly due to an increase in education and the return to skills as López-Calva and Lustig (2010) suggest, but it is also the result of the creation of formal jobs – which shifted workers from the more unequal self-employment jobs to waged employment – as well as from a strengthening of labour market institutions, particularly increases in the real value of the minimum wage, but also a strengthening of collective bargaining, especially in Uruguay, Brazil and Argentina. Indeed, in Argentina, Brazil, Mexico and Uruguay, reduced inequality in labour incomes accounted for over 60 per cent of the fall in inequality, most of which occurred amongst registered wage earners (formal workers). Public cash transfers were important – particularly in Chile and Mexico where they contributed over 25 per cent to the reduction in inequality – but the main driver was the reduction in inequality in labour income. In Mexico, where informal employment is particularly large, most of the declines in inequality were amongst unregistered waged workers; self-employed earnings contributed to inequality (Keifman and Maurizio, 2012).

In Africa, the picture has been mixed. There are some countries, such as Ethiopia, with very low levels of recorded inequality, reflecting in part the low levels of income per capita, and other countries, such as South Africa, which boasts the highest income inequality in the world. South Africa had made some headway in lowering inequality at the end of the 1990s, but this was reversed in the 2000s as wage dispersion increased to the benefit of the largely white workers at the top of the wage distribution; wages at the bottom have been negatively affected by the rise of contract work. However, two cash transfer programmes have helped to alleviate poverty in the bottom deciles, which remain affected by high rates of unemployment (Bhorat et al., 2013). In Kenya, the relatively successful economic performance of the 2000s did not translate into labour force gains, as contract work and informal work proliferated, leading to a greater dispersion of income (Wambagu and Kabubo-Mariara, 2013).

Although the causes for rising income inequality differ among countries, the weakening of labour market institutions has played either a leading or supporting role in bringing about these trends in many parts of the world. In Latin America, these institutions figured prominently in helping to redress the large inequalities that exist in the region. Still, for the greater part of the last three decades, labour market institutions have come under attack, blamed for the less than stellar economic and labour market performance experienced in many parts of the world.

1.3 THE DEBATE ON LABOUR MARKET INSTITUTIONS

The weakening of labour market institutions in many parts of the industrialized and developing world over the past several decades is often attributed to globalization. The widespread integration of financial and goods markets that began in the 1980s, coupled with improvements in information technology, the rise of democratization, and overall improvements in literacy and education throughout many parts of the world, facilitated shifts in production to countries that had formerly been excluded from the world economy.

Although globalization has brought prosperity to some, there have been important political effects from greater economic integration that were largely unforeseen (Acemoglu and Robinson, 2013). One important effect was the widespread weakening of the political power of labour, as manifest in the decline of unionization rates in much of the industrialized world and some developing countries (Chapter 4). As Hayter explains in Chapter 4, labour's weakened ability to act as a 'countervailing force' meant that in some countries, reforms were instituted that negatively affected workers, including trade reforms, financial deregulation, orthodox monetary policies[4] and the scaling back of the welfare state. Moreover, even where labour's voice in national affairs remained strong, because capital became global but the scope of policy intervention remained national, many countries had difficulty in responding to the challenges brought about by globalization.

In developing countries, globalization did sometimes lead to the creation of new jobs in employment-intensive export industries, but governments often held down wages and repressed unions, out of concern that wage increases would lessen their countries' competitive edge. Moreover, in countries where the economic reforms had less than satisfactory results with regard to economic performance and employment, 'rigid' labour markets were blamed for impeding the potential of globalization. In industrialized countries, the debate on labour market flexibility came to the fore with publication of the 1994 OECD *Jobs Strategy*, which argued that the lower unemployment rates of the United States of the early 1990 were due to its more flexible labour market. Thus, if Europe wanted to lower its unemployment rates it would need to flexibilize its labour market, particularly its employment protection laws, restrictions on working time, wage policies and unemployment benefit systems. It was argued that wages needed to respond to signals in the market, thus decentralized collective bargaining was preferred, or in its absence, a system that allowed opt-out clauses at the firm level. Minimum wages were discouraged and the report suggested that countries should ease restrictions on dismissal and permit the use of fixed-term contracts (OECD, 1994).

In developing countries, a similar viewpoint was espoused.[5] Here again many of the same institutions attacked in the OECD *Jobs Strategy* became targets for labour reforms in developing countries.[6] Furthermore, labour market reforms were often included as part of conditions on loan agreements, such that, even in countries where reforms were not supported or deemed necessary by the government, the countries were urged to implement them in order to receive bail-outs.[7] This occurred in the Asian crisis of the late 1990s, and is occurring in the 2010s in Southern Europe under the troika (comprising the European Central Bank, European Commission and International Monetary Fund).

Perhaps the most emblematic of efforts to deregulate labour markets was the World Bank's 'Doing Business' indicators. Launched in 2002, the index ranks countries according to their 'ease of doing business', and includes a sub-index on labour laws, known as the 'Employing Workers' index. The Employing Workers index assessed the degree of regulation in labour markets in the areas of working time, minimum wages, dismissal protection, severance pay and non-wage labour costs, based on a benchmark of no regulation and zero cost. As a result, countries with more regulated labour markets were ranked lower in the index.

Support for the deregulatory stance of the multilateral organizations came largely from economic theory, as empirical evidence on the effect of institutions was mixed (Nickell and Layard, 1999). Under the standard (neoclassical) economic model of labour markets, wages are determined by the intersection of demand and supply in the labour market; the labour market clears – meaning that there is full employment – as long as there are no impediments. As a result, unemployment is viewed as a problem of the labour market, rather than as a problem of insufficient aggregate demand. Policy-makers, unfortunately, came to depend on the predictions of this simplistic model, ignoring its numerous critiques.[8]

In the 2000s, there seemed to be some recognition that the push to deregulate labour markets had gone too far. In 2006, the OECD published a reassessment of the *Jobs Strategy*, which, although nuanced, gave greater scope to minimum wages, softened the position on employment protection legislation, and recognized the positive economic and employment performance of economies with centralized collective bargaining (OECD, 2006; Watt, 2006). In 2011, the World Bank revised its

Employing Workers index based on criticisms from trade unions, the ILO and some governments, and dropped the score of this index from the calculation of overall country rankings under the Doing Business indicators.[9] While there was political pressure against the calls for labour market deregulation, a prime motivation was the new empirical evidence, discussed in Part II of this volume, which showed that minimum wages were not detrimental to employment creation, that more flexible employment protection legislation had resulted in more segmented labour markets, and that encompassing collective bargaining systems delivered beneficial outcomes to workers, firms and economies. This debate was also addressed in the 2013 *World Development Report: Jobs*, in which the World Bank concluded that 'the impact of labour policies and regulations on the labour markets of developing countries was modest' and 'certainly more modest than the intensity of the debate would suggest' (World Bank, 2012, p. 26).

1.4 THE WORKINGS OF LABOUR MARKET INSTITUTIONS

An underlying thesis of this book is that labour market institutions do not work independently but have important interaction effects. Thus, when designing policies it is important to not only understand that there may be secondary effects from the policies, but also to consider how to take advantage of these secondary effects in policy design. These effects may be economic, but they can also be social or political, by changing the balance of power in society, thus affecting future policy design (see Acemoglu and Robinson, 2013). Tinbergen (1967) famously argued that we need as many instruments as targets in order to reach a policy goal. But just as we are better off having more tools than goals, we also should not expect so much from just one tool. Too often policies are criticized for failing to reach goals that were never prescribed to them in the first place. Some examples include unemployment insurance, which is criticized for not covering the poor when its intention is to smooth the income of displaced workers during labour market transitions. If it fails to help the poorest in society, the policy response should be to enact policies that help the poor, not destroy unemployment insurance.

Similar arguments can be made regarding the minimum wage. In the USA, as elsewhere, the minimum wage is criticized for not 'lifting families out of poverty' when its stated objective under the US Fair Labor Standards Act (1938) was to prevent and eliminate low labour standards that harm workers and undermine fair competition (Kaufman, 2010). We should therefore assess its effectiveness on these grounds. In other cases, the minimum wage is over-used, often to compensate for underdeveloped collective bargaining and industrial relations' systems.[10] Examples include the Dominican Republic, which has minimum wages by sector, occupational category, and in some cases for the task at hand – for example, there are varying wages for construction workers who install beams of different sizes or operate machinery with greater horsepower. This complex and fragmented system hinders compliance by making it more difficult for workers and employers to know the correct wage, and also makes monitoring more difficult (OIT, 2013a). Countries with weak or non-existent collective bargaining also run the risk of setting their minimum wage too high, at a level that benefits the average worker, rather than as a floor to prevent low standards. Too high a minimum wage can result in non-compliance, as well as weaken the productivity–pay link (Lee and Gerecke, 2013; Rani et al., 2013).

Labour Institutions and the Production Process

Labour market institutions can affect firms' decisions on how (or where) to structure production, including how much to invest in training or technological upgrading. In their seminal study, *Industrial Democracy*, Webb and Webb (1902) argued that wage floors were an effective policy for preventing what they termed 'parasitic' industries, or industries that paid wages that were insufficient to cover the social costs of the worker. Similar arguments were advanced in the 1950s by the Swedish trade union economists Rudolf Meidner and Gösta Rehn who argued about the importance of collective bargaining and minimum wages for putting 'technological laggards' out of business, coupled with policies to boost investment and aggregate demand (Galbraith, 2012).

Piore (2004) explains how many of the first labour standards in the USA were directed against the sweatshop production model and industrial homework. As he explains, under a piece-rate system, employers have little incentive to invest in technological or organizational improvements, or worker health and safety, since it is the workers' earnings that fall if they are less productive. But state regulation of working conditions, including health and safety laws, minimum age requirements, minimum wages, and employment protection, altered the incentives of employers.[11] By mandating health and safety and requiring that a minimum wage be paid, employers had no choice but to upgrade production processes and make technological improvements, contributing to the decline of sweatshops in the USA in the first part of the 20th century. Yet under the current model of globalization, with the ease and low cost of communication and shipping, sweatshops have re-emerged as businesses in many industrialized countries have subcontracted their manufacturing to countries with weak and unenforced standards on health and safety, wages and working time, as well as constraints on freedom of association and collective bargaining rights. The April 2013 collapse of the Rana Plaza Building in Bangladesh, which left over 1200 garment workers dead in one of the deadliest industrial accidents of all time, is a grim and shocking reminder of the need for regulating working conditions.

Labour Institutions and Workers' Access to the Labour Market

Institutions also affect workers' access to the labour market, influencing their decision to participate in or withdraw from the labour market, as well as affecting the types of jobs they pursue. Several chapters in this volume address this theme. One emblematic example concerns the provision – or lack of provision – of care services, which can determine women's ability to enter or remain in the labour market, with consequences for both gender and income inequality. As discussed in Chapters 11 and 12, most women shoulder the primary burden of care responsibilities. If care services are not provided publicly, then women either outsource these services if they can afford to do so, or withdraw from the labour market. Alternatively, they choose professions that allow them to balance their work and family responsibilities, or work in part-time and informal employment, often with marked differences in wages, hours and access to benefits (see Chapter 7 on part-time work).

Reconciling care responsibilities with work is most difficult for lower-income women. Women from higher-income quintiles have the financial means to outsource or 'commodify' care responsibilities, thus perpetuating inequality between groups. Among women with children under six years of age in Latin America, the labour force participation rates of women from the poorest quintile are just 40 per cent compared with 70 per cent for the richest (Chapter 11). Moreover, those of the poorest income quintile who do work may either be exacerbating 'time poverty' or redistributing responsibilities to other, typically female, household members. This finding is substantiated by the higher share of young female NEETs (not in education, employment or training) from lower-income families, as demonstrated in Chapter 14 on youth.

In other cases, labour institutions, particularly social policies, can be an effective means for reducing labour supply. Increased access to secondary and tertiary education can help postpone youth entry into the labour market, allowing young people to further their education and training, thereby boosting their human capital formation and relieving pressure on the labour market. The availability of social protection, especially old-age pensions, affects the labour supply decisions of the elderly. Chapter 9 documents the significant negative relationship between coverage and benefit levels of pensions and the labour force participation of the elderly. Social assistance programmes, by raising family incomes, can also mitigate desperation and thus the likelihood of falling victim to forced labour or other forms of exploitative work. In Brazil, the decline in forced labour in the country has been partly attributed to the conditional-cash-transfer programme, Bolsa Família (OIT, 2013b).

Labour Institutions and Wage Determination

The relationship between earnings on the job and institutions that regulate the labour market such as collective bargaining, minimum wages and contract type is relatively straightforward, but earnings are also mediated by the existing social policies of a country. As Figure 1.2 illustrates, a household's income is not just the sum of market income plus transfers – transfers can influence wage-setting.

A good example is employment guarantee programmes (also known as employer-of-last-resort programmes). Since India instituted the Mahatma Gandhi National Rural Employment Guarantee Scheme in 2005, which entitles rural households to 100 days of employment per year, paid at the state-level minimum wage, compliance with the minimum wage has improved. Between 2004/05 and 2009/10, the number of waged workers earning less than the minimum fell from 73 million to 62 million. In the state of Maharashtra, which has had an employment guarantee programme since the 1970s, the proportion of workers paid below the

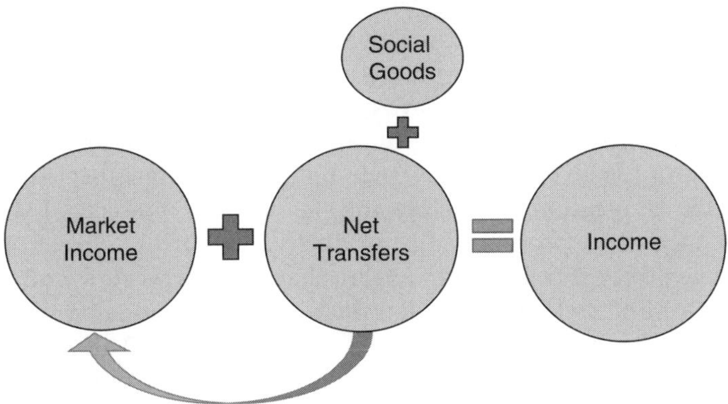

Source: Author's elaboration.

Figure 1.2 Net transfers and social goods affect market income

state-level minimum wage was much lower than the levels recorded for other states in India (Belser and Rani, Chapter 5 of this volume).

Unemployment insurance is another institution that can affect market earnings. One of the policy goals of unemployment insurance is to allow displaced workers sufficient time for job search, so that they can find a job that better matches their skills, thereby reducing the likelihood or degree of a wage reduction (Chapter 10). Other social policies, such as employment subsidies can have the opposite effect by lowering market wages. In times of economic crisis some countries respond to rising unemployment by offering employment subsidies to employers to encourage hiring. Although a reasonable policy during times of slack demand and falling profits, permanent employment subsidies, either paid directly to employers, or to workers in the form of in-work benefits, can provide incentives to employers to underpay their workers, thereby lowering market earnings.

Finally, a large determinant of wage setting is the relative tightness of the labour market. An explicit government commitment to full employment that relies on aggregate demand management to relieve slack in the labour market is likely to influence wages. Given the importance of the macroeconomic setting on workers' welfare, the next section discusses how full employment policies contribute to greater equity and thus of the need to direct macroeconomic policy towards this goal.

1.5 MACROECONOMIC POLICIES AND FULL EMPLOYMENT

The promotion of full, productive and freely chosen employment is a central tenet of the ILO, enshrined in its 1944 Declaration of Philadelphia, which states that nations should '[further] programmes to achieve full employment and [raise] standards of living'. Two decades later, the International Labour Conference approved the Employment Policy Convention, 1964 (No. 122), which obliged ILO member States that ratified the convention to 'declare and pursue, as a major goal, an active policy designed to promote full, productive and freely chosen employment'. The policy should aim to ensure that 'there is work for all who are available for and seeking work' that the work is 'as productive as possible' and that it is freely chosen. In 2008, Convention No. 122 along with three other conventions[12] were designated by the ILO's Governing Body as 'priority instruments', given their significance for labour market governance. By designating the convention as a priority instrument, the ILO sought to encourage ratification and thus, compliance, by its member states; by 2014, 108 of the ILO's 185 member States had ratified the convention.[13]

Full employment policies are cornerstones for ensuring equitable societies. Persons who are unable to find waged work or promising opportunities for self-employment will suffer want unless they have income from other sources, be it income-bearing assets, family or social networks, or transfers from the government. Yet even with private or public transfers, there is an income loss to the individual and the household, as well as a loss to society by not benefiting from that person's productive potential.

Moreover, the incidence of unemployment among workers differs, with less-educated, poorer workers having a greater probability of experiencing unemployment when compared with the well off and more highly educated workers. This is particularly true in industrialized countries, where unemployment rates are two to three times higher for lower-educated workers, but also higher for women and other minority groups. (In developing countries, it is the more educated who experience higher unemployment rates, as the less educated typically turn to self-employment in the informal economy, and thus do not show up in unemployment statistics.)[14] Thus, the policy to raise interest rates to contain inflation when unemployment drops below a certain level (the so-called NAIRU, non-accelerating inflation rate of unemployment), is particularly harmful to specific groups in the labour market. For this reason, policies directed at reducing unemployment are beneficial for reducing overall income inequality as well as inequality among groups. Indeed, in a recent analysis of 24 OECD countries, the OECD finds that a one percentage point increase in the share of employment reduces the overall Gini coefficient of the working-age population by 0.65 percentage points (OECD, 2011).

Unemployment, in addition to hurting individuals who cannot find work, can also have a dampening effect on the wages of those who remain employed, as both individual and collective bargaining positions are weakened. The extensive literature on the wage curve (Blanchflower and Oswald, 1995) documents the responsiveness of pay to shifts in the level of unemployment, with findings for most countries that a doubling of unemployment leads to a real wage drop of between 7 to 9 per cent. Figures vary slightly among countries depending on the strength of certain labour market institutions, particularly employment protection legislation. If a worker is not concerned about unemployment because there are employment protection laws that limit a firm's ability to dismiss a particular worker, then the worker will be in a better negotiating position and wage levels may not fall as sharply. Thus, the more flexible the labour market, the more susceptible is workers' pay to changes in the level of unemployment, potentially affecting the distribution of wages in an economy. The relationship between unemployment and falling wages is also due to the decline in hours that occurs during downturns in the business cycle. Thus, even if workers are able to retain their hourly wage rate, the reduction of hours worked during periods of lax demand can contribute to declining overall and average wages (Galbraith, 2012).

Unemployment can also be detrimental to the sustainability of welfare states. It is for this reason that countries that have pursued universal social policies, such as the Nordic countries, have made increasing employment rates, particularly among women, a cornerstone of their economic and social development strategies (Esping-Andersen, 1990). These countries recognize that unemployment puts pressure on the fiscal resources needed to sustain the programmes, but also on societies' willingness to support transfer policies. By assuming responsibility for the welfare of children and the elderly, the Scandinavian countries are able to encourage greater labour force participation of women who, less burdened by care responsibilities, can more easily enter the labour market.[15] Moreover, the many public services offered provide numerous decent employment opportunities, and the high quality of these services ensures support from society as a whole.

Instituting policies that allow people to work is one important piece of the puzzle, but these policies must also be complemented by policies to sustain and boost aggregate demand.[16] Achieving full employment requires supportive monetary and fiscal policies that can stabilize the business cycle and ensure productive investments that create jobs. In most countries in the world, there are fewer jobs than there are workers who would like, or who need, to work – full employment is not the natural outcome of market forces. But unfortunately, over the past several decades, job creation has fallen off the macroeconomic policy agenda. Price stability has been the sole policy goal of monetary policy, as attested to by the large number of central banks that have adopted inflation targeting as their sole mandate (Epstein, 2007). While controlling inflation is important, it should not come at the expense of unemployment and underemployment; rather it should be considered alongside policies to boost investment and job creation (Islam and Kucera, 2014).

In Chapter 3 of this volume, Islam and Hengge argue for the need to revive the 'full employment compact' that held sway during the golden age of capitalism. To do so, countries in the developed world will need macroeconomic policies that emphasize both price stability and an employment objective, whereas low- and middle-income country governments 'need to act as guardians of stability as well as agents of inclusive development' (p. 66). Achieving these objectives will require an array of both monetary and fiscal policies.

As the authors explain, too often interest rates have been set high to stave off inflation, and in the case of many developing countries, to attract foreign investment in order to roll over liabilities. As a result, credit for domestic investment is not only squeezed, but is also too expensive. It is thus not surprising that firms in low- and middle-income countries often report access to finance as a major constraint to their businesses (Islam and Hengge, Chapter 3). But these problems can be overcome by having central banks or national development banks use policy tools that promote lending to key economic sectors for employment creation and growth (Epstein, 2007).

Also important is the need to institute fiscal policies that boost aggregate demand, particularly during downturns, but which also provide funds for public investment in both physical and social infrastructure. Unfortunately, in many developing countries, tax-to-GDP ratios are low (in some cases around 10 per cent of GDP) limiting the ability of governments to invest in infrastructure that is fundamental for economic development, as well as important sources of employment creation (Chapter 3). Low tax revenues also limit the ability of governments to invest in public services, with implications for the quality of the labour force and workers' ability to access the labour market (Chapter 11), but also on the amount of redistribution that is possible (Chapter 8). Moreover, fiscal policy is not only limited in many developing countries (and some developed countries as well), but has tended to be pro-cyclical, augmenting boom-and-bust cycles and further harming the labour market.

Managing financial flows is also necessary for ensuring that finance is directed at productive investments, but also for avoiding financial crises, which plagued the developing world in the 1990s and ushered in the Great Recession in 2008. Indeed, a disturbing trend over the past several decades has been the growing 'financialization' of many economies. Epstein (2006) defines 'financialization' as the increasing importance of financial markets, financial motives and financial actors in the operations of the economy; Freeman (2011) refers to it as the '800-pound gorilla'. It is clear that in the case of the United States, the rise in finance – both in the power of its actors and in the importance of finance in the domestic economy – was the result of financial deregulation in the 1980s and 1990s that permitted the development of large and powerful financial institutions. The influence of these institutions, coupled with an ideological belief in efficient markets by economists and policy-makers alike, permitted the blocking of regulation of the derivatives market and the development of a shadow banking system, further increasing the size and the degree of pooled risk of the large financial institutions. The deregulatory stance was also a feature of the Federal Reserve, which lowered bank reserve requirements and refused to use regulatory tools such as stock margin requirements or credit controls to temper the growth of risky financial practices (Palley, 2012).

Financialization was also supported by the rise of 'shareholder capitalism', which shifted company strategies toward focusing on the value of their share price, in order to increase the market value of the firm and subordinate management exclusively to the interests of owners. Management came to be rewarded with share options and bonus payments based on profits, thereby fuelling a business model of short-run 'profits without investment' (Dullien et al., 2011). Flexibilization of labour practices, including outsourcing, helped to cut costs and boost profits, but weakened the employment relationship, ultimately hurting labour (Weil, 2014). These practices were not disconnected from developments in financial markets since the deregulatory reforms spawned a mutual fund industry that sought ever-increasing returns on its investments and pressured firms to pay dividends.

The result of these interconnected forces is manifest in the declining wage shares and the growth of the income of the top 1 per cent, as well as the growing divergence between labour productivity and wage growth, as discussed earlier in the chapter. These trends have had feedback effects on economic growth as falling labour shares negatively affect private consumption (ILO, 2013a).[17] The determination of wages goes beyond firm-level negotiations between a worker and his or her employer; macro- and mesoeconomic structures play a determining role. Moreover, both the personal and the functional distribution will determine the course of economic growth. Nevertheless, it is not possible to isolate specific causes for why wage shares have fallen in recent decades. This is probably because ultimately the causes are inter-related: financialization, globalization, technological change and the weakening of labour institutions have all played off one another, contributing to declining wage shares. And just as financialization has affected management practices that have weakened labour, what is needed are supportive labour institutions that can allow labour to be a countervailing force (Freeman, 2011).

1.6 INCOME FROM WORK

An individual's well-being is, for the most part, dependent on the income that the individual and the individual's family earns from work. As discussed earlier in the chapter, the labour market and how workers fare from the market is not simply the result of market forces, but depends on the myriad of institutions that guide the labour market. Part II of this volume analyses some of the labour institutions that determine earnings, including unions and collective bargaining (Chapter 4), minimum wages (Chapter 5), and the different forms of contractual engagement in the labour market (temporary contracts, Chapter 6; part-time work, Chapter 7).

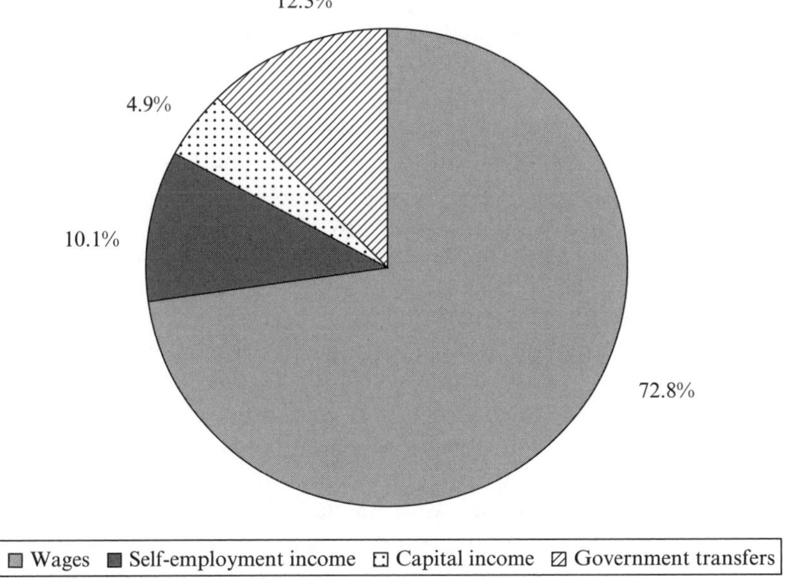

Note: Data are standardized by applying average tax rate of the 30 OECD countries for which information is available.

Source: OECD (2011).

Figure 1.3 Components of disposable income, working-age population, mid-2000s, OECD-30

Income from waged work and self-employment accounts for the vast majority of individual and family incomes across the world. According to the OECD (2011), based on data for 30 countries, 83 per cent of household disposable income amongst the working-age population is earnings from work, with 73 per cent stemming from waged work and 10 per cent from self-employment. The remaining income sources include rents (4.9 per cent) and government transfers (12.3 per cent) (Figure 1.3). Among countries there is wide variation in income sources. In Chile, Italy and the Republic of Korea, self-employment income accounts for over one-quarter of income, with waged income playing a less important role. Similarly, government transfers are nearly negligible in Chile (0.81 per cent), low in the United States (4.9 per cent), but comprise 15–20 per cent of income in Continental Europe (Austria, 20 per cent; France, 18 per cent; Sweden, 15 per cent).

In countries where labour markets are less regulated, there is a wider dispersion of labour market earnings. Collective bargaining and minimum wages are two institutions that directly affect workers' earnings, compressing the overall wage distribution by propping up wages at the bottom of the wage pyramid.

Chapter 4 of this volume by Susan Hayter addresses the role of unions and collective bargaining in reducing wage inequality. Unions' influence on wage distribution in an economy can come from their role as 'actors' representing labour in broader economic and social policy debates, but also as parties to collective bargaining agreements negotiated at either the firm or sectoral level. In her extensive review of the impact of collective bargaining on wages, Hayter distinguishes between collective bargaining systems that are narrow, or limited to the parties or bargaining unit, versus encompassing systems, in which collective bargaining agreements are extended to workers in the broader economic sector who are not members of the union. Under both systems there will be wage compression, but because narrow systems are limited to unionized firms the effect of the wage compression on broader wage inequality in the labour market will depend on the degree of unionization in the economy. Hayter gives data showing that trade union density has, in general, fallen in both developed and developing countries. As a result, the wage compression effects of the narrow systems have become even more limited. Under encompassing systems, collective bargaining agreements continue to be extended despite declines in trade union density, though movements from centralized to decentralized systems and opt-out clauses have eroded some coverage. Nevertheless, extension has allowed these systems to have a greater effect on compressing wages in the overall economy.

Hayter argues that debates on the equity versus efficiency of unions and collective bargaining has distracted attention from the decline in labour's share in the national income, the growing dispersion of personal incomes, as well as the overall decline in unionization. Moreover, her review shows that there is no systematic evidence to support the claim that unions help 'insiders' to the detriment of 'outsiders'. Rather, unions, as representatives of workers in larger social and economic debates, have played an important role in influencing policies to the benefit of workers, particularly those at the bottom of the pay scale. This is particularly true for tripartite negotiations on the minimum wage, working time, as well as public spending on social protection and social services. But the declining influence of labour has affected its ability to act as a countervailing force in many countries. The financial crisis of 2008, the Great Recession, the austerity measures being imposed in many parts of the world, and the deregulation of labour laws and collective bargaining in Europe in the 2010s, are manifestations of its weakening voice.

Chapter 5 of this volume by Patrick Belser and Uma Rani concerns the relationship between minimum wages and wage inequality. According to the ILO, approximately 90 per cent of countries have minimum wages though there is a wide diversity in the systems, including the wage-setting process, as well as in their scope, complexity and effectiveness, and their absolute and relative values (ILO, 2008). Minimum wages, by ensuring a minimum level of earnings for those at the bottom of the pay scale, are an effective tool for compressing the wage distribution as well as lessening the incidence of low pay in both developed and developing countries.[18] In their chapter, Belser and Rani review the extensive empirical evidence of the effect of minimum wages on inequality and employment, supplementing discussion with their own empirical analysis of 11 developing countries. They find that even in developing countries where enforcement is lax, minimum wages help to reduce inequality. In most countries, this occurs at the bottom of the distribution (D5/D1), though in some countries where minimum wages are higher relative to average wages, the compression occurs in the middle of the distribution (D75/D25). They attribute the important wage compression impacts at the bottom of the distribution in part to 'lighthouse effects', whereby formal minimum wages provide a reference for bargaining among informal waged employees and their employers.

Despite the benefits of minimum wages on inequality, there has been considerable debate in the economics profession on its employment effects, specifically whether raising the minimum wage leads to job losses as the competitive labour market model suggests. Yet as Belser and Rani document in their chapter, there exists substantial empirical evidence to the contrary, demonstrating negligible effects on employment and sometimes positive effects as a result of encouraging workers to enter the labour market. Moreover, at the macroeconomic level, higher minimum wages can stimulate consumption and thus, aggregate demand. Here again, they complement the extensive literature review with their own analysis from five developing countries, and find no significant disemployment effects. Belser and Rani caution, however, that minimum wages must not be set at a level that is too high, as then it ceases to help the poorest workers and promotes non-compliance, nor at too low a level, which negates the effectiveness of this important policy tool.

The type of employment contract that a person works under affects the pay and working conditions of the worker, including his or her sense of job and income security. The decline of the standard employment relationship, witnessed by the rise in temporary employment contracts, dependent self-employment, temporary agency work, or other forms of subcontracted work, is just beginning to be understood.[19] Moreover, in many parts of the world, large parts of the labour force continue to work under informal employment contracts with scant protection by the law and access to social security. Two chapters in the volume address employment contracts: Chapter 6 on temporary contracts and wage inequality and Chapter 7 on part-time work. In both chapters it is clear that the type of contracts that exist in a country is an outcome of the regulations of the country. This implies that the law, if well designed and enforced, can be an effective tool for improving working conditions.

In Chapter 6 of this volume, Sandrine Cazes and Juan Ramón de Laiglesia document the increase over the past several decades in temporary contracts in both advanced and emerging economies, with temporary contracts becoming a notable feature of labour markets in Southern Europe, the Andean countries, and parts of Asia. In Europe, temporary contracts cover approximately 15 per cent of the labour force and in some countries, such as Spain, over one-quarter of the labour force is on temporary contracts. Temporary contracts entail significant wage penalties for the individual workers. Moreover, in countries with high shares of these contracts, there are low transitions between fixed-term and indefinite contract jobs, with the risk that workers become trapped in these jobs. As the authors argue, this is problematic not just for the individual, but for the labour market as a whole, as it leads to segmented labour markets and inhibits investments in training that are important for improving productivity. Moreover, workers employed under temporary contracts are often excluded from legislated benefits, and in some cases, are not covered by collective agreements.

In Chapter 7, Jon Messenger and Nikhil Ray tackle the issue of part-time work and inequality. Whether part-time work will be a source of inequality will depend largely on how it is regulated in national labour markets. In countries where the laws reflect the principle of equal treatment of part-time workers, wages and benefits will be on a pro-rata basis. Moreover, some countries grant employees the right to switch into and out of part-time work, mitigating the risk of the job becoming a career trap. Under these conditions, part-time work can be an attractive option for workers who need to reconcile work with care responsibilities or schooling, as these workers may otherwise not have participated in the labour market. However, in other countries, unregulated part-time work is sometimes a strategy on the part of employers to evade paying social security contributions, health insurance, or paid leave, resulting in lower earnings and poorer job quality. Many of these jobs also suffer from unpredictability in work schedules, hindering the principal positive attribute of part-time work. Part-time work can also be associated with less investment in training, adding to the potential scarring effects of part-time work on career development. In developing countries, part-time work is also commonly found among informal, self-employed workers, at times reflecting a strategy for reconciling domestic responsibilities with work, but also reflecting insufficient opportunities for work.

1.7 THE REDISTRIBUTION OF INCOME

Market income constitutes the bulk of income for persons of working age, but there are times in life when we are either not of working age or are not employed. Societies have to find a way to smooth income across the different stages of life as well as prepare for possible contingencies that may arise. Redistributive social policies are the principal means that governments have to alter the distribution of income. However, the reasons for, and commitment to redistribution vary widely across countries, as does the degree of redistribution. Part III of this volume addresses redistributive social policies and their effect on inequality.

In Chapter 8, Malte Luebker analyses how redistributive policies, in the form of taxes and transfers, can reduce overall income inequality in a society. He reviews some of the problems with measuring redistribution and presents findings on trends and cross-country differences in redistribution. Luebker cautions that fiscal redistribution measures are a 'snapshot' that cannot account for the contributions of some policies, particularly the provision of public goods. Moreover, as discussed previously, there are important interaction effects from social policies, such that the 'design of welfare states will affect market inequalities', by, for example, affecting decisions to participate in the labour market (Esping-Andersen and Myles, 2009, p. 640).

Nevertheless, there are notable differences between countries, indicating divergence in the commitment and political will to build just societies. According to Luebker's calculations, in Latin America and East Asia, taxes and transfers have little impact on reducing the Gini coefficient (a reduction of a mere 0.02 percentage points), indicating how this is an underdeveloped policy tool. Comparing Europe with Australia, Canada, Israel and the United States, both groups' initial levels of inequality were about the same, but transfers in Europe had twice the impact as in the other four countries. In Australia, Canada, Israel and the United States, tax policy had a more significant effect in reducing inequality, but as redistributive policies were less important, the final level of inequality was nearly 25 per cent higher than in Continental Europe.

Tax policy is a critical component of fiscal redistribution. In developing countries, tax systems are less developed and tax revenues as a percentage of GDP are usually much lower than in industrialized countries, ranging from 18 per cent in Thailand, 12 per cent in Bangladesh, 15 per cent in Peru and 13 per cent in Dominican Republic. The low tax base explains, in part, the limited redistributive impact in Latin America and East Asia. Amongst industrialized countries, tax revenues as a percentage of GDP are higher, but there is also much variation, ranging from 25 per cent in the USA and the Republic of Korea, to 36 per cent in Germany. With lower tax bases, there is less scope to use taxes as a means to redistribute incomes and less money available for investment in public goods that are needed for social and economic development. Moreover, the design of tax policy – whether it is progressive or regressive – will affect the ability of taxes to alter the distribution of income.

Indeed, the design of tax policy, as well as transfer policy, is an important distinguishing element among countries. Luebker shows, for example, that the amount of money spent, as a percentage of national income, on the welfare state only accounts for one-third of the overall variation in redistribution – the rest is due to the design of tax and transfer systems. The chapters that follow in Part III discuss different social policies, how they are characteristic of specific welfare state models as well as the degree to which they attenuate inequality in income as well as among groups.

Pensions are long-term social security benefits that are paid over prolonged periods in situations of old age, disability and loss of breadwinner. They are the most important redistributive policy, in some countries accounting for up to 80 per cent of total transfers. Their budgetary importance varies among countries, however, depending on the share of elderly in the population, but also the design of the social security system, particularly the availability and importance given to other transfers such as social assistance. In Chapter 9, Christina Behrendt and John Woodall analyse how the design of pension and other social security income transfer systems affects overall income inequality in a country as well as inequality between groups, namely the elderly and those of working age, and women and men. Pension coverage varies across regions of the world, with 90 per cent of older persons in Europe receiving a pension compared with 75 per cent in North America, 50 per cent in Latin America and the Caribbean, 25–30 per cent in Asia and the Pacific, the Middle East and North Africa and only 15 per cent in Sub-Saharan Africa. These differences largely reflect the percentage of formal waged employment in the particular countries, thus countries with large informal economies generally have lower pension coverage of the elderly, unless non-contributory pensions form part of the system.

As Behrendt and Woodall explain, how redistributive a pension system is will depend on its design, including the mix between public and private pensions, whether there are non-contributory elements of protection, and if there are minimum pension guarantees for those who are unable to build up sufficient entitlements. Contributory pensions tie coverage and benefit levels to employment and as a result often perpetuate inequalities in the labour market. This is particularly true for women, who as a result of shorter work histories, make fewer contributions and ultimately receive lower benefits. But the same could be argued for all workers who have more erratic work histories, thus the growing share of workers in temporary contracts, as discussed in Chapter 6, may have important impacts on future pension coverage. Non-contributory pensions can compensate shortfalls in contribution by providing coverage to those who normally would not qualify for benefits and, indeed, women are the principal recipients of non-contributory pensions. But these pensions are often means-tested and benefits tend to be low.

Like many contributory pension systems, unemployment insurance can perpetuate existing inequalities in the labour market, as workers with stronger labour force attachment are the ones who benefit if displaced. In Chapter 10, Janine Berg analyses the different forms of income support for the unemployed and the poor and their contribution to mitigating inequality. She begins with an analysis of unemployment benefit schemes, noting how only 42 per cent of countries have schemes and amongst those countries that do, coverage rates are low, with only 61 per cent of the unemployed in high-income countries receiving benefits. She argues for the need to adapt unemployment insurance systems to changes in the world of work, including the rise of new forms of contractual arrangements as well as the increased participation of women in the labour market, some of whom have weaker labour force attachment, and thus may not qualify for benefits under existing systems.

Social assistance programmes are an important complement to unemployment benefit systems, as they can provide income to the long-term unemployed, but also to workers who do not earn enough to support themselves and their families. Countries differ, however, with respect to the importance that they assign to social assistance, as well as how social assistance programmes fit into the broader social protection system. In more universal welfare states, proportionally fewer resources are devoted to social assistance, given the wider range of programmes available, including family allowances. Developing countries have recently expanded social assistance programmes, which is a welcome development given their effectiveness at reducing poverty. But because of the low level of benefits, and the lack of other complementary social protection policies, the programmes are less likely to alter the distribution of income in a society.

The latest trend is conditional-cash-transfer programmes, which require families to attend to the educational and health needs of their children. While certainly laudable goals, the programme requirements can have the unintended consequence of excluding those who are most in need. It does, however, have the benefit of putting pressure on governments to provide health and education services for its citizens, a necessary social good that is fundamental to both human and economic development. Moreover, it represents an important step in filling a void in the existing social protection systems of many developing countries.

As discussed previously, public social services can have an important bearing on access to the labour market, particularly of women. The availability (or lack) of public social services also has a direct bearing on household incomes, as lower-income households who are forced to purchase these services of the market will pay a proportionally larger share of their income than higher-income households. Chapter 11 on public social services by Juliana Martínez Franzoni and Diego Sánchez-Ancochea analyses the relationship between the provision of public social services in the areas of healthcare, education, early childhood education and care (ECEC), and income inequality. The provision of high-quality public services in these areas is not only fundamental for breaking the inter-generational cycle of poverty by providing better opportunities for the next generation, but also in minimizing present inequality between different groups.

The authors cite data from the OECD that shows that public services increase disposable income more than transfers, with the greatest impact occurring in the Scandinavian countries. Indeed, the differences in income inequality between the USA and Sweden partly reflects the provision of care services; in Sweden these are provided publicly, compared with the USA where they are attained, for the most part, through private means. As the authors argue, public social services democratize access to services, allow families to re-allocate income to other needs, and release time from unpaid work.

When health, education and ECEC services are only provided through the market, the inequality of market incomes is propagated as lower-income families either cannot afford the health and care services, or spend disproportionate amounts of their income on these services when they do buy them, and attain services of inferior quality. Moreover, the lack of public care services affects women's ability to engage in paid work, and their more tenuous attachment to the labour market translates into lower earnings and benefits. An important conclusion to draw from this chapter, and which relates to the wider theme of this book on the interaction of institutions, is that market incorporation alone will not be a sufficient condition for reducing inequality; other policies, including the provision of quality public services, but also broader social welfare policies, are needed.

1.8 DO LABOUR INSTITUTIONS HURT OR HELP VULNERABLE GROUPS?

As mentioned previously, the World Bank's *World Development Report 2013: Jobs* (World Bank, 2012) concluded that the effect of labour market institutions on employment performance was negligible. The report, however, went on to argue that most of the impact was redistributive, but 'generally to the advantage of middle-aged male workers (as opposed to owners of capital, women and younger workers)' (p. 26). In this conclusion, the World Bank is essentially putting forth the argument that labour market institutions benefit 'insiders' to the detriment of 'outsiders', who are typically women, youth and migrants. But this is ironic, given that women fare worse when the labour market is less regulated (Rubery, 2011), as do youth and migrants. For this reason, and because of the important relationship between group inequality and overall income inequality, this volume included a fourth part addressing the impact of labour market institutions on gender equality (Chapter 12), migrant workers (Chapter 13) and youth (Chapter 14).

In Chapter 12, Sarah Gammage explains how women generally have a more tenuous attachment to the labour market, due to the unequal distribution of care responsibilities within the household. Women are more likely to transit in and out of paid work as a result of these responsibilities and many women require more flexible forms of employment that allow them to better balance work and family life, if they are to engage in paid work. Moreover, there are greater fixed costs for women in entering the labour market as they may have to pay for those tasks that they are currently doing at the home. Labour market institutions can mediate women's entry into the labour force by providing public care services but also by legislating more flexible forms of employment.

Once in the labour market, women are more likely to work in feminized occupations, including informal or part-time work, with marked differences in wages, hours and access to benefits. Moreover, like other minority groups, they are more often found in low-waged work and in sectors that have lower collective bargaining coverage. As a result, minimum wages are sometimes the only policy tool available; by raising the wages of low-wage workers, they reduce gender wage gaps as well as overall wage inequality. Minimum wages can also correct for discriminatory practices that set differential wages for work of equal value.[20] Moreover, by raising wages at the lower end of the income distribution, minimum wages may increase labour force participation rates of lower-income women who need to cover the fixed costs of going to work.

Collective bargaining is an important institution for compressing the wage distribution and improving working conditions and thus can help to improve gender and wage equality (Chapter 4). Gammage, while citing the important benefits of collective bargaining for compressing the wage distribution and lowering gender wage gaps cautions that women generally have lower union membership. She argues that gender concerns are often excluded in collective bargaining negotiations and thus, for the need to improve women's voice in unions and at the bargaining table.

Gammage concludes by arguing that labour market institutions have a significant role to play in fostering gender equality in the labour market, but that there is also a need for explicit policies to change the gender distribution of labour within the household, which is not immutable. She argues that the state has a role to play in actively encouraging men to take on more domestic responsibilities, particularly with regard to care duties, through parental benefit and leave policies, gender equity laws and non-discrimination laws. She argues that without addressing this fundamental inequality, there will be limits to what minimum wages, collective bargaining and other labour institutions can correct.

Chapter 13 by Christiane Kuptsch tackles the difficult issue of providing equal protection to low or semi-skilled migrant workers, some of whom have irregular status. Kuptsch reminds us that the eight fundamental conventions of the ILO on freedom of association and collective bargaining, freedom from discrimination and the elimination of forced and child labour apply to all workers, regardless of their status or location. She cites the example of Spain where trade union rights of illegal migrant workers were upheld on account of these conventions. Yet with few exceptions, it has been difficult to ensure the rights of migrants, making them vulnerable to exploitation. Low-skilled migrant workers tend to be employed in sectors that are often less protected, such as agriculture and domestic work. Moreover, some countries with sizeable migrant populations, such as the Gulf States, lack fundamental labour institutions that can guarantee protections for the workers. In some cases, countries overtly discriminate against migrant workers, by, for example, setting lower minimum wages for non-nationals, or tying migrants to particular employers, thus negating all possibility for bargaining and leaving the workers more exposed to abuse.

This chapter is interlinked with the chapters on public social services (Chapter 11) and gender (Chapter 12), as many low-skilled migrant workers form part of the international 'global care chain', whereby families in destination countries hire migrant domestic workers to compensate for the lack of publicly available quality daycare – the so-called 'pull for care'. Labour shortages in key occupations such as nursing have also led to important migrant flows, at times involving several countries. These examples serve to demonstrate the inter-connectedness, and thus responsibility, that national governments as well as the international community have in regulating and respecting the rights of migrant workers.

In Chapter 14, Gerhard Reinecke and Damian Grimshaw analyse the inequality between youth and adults as well as between youth, and assess how labour market institutions contribute to shaping the employment prospects and conditions of young workers. In some countries of the world, youth unemployment has reached alarming levels, raising concerns about the prospects of a lost generation (ILO, 2013b). The dramatic fears on one end of the debate contrast markedly with more dismissive positions that argue that the problems that youth face are transitional and will go away with age. As in most labour market debates, so much depends on where the worker – in this case the young worker – lives, and the labour market that the individual faces. Also, in countries where social mobility is constrained, the inequalities present in the young workers' upbringing will likely manifest in their transition to the labour force and the conditions under which they work.

As the authors explain, in some countries, notably those with developed vocational training systems and regulated apprentice programmes, the transition from school to work is relatively seamless; in other countries, youth struggle to find a first job in their chosen field, or work in jobs with precarious conditions and few prospects. That youth earn less than adults is to be expected given their lack of experience; the concern, however, is whether youth get trapped in poor-quality jobs. Thus, an important policy question is who transits and what policies support the transition. In countries where a smaller proportion of the labour force is low wage (defined as earning less than two-thirds the median wage), there is greater probability of these jobs serving as stepping stones. This is the case in Denmark, for example, where many youth are employed in low-wage jobs, often in part-time positions, but the youth transit out of low wage over time (Esbjerg et al., 2008). This differs from other countries, such as the USA, where low-wage employment is a problem for the core workforce, particularly prime-age women. In these countries, youth employed in low-wage work are less likely to transit out (Gautie and Schmitt, 2010). This is partly due to the lack of collective bargaining in many low-wage sectors, which implies that if workers remain in the same firm, even though they are gaining experience, they are not likely to advance much in pay. In contrast, where unionization is stronger, less-educated workers receive more training and rewards from experience, allowing them to advance further in pay scales.

The chapter surveys the literature on the impact of employment protection legislation on youth unemployment and concludes that the results are mixed, and when positive, are negligible – much like the general literature on the topic. Regarding youth minimum wages, the authors note that there is a policy divide on this topic, with many countries legislating specific wages for youth. The authors conclude that youth minimums are unlikely to be a panacea for employment problems, and that if instituted, countries should use wider age bands with smaller differentials, thereby lessening the problem of annual wage increases.

Many of the policies addressed in this book come to the fore in the discussion of youth. Policy debates on equality of opportunity and the use of conditional-cash-transfer programmes to upgrade educational levels, labour market transitions, the effect of wages, temporary contracts, and collective bargaining on working conditions, the inequalities that exist between groups and how they translate into overall earnings inequality, emerge from this discussion. The chapter reveals the complexity of the debate on labour market institutions, but also the importance of good policy design in improving the well-being of workers – both young and old.

1.9 CONCLUSION

The chapters in this volume make clear that 'inequality is . . . a matter of political choice and institutional design' (Luebker, Chapter 8, p. 236) and that the enactment and design of labour market institutions is a manifestation of a society's commitment to greater equity. Thus, to be successful, countries must institute a wide range of policies that can support this objective. This book addresses the labour market institutions that are needed. It discusses the importance of having explicit macroeconomic policies to support full employment, of having well-designed institutions that govern work contracts, as well as the need for social policies and public social services that support the working and non-working alike.

While it may seem odd to have a discussion of macroeconomic policies in a book on labour market institutions, achieving full employment will only occur if there are explicit macroeconomic policies that support aggregate demand and job creation. Removing 'rigidities' in the labour market will not bring about full employment; it will only worsen workers' well-being, increase inequality and insecurity, and promote industries that compete on cheap labour rather than technological innovation. Countries must also regulate finance to ensure that investments are directed at productive activities that better societies and create jobs. Finance needs to return to being a means to fund these investments rather than being a source of its own profits.

Highly skilled workers have benefited from the rising share of capital of the past decades. Less skilled workers, however, have seen their wages and working conditions decline as unions have lost power, minimum wages have weakened and non-standard employment contracts have proliferated. The chapters in this volume provide evidence on how these labour market institutions, when designed well, can promote greater equality and support the earnings of those at the bottom of the pay scale and of more equitable societies in general.

Redistributive social policies, including public social services, improve workers' access to the labour market, remove workers from the labour market who should not be there (adolescents, the elderly), and help in wage bargaining by setting a reference wage. They can protect those who cannot work or are unable to find work as well as those who earn too little from work. Countries differ exceedingly on the resources that they collect as well as those that they dedicate to social policies. But even countries with similar budgets will have different outcomes in income distribution depending on the other policies discussed in the book as well as the design of their welfare states.

Women, migrants and youth face distinct hurdles in the labour market. Women's weaker labour force attachment emanates from the unequal distribution of care responsibilities. Migrants are either not protected, or are not aware of the protections that they may have in host countries; they are also in an even more unequal position vis-à-vis their employers. Youth have difficulty getting their foot in the doorway and risk getting stuck in precarious and low-wage jobs when labour markets are less regulated. The chapters discuss how labour market institutions can protect vulnerable groups in the labour market, calling into question the assumption that labour market regulations hurt these 'outsider' groups. Rather, what is needed are labour markets that are well-regulated, and policies that are designed, instituted and enforced to take into account the specific constraints that vulnerable groups face in the labour market.

There is a wide range of distributive and redistributive policies that countries can adopt if they want to build just societies. There is no one-size-fits-all model; rather, policies should be designed to reflect the economic, social and institutional characteristics of the country. Building just societies, however, requires an explicit commitment to this goal. It remains to be seen whether this commitment will be supported in the 21st century.

NOTES

* I would like to thank David Howell, Rolph van der Hoeven, Frank Hoffer, Uma Rani and four anonymous referees for valuable comments on a previous draft of this chapter.

1. Belgium, Chile, France, Greece, Ireland, Portugal, Spain and Turkey. The deregulation of the labour market and austerity policies enacted during the Great Recession, with the stated goal of making unit labour costs competitive, have likely eroded the gains of the bottom quintile in Greece, Ireland, Portugal and Spain.
2. Data is from the Standardized World Income Inequality Database (SWIID). Trends in income distribution are sensitive to the indicator used (Gini, Theil, decile comparisons), the unit of analysis and the data chosen. Thus, particular country trends may differ under alternative measures.
3. Data from the Congressional Budget Office and cited in *Economic Report of the President* (2012).
4. See Epstein (2007).
5. See, for example, the World Bank 1995 *World Development Report: Workers in an Integrating World.*
6. In countries where the political environment did not allow deregulation, there was still de facto flexibilization of the labour market, as a result of the scaling back of budgets on labour administration and inspection. For example, Mexico in the 1990s and 2000s.
7. For a more recent evaluation of policies recommended under Article IV consultations, see Islam et al. (2012).
8. See, for example, Manning (2003) and Fine (1998).
9. See http://www.doingbusiness.org/methodology/employing-workers for a discussion of the changes made to the methodology; last accessed 24 August 2014.
10. Lee and Gerecke (2013) refer to this problem as 'regulatory indeterminacy'.
11. Many of the health and safety laws in the United States were enacted in response to the 1911 Triangle Shirtwaist Factory Fire in New York City, which caused the deaths of 146 garment workers.
12. The other conventions concern labour inspection (the Labour Inspection Convention, 1947 (No. 81) and the Labour Inspection (Agriculture) Convention, 1969 (No. 129)) and the Tripartite Consultation (International Labour Standards) Convention, 1976 (No. 144).
13. To read the full convention, see ILO Normlex at https://www.ilo.org/dyn/normlex/en/f?p=1000:11300:0::NO:11300:P11300_INSTRUMENT_ID:312267; last accessed 24 August 2014.
14. In the Arab States, there are high rates of unemployment among tertiary-educated workers, particularly youth.
15. Alva Myrdal explains the comprehensive set of policies that are needed to ensure family security and women's access to the labour market in a 1939 article in the *International Labour Review* (Myrdal [1939] 2013).
16. Sweden, which pioneered policies to boost women's participation in the labour market, was also the first country to pursue Keynesian policies during the Great Depression. See Ohlin ([1963] 2013).
17. Indeed, stagnating real wages and growing inequality are often advanced as an explanation of the current crisis, particularly in the USA. Households compensated for their falling incomes by increasing debt, which was sustained initially because of rising home prices, but which eventually collapsed when the bubble in the US housing market burst (see Stiglitz, 2010; Islam and Kucera, 2014).
18. See the two special editions of the *International Labour Review* on low-pay work in industrialized countries (Vol. 148, No. 4) and emerging economies (Vol. 151, No. 3).
19. For an in-depth discussion of the causes and implications of subcontracted work, see Weil (2014).
20. Unfortunately, in some countries where minimum wages are set by occupation, the wage floors sometimes institute discriminatory policies by setting lower wages for jobs that are typically held by women.

REFERENCES

Acemoglu, D. and J. Robinson (2013), 'Economics versus politics: pitfalls of policy advice', *Journal of Economic Perspectives*, **27**(2), 173–92.

ADB (2012), *Asian Development Outlook: Confronting Rising Inequality in Asia*, Manila: Asian Development Bank.

Bhorat, H., N. Mayet, N. Tian and D. Tseng (2013), 'The determinants of wage inequality in South Africa', unpublished draft discussion paper for the International Labour Office.

Blanchflower, D. and A. Oswald (1995), *The Wage Curve*, Cambridge, MA: MIT Press.

Corak, M. (2013), 'Income inequality, equality of opportunity and intergenerational mobility', *Journal of Economic Perspectives*, **27**(3), 79–102.

Dullien, S., H. Hansjorg and C. Kellermann (2011), *Decent Capitalism: A Blueprint for Reforming Our Economies*, London: Pluto Press.

Economic Report of the President (2012), transmitted to the Congress February 2012 together with the *Annual Report of the Council of Economic Advisers*, Washington, DC: US Government Printing Office, accessed 24 August 2014 at http://www.whitehouse.gov/sites/default/files/microsites/ERP_2012_Complete.pdf.

Epstein, G. (2006), *Financialization and the World Economy*, Cheltenham, UK and Northampton, MA, USA: Edward Elgar Publishing.

Epstein, G. (2007), 'Central banks, inflation targeting, and employment creation', *ILO Economic and Labour Market Papers No. 2007/2*, accessed 24 August 2014 at http://www.ilo.org/public/english/employment/download/elm/elm07-2.pdf.

Esbjerg, L., K. Grunert, N. Buck and A.M. Sonne Andersen (2008), 'Working in Danish retailing: transitional workers going elsewhere, core employees going nowhere, and career-seekers striving to go somewhere', in N. Westergaard-Nielsen (ed.), *Low-wage Work in Denmark*, New York: Russell Sage Foundation.

Esping-Andersen, G. (1990), *The Three Worlds of Welfare Capitalism*, Cambridge, UK: Polity Press.

Esping-Andersen, G. and J. Myles (2009), 'Economic inequality and the welfare state', in W. Salvedra, B. Nolan and T. Smeeding (eds), *The Oxford Handbook of Economic Inequality*, Oxford: Oxford University Press.

Freeman, R. (2011), 'New roles for unions and collective bargaining post the implosion of Wall Street capitalism', in S. Hayter (ed.), *The Role of Collective Bargaining in the Global Economy, Negotiating for Social Justice*, Cheltenham, UK and Northampton, MA, USA/Geneva: Edward Elgar Publishing/International Labour Office.

Fine, B. (1998), *Labour Market Theory: A Constructive Reassessment*, London: Routledge.

Galbraith, J. (2012), *Inequality and Instability: A Study of the World Economy Just Before the Great Crisis*, Oxford: Oxford University Press.

Gautie, J. and J. Schmitt (2010), *Low-wage Work in the Wealthy World*, New York: Russell Sage Foundation.

ILO (2008), *Global Wages Report 2008/2009: Minimum Wages and Collective Bargaining: Towards Policy Coherence*, Geneva: International Labour Office.

ILO (2010), *Labour and Social Trends in the ASEAN 2010*, Bangkok: ILO Regional Office for Asia and the Pacific.

ILO (2013a), *Global Wage Report 2012/13: Wages and Equitable Growth*, Geneva: International Labour Office.

ILO (2013b), *Global Employment Trends for Youth 2013: A Generation at Risk*, Geneva: International Labour Office.

ILO/IILS (2011), *World of Work Report: Making Markets Work for People*, Geneva: International Institute of Labour Studies/International Labour Office.

IMF (2007), *World Economic Outlook: Globalization and Inequality*, Washington, DC: International Monetary Fund.

IPEA (2010), 'Efeitos econômicos do gasto social no Brasil' [Economic effects of social spending in Brazil], in *Perspectivas da Política Social no Brasil, Livro 8 do Projeto Perspectivas do Desenvolvimento Brasileiro*, Brasilia: Instituto de Pesquisa Econômica Aplicada.

Islam, I. and D. Kucera (2014), *Beyond Macroeconomic Stability: Structural Transformation and Inclusive Development*, Basingstoke/Geneva: Palgrave Macmillan/International Labour Office.

Islam, I., I. Ahmed, R. Roy and R. Ramos (2012), 'Macroeconomic policy advice and the Article IV consultations: a development perspective', *ILO Research Paper No. 2*, Geneva: International Institute for Labour Studies/International Labour Office.

Kaufman, B. (2010), 'Institutional economics and the minimum wage: broadening the theoretical and policy debate', *Industrial and Labor Relations Review*, **63**(3), 427–53.

Keifman, S. and R. Maurizio (2012), 'Changes in labour market conditions and policies: the impact on wage inequality during the last decade', *UNU-WIDER Working Paper No. 2012/14*, Helsinki: UN University World Institute for Development Economics Research.

Kuznets, S. (1955), 'Economic growth and income inequality', *The American Economic Review*, **45**(1), 1–28.

Lee, S. and M. Gerecke (2013), 'Regulatory indeterminacy and institutional design in minimum wages: decentralization, coordination and politics in Asian minimum wages', paper presented at the 3rd Regulating for Decent Work Conference, Geneva, 3–5 July.

Le Temps (6 July 2013), 'Si vous souhaitez une société juste, prenez exemple sur les Scandinaves' [If you want a just society, take the example of the Scandinavians], *Le Temps*, weekend edition, accessed 24 August 2014 at http://www.letemps.ch/Page/Uuid/9b9b1bfa-e589-11e2-99fe-9d7442c3ec89/Si_vous_souhaitez_une_soci%C3%A9t%C3%A9_juste_prenez_exemple_sur_les_Scandinaves.

Lewis, W.A. (1954), 'Economic development with unlimited supplies of labour', *The Manchester School*, **22**(2), 139–91.

López-Calva, L. and N. Lustig (eds) (2010), *Declining Inequality in Latin America: A Decade of Progress?*, New York and Washington, DC: United Nations Development Programme and Brookings Institution Press.

Manning, A. (2003), *Monopsony in Motion: Imperfect Competition in Labor Markets*, Princeton, NJ: Princeton University Press.

Myrdal, A. ([1939] 2013), 'A programme for family security in Sweden', *International Labour Review*, **152**(S1), 51–61.

Nickell, S. and R. Layard (1999), 'Labour market institutions and economic performance', in O. Ashenfelter and D. Card (eds), *Handbook of Labor Economics, Vol. 3, Part C*, Amsterdam: North-Holland, pp. 3029–84.

OECD (1994), *The OECD Jobs Strategy: Facts, Analysis, Strategies*, Paris: Organisation for Economic Co-operation and Development.

OECD (2006), *OECD Employment Outlook: Boosting Jobs and Incomes*, Paris: Organisation for Economic Co-operation and Development.

OECD (2011), *Divided We Stand: Why Inequality Keeps Rising*, Paris: Organisation for Economic Co-operation and Development.

Ohlin, B. ([1963] 2013), 'Economic recovery and labour market problems in Sweden: II (1935)', *International Labour Review*, **152**(S1), 20–36.

OIT (2013a), *Crecimiento, empleo y cohesión social en República Dominicana* [Growth, Employment and Social Cohesion in the Dominican Republic], San José: Organización Internacional del Trabajo (ILO).

OIT (2013b), *Informe para la discusión en la reunión tripartita de expertos sobre la posible adopción de un instrumento de la OIT que complemente el Convenio sobre el trabajo forzoso, 1930 (núm. 29)* [Report for Discussion at the Tripartite Meeting of Experts Concerning the Possible Adoption of an ILO Instrument to Supplement the Forced Labour Convention, 1930 (No, 29)], San José: Organización Internacional del Trabajo (ILO).

Palley, T. (2013), *From Financial Crisis to Stagnation: The Destruction of Shared Prosperity and the Role of Economics*, New York: Cambridge University Press.

Piketty, T. (2014), *Capital in the Twenty-first Century*, Cambridge, MA: Harvard University Press.

Piore, M. (2004), 'Rethinking international labor standards', in W. Milberg (ed.), *Labor and the Globalization of Production: Causes and Consequences of Industrial Upgrading*, Basingstoke, UK: Palgrave Macmillan.

Rani, U., P. Belser, M. Oelz and S. Ranjbar (2013), 'Minimum wage coverage and compliance in developing countries', *International Labour Review*, **152**(3–4), 381–410.

Rubery, J. (2011), 'Towards a gendering of the labour market regulation debate', *Cambridge Journal of Economics*, **35**(6), 1103–26.

Stiglitz, J. (2010), *Freefall: America, Free Markets, and the Sinking of the World Economy*, New York, W.W. Norton & Co.

Tinbergen, J. (1967), *Economic Policy: Principles and Design*, Amsterdam: North-Holland.

UNCTAD (2012), *Trade and Development Report: Policies for Inclusive and Balanced Growth*, Geneva: United Nations Conference on Trade and Development.

Wambagu, A. and J. Kabubo-Mariara (2013), 'Labour market institutions and earnings distribution in Kenya', unpublished draft discussion paper for the International Labour Office.

Watt, A. (2006), 'Assessing the reassessment of the OECD Jobs Strategy: eppur si muove?', *European Economic and Employment Policy No. 2/2006*, Brussels: European Trade Union Institute.

Webb, S. and B. Webb (1902), *Industrial Democracy*, London: Longmans, Green & Co.

Weil, D. (2014), *The Fissured Workplace*, Cambridge, MA: Harvard University Press.

World Bank (1995), *World Development Report: Workers in an Integrating World*, Washington, DC: World Bank.

World Bank (2012), *World Development Report 2013: Jobs*, Washington, DC: World Bank.

PART I

Macroeconomic policies, development and inequality

2. Economic development and inequality: revisiting the Kuznets curve*

Sangheon Lee and Megan Gerecke

> The importance of inequality lies in its economic rationale, in its origins in production, and in its consequences in consumption, with due cognizance of the limits and political tolerance for such inequality in roles in production and shares in consumption.
>
> (Kuznets, 1965)

2.1 INTRODUCTION

Why is income inequality widening or narrowing? Does it matter? These questions have not attracted much attention from conventional economic theory, also known as 'neoclassical' theory. The theoretical model assumes that the market efficiently allocates and compensates resources, so that, as Bertola (2000, p. 480) points out, 'the dynamics of income and consumption distribution have no welfare implications'. However, this approach has been challenged in recent years by growing evidence that income inequality has been widening in terms of both personal and functional income distributions (IMF, 2007; ILO/IILS, 2008; OECD, 2008, 2011). Over the period 1980–2007, labour income grew at a slower rate than productivity in many countries, with the gap expanding particularly strongly in the regions of Asia and North Africa (ILO/IILS, 2008; ILO, 2010). At the same time, the distribution of labour income became more and more unequal, mushrooming among top earners and stagnating among the rest (ILO, 2010; also see ILO/IILS, 2012). Not surprisingly, the issue of inequality is now back at the centre of global debates as a growing number of economists suspect that widening inequality has been an important cause of the Great Recession (see van Treeck and Sturn, 2012 or Kucera et al., 2014 for a review).

Another reason for complacency in economic thinking about inequality is the rather politically loaded argument that 'growth should be in the driver's seat and distribution in the backseat' particularly in the context of developing countries. The Kuznets curve, which postulates an inverted-U-shaped relationship between inequality and income level, is often used to bolster this view: income inequality starts to widen with industrialization and structural transformation, but will automatically narrow at higher income levels. The Kuznets curve has often been understood as a 'natural law' of inequality that does not allow room for policy interventions to mitigate inequality. Yet empirical evidence is at best mixed.

This chapter will challenge these 'conventional wisdoms' (which are already questioned on their empirical accuracy) by returning to Kuznets's original, more nuanced view of inequality. While the standard interpretations assume a universal inverted-U-shaped relationship between growth and inequality, the latter emphasizes that socio-political factors affect inequality and thus considers inequality as part of a broader 'political and social economy'. Building on Acemoglu and Robinson's (2002) 'political economy of the Kuznets curve' and Milanović's (1994) 'augmented Kuznets curve', among others, we argue that a socio-political understanding of the recent developments in inequality and growth is far more convincing.

More precisely, we argue that once inequality becomes too wide it will generate socio-political pressures that cannot be ignored and will rather enter into policy debates. This creates a political opening that we term a 'Kuznets *moment*' where societies must choose how they move forward: they can ignore the moment and continue on the previous path, or they can implement distributive and redistributive policies that will eventually reverse the trend of widening inequality. Those societies that choose to ignore this window of opportunity are prone to suffer from the 'revenge of the Kuznets moment', namely economic instability, decline or stagnation.

The remainder of this chapter is organized into four sections. The first examines the growth–inequality nexus, presenting the conventional interpretation of the Kuznets curve, the mixed empirical evidence for this curve and some alternative factors that are thought to influence growth and inequality. The second section explores how the socio-political economy influences growth and inequality, echoing Kuznets's argument that it is an important factor in determining whether inequality widens or narrows. The third section reviews the experience of several developed and developing countries, highlighting the role of policy and institutional failures in explaining the recent trends of widening inequality. The fourth section concludes, echoing Kuznets's 1955 call to researchers and policy-makers to move beyond strict economics to a 'political and social economy' and embrace a broader range of social and political factors in explaining inequality and growth.

In following this line of argument we highlight that inequality is both a cause and a product of policy decisions. As the various contributions to this volume clearly demonstrate, well-designed labour market institutions and policies can promote equality.[1] All too often, policy-makers assume that in choosing to promote equality, they must concede efficiency and growth. This chapter challenges the notion of a 'natural' trade-off between growth and equality. It suggests that moderate levels of inequality are compatible with growth, while extreme levels – on either end – are not. As country case studies show, choice is possible, however constrained it may be.

2.2 DOES GROWTH REDUCE INEQUALITY? THE CONVENTIONAL KUZNETS CURVE – THEORY AND EVIDENCE

Kuznets never intended to offer an immutable law of inequality and development. Yet, his 1955 article nonetheless sparked a plethora of attempts to determine a linear relationship between income distribution and growth (which we call the 'conventional' Kuznets curve).[2] This section will explain the theoretical and empirical underpinning of this conventional approach and argue that the relationship between growth and inequality is contentious both theoretically and empirically. Indeed, as we will show, the 'economic' explanations behind the conventional Kuznets curve lack sufficient empirical support.

The Conventional Kuznets Curve

The key channel underlying the 'Kuznets process' is structural transformation, which essentially involves shifting human resources from agriculture to industry and from rural to urban areas – in short, industrialization and urbanization (Kanbur, 2000). In fact, Lewis's model of economic development (Lewis, 1954), which preceded Kuznets's work, had already suggested that industrialization requires labour inflow from labour surplus sectors (i.e., the rural/traditional sector with low labour earnings) to labour shortage sectors (i.e., the urban/modern sector) and that this process would inevitably widen income inequality. Lewis predicted that this inequality-widening process would continue until the pool of labour surplus was exhausted and wages in that sector began to catch up with urban wages (reaching a 'Lewisian turning point'). More generally and intuitively, he concluded that 'development must be [at least temporarily] inegalitarian because it does not start in every part of an economy at the same time' (1976, p. 26).

Kuznets extended Lewis's simple two-sector model to examine personal

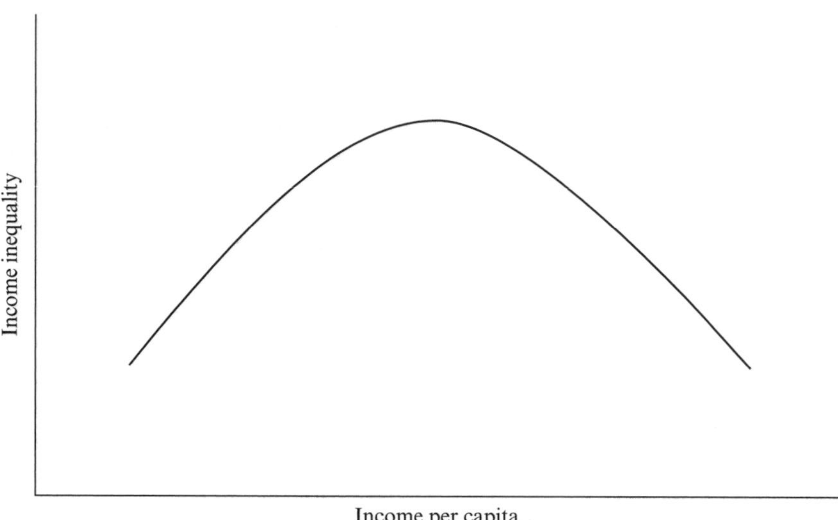

Figure 2.1 Kuznets curve: a simplified version

income distribution (e.g., percentile distribution of income). Starting from the observation that the rural sector had a relatively low average income and narrow income inequality, he incorporated two 'stylized' facts: (1) that the urban sector had an increasing share of the population; and (2) that the average income gap between the rural and urban sector was stable or widening. With these assumptions, he easily showed that personal income distribution will widen when sectoral shifts first begin. However, much like the 'Lewisian turning point', this process will be limited, ending as the process of structural transformation nears completion. As this happens, inequality will start to narrow. He models this sectoral shift to produce the inverted-U curves shown in Figure 2.1 (Kuznets, 1955).[3] In short, income inequality widens first with economic development and then narrows once it reaches a turning point. Hence, an inverted-U-shaped relationship between income inequality and economic development. Some empirical support was provided in Kuznets (1955) and further elaborated in his later work (1965).

In the rest of his article, Kuznets considers other factors that affect this relationship (e.g., demographic trends,[4] the political economy, etc.), but it was this structural explanation and the relevant empirical observations that were quickly taken up and used to challenge the relevance of distributional policy interventions. If inequality inevitably widens as a by-product of early economic development and is automatically addressed as the economy matures to a 'sufficiently' high level, there is very little room for policies. One could even argue that distributional policies are counter-productive in that they may reduce economic growth or slow industrialization.

This approach to policy also gained support from certain macroeconomic arguments that emphasized the importance of the savings-investment channel for industrialization and economic growth. In the classical view (e.g., Kaldor, 1955), wider inequality should spur growth through increasing net savings and investment since the rich have a higher marginal propensity to save; this would imply a positive correlation between initial inequality and subsequent growth. This dynamic will be stronger if efficient stock markets do not exist and thus large investments are 'indivisible' (Aghion et al., 1999). This view can be used to support the notion of a trade-off between equity and efficiency (Okun, 1975): efforts to redistribute wealth towards equality are seen as distortionary; they harm growth through reducing people's incentive to work and save.

Empirical Evidence

With this theory in mind, what does the empirical evidence tell us? Given the great policy implications of the Kuznets curve, it is not surprising that many empirical studies and literature reviews have been written on this topic (see, for example, Kanbur, 2000; Bourguignon, 2004; Isagiller, 2011 for reviews).

Interestingly, the Kuznets curve was generally accepted as a stylized fact until the 1980s (though, of course, with some exceptions).[5] For instance, Paukert (1973) updated Kuznets's dataset to cover low-income countries up to the 1960s and then confirmed the existence of an inverted-U-shaped relationship between national income and inequality (with a possible turning point around US$250–600 GDP per capita). Its widespread acceptance as an empirical regularity was partly due to data limitations. Kuznets himself warned of the limited availability of aggregate income data and its questionable reliability. Indeed, any empirical analysis concerning the Kuznets curve was vulnerable to data quality, particularly in the case of comparative analysis for countries with different income levels.

However, perhaps more importantly, the growing popularity of the Kuznets curve also reflected actual trends in income inequality at the time, particularly the experience of industrialization in Latin America in the 1960s and 1970s. In fact, the precipitous rise in inequality did not begin in many countries until the 1980s (as seen in Figure 2.2). With these secular upward changes in inequality in recent years, the findings of empirical analysis have also changed dramatically (as have their empirical techniques). By the mid-1990s, the evidence was more mixed, though often a

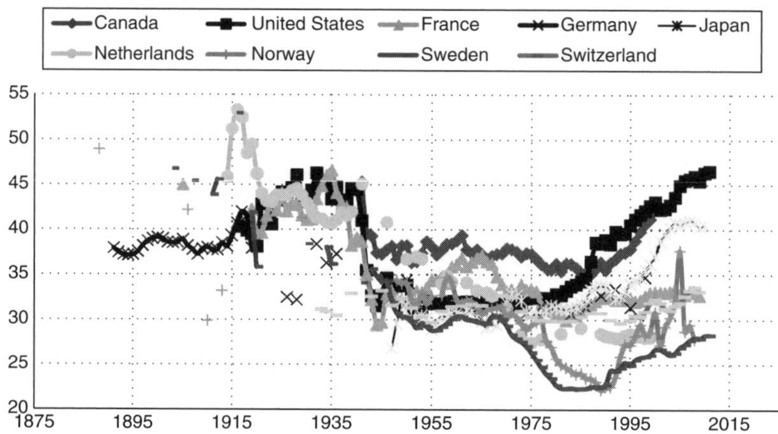

Source: The World Top Incomes Database (http://topincomes.g-mond.parisschoolofeconomics.eu/, last accessed 29 April 2013).

Figure 2.2 Trends in the top 10% income share in selected countries(1870-2011)

negative relationship between inequality and growth was reported across countries (see Benabou, 1996 or Isagiller, 2011 for a review).

Deininger and Squire's (1996) dataset changed the terms of the debate. Substantially expanding on the data of the time, the authors found no systematic relationship between growth and inequality within most countries; while their cross-section regressions supported the inverted U, this was deemed to be the result of regional exceptionalism, reminiscent of old critiques that Latin America, with its wide inequality and middle-income levels, was driving the Kuznets curve. This, of course, sparked new debate, which was again largely mixed (see Isagiller, 2011 for a brief review). Some studies found the curve to be empirically consistent, but that it did not explain much of the observed variance in inequality (Barro, 2008); others noted a positive correlation among high-income countries.[6] Banerjee and Duflo (2003, p. 268) perhaps put it best when they say, 'without imposing a linear structure, it quickly becomes clear that the data does not support the linear structure that has routinely been imposed on it'.

Data concerns continue to drive much of the debate. Datasets have evolved but remain markedly imperfect.[7] Efforts to update and extend them will, of course, be limited by historical data. And this limitation undermines their utility, because changes in both inequality and development are slow – usually occurring over a long period of time. Unsurprisingly, findings are sensitive to the chosen data source, measurement indicator (e.g., Gini, Theil, quintile and decile distribution, etc.) and unit of analysis, including the 'who', 'what' and 'when' of inequality (i.e., household, individual; net or gross income, land, wealth, etc.; length of time period, choice of timing for initial inequality).[8]

Methodological concerns have also played an important role in the debate. Statistical techniques and whether the relationship is measured across countries or across time significantly affect the results. Summarizing previous studies, Banerjee and Duflo (2003) highlight that OLS regressions tend to find a negative correlation and fixed effects' estimates tend to find a positive relationship. They note that Barro (2000), using a three-stage least squares regression (random effects) finds no relationship unless poor and rich economies are separated. As noted above, studies relying on cross-national data often find an inverted-U relationship across countries, whereas the theory describes changes in inequality over time (see Deininger and Squire, 1998 for a discussion).[9] All in all, measuring the relationship between inequality and growth remains a complicated task and existing studies do not provide strong evidence of a consistent or systematic relationship.

Case studies add a level of detail that is missing in macro-discussions. They often highlight multiple factors that affect growth and inequality in contradictory ways (Kanbur, 2000; Bourguignon et al., 2005). For instance, the ambitious World Bank study on the 'microeconomics of income distribution' analyses the changes in Argentina, Brazil, Colombia, Mexico, Indonesia, Malaysia and Taiwan (China). The coordinators conclude that 'in all but one country . . . [there were] countervailing forces acting on the distribution of income [in both positive and negative ways]' (Bourguignon et al., 2005, p. 389). Once again this conclusion undermines the idea of a 'natural law' on growth and inequality.

Explaining Why the Conventional Kuznets Curve Fails: The Economic Approach

Given the questionable empirical basis of the conventional Kuznets curve, it is natural to ask where it went wrong. A wide range of factors have been put forward. Let us review them quickly, focusing in on economic factors.

First, questions can be raised to the claim that inequality is 'necessary' for economic development (i.e., the claim made by introducing 'causality' to the empirical 'regularity' that Kuznets observed). This view has been challenged by the Keynesian critique that growth can also be constrained by a lack of consumption and demand – the other face of high savings and investment. Based on the same assumptions – that is, the rich saving more and the poor saving less – more equality could increase consumption and thus demand. Recent debates on whether growth is driven by wages or profit echo this critique (see, for example, ILO, 2013 and background papers: Hein and Mundt, 2012; Stockhammer, 2012; Onaran and Galanis, 2012; Storm and Naastepad, 2012). However, even if we leave this debate aside and temporarily accept the idea that savings and investment drive growth, there are still several problems with this argument. First, there is an 'adding up' problem. While at the micro-level, empirical evidence confirms that the propensity to consume diminishes across the income distribution, the aggregate impact on savings and consumption is ambiguous (see Schmidt-Hebbel and Serven, 2000 for a review). If consumption and savings are determined by *relative* rather than *absolute* income, a declining propensity to consume will not necessarily affect the aggregate rates of saving and consumption (on the topic of relative income, see Duesenberry, 1949; Easterlin, 1974; Oswald, 1997; Carroll et al., 2000 among others).

Second, the underlying assumption that income is distributed in a way that rewards the most productive elements of society is tenuous. In practice, asymmetric information and problems guaranteeing collection upon default create imperfect credit markets, so that access to credit depends on assets or collateral (see Aghion and Bolton, 1992 or Piketty, 1997 for a review). With rationed credit, wealth inequalities may endure over time (Piketty, 1997, 2014).[10] In addition to harming the poor, such a system is economically inefficient since potentially high-return investments may not be pursued. Such credit constraints have been explored on many topics such as education (Galor and Zeira, 1993), land and other agricultural inputs (Deininger and Squire, 1998).

In a way, this discussion parallels that of Chaudhuri and Ravallion (2006) on 'good' and 'bad' inequalities.[11] According to these authors, 'good' inequalities 'reflect and reinforce market-based incentives . . . to foster innovation, entrepreneurship and growth', while 'bad' inequalities stem from market, coordination and governance failures and 'prevent individuals from connecting to markets and limit investment in human and physical capital'.[12] In practice, this distinction is not so easy to make (i.e., what begin as 'good' inequalities may lead to 'bad' ones), but it nonetheless highlights that *some* level of inequality may be efficient. As explored in more depth below, extremely wide or narrow inequality may damage growth and macroeconomic stability.

Second, as regards the causes of growing inequality in recent years, many scholars have pointed out the emergence of new economic and structural factors that did not exist when the conventional Kuznets curve was developed. In a sense, they refer to the new types or waves of structural transformation. Arguably, the two key factors in this regard have been new technological changes and globalization, both of which can affect the sectoral and occupational distribution of employment (or Kuznetsian inter-sectoral shifts of population) and eventually affect the income distribution.

First, technological progress promotes growth but may polarize jobs and earnings by hollowing out middle-layer jobs, because these jobs often consist of routine tasks that are relatively easy to replace with technology (e.g., clerical and craft work; see Autor et al., 2003). Technology may generate demand for high-skilled workers or jobs (see literature on skill-biased technological change [SBTC]), but it cannot replace certain non-routine and location-specific jobs, even if they are low paid or low skilled (e.g., live-in nanny). In fact, it may boost demand for these jobs by increasing the earnings of high-skilled workers and, in doing so, increasing their opportunity cost for time spent cooking, cleaning, caring, doing repairs, and so on (Mazzolari and Ragusa, 2013). These hypotheses of 'routinization' and job polarization are in line with recent evidence from the USA, the UK and Europe (see Autor et al., 2006; Goos et al., 2009; Hurley et al., 2013 among others). Technological progress may also change the functional distribution of income in favour of capital and thus widen personal income inequality, because owners of capital are typically among the upper half of the income distribution (see ILO, 2013 for a deeper discussion of functional income distribution). However, while technological changes, especially SBTC, are of potential importance in explaining inequality, the magnitude of their roles is still subject to debate and there is evidence that the contribution of SBTC to job polarization has been rather limited (see Mischel et al., 2013).

Another hypothesis is that globalization is responsible for widening income inequality (see Jansen and Lee, 2007 for a review of this debate). Traditional theories suggest that trade will reward the abundant factors of production – namely capital and skills in industrialized economies and unskilled labour in developing economies; it should thereby widen inequality in industrialized economies and narrow it in developing economies (though, of course, the exact effect will depend on the economy's factors of production).[13] At the same time, more open trade could narrow consumption inequality by increasing price competition and reducing tariffs and other trade barriers. However, as Jansen and Lee (2007) review, several anomalies exist that are at odds with this traditional perspective: first, industrialized countries mainly trade amongst themselves; second, most restructuring has occurred within sectors instead of across them (as the traditional theories would have predicted); and third, skills premiums have increased in some developing countries despite the fact that these are not abundant factors (e.g., Latin America in the 1990s). Even taking these anomalies into account, globalization could still widen income inequality if mid-layer jobs are easier to trade (polarization due to offshoring) or if trade, openness and FDI reduce the bargaining power of workers by increasing their sense of insecurity, making them easier to substitute with foreign labour and increasing the sensitivity of sales to wage increases through competition. Finally, as discussed above, by favouring capital over labour, globalization may widen income inequality. In any case, the evidence of globalization's effect on wage and income inequality is mixed, though both wage and income inequality have widened alongside a shift in functional income distribution towards capital (Jansen and Lee, 2007).

2.3 THE SOCIO-POLITICAL ECONOMY OF THE KUZNETS CURVE: KUZNETS MOMENT

So then, how can we make sense of the empirically ambiguous relationship between growth and inequality? Does this mean that Kuznets was simply wrong?

We argue that he was not. Rather, the conventional interpretation of the Kuznets curve fails because it only captures part of Kuznets's theory. In particular, it fails to recognize the importance of socio-political dimensions on which Kuznets placed great emphasis. In fact, while he did suggest that the initial period of widening inequality was driven by industrialization, urbanization and the concentration of savings among high earners, he went on to say that the subsequent period of narrowing inequality was driven by 'legislative interference and "political" decisions' brought about by 'the growing political power of the urban lower-income groups' (Kuznets, 1955, pp. 9, 17). In other words, the U-turn in income inequality is to a large extent driven by policy shifts in response to political pressure from society. Moreover, Kuznets was extremely cautious about applying the experiences of advanced countries (e.g., Germany) to less-developed countries for fear of a 'failure of the political and social systems of underdeveloped countries to initiate the governmental or political practices that effectively bolster the weak positions of the lower-income classes' (Kuznets, 1955, p. 24).

In short, widening income inequality in the market may spark a socio-political reaction that opens up a window of opportunity for a policy choice that directly or indirectly rebalances income distribution. We call this socio-political opening a 'Kuznets moment'. The Kuznets moment has a wide range of implications for theories around growth and inequality and the role policy and institutions can play.

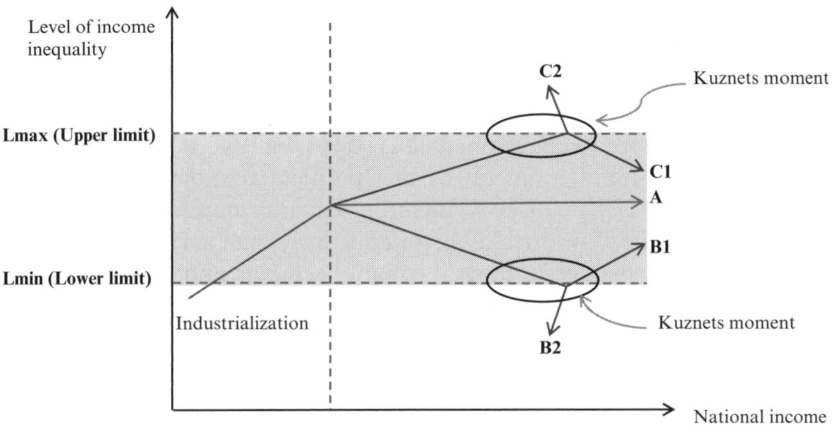

Figure 2.3 Economic development and the Kuznets moment

Defining the Kuznets Moment

Our socio-political interpretation of the Kuznets curve is summarized in Figure 2.3. As Kuznets noted, income inequality tends to be narrow before capitalist industrialization begins. Yet, industrialization, which involves a series of structural transformations with massive reallocation of resources (e.g., from rural to urban areas), creates upward pressures on inequality along with higher income growth. The widening trend in inequality will continue unless policy actions are taken from the early stage (Case A).

In a typical historical situation, inequality widens until it reaches a Kuznets moment at which point socio-political pressures relating to income inequality cannot be ignored and are brought into policy debates. Faced with the Kuznets moment, the society may *choose* to adopt distributive and redistributive policies, which will eventually mark a U-turn in inequality (Case C1) – hence, the conventional shape of the Kuznets curve. However, as emphasized earlier, there is no guarantee that such change will take place. If there is insufficient bottom-up pressure and rent-seeking activities among top-income groups are further strengthened, a 'Robin Hood paradox' could play out such that inequality may further widen (Lindert, 2004). These policy failures will have negative political and social consequences, which will damage the production potential of the economy and reduce the overall income level (Case C2). In other words, Kuznets 'revenge' will kick in, with the worst-case scenario being an extended period of economic depression.

Theoretically, this scenario is applicable to the case of 'too much equality', although Kuznets did not discuss this explicitly. If distributive and redistributive policies are pursued to the other extreme (e.g., former communist countries), an inverted Kuznets moment could occur where incentives to work diminish, growth stagnates and economic and political crises become more likely. Nonetheless, this narrative is less convincing than the 'upper limit' moment, as the 'political economy' of complete equality is difficult to conceive. Ensuring equality necessitates a certain degree of centralized political control and thus some sort of 'vanguard'. By extension, this suggests some inequality remains and raises the more fundamental question of whether economic stagnation is due to inefficient central planning rather than 'equality'.

The Implications of the Kuznets Moment

The Kuznets moment has a wide range of implications for theories around growth and inequality and the role policy and institutions can play.

First, it clearly highlights the importance of socio-political factors in influencing income distribution. Admittedly, this socio-political dimension of the Kuznets curve has not been completely ignored in economic studies; it has been recognized by some scholars in recent years. Milanović (1994) observed substantive variations in income inequality between countries and over time that called into question the relevance of the Kuznets curve. To explain these trends, he proposed an 'augmented Kuznets curve' in which income inequality is not just the function of income levels (or growth) but also 'the product of *social choices* mediated through elections, lobbying of various social groups, societal preferences or historical developments' (p. 5; original emphasis). More recently, Acemoglu and Robinson (2002) have taken a further step to develop a 'political economy of the Kuznets curve'. Based on the historical evidence concerning income inequality between the early 19th century and early 20th century, they concluded that the observed decline in income inequality 'was not an unavoidable consequence of economic development, but an outcome of political changes forced on the system by the mobilization of the masses' (p. 184). Then they hypothesized that 'capitalist industrialization tends to increase inequality, but this inequality contains the seeds of its own destruction, because it induces a change in the political regime toward a more redistributive system' (ibid.). Their arguments are strikingly similar to those of Polanyi (1957, p. 127), where society 'inevitably . . . [takes] measures to protect itself' against the 'self-adjusting market' (though he argues there will be a pendulum – where the self-protection will also trigger counter-reactions).

Second, as Kuznets (1955, 1965) recognized, this change toward redistribution is not guaranteed; the political forces will not necessarily mobilize and, if they do not, no political juncture will arise. In Kuznets's (1955, p. 17) narrative, 'the growing political power of the urban lower-income groups' drove the policy responses. But as Acemoglu and Robinson (2002) recognize, political pressure for change may not arise, even in democratic societies that are naturally the most conducive environment. Rather, for political pressure to arise those at the bottom end of the income distribution must be politically literate, active, motivated and able to overcome collective action problems to present an organized front.[14]

The political reaction will also depend on existing social and political institutions, whose features are themselves likely endogenous to the distribution of political power (see discussion below and Savoia et al., 2010 for a review). For instance, inequality may make democracy and thus political voice less likely (though as Savoia et al., 2010 review, the link is under-researched and the evidence, mixed). Freedoms that are fundamental to organization – for instance, freedom of association or of expression – may or may not be protected by laws and institutions. Seemingly innocuous decisions on electoral systems (majoritarian, proportional, etc.) or geographical divisions of electorates will affect who organizes and how effective they are. Social policies such as accessible education may improve the political literacy of the poor. The list goes on.

Third, even when widening inequality does trigger political mobilization and unrest, the actions and reactions this unrest causes cannot be determined a priori. Many authors fail to recognize this; instead they suggest that in democracies, inequality will generate inefficient redistribution away from the rich, which limits growth by reducing the rewards to investment and harming property rights (Alesina and Rodrik, 1994; Persson and Tabellini, 1994).[15,16] Leaving aside for the moment the questionable assumption that redistribution towards the poor is bad for growth, it is unclear whether redistribution will even occur. Recent revisionist versions of the Kuznets curve recognize this uncertainty (see Milanović, 1994; Acemoglu and Robinson, 2002). For instance, Acemoglu and Robinson (2002, p. 184) suggest that in the face of political unrest, the established elite may choose from a number of actions, 'ranging from income redistribution, to repression, or to fundamental political change'.

If 'the people' fail to mobilize or if the elite seek to maintain or strengthen their political and economic advantage, the policy choice will likely widen rather than narrow inequality. This rather familiar real-world phenomenon was well illustrated by Vilfredo Pareto a long time ago:

> If a certain measure A is the case of the loss of one franc to each of a thousand persons, and of a thousand franc gain to one individual, the latter will expend a great deal of energy, whereas the former will resist weakly; and it is likely that,

> in the end, the person who is attempting to secure the thousand francs via A will be successful. (Vilfredo Pareto, 1927, *Manual of Political Economy*, New York: Kelley, p. 379, quoted in Sen, 1999, p. 122)

This may explain why we sometimes observe what Lindert (2004) has coined as the 'Robin Hood paradox': that redistribution is most common where it is least needed – namely, in more equal societies. Instead of triggering redistribution, widening inequality can lead to institutions and policies that perpetuate or accelerate it (see Savoia et al., 2010 for a detailed review). As Robert Dahl (1961, p. 1) provocatively demands, even in a democracy 'where nearly every adult may vote but where knowledge, wealth, social position, access to officials, and other resources are unequally distributed, who actually governs?' In concentrating resources among a small group of individuals, inequality strengthens their capacity and incentive to maintain or create inefficient institutions, policies and practices that benefit them at the cost of others. Simply put, inequality in economic resources can lead to inequality in political power, which in turn leads to unequal policies that impede efficient incentives and access to opportunities to invest and innovate (World Bank, 2005; Bebbington et al., 2008).[17]

Globalization and financialization have likely worsened this power imbalance: the increasing mobility of capital but not labour has strengthened capital's bargaining power[18] (OECD, 2011; ILO, 2013); the atomization of workers in value chains stretching across borders and linguistic and cultural barriers have made worker mobilization much more difficult. International financial institutions, such as the IMF, the World Bank and so on, have also introduced a new political force into countries' political economies (Stewart, 2010).

This brings us to our final point: the failure to take proper policy actions to narrow inequality during a Kuznets moment is not without consequences. Rather, a 'revenge' of the Kuznets moment occurs, where it is the lack of policy counter-measures that actually plants the seeds of a system's destruction. Kuznets revenge will either occur through inefficiency or by triggering unrest and instability.

Inefficient institutions that advantage the rich have been shown to harm growth prospects over the long term. For instance, Engerman and Sokoloff (1997, 2002) compare the Americas, arguing that the 'reversal of fortunes' between Latin America and Canada and the United States was because of greater initial equality in the North, which led to more egalitarian institutions, such as suffrage, schooling, land policy, taxation, patents and banking, that improved its long-term growth prospects (see authors' later publications and also Easterly, 2007). Similarly, Lindert (2004) emphasizes that more equal societies provide more equal access to education, which in turn creates more productive workers who are more politically active and capable.

Redistribution is not necessarily economically inefficient. Even from a neoliberal viewpoint, redistribution may compensate for imperfect credit markets (which prevent the poor from investing in human capital and other opportunities), unequal protection of property rights across income groups or other market policies that redistribute towards the rich (Saint-Paul and Verdier, 1996; see Luebker, Chapter 8 in this volume for a broad definition of redistribution). Bourguignon puts it nicely when he says: 'Good policies for growth and poverty reduction generally involve redistribution – of influence, government expenditures, current income . . . away from dominant groups'.[19] When inequality is wide and enduring, it likely reflects 'bad' inequalities (Chaudhuri and Ravallion, 2006) or structural inequality (Easterly, 2007), both of which are bad for growth. Kuznets's own work has strong parallels. He states that: 'a highly unequal distribution of income may in one case be most conducive to economic growth whereas in another case it may constitute a major obstacle, even if it does not go so far as to threaten political breakdown'; what matters is:

> the junction at which the production and the use of income meet within the family or consuming unit, the latter acting in two roles, as producer and a consumer. This distribution represents an intersection of the system of rewards for productive activity with the system of allocation of these rewards, or the use of income, and both systems affect the relation between actual and potential economic growth. (Kuznets, 1965, p. 303)

At a global level, a new wave of studies building on post-Keynesian economics also suggest a Kuznetsian 'revenge' (see ILO, 2013 for a review). They have shown that the shifts in income away from labour have actually reduced the level of economic growth and made growth more unstable. It is now widely believed that these distributional changes with economic consequences have contributed to the Great Recession (see, for instance, Stiglitz, 2012).

Aside from leading to economic inefficiency, elite overreach and the accompanying inequality can harm growth through macroeconomic volatility, either by eventually sparking political unrest and in turn damaging the investment climate[20] or through the mechanisms described above (credit market failures, underinvestment in education, infrastructure, etc.) (Berg and Ostry, 2011; Berg et al., 2012; see Aghion et al., 1999 for an early review). Elite overreach has been argued to be behind many economic crises (see, for instance, Johnson, 2009 or the literature reviewed in Kucera et al., 2014).

2.4 KUZNETS MOMENT IN ACTION: RECENT COUNTRY EXPERIENCES

Our view of the Kuznetsian approach to inequality and growth, in which a Kuznets moment plays a critical role in shaping the relationship between the two, implies the inherent limitations of comparative econometric analysis of a large group of countries and the critical importance of country-level analysis. In this approach, while it is possible to identify common factors that can influence inequality, these factors will be channelled through socio-political mechanisms and may trigger policy responses – thus, it is not possible to establish or predict the relationship between growth and inequality at the aggregate level. Paradoxically, the Kuznetsian approach, as we understand it, does not allow for the conventional Kuznets curve but instead emphasizes policies and the socio-politics that surround them. This perspective is particularly useful in understanding different (even contrasting) dynamics of inequality in recent years across countries. Our central observation here is that shifts in equality tend to be related to socio-political changes (which in themselves may be sparked by domestic and global economic crisis). This section highlights different possible combinations of growth and inequality by *illustrating* trends in a selected number of country cases, without attempting to identify the exact mechanism underlying these combinations (a topic that merits future research).

Figure 2.4 shows trends in income inequality (measured by Gini coefficients) over more than 30 years in different parts of the world. The selection of countries is intended to reflect *roughly* three generations of economic development: the first generation of 'old' industrialized countries (Sweden and USA, OECD countries); the second generation of Asian countries (particularly 'Asian tigers'); and the third generation of newly (re-)emerging Latin American countries. Interestingly, inequality dynamics differ considerably between the three groups of countries.

Revenge of the Kuznets moment

The trends in the 'old' industrialized countries are all well known. Inequality was stable or narrowing until the 1970s and it began to widen from the 1980s. This reversal has affected countries regardless of whether they began with wide or narrow inequality (e.g., United States versus Sweden). On average among OECD countries, this historical reversal took place in the early 1980s, but the exact timing varies between countries. For instance, in the United States trends in inequality reached a turning point in the early 1980s when major political and policy shifts were made. In Sweden, the turning point came a decade later in the early 1990s when

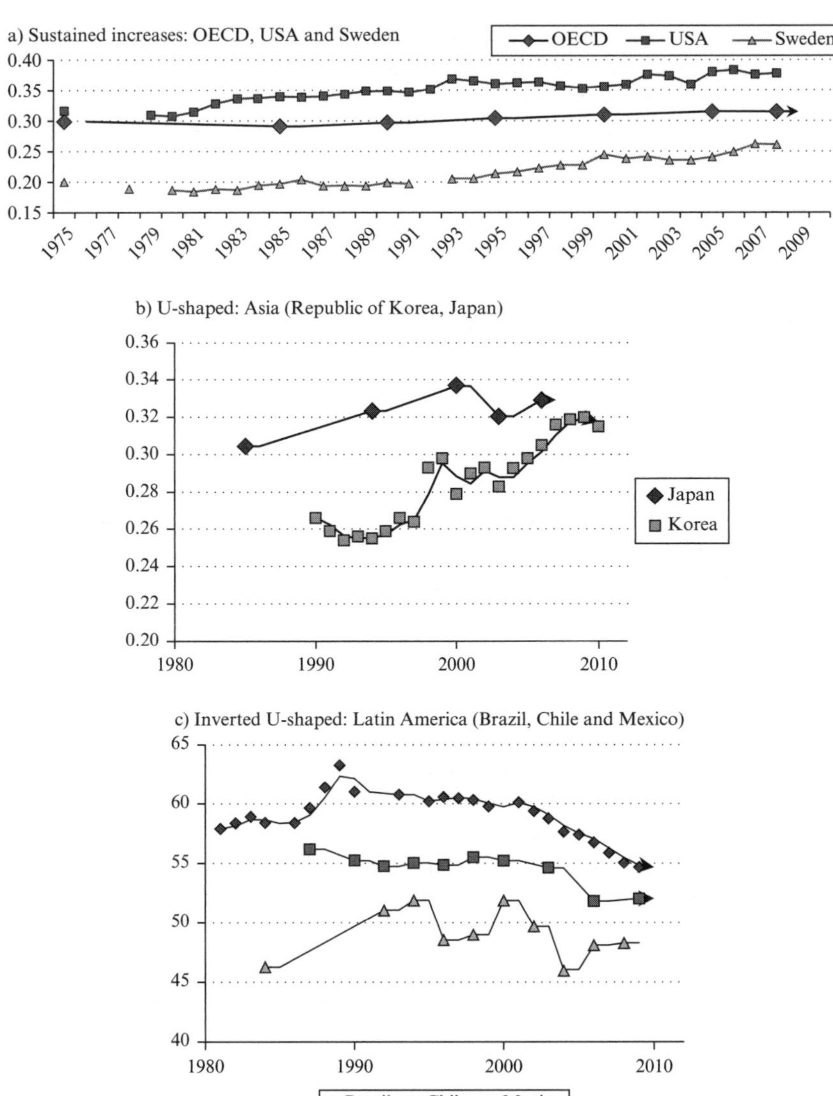

Sources: OECD statistics for OECD and Japan (OECD, 2011); KLI Labour Statistics (in Korean) for Republic of Korea; World Bank statistics for Latin American countries (http://data.worldbank.org/indicator/SI.POV.GINI; last accessed 3 September 2014).

Figure 2.4a–c Trends in income inequality (Gini coefficients, household disposable income)

the country was hit by a financial crisis. The case of the USA is striking in many respects. Around the turning point, the Gini coefficient was at about the OECD average, but since this time, the USA has steadily diverged from the average. As many have pointed out (e.g., Stiglitz, 2012), this continued widening of inequality in the USA produced socio-political tensions creating a Kuznets moment before the crisis. However, no significant policy responses were introduced due to powerful 'rent-seeking' of the top income group and the relatively limited 'political power of . . . the lower-income groups' (Kuznets, 1955, p. 17). As discussed earlier, this has eventually led to what we call the 'revenge of the Kuznets moment' (e.g., the Great Recession; see Kucera et al., 2014 for an overview of research linking inequality to the financial crisis).

Kuznets moment in action with uncertain direction

Given our focus on economic development, the experience of developing countries is even more relevant. Among them, the case of the 'Asian tigers' is particularly interesting. In fact, the proponents of the conventional Kuznets curve used to argue that the Asian experiences validated their views, since these countries experienced a relatively short period of widening inequality, followed by a period of high growth and narrow inequality. They have often been praised as the 'champion[s] of equitable growth' (e.g., see Page, 1994). However, this is no longer the case. With the bursting of the 'bubble economy', the 'old tiger' Japan started to see a rapid expansion of inequality. The Republic of Korea, as one of the new Asian tigers, followed suit. The turning point in the Republic of Korea was also an economic crisis – the Asian financial crisis of 1997. Driven by their respective crises, both countries shifted their policies towards neoliberal market reforms, and the Great Recession has accelerated the expansion of inequality in both countries. It is plausible that these significant trends have opened a Kuznets moment in both countries, but, as emphasized earlier, it has yet to be seen if it will lead to an egalitarian policy or to a Kuznetsian revenge.

Kuznetsian turning point

While many countries have not capitalized on the Kuznets moment to create a turning point in inequality, some other countries, particularly in Latin America, have demonstrated that a Kuznetsian policy shift is indeed a viable option. Inequality in this region (e.g., Brazil, Chile and Mexico in Figure 2.4) has been declining since the mid- to late 1990s. This period coincides with important policy shifts away from the dominant policy thinking of the 1980s and early 1990s. In Brazil in particular, the new political challenges prompted a series of policy interventions, notably significant real increases in the minimum wage and an expansion of the social security system, including the well-known Bolsa Família (Family Allowance) programme, but also a rural pension. In addition, there were greater investments in education and health (de Souza, 2012). In Mexico, where policy interventions were largely limited to social assistance programmes, the reduction in inequality has been more tempered.

2.5 CONCLUDING REMARKS

This chapter examined the relationship between economic growth and inequality, which has been subject to much debate and controversy and which has often centred on Kuznets's inverted-U-shaped curve. While the Kuznets curve has often been used to deny the need for distributive/redistributive policies, we have argued that this conventional interpretation lacks empirical grounds and that it is based on an incomplete understanding of Kuznets's original analysis. In our view, Kuznets never intended to present a general *economic* law of inequality but rather highlighted the importance of socio-politics in determining inequality outcomes. His emphasis on the political empowerment of lower-income groups and progressive legislation toward rebalancing income distribution is particularly important in this respect.

Inspired by Kuznets's original views and by recent attempts to bring his perspective back into debates on inequality (e.g., Acemoglu and Robinson, 2002), this chapter presents a political economy of inequality and growth in which political and social factors play a critical role in shaping the relationship. Using the concept of a Kuznets moment, we have shown that the tensions that come from growing inequality do not necessarily lead to mitigating policy measures. Indeed, some regressive political dynamics did not receive much attention in Kuznets's analysis: along with widening inequality, 'rent-seeking' by the top income group may get stronger and 'collective action' by low-income groups may become more and more difficult to achieve. This asymmetry in political mobilization between income groups has typically widened in recent years under the pressure of globalization and financialization. The failure of policy shifts during the critical period of a Kuznets moment may lead, in an extreme case, to an economic and/or political crisis: what we call the 'revenge' of the Kuznets moment.

The Kuznetsian socio-political economy of inequality means that there is no 'natural' relationship between growth and inequality. Instead, various combinations are entirely plausible, depending on policies and related institutions. In this perspective, considerable variations in inequality trends between countries and regions should not come as a surprise. As the following chapters of this book show, institutions matter in mitigating inequality.

NOTES

* The views expressed here are solely those of the authors and do not necessarily reflect those of the International Labour Organization. Sections 2.2 and 2.3 of this chapter draw on the authors' paper, 'Inequality and economic growth: revisiting the Kuznetsian political economy of inequality', *Indian Journal of Labour Economics*, **56**(1). The authors are grateful to Janine Berg for her insightful comments and to the participants of the ILO Workshop on Labour Market Institutions and Inequality (7–8 February 2013) for helpful comments on the earlier version of this chapter.

1. See, in this volume, Belser and Rani on minimum wages, Hayter on unions and collective bargaining, Martínez Franzoni and Sánchez-Ancochea on public social services, Luebker on redistribution through taxes and transfers, Behrendt and Woodall on pension systems, Berg on income support for the unemployed and the poor, Islam and Hengge on full employment policies, Cazes and de Laiglesia on contractual segmentation, and Messenger and Ray on working time.
2. Despite the fact that Kuznets emphasized economic development, much of the discussion has focused on growth rates.
3. This curve will be more or less pronounced depending on the productivity gap and the income dispersion within the sectors. The new sector – for example, industry – is assumed to be more productive.
4. Though often overlooked, demographics can also be a channel linking inequality and growth. A correlation has been observed between high inequality and high fertility, which is argued to harm growth through increasing family size and thus reducing investment in human capital (dubbed as 'endogenous fertility' channel by Perotti, 1996; see also Galor and Zang, 1997). Vogl (2013) provides an interesting critique of this perspective, showing that family size and human capital investment were not always (and in some cases are not) negatively correlated. Some authors nuance this, drawing attention to 'differential fertility' rates across skill/earning groups rather than total fertility (Kremer and Chen, 2002; de la Croix and Doepke, 2003). They argue that total fertility only increases because poorer individuals have larger families in situations of inequality, because they face lower opportunity costs of children (and perhaps also lower direct costs such as investment in education). In unequal societies, less-educated workers have larger families, but suffer from an alleged 'quality–quantity' trade-off, meaning growth suffers (Kremer and Chen, 2002; de la Croix and Doepke, 2003). It should be noted this relationship does not seem to be monotonic: fertility differentials are small in high-income countries (because fertility is low across the skill distribution) and follow a hump-shaped pattern in the poorest developing countries because of subsistence constraints or access to education (Kremer and Chen, 2002; Vogl, 2013). Similarly, de la Croix and Doepke (2003) suggest that differential fertility and inequality will follow an inverted-U curve over the course of development.
5. See Kravis (1960); Kuznets (1965); Paukert (1973); Ahluwalia (1976).
6. For high-income countries, see Barro (1999); List and Gallet (1999); and Tribble (1999).
7. The Deininger and Squire dataset was extended by UNDP and the UN University World Institute for Development Economics Research (UNU-WIDER) into the World Income Inequality Database (WIID), and further extended and standardized by Frederick Solt (2008) into the Standardized WIID (SWIID). An alternative to these Gini-based datasets is the University of Texas Inequality Project-UN

Industrial Development Organization (UTIP-UNIDO), which compiles Theil indexes of manufacturing wages.

8. For example, measuring over different time periods may affect the results. Concentrating on shorter time periods with Deininger and Squire's (1996) data, Forbes (2000) finds a positive, rather than negative, relationship between inequality and growth. Exploring this issue of timing, Galbraith (2012) highlights that studies that compare initial inequality at one point of time to growth rates over time fall into the trap of comparing apples to oranges, as the choice of starting point cannot avoid being arbitrary.
9. Indeed, using panel data, Li et al. (2001) show that cross-country differences explain 90 per cent of the variance in inequality, with hardly any role for intra-country changes over time.
10. Whereas with perfect credit markets, as in Solow's (1956) model, inheritance should not play a determining role in income generation.
11. See also Easterly (2007) on market-based and structural inequality; he qualifies the latter as unambiguously bad for growth.
12. Chaudhuri and Ravallion (2006, pp. 16, 17). In other words, the authors argue for equality of opportunity rather than equality of outcome – or, in other words, Roemer's distinction between circumstance and effort (Bourguignon et al., 2007). They acknowledge that efficient unequal outcomes may restrict opportunities through facilitating corruption, rent-seeking or crony capitalism, whereby individuals who benefit early on in the development process restrict opportunities for others.
13. If the South is engaged in technological catch-up, income inequality may widen in both sets of countries, since jobs that were low skilled in industrialized economies may be relatively high skilled in developing economies (see discussion of literature in Jansen and Lee, 2007).
14. Because of collective action problems and the lower likelihood of the poor (or uneducated) to be politically active, organization of and by the poor will likely depend on them having some shared sense of identity – for instance, 'class characteristic (being peasants or workers)' that they can organize around (Stewart, 2011, p. 542). Nonetheless, one should not ignore out of hand that the rich can also face collective action problems (Elster, 1982).
15. Assuming a flat tax rate and universal transfers, Meltzer and Richard (1981) show the median voter benefits more and more from redistribution as inequality widens and should thus rationally increase their support for such policies. Alesina and Rodrik (1994) suggest that even dictatorships must respond to the demands of the majority to avoid being overthrown.
16. Inequality could also encourage illegal activities such as 'appropriation' and rent-seeking that damage the investment climate and increase vulnerability to external shocks (see Benhabib and Rustichini, 1996 among others).
17. There are many ways this may happen. To name a few: (1) senators and politicians may vote for the preferences of the rich (Gilens, 2005); (2) the range of choices presented by parties may not reflect 'lower-income' interests, but rather areas where the disagreement exists among the elite (i.e., the left represents interests of the wealthier constituents such as civil rights, gender equality and environment regulation (Solt, 2008; Hacker and Pierson, 2010)); (3) politics reflects *organized* interests and business has organized politically while unions have been undermined (Hacker and Pierson, 2010); (4) the careers of politicians and bureaucrats start off or end within elite industries, resulting in close ties between these worlds (see Johnson, 2009 on American finance); (5) poverty and lack of education reduce the likelihood of the poor to participate politically (though this may not hold across developing countries; see, for instance, Isaksson, 2010). See also (Kucera et al., 2014) for a discussion of the literature on the role politics played during the crisis.
18. As Jansen and Lee (2007) note, employers do not actually have to leave for their bargaining power to increase; rather, the mere threat may be enough to make mobilization and protest too risky or high stake.

19. See http://siteresources.worldbank.org/EXTPREMNET/Resources/489960-133899724 1035/Growth_Commission_Workshops_Equity_Bourguignon_Presentation.pdf; last accessed 25 August 2014.
20. For instance, riots, protests, strikes, mass violence and revolutions will lead to uncertainty (e.g., government turnover, regime change, risk of expropriation, nationalization or sovereign default, deteriorating rule of law, corruption, contract enforceability, and so on; for a brief overview, see Benabou, 1996; Acemoglu and Robinson, 2002).

REFERENCES

Acemoglu, D. and J.A. Robinson (2002), 'The political economy of the Kuznets curve', *Review of Development Economics*, **6**(2), 183–203.

Aghion, P. and P. Bolton (1992), 'Distribution and growth in models of imperfect capital markets', *European Economic Review*, **36**(2–3), 603–11.

Aghion, P., E. Caroli and C. Garcia-Penalosa (1999), 'Inequality and economic growth: the perspective of the new growth theories', *Journal of Economic Literature*, **37**(4), 1615–60.

Ahluwalia, M.S. (1976), 'Inequality, poverty and development', *Journal of Development Economics*, **3**(4), 307–42.

Alesina, A. and D. Rodrik (1994), 'Distributive politics and economic growth', *Quarterly Journal of Economics*, **109**(2), 465–90.

Alvaredo, F., A.B. Atkinson, T. Piketty and E. Saez (n.d.), *The World Top Incomes Database*, accessed 25 August 2014 at http://topincomes.g-mond.parisschoolofeconomics.eu/.

Autor, D.H., L.F. Katz and M.S. Kearney (2006), 'The polarization of the US labor market', *NBER Working Paper No. 11986*, Cambridge, MA: National Bureau of Economic Research.

Autor, D.H., F. Levy and R.J. Murnane (2003), 'The skill content of recent technological change: an empirical exploration', *Quarterly Journal of Economics*, **118**(4), 1279–333.

Banerjee, A.V. and E. Duflo (2003), 'Inequality and growth: what can the data say?', *Journal of Economic Growth*, **8**(3), 267–99.

Barro, R.J. (1999), 'Inequality, growth, and investment', *NBER Working Paper No. 7038*, Cambridge, MA: National Bureau of Economic Research.

Barro, R.J. (2000), 'Inequality and growth in a panel of countries', *Journal of Economic Growth*, **5**(1), 5–32.

Barro, R.J. (2008), 'Inequality and growth revisited', *Working Paper Series on Regional Economic Integration, No. 11*, Manila: Asian Development Bank.

Bebbington, A.J., A.A. Dani, A.D. Haan and M. Walton (eds) (2008), *Institutional Pathways to Equity: Addressing Inequality Traps*, Washington, DC: World Bank.

Benabou, R. (1996), 'Inequality and growth', in B.S. Bernanke and J.J. Rotemberg (eds), *NBER Macroeconomics Annual, Vol. 11*, Cambridge, MA: MIT Press, pp. 11–74.

Benhabib, J. and A. Rustichini (1996), 'Social conflict and growth', *Journal of Economic Growth*, **1**(1), 125–42.

Berg, A. and J.D. Ostry (2011), 'Inequality and unsustainable growth: two sides of the same coin?', *IMF Staff Discussion Note, SDN/11/08*, Washington, DC: International Monetary Fund.

Berg, A., J.D. Ostry and J. Zettelmeyer (2012), 'What makes growth sustained?', *Journal of Development Economics*, **98**(2), 149–66.
Bertola, G. (2000), 'Macroeconomics of distribution and growth', in A.B. Atkinson and F. Bourguignon (eds), *Handbook of Income Distribution*, Amsterdam: Elsevier, pp. 477–540.
Bourguignon, F. (2004), *The Poverty–Growth–Inequality Triangle*, New Delhi: Indian Council for Research on International Economic Relations.
Bourguignon, F., F.H.G. Ferreira and N. Lustig (eds) (2005), *The Microeconomics of Income Distribution Dynamics in East Asia and Latin America*, New York: World Bank and Oxford University Press.
Bourguignon, F.O., F.H.G. Ferreira and M. Walton (2007), 'Equity, efficiency and inequality traps: a research agenda', *Journal of Economic Inequality*, **5**(2), 235–56.
Carroll, C.D., J. Overland and D.N. Weil (2000), 'Saving and growth with habit formation', *American Economic Review*, **90**(3), 341–55.
Chaudhuri, S. and M. Ravallion (2006), 'Partially awakened giants: uneven growth in China and India', *World Bank Policy Research Working Paper No. 4069*, Washington, DC: World Bank.
Dahl, R.A. (1961), *Who Governs? Democracy and Power in an American City*, New Haven, CT: Yale University Press.
Deininger, K. and L. Squire (1996), 'A new data set measuring income inequality', *The World Bank Economic Review*, **10**(3), 565–91.
Deininger, K. and L. Squire (1998), 'New ways of looking at old issues: inequality and growth', *Journal of Development Economics*, **57**(2), 259–87.
de la Croix, D. and M. Doepke (2003), 'Inequality and growth: why differential fertility matters', *American Economic Review*, **93**(4), 1091–13.
de Souza, P.H.F. (2012), 'Poverty, inequality and social policies in Brazil, 1995–2009', *Working Paper No. 87*, Brasilia: International Policy Centre for Inclusive Growth.
Duesenberry, J.S. (1949), *Income, Savings and the Theory of Consumer Behavior*, Cambridge, MA: Harvard University Press.
Easterlin, R.A. (1974), 'Does economic growth improve the human lot? Some empirical evidence', in P.A. David and M.W. Reder (eds), *Nations and Households in Economic Growth: Essays in Honour of Moses Abramowitz*, New York: Academic Press, pp. 89–125.
Easterly, W. (2007), 'Inequality does cause underdevelopment: insights from a new instrument', *Journal of Development Economics*, **84**(2), 755–76.
Elster, J. (1982), 'The case for methodological individualism', *Theory and Society*, **11**(4), 453–82.
Engerman, S. and K. Sokoloff (1997), 'Factor endowments, institutions and differential paths of growth among the New World Economies', in S. Haber (ed.), *How Latin America Fell Behind*, Stanford, CA: Stanford University Press.
Engerman, S.L. and K. Sokoloff (2002), 'Factor endowments, inequality, and paths of development among new world economies', *NBER Working Paper No. 9259*, Cambridge, MA: National Bureau of Economic Research.
Galbraith, J.K. (2012), *Inequality and Instability: A Study of the World Economy Just Before the Great Crisis*, Oxford: Oxford University Press.
Galor, O. and H. Zang (1997), 'Fertility, income distribution, and economic growth: theory and cross-country evidence', *Japan and the World Economy*, **9**(2), 197–229.

Galor, O. and J. Zeira (1993), 'Income distribution and macroeconomics', *The Review of Economic Studies*, **60**(1), 35–52.
Gilens, M. (2005), 'Inequality and democratic responsiveness', *Public Opinion Quarterly*, **69**(5), 778–96.
Goos, M., A. Manning and A. Salomons (2009), 'Job polarization in Europe', *The American Economic Review*, **99**(2), 58–63.
Hacker, J.S. and P. Pierson (2010), 'Winner-take-all politics: public policy, political organization, and the precipitous rise of top incomes in the United States', *Politics and Society*, **38**(2), 152–204.
Hein, E. and M. Mundt (2012), 'Financialisation and the requirements and potentials for wage-led recovery – a review focusing on the G20', *Conditions of Work and Employment Series No. 37*, Geneva: International Labour Office.
Hurley, J., E. Fernández-Macías and D. Storrie (2013), 'Employment polarisation and job quality in the crisis', in Eurofound (ed.), *European Jobs Monitor 2013*, Dublin: European Foundation for the Improvement of Living.
ILO (2010), *Global Wage Report 2010/11: Wage Policies in a Time of Crisis*, Geneva: International Labour Office.
ILO (2013), *Global Wage Report 2012/13: Wages and Equitable Growth*, Geneva: International Labour Office.
ILO/IILS (2008), *World of Work Report 2008: Income Inequalities in the Age of Financial Globalization*, Geneva: International Labour Office/International Institute for Labour Studies.
ILO/IILS (2012), *World of Work Report 2012: Better Jobs for a Better Economy*, Geneva: International Labour Office/International Institute for Labour Studies.
IMF (2007), *World Economic Outlook: Globalization and Inequality*, Washington, DC: International Monetary Fund.
Isagiller, A. (2011), 'A cross-country investigation of inequality and growth with Theil indexes', *Iktisat Fakültesi Mecmuası*, **61**(2), 111–42.
Isaksson, A.-S. (2010), 'Political participation in Africa: participatory inequalities and the role of resources', *University of Gothenburg Working Papers in Economics No. 462*.
Jansen, M. and E. Lee (2007), *Trade and Employment: Challenges for Policy Research*, Geneva: World Trade Organization and International Labour Office.
Johnson, S. (2009), 'The quiet coup', *The Atlantic*, 1 May.
Kaldor, N. (1955), 'Alternative theories of distribution', *The Review of Economic Studies*, **23**(2), 83–100.
Kanbur, R. (2000), 'Income distribution and development', in A.B. Atkinson and F. Bourguignon (eds), *Handbook of Income Distribution*, Amsterdam: Elsevier, pp. 791–841.
Kravis, I.B. (1960), 'International differences in the distribution of income', *The Review of Economics and Statistics*, **42**(4), 408–16.
Kremer, M. and D.L. Chen (2002), 'Income distribution dynamics with endogenous fertility', *Journal of Economic Growth*, **7**(3), 227–58.
Kucera, D., R. Galli and F. Al-Hussami (2014), 'Keeping up with the Joneses or keeping one's head above water? Inequality and the post-2007 crisis', in I. Islam and D. Kucera (eds), *Beyond Macroeconomic Stability: Inclusive Growth and Structural Transformation*, Basingstoke, UK/Geneva: Palgrave Macmillan/International Labour Office.

Kuznets, S. (1955), 'Economic growth and income inequality', *The American Economic Review*, **45**(1), 1–28.

Kuznets, S. (1965), 'Inequalities in the size distribution of income', *Economic Growth and Structure: Selected Essays*, London: Heinemann Educational Books Ltd, pp. 288–303.

Lewis, W.A. (1954), 'Economic development with unlimited supplies of labour', *The Manchester School*, **22**(2), 139–91.

Li, H., L. Squire and H. Zou (2001), 'Explaining international and intertemporal variations in income inequality', *The Economic Journal*, **108**(446), 26–43.

Lindert, P.H. (2004), *Growing Public: Social Spending and Economic Growth Since the Eighteenth Century*, New York: Cambridge University Press.

List, J.A. and C.A. Gallet (1999), 'The Kuznets curve: what happens after the inverted-U?', *Review of Development Economics*, **3**(2), 200–206.

Mazzolari, F. and G. Ragusa (2013), 'Spillovers from high-skill consumption to low-skill labor markets', *The Review of Economics and Statistics*, **95**(1), 74–86.

Meltzer, A.H. and S.F. Richard (1981), 'A rational theory of the size of government', *The Journal of Political Economy*, **89**(5), 914–27.

Milanović, B. (1994), 'Determinants of cross-country income inequality: an "augmented" Kuznets' hypothesis', *Policy Research Working Paper No. 1246*, Washington, DC: World Bank.

Mischel, L., J. Schmitt and H. Shierholz (2013), 'Assessing the job polarization explanation of growing wage inequality', *Economic Policy Institute Discussion Paper*, October 2013.

OECD (2008), *Growing Unequal? Income Distribution and Poverty in OECD Countries*, Paris: Organisation for Economic Co-operation and Development.

OECD (2011), *Divided we Stand: Why Inequality Keeps Rising*, Paris: Organisation for Economic Co-operation and Development.

Okun, A.M. (1975), *Equality and Efficiency: The Big Tradeoff*, Washington, DC: Brookings Institution Press.

Onaran, O. and G. Galanis (2012), 'Is aggregate demand wage-led or profit-led? National and global effects', *Conditions of Work and Employment Series No. 40*, Geneva: Conditions of Work and Employment Branch, International Labour Office.

Oswald, A.J. (1997), 'Happiness and economic performance', *The Economic Journal*, **107**(445), 1815–31.

Page, J. (1994), 'The East Asian miracle: four lessons for development policy', in S. Fischer and J.J. Rotemberg (eds), *NBER Macroeconomics Annual*, Cambridge, MA: MIT Press, pp. 219–82.

Paukert, F. (1973), 'Income distribution at different levels of development: a survey of evidence', *International Labour Review*, **108**(2), 97–125.

Perotti, R. (1996), 'Growth, income distribution, and democracy: what the data say', *Journal of Economic Growth*, **1**(2), 149–87.

Persson, T. and G. Tabellini (1994), 'Is inequality harmful for growth?', *The American Economic Review*, **84**(3), 600–621.

Piketty, T. (1997), 'The dynamics of the wealth distribution and the interest rate with credit rationing', *The Review of Economic Studies*, **64**(2), 173–89.

Piketty, T. (2014), *Capital in the Twenty-first Century*. Cambridge: Harvard University Press

Polanyi, K. (1957), *The Great Transformation: The Political and Economic Origins of Our Time*, Boston, MA: Beacon Press.

Saint-Paul, G. and T. Verdier (1996), 'Inequality, redistribution and growth: a challenge to the conventional political economy approach', *European Economic Review*, **40**(3), 719–28.
Savoia, A., J. Easaw and A. Mckay (2010), 'Inequality, democracy, and institutions: a critical review of recent research', *World Development*, **38**(2), 142–54.
Schmidt-Hebbel, K. and L. Serven (2000), 'Does income inequality raise aggregate saving?', *Journal of Development Economics*, **61**(2), 417–46.
Sen, A. (1999), *Development as Freedom*, Oxford: Oxford University Press.
Solow R. (1956), 'A contribution to the theory of economic growth', *Quarterly Journal of Economics*, **70**(1), 65–94.
Solt, F. (2008), 'Economic inequality and democratic political engagement', *American Journal of Political Science*, **52**(1), 48–60.
Stewart, F. (2010), 'Power and progress: the swing of the pendulum', *Journal of Human Development and Capabilities*, **11**(3), 371–95.
Stewart, F. (2011), 'Inequality in political power: a fundamental (and overlooked) dimension of inequality', *The European Journal of Development Research*, **23**(4), 541–5.
Stiglitz, J.E. (2012), 'Macroeconomic fluctuations, inequality, and human development', *Journal of Human Development and Capabilities*, **13**(1), 31–58.
Stockhammer, E. (2012), 'Why have wage shares fallen?: A panel analysis of the determinants of functional income distribution', *Conditions of Work and Employment Series, No. 35*, Geneva: International Labour Office.
Storm, S. and C.W.M. Naastepad (2012), 'Wage-led or profit-led supply: wages, productivity and investment', *Conditions of Work and Employment Series No. 36*, Geneva: International Labour Office.
Tribble, R. (1999), 'A restatement of the s-curve hypothesis', *Review of Development Economics*, **3**(2), 207–14.
van Treeck, T. and S. Sturn (2012), 'Income inequality as a cause of the great recession? A survey of current debates', *Conditions of Work and Employment Series No. 39*, Geneva: International Labour Office.
Vogl, T. (2013), *Differential Fertility, Human Capital, and Development*, Princeton, NJ: Princeton University and National Bureau of Economic Research.
World Bank (2005), *World Development Report 2006: Equity and Development*, Washington, DC: World Bank.

3. Renewing the full employment compact: issues, evidence and policy implications

Iyanatul Islam and Martina Hengge

3.1 INTRODUCTION

The basic premise of this chapter is that governments across the world have a responsibility to ensure that all those willing and able to work have ample opportunities to do so at living wages and under safe and secure working conditions. This might be called the 'full employment compact'. It bears the intellectual imprint of Keynesian economics. The compact was ushered in in the wake of the *Beveridge Report* in the UK just after World War II (Abel-Smith, 1992). It also inspired the United States government to adopt the notion of 'maximum employment' as a key policy goal.[1] In the mid-1960s, the International Labour Organization (ILO) enshrined the notion of 'full, productive and freely chosen employment' in one of its key conventions.

The chapter argues that the full employment compact that held sway from the end of World War II to the early 1970s coincided with a golden era of equitable growth in the developed world. The oil price shock-induced 'stagflation' of the 1970s eventually led to the emergence of a conservative strain of macroeconomics that displaced full employment as a core policy goal. Ironically, this displacement also coincided with an increase in inequality in most OECD countries between the mid-1980s and the late 2000s, insufficient supply of good jobs as well as the steady erosion of the bargaining power of workers.

How did the full employment agenda evolve in the case of developing countries? The traditional discourse in development economics paid little attention to the importance of the full employment compact, focusing instead on issues of underemployment and poverty. Yet these issues receded into the background with the onset of the structural adjustment era of the 1980s and 1990s when the preoccupation of international financial institutions and the donor community was with the rectification of macroeconomic imbalances as a pre-condition for growth and employment creation. By the 2000s, the structural adjustment era was terminated, but what emerged eventually as the Millennium Development Goals (MDGs) entailed a benign neglect of full employment. This changed in the late 2000s, thanks to activism by the ILO. Aiming for 'full and productive employment' eventually became a core plank of the global development agenda.

The revival of the 'full employment compact' will entail more than mere aspirational statements. It will mean the adoption of a 'dual mandate' in both developed and developing countries that should guide specific policy actions. In the case of developed countries, much greater attention would need to be given to both macroeconomic stability and the employment objective, while in the case of low- and middle-income countries, governments would need to act as guardians of stability as well as agents of inclusive development. How this dual mandate can be operationalized in a development context is a core message of this chapter.

There is a range of pertinent issues that impinge on the scope of this chapter. It is appropriate to raise these issues at this juncture. To start with, despite explicit references to wages and working conditions in the definition of the full employment compact, the chapter does not discuss the role of wage policy. This is because wage policy is discussed at some length in other chapters of this volume. Furthermore, in the case of many developing countries where the informal sector and self-employment loom large, the remit of wage policy in influencing aggregate demand as a vehicle for promoting growth and employment is understandably limited. Other policy instruments – such as cash transfers – are likely to be more effective in reaching groups outside the formal sector.

Even in developed countries with well-established formal labour markets, the nexus between wages and aggregate demand is not as obvious as it seems.[2] This ambiguity is understandable because wages play a dual role: they are a source of income (and hence consumption); they influence competitiveness through changes in the cost of production. Getting the balance right in the design and implementation of wage policies is crucial, but a detailed exposition of this topic is beyond the scope of this chapter. Nevertheless, the authors are steadfast in their conviction that empowering labour market institutions is a prerequisite for enabling workers and their families across the world to enjoy the fruits of living wages and acceptable working conditions.

The chapter proposes employment-friendly macroeconomic policies but makes the assumption that implementation is the preserve and privilege of national governments. The astute reader might argue that this is an optimistic assumption for developing countries. After all, one might argue, knowledge about good policies is readily available because they are akin to a global 'public good', but the primary challenge for developing countries is weak administrative and institutional capacity to implement good policies. The issue of administrative and institutional capacity is more complex than it appears. Even in low-income countries, implementation capacity is not uniformly low, but unevenly distributed. It might be limited in specific ministries, but institutions entrusted with macroeconomic policy-making obligations – central banks, finance ministries, and ministries responsible for coordination of economic policies – are likely to be well endowed with appropriate competencies. These institutions also receive considerable technical assistance from key multilateral agencies, most notably the International Monetary Fund (IMF), World Bank and United Nations Development Programme (UNDP). Furthermore, many developing countries have demonstrated that they are capable of institutional innovations even in the presence of seemingly constrained implementation capacity. Examples include conditional cash transfers, employment guarantee schemes and mobile banking.

Finally, one should readily acknowledge that the chapter does not discuss the issue of 'rebalancing' of aggregate demand and its role in reviving the full employment compact. One could argue that many developing countries, including systemically important ones such as China, rely excessively on export demand to drive growth and employment and that one should focus more on domestic sources of aggregate demand. This is clearly a highly topical issue, but it is not obvious that the policy advice of 'rebalancing' of aggregate demand can be uniformly applied to all countries. The topic is particularly worthy of debate for large and populous developing countries, such as Brazil, China, Indonesia, India, and South Africa, which have expansive domestic markets. 'Rebalancing' as a new macroeconomic and growth strategy might be less relevant for small, open economies in both the developing and developed world.

3.2 THE RISE AND DECLINE OF THE FULL EMPLOYMENT COMPACT IN THE DEVELOPED COUNTRIES: AN OVERVIEW[3]

As noted in the introduction, the full employment compact held sway throughout the 1960s. A notable development during this period was the promulgation of a convention by the ILO, known popularly as Convention No. 122, on employment policy (Employment Policy Convention, 1964). It called on its member states to 'declare and pursue, as a major goal, an active policy designed to promote full, productive and freely chosen employment'. To date, 107 member States of the ILO have ratified this convention.[4] Of course, the convention drew attention to the need to ensure the consistency of the employment policy goal with other economic and social objectives and to ensure that its pursuit was sensitive to variations in national economic circumstances.

The era of the full employment compact coincided with a 'Golden Age' of growth in the developed world characterized by 'rising employment (and) fairly equitable . . . growth' (van der Hoeven, 2010, p. 80).[5] It was possible because governments genuinely believed that employment and equitable distribution were part of a virtuous circle. In 1956, for example, the Social Economic Council of the Netherlands formulated an economic policy framework based on five objectives: (1) full employment; (2) equitable income distribution; (3) shared economic growth; (4) price stability; and (5) sustainable balance of payments. These objectives were agreed in a 'social compact between workers, employers and governments of various political natures' (ibid., p. 79).

The full employment compact began to unravel in the 1970s, which saw two oil shocks and stagflation in the industrialized world. These turbulent global circumstances and the ascendency of conservative governments in the UK and the United States led to the emergence of a conservative strain of macroeconomics. This paradigm did not allow for involuntary unemployment caused by an aggregate demand deficit. Market forces ensured that labour markets would 'clear' under normal circumstances. Any observable incidence of significant and persistent unemployment was either voluntary (optimizing economic agents collectively prefer to consume more leisure) or caused by labour market rigidities.

Thus, the emphasis was on either attenuating labour market rigidities or making work more attractive relative to consumption of leisure through fiscal incentives and by scaling back 'generous' unemployment benefits that allegedly induce long periods of job search. Of course, this paradigm allowed for support to particular groups within the labour market (such as low-skilled workers) who might find it difficult to gain a foothold in the labour market, but the preferred policy response was to enhance employability of such groups through appropriate training and retraining. Full employment was largely replaced as a key macroeconomic goal, with central banks (whether independent or not) pursuing inflation targeting and finance ministries supporting such a policy regime through fiscal prudence. These ideas arguably influenced the OECD *Jobs Study* of the mid-1990s (OECD, 1994).

The decline of full employment as a policy objective that was quite evident by the 1980s also coincided with a rise in inequality in most OECD countries. For example, the average income growth of the bottom decile in

27 OECD countries was 1.3 per cent vis-à-vis 1.9 per cent for the top decile between the mid-1980s and the late 2000s.[6] Our estimates, drawing on data from a sample of 32 European countries, suggest a strong and negative correlation between the employment rate and the incidence of social exclusion and poverty. This means that reduced employment opportunities that prevail most notably in Europe today are expected to be associated with rising incidence of poverty and social exclusion.[7] While several reasons have been advanced to explain the phenomenon of rising inequality, deprivation and shrinking employment opportunities, one factor that cannot be ignored is that the 1980s and subsequent decades saw the steady erosion of the bargaining power of workers in advanced countries. Recent research by the ILO has shown that the incidence of low pay and vulnerability is closely related to the sustained decline in the bargaining power of workers since the ascendency of economic conservatism in the last two to three decades (ILO, 2010a).

3.3 TRADITIONAL DEVELOPMENT ECONOMICS, THE STRUCTURAL ADJUSTMENT ERA AND BEYOND: THE LONG ROAD TO MILLENNIUM DEVELOPMENT GOAL 1B[8]

The rise and decline of the full employment compact in the industrialized world and the popularity of the focus on employability, inflation targeting and fiscal prudence sets an appropriate context to the evolution of full employment as part of the global development agenda. The first-generation development economists did not really induct the full employment compact as part of the development literature. The primary challenge was seen as one of underemployment and poverty rather than open unemployment. The answer to this was growth and structural change that would absorb 'surplus labour' from rural-based agriculture at a constant real wage à la Lewis in a modern, urban-based industrial sector (Lewis, 1979).

Of course, an alternative tradition – the Harris-Todaro model – emerged to question this benign process of change (Harris and Todaro, 1969). The model allowed for open unemployment in urban areas as well as underemployment in the informal sector due to labour market rigidities. However, this alternative tradition focused on rural development as a way of stemming uncontrolled rural–urban migration so that it would keep pace with the capacity of the urban formal sector to absorb new entrants to the workforce through a combination of migration and natural increase in the labour force.

As the 1970s progressed, the tussle between the benign view of the Lewisian framework and the grim prognosis of the Harris-Todaro model seemed to give way to the notion that a reliance on growth alone neither offered sustained structural change nor did it alleviate the problems of pervasive poverty and underemployment. Thus, the World Bank advocated its 'redistribution with growth' strategy, while others outside the bank argued in favour of a 'basic needs strategy' (Chenery, 1974; Streeten, 1982).

In neither of these conceptualizations of a grand development strategy did the notion of sustained job creation receive pride of place until the ILO came up with its World Employment Programme (WEP) (Rodgers et al., 2009). While the WEP lasted, there was considerable enthusiasm for inducting employment concerns in development policy. But the momentum created by the WEP did not last long enough to change the development paradigm. It faded away as the agenda of economic conservatism in the industrialized world eventually left its intellectual footprint in the form of 'structural adjustment programmes' (SAPs) under the auspices of the Bretton Woods institutions. The ILO responded with a critique of structural adjustment programmes, while other UN agencies called for 'structural adjustment with a human face' (Jolly, 1991).

Between 1980 and 1998, over 950 structural adjustment programmes were implemented in developing countries (Easterly, 2001, p. 36). The challenges of development were seen as the product of dual policy failures: macroeconomic mismanagement and structural and labour market rigidities that sapped efficiency and productivity as a result of an ill-conceived strategy of state-led, import-substituting industrialization. Hence, the grand development strategy became one of ensuring macroeconomic stability through (explicit and implicit) inflation targeting, fiscal prudence and efficiency-enhancing structural and labour market reforms to unleash the productive potential of the economy by encouraging global economic integration. It was felt that sustained job creation and poverty reduction would be a natural outcome of such a policy framework that emphasized both macroeconomic and microeconomic dimensions of development. The era of the structural adjustment programmes came to a formal closure in 1998. It was replaced by 'poverty reduction strategies' (PRSs) led by the Bretton Woods institutions. This renewed emphasis on poverty reduction was an admission of the inadequacies of the structural adjustment era either to unleash growth or to reduce poverty on a sustained scale, although there were notable exceptions. While the emphasis on macroeconomic stability remained, it was felt that growth had to be 'pro-poor' and public resources should be directed towards specific programmes and interventions pertaining to health, education and infrastructure, while the private sector would take care of investment and job creation. The PRSs were the forerunner to the MDGs that were adopted by UN Millennium Summit in 2000. The international community supported target reductions in both income and non-income dimensions of poverty by 2015 across the developing world.

The MDGs were preceded by two landmark events: the 1995 United Nations World Summit for Social Development and an influential 1996 OECD publication on development partnership that first drew attention to the need for making a global commitment to target and time-bound reductions in income and non-income dimensions of poverty (United Nations, 1995; OECD, 1996). The OECD approach did not include any employment dimensions in its call for a renewed commitment to poverty reduction, while the 1995 World Summit made a renewed commitment to full employment as a core part of its mandate. The 1996 OECD version seemed to prevail in the 2000 version of the MDGs: any reference to employment, far less full employment, was conspicuously absent.[9]

It took another five years for the UN system to accept an ILO proposal to induct employment concerns in the MDGs and another three for it to unveil MDG 1B that set as a target 'full and productive employment and decent work for all' supported by four indicators to monitor progress: labour productivity, employment-to-population ratio (EPR), working poverty and vulnerable employment.

Despite these laudable developments, there is always the risk that the global community might end up paying lip service to full employment as part of the MDGs that will formally come to a close at the end of 2015. How does one avoid such a risk? The discussion in the subsequent sections suggests some specific policy actions that can be undertaken to promote the cause of 'full, productive and freely chosen employment' in both developed and developing countries. It is guided by the notion of a 'dual mandate' in which policy-makers care both about economic stability and employment.

3.4 REVIVING THE FULL EMPLOYMENT COMPACT: SOME SUGGESTIONS

The Role of the Dual Mandate: A Developed Country Perspective

In order to argue the case for reviving the full employment compact, it is useful to highlight the limits of a policy framework that has a de facto 'single mandate'. In this framework, what matters are price stability and sustainable public finances. Ensuring them will ensure investor confidence and foster growth and employment. In 1990, this framework was enshrined by the central bank of New Zealand, which declared a commitment to low single-digit inflation (below 3 per cent). Two years later, the Maastricht Treaty became the most famous example of both inflation targets and fiscal rules that were formally adopted by a group of developed countries (the members of the Eurozone).[10]

The pitfalls and perils of focusing on inflation targeting at the expense of employment can be illustrated in three cases: Canada of the 1990s, the European Central Bank (ECB) and Sweden today. In 1987, the newly appointed governor of the Canadian central bank took the mandate of attaining very low inflation targets seriously. When he took office, the inflation rate was 4.8 per cent. In 1993, inflation eventually fell to 1.8 per cent as a result of the vigorous application of restrictive monetary policy. By then, the unemployment rate stood at 11.3 per cent, the worst since the Great Depression. The distinguished Canadian economist Pierre Fortin called it the 'Great Canadian slump'. It took the economy another seven years to recover (Akerlof and Shiller, 2009).

Consider the case of Sweden today. Leading Swedish economist and former deputy governor of the Swedish central bank, Lars Svensson, points out that over the last 15 years the Swedish central bank has, on average, undershot its target rate of inflation of 2 per cent. This has resulted in an unemployment rate that is significantly above what it ought to be. This represents a 'very large cost to the real economy'. The author argues that a proper interpretation of the relevant act (Sveriges Riksbank Act) and the associated government bill on fiscal policy confers on the Swedish central bank a 'dual mandate' for monetary policy that should focus on both 'price stability and highest sustainable employment'. Instead, by running a stricter than necessary monetary policy, the Swedish central bank has failed to meet its obligations under the dual mandate (Svensson, 2012, p. 17).

Consider now the case of the ECB, which emphasizes price stability above all other goals. As the EU Treaty puts it, 'the primary objective' of the ECB is to 'maintain price stability and, without prejudice to this objective, to support the general economic policies in the Community'.[11] This preoccupation of the ECB has led it to run pro-cyclical monetary policy at various times: for example, July 2008, when the interest rate was raised on the eve of the global recession; upward adjustments to interest rates on two occasions in 2011, despite rather weak macroeconomic conditions. On all these occasions, the ECB raised concerns about imported inflation even though it is well known that one should not respond to imported inflation unless it becomes embedded in core inflation. It is difficult to dismiss the possibility that these pro-cyclical monetary policy initiatives by the ECB adversely affected growth and employment in the EU.

How does one make the transition to a dual mandate? The US central bank (the Federal Reserve) offers one approach. It has suggested a renewal of the dual mandate by offering 'forward guidance' on the course of monetary policy. It has explicitly stated that the current ultra-low interest environment will last until the economy approaches full employment (defined as an aggregate unemployment rate that is below 6 per cent).[12]

The approach adopted by the US Federal Reserve is promising, but it has important limitations. There is a growing realization that advanced country central banks, including the US Fed, have set the inflation target too low. The standard preference seems to be a 2 per cent inflation rate as the appropriate target. The problem is that this makes monetary policy susceptible to the 'liquidity trap' or the so-called 'zero lower bound' (ZLB). If a negative demand shock hits an economy, as in the case of the recent global economic and financial crisis, expansionary monetary policy can quickly reach its limits, as nominal interest rates cannot go below zero. Of course, there is ongoing preoccupation with 'quantitative easing' as a means of propping up aggregate demand, but the bulk of the evidence suggests limited effectiveness.[13] In the case of the USA, a study by Ball (2013) has shown that had the targeted inflation rate been set at 4 per cent, unemployment would have been lower than it is now and the Fed could have exited the ZLB quite readily. Instead, the Fed and a number of other advanced country central banks appear to have been mired in a ZLB for about five years now and they are having difficulty even meeting the 2 per cent inflation target.[14]

When one assesses the prospects for implementing the dual mandate from the perspective of fiscal policy, the challenges are considerable. There was a short-lived enthusiasm for fiscal stimulus packages to stave off the Great Recession of 2008–09 (ILO/World Bank, 2013). Once the worst was over, the policy elite in Europe shifted from fiscal stimulus to austerity programmes, while in the United States the fiscal stimulus package was wound down. The IMF lent its support to this shift on the grounds that rising public indebtedness was the major challenge in the post-crisis era and continuation of expansionary fiscal policy would trigger the risk of sovereign debt defaults (Blanchard et al., 2013).

In retrospect, the shift to fiscal austerity programmes was premature and based on fragile empirical evidence (Chowdhury and Islam, 2012; Herndon et al., 2013). Admittedly, a sovereign debt crisis broke out in the peripheral economies of the Eurozone between late 2009 and mid-2010, but it did not engulf the developed world as a whole. Indeed, the core economies of the Eurozone remain immune from a sovereign debt crisis. Countries such as the UK, United States and Japan that can issue public debt in credible domestic currencies face historically low interest rates despite high and rising public debt-to-GDP ratios. The current policy package of fiscal austerity, quantitative easing or asset-buying programmes by central banks to boost economic activity, and so-called structural reforms, have turned out to be ineffective in coping with the mass unemployment that has emerged in various parts of Europe. The European Union has already suffered its longest recession since its inception. The renewal of the full employment compact in developed countries will remain crucially incomplete unless there is a fundamental shift away from the fiscal austerity agenda.

Dual Mandate and Structural Transformation: A Developing Country Perspective

One needs a 'dual mandate' for macroeconomic policy managers in developing countries that goes beyond a focus on unemployment. This is appropriate for developed countries with a high incidence of formal labour markets. The structural realities of developing economies are such that low productivity employment is the norm rather than the exception. In such a setting, the notion of the dual mandate emphasizes the role of macroeconomic policy managers along two dimensions: (1) as guardians of stability; (2) as agents of inclusive development.

Being a guardian of stability does not merely mean passively accepting exogenous targets on debts, deficits and inflation derived from a 'one-size-fits-all' approach. It means upholding the principles of price stability, fiscal and financial sustainability using a country-specific approach. It means protecting people from the vagaries of business cycles and other exogenous shocks through sustainable counter-cyclical policies based on a mix of automatic stabilizers and discretionary interventions. This point is particularly important because developing countries, on average, suffer from greater output and inflation volatility than their developed counterparts (Agenor and Montiel, 2008, p. 5). To make matters worse, developing economies are prone to running pro-cyclical macroeconomic policy (Ilzetski and Veigh, 2008).

The notion of macroeconomic policy managers as agents of inclusive development entails various obligations on developing country macroeconomic policy managers. At the very least, it entails an emphasis on a sustainable resource mobilization strategy to support the attainment of core development goals. It should also be interpreted to suggest how policy-makers can facilitate the process of structural transformation. One way of engaging with this issue is to identify binding constraints on sectors with the most potential for productive job creation. As will be argued later, promoting financial inclusion and attenuating infrastructure deficits can enhance the job creating potential of various sectors. This is best done by using standard macroeconomic policy instruments, such as giving priority to raising adequate domestic revenue, incentive-compatible credit allocation schemes, and appropriate regulatory changes by monetary and financial authorities.

The exchange rate regime can also be used to forge closer links between macroeconomic policy, structural transformation and inclusive development. This can happen when the exchange rate is kept at a stable and competitive level that is consistent with economic fundamentals. It can stimulate growth and effectively operate as a tool of industry policy that supports structural transformation by shifting resources from the non-traded to the traded goods sector. On the other hand, the use of exchange rate policy to promote structural transformation and employment creation requires prudent capital account management. These issues are explored in greater depth at a later juncture.

The subsequent sections will elucidate some practical policy implications arising from the above assessment, particularly in a developing country context. The analysis will start with exchange rate policies and capital account management, followed by monetary and financial policies and subsequently turns to fiscal policy.

3.5 EXCHANGE RATE POLICY AND CAPITAL ACCOUNT MANAGEMENT: IMPLICATIONS FOR EMPLOYMENT CREATION

Central banks can promote economic diversification and employment creation through appropriate management of the exchange rate. The latter can play a dual role: as an anti-inflation tool and as a tool for resource allocation between the traded and non-traded sectors. Managing the dual role is a core macroeconomic policy task, especially as recent evidence has shown that so-called ‘hard pegs’ (entailing fully fixed exchange rates) can significantly increase the vulnerability of countries to ‘growth collapses’ (Ghosh et al., 2013).

What matters is to manage nominal exchange rate flexibility in a way that avoids real exchange rate misalignments on a sustained basis. Concerns about real exchange rate misalignments have become central to the debate on how to achieve sustained growth both by tempering economic volatility and by encouraging structural transformation. In general, an overvaluation of the real exchange rate is expected to impede economic growth; it can harm domestic firms’ competitiveness in international markets and lead to an unsustainably high current account deficit

(IMF, 2013). Beyond that, it has been argued, among others by Freund and Pierola (2008), Rodrik (2008) and Steinberg (2011), that currency undervaluation can facilitate growth and employment. The rationale is that it delivers cost competitiveness in a way that avoids the cumbersome and contentious nature of other policy instruments, such as selective taxes and subsidies, geared towards specific sectoral activities.

A number of studies have analysed the effect of real exchange rate movements on employment. In an open economy, currency appreciations can have negative employment effects through three major channels. First, an appreciation of the real exchange rate can lead to a contraction in employment in the traded goods sector caused by the deterioration of the economy's competitiveness and thus lower net exports. Second, currency appreciation translates into higher real wages (measured in international currency) resulting from a reduction in the cost of imported goods. This can lead to a shift from labour to capital goods, particularly if the latter have a significant import component. The change in relative prices of labour to capital goods affects both the traded and non-traded sectors. Third, the exchange rate can affect employment through the development channel. Given that an appreciation can lead to lower profitability in the traded goods sector, it prevents a shift in resources from the non-traded to the traded sector (a process that can effectively act as an industrial policy). Since the expansion of the traded goods sector is commonly believed to bring about growth and modernization in the economy, real exchange rate appreciation can hinder structural transformation (Frenkel and Ros, 2006). Although not exhaustive, Table 3.1 provides an overview of empirical studies that have found negative (positive) effects of real exchange rate appreciations (depreciations).

As illustrated in Table 3.1, there is considerable evidence that real exchange rate depreciations have an employment-enhancing effect. These findings, however, neglect the potentially adverse impact that currency depreciations can have in economies with high liability dollarization, that is, when private sector debt is denominated in foreign currency while assets are denominated in domestic currency. This renders the private sector sensitive to balance sheet effects – increased indebtedness of firms through a currency mismatch of assets and liabilities – through real exchange rate depreciations. Such negative effects can exceed the positive effects of domestic firms' increased competitiveness (Islam, 2011).

A study by Galindo et al. (2006) analyses the impact of real exchange rate movements on employment, with varying degrees of trade openness and debt dollarization. Based on a panel dataset for nine Latin American countries, the authors show that the positive effect of real exchange rate depreciations is reversed, and can be negative, with increasing liability

Table 3.1 Effect of real exchange rate (RER) movements on employment

Source	Effect on Employment	Sample of Countries
Bahamani-Oskooee et al. (2007)	RER depreciation has a significant employment-enhancing effect in the short run, but not in the long run	USA
Burgess and Knetter (1998)	Appreciation leads to a decline in manufacturing employment	G-7 countries
Campa and Goldberg (2001)	Depreciation increases employment in the manufacturing industry (significant for low mark-up industries, but insignificant for high mark-up industries)	USA
Eichengreen (2008)	RER depreciation has a statistically significant positive effect on industry employment	40 emerging market countries
Faria and León-Ledesma (2005)	In the USA, an appreciation leads to a decrease in employment. In the UK, the employment effect is positive, albeit not statistically significant	UK, USA
Filiztekin (2004)	Depreciation has a negative employment effect in the manufacturing industry[a]	Turkey
Frenkel and Ros (2006)	RER appreciation is associated with an increase in the unemployment rate	Argentina, Brazil, Chile, Mexico
Gourinchas (1999)	RER appreciation leads to job reduction	France
Hua (2007)	Statistically significant negative effect of RER appreciation on manufacturing employment	China
Kandil and Mirzaie (2003)	Decrease in employment growth in several industries in response to dollar appreciation, but increase in employment growth in the mining sector	USA
Klein et al. (2003)	RER appreciation significantly affects net employment through job destruction and reduction of net employment growth rate in the manufacturing industry	USA
Ngandu (2009)	Appreciation can have a negative employment effect in the traded sector, but not in the non-traded sector	South Africa

Note: a. This finding can be ascribed to the high dependency on foreign inputs of production.

dollarization (where both the government and the private sector borrow on a significant scale in foreign currencies while assets are denominated in national currencies). Similarly, for Mexico, Lobato et al. (2003) find that the balance sheet effect outweighs the competitiveness effect engendered currency depreciations. While the balance sheet effect is not undisputed (see, for instance, Bleakley and Cowan, 2002; Luengnaruemitchai, 2003), liability dollarization poses a risk to contractionary depreciation and thus a decline in employment.

It is thus clear that movements in real exchange rates can have a substantial impact on employment. There seems to be consensus that currency appreciations have a negative impact on employment, whereas depreciations support growth and employment. Does this imply that governments should pursue a policy of deliberate exchange rate undervaluation? Some countries have indeed maintained an undervalued currency over a long period of time, such as China whose currency has been undervalued for a substantial part of the last two decades.[15] Such policy can facilitate growth-enhancing structural transformation, ultimately leading to employment creation (McMillan and Rodrik, 2011). Yet, as emphasized by Rodrik (2008) and the IMF (2013), sustained undervaluation of the exchange rate can lead to global current account imbalances and produce 'beggar-thy-neighbour' effects. Hence, a more reasonable policy to avoid the adverse effect of overvaluation could consist in keeping the real exchange rate at a stable and competitive level that is consistent with economic fundamentals.

It must be reiterated that the presence of liability dollarization acts as a constraint on the central bank's ability to influence the path of the exchange rate. This happens because of the reluctance of central banks to engage in depreciation because it leads to potentially negative balance sheet effects that can outweigh the expansionary impact of depreciations. It is thus crucial to attenuate high levels of liability dollarization through active capital account management and prudential regulation of the financial system (Islam, 2011). Expansions and contractions in the money supply can be controlled through the use of quantitative credit controls, interest rate ceiling and reserve requirements on bank deposits. But countries must also be willing to impose capital controls if needed when flows reach levels that prevent the central bank from properly conducting its operations. Capital controls enable the central bank to counteract appreciations that move the currency away from its stable and competitive level and thus support employment.

It has to be acknowledged that there is still continuing ambivalence pertaining to official views – as represented by the IMF – on the use of capital controls. There was a time when the IMF was an advocate of full capital account liberalization, but now has offered qualified support to its use (Ostry et al., 2010). The theoretical case for prudential capital controls is well understood. There is recognition that counter-cyclical taxes on short-term capital inflows during a boom can reduce the severity of busts. It is also recognized that there is little evidence supporting the notion that free capital mobility can raise economic growth sustainably (Jeanne et al., 2012).

Country-specific examples can be given of successful cases of prudent capital account management, such as Chile, but what is needed are transparent and widely agreed international rules for capital controls. These controls include price-based measures, such as counter-cyclical taxes on certain types of capital flows. The international community could agree on the type, composition and ceiling on price-based measures pertaining to capital mobility in order to limit any possible harmful side-effects of such measures on economic growth. These codes of conduct could be developed under the auspices of the IMF. The lack of such a global framework means that 'capital controls are still marked by a certain stigma' leading to less than optimal outcomes, with some countries, such as China, pursuing capital controls with vigour, while others are much more ambivalent about it.[16]

3.6 MONETARY POLICY AND FINANCIAL POLICIES: THE IMPORTANCE OF FOSTERING FINANCIAL INCLUSION

Central banks and financial authorities can support structural transformation and job creation through promoting financial inclusion. Lack of access to finance has been found to constitute a major hindrance to business operations and expansion. According to the World Economic Forum (2012), access to finance is among the five most problematic factors for businesses in 76.5 per cent of the sample of low- and middle-income countries and 79.9 per cent of the sample that cuts across all income groups. Similarly, the World Bank (2012a) shows that lack of access to finance is an obstacle for firms in low- and middle-income countries across all regions of the world. In Sub-Saharan Africa, the Middle East and North Africa (MENA) and Latin America and the Caribbean, more than 30 per cent of the surveyed firms have cited access to finance as a major constraint (Figure 3.1).[17]

At the household level, more than 2.5 billion people around the world, corresponding to roughly half of the world's adults, remain unbanked. Among those who are adults earning less than US$2 a day, 75 per cent

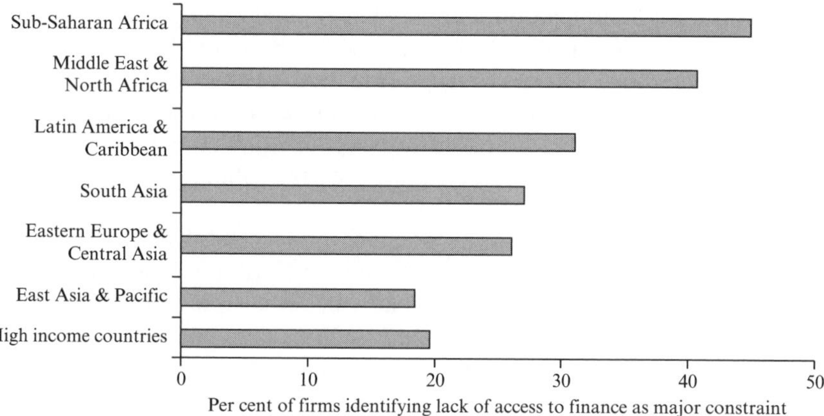

Note: Regional averages were calculated by taking the mean of country-level indicators, including only those country surveys for which the global methodology has been used.

Source: World Bank (2012a).

Figure 3.1 Lack of access to finance as a major constraint for firms in low- and middle-income countries across regions of the world

are without a bank account (Demirgüç-Kunt and Klapper, 2012; World Bank, 2013). Yet, the poorer a household, the greater their need for protection against vulnerabilities – such as illness or unemployment – and for investment in education and health, and thus their need for financial services, such as savings, credit, insurance and remittances. Financial inclusion can also contribute to increasing people's livelihood through enabling them to engage in entrepreneurial activities (Allen et al., 2012; Fine et al., 2012; World Bank, 2012b).

Overcoming barriers to financial inclusion requires a variety of comprehensive actions, including appropriate changes in the design of monetary and financial policies. While price stability remains an important objective for central banks, promoting an inclusive financial sector, most notably through steering the allocation of credit to underserved areas and targeted sectors, should also be an integral component of their mandate. It is encouraging to note that 67 per cent of central banks across the world cite the promotion of financial inclusion as part of their mandate (Allen et al., 2012). Possible measures include lowering interest rates and providing credit guarantees and subsidized credit to sectors that can contribute to productivity and employment growth, such as small- and medium-sized enterprises and export-oriented sectors.[18]

Some country-specific examples can be used to illustrate the importance of financial inclusion as a key part of a central bank's mandate. In Nigeria, for instance, an agricultural lending facility provides loan guarantees that cover up to half of financial institutions' losses incurred from loans to both small farmers and large enterprises in the agricultural sector. The facility also provides incentives to banks to allocate a large share of their credit to agribusiness. In addition, it provides assistance in credit risk assessment for banks as well as in financial management for borrowers. The programme aims at raising lending to the agribusiness from 1 to 7–10 per cent of total loans by 2020 (Fine et al., 2012).[19] In Rwanda, a donor-supported credit guarantee scheme played an important role in enabling the country to become a significant exporter of speciality coffee in the 2000s. The credit guarantee scheme was able to overcome the risk aversion of traditional lenders who focused on the seasonal financing of large traders and exporters and eschewed support for the investment needs of the speciality coffee sector (ILO, 2011b, pp. 174–7).

Public ownership of parts of the banking system can be a vehicle to realize measures aimed at increasing financial inclusion and supporting employment. In some developing countries, for example Argentina, Brazil, the Republic of Korea, Malaysia and Taiwan (China), investment banks have played a central role in directing credit to targeted sectors (Epstein, 2007).

Can developing countries promote financial inclusion effectively within a reasonable time period? A good example is Ecuador. Following the 1998–2000 financial and economic crisis, policy-makers embraced the opportunity to face the downturn through a set of financial, economic and social policies, including policies to boost financial inclusion. Major changes to the country's institutional arrangements were undertaken, including to the orientation and functions of the Ecuadorian Central Bank, which has incorporated financial inclusion into its strategic goals. The institutional capacity of the bank to orchestrate the government's financial inclusion policy is grounded in (1) its responsibility for financial regulation; (2) its participation in financial supervisory bodies; (3) the incorporation of financial inclusion projects in its organizational structure; and (4) the National Payment System, one of the bank's principal instruments to conduct monetary policy. These policy initiatives appeared to bear fruit. Over 2005 to 2011, the percentage of the population with a bank account in the national financial system increased from 28.9 to 83.2 per cent, which is quite a dramatic transformation. The share of the population with a bank account in private banks and credit holdings doubled during the same period. Together, private banks and credit unions provided more than 70 per cent of all bank accounts in 2011. Public banks recorded the largest relative increase, up from 1.3 per cent in 2005 to 9.6 per cent in 2011. In addition, regulatory reforms have led to a decline in both real interest rates and consumers' cost for financial transactions (Banco Central del Ecuador, 2012).[20]

3.7 FISCAL POLICY: REINFORCING THE REDISTRIBUTIVE CAPACITY OF THE STATE AND SUPPORTING STRUCTURAL TRANSFORMATION

The role of macroeconomic policy-makers as agents of both economic stabilization and development entails the pursuit of counter-cyclical policies on the one hand and the implementation of policies that support structural transformation and core development goals on the other hand. We commence with a brief reference to the ways in which fiscal policy can shape secondary income distribution in a positive direction. Redistribution through fiscal instruments (defined as direct taxes, mandatory social security contributions and transfer payments) across the developing world is limited. In high-income countries on the other hand, fiscal policy plays a major role in income redistribution (Bastagli et al., 2012). A more detailed analysis on redistribution policies, including the decomposition of fiscal redistribution, is provided by Luebker in Chapter 8.

Perhaps the major reasons behind this discrepancy between developed and developing countries are low tax-to-GDP ratios and insufficiently progressive, or even regressive, tax structures in low- and middle-income countries. Low tax-to-GDP ratios can either reflect low tax rates or narrow tax bases that can result from a number of factors, including a large informal sector, a high degree of tax evasion, and weak tax administration. Tax ratios tend to be lower in low- and middle-income countries than in high-income countries. Over 1992 to 2010, for instance, the average tax ratio in OECD countries amounted to 34.5 per cent of GDP compared to 12.4 per cent for a sample of 13 Latin American non-OECD countries.[21] The Asia-Pacific region has the lowest tax burden across the developing regions of the world, despite rapid economic growth (UN-ESCAP, 2013).

Low tax revenues limit governments' fiscal space, and consequently its capacity to foster structural transformation and support core development goals. An important aspect pertaining to the relevance of fiscal policy as an instrument to promote structural transformation relates to the role that infrastructure deficits play in inhibiting growth and employment in developing countries. Evidence suggests that lack of adequate infrastructure undermines growth and employment creation (Asian Development

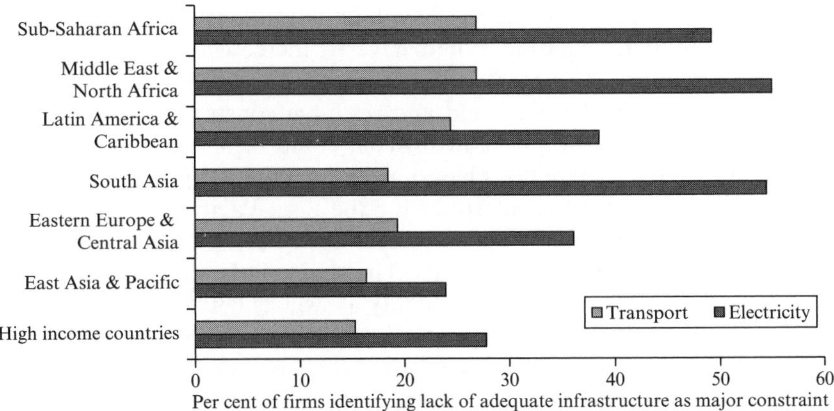

Note: Regional averages were calculated by taking the mean of country-level indicators, including only those country surveys for which the global methodology has been used.

Source: World Bank (2012a).

Figure 3.2 Inadequate infrastructure as a major constraint for firms in low- and middle-income countries across regions of the world

Bank, 2012; Fine et al., 2012; World Bank, 2012a; World Economic Forum, 2012). For instance, enterprise surveys undertaken by the World Bank (2012a) show that inadequate infrastructure, as proxied by the supply of electricity and transport, is a major hindrance to doing business in low- and middle-income countries across all regions of the world. Roughly 50 per cent of the surveyed firms in Sub-Saharan Africa, South Asia and the MENA region identified major constraints related to the supply of electricity. Lack of transport is a major constraint for more than one-fifth of the surveyed enterprises in Sub-Saharan Africa, the MENA region and Latin America and the Caribbean (Figure 3.2). Further studies have provided similar findings. *The Global Competitiveness Report* by the World Economic Forum (2012) shows that inadequate supply of infrastructure is among the top five problematic factors for doing business in more than half of the surveyed low- and middle-income countries.[22]

Estimates suggest that the infrastructure spending gaps are vast. In Sub-Saharan Africa, for instance, infrastructure spending needs are estimated to amount to US$94 billion a year, corresponding to approximately 9 per cent of GDP (Yepes, 2008 as cited in Lin and Doemeland, 2012). CEPAL (2011) estimates that Latin America and the Caribbean needs to invest roughly 5.2 per cent of the region's GDP per year to meet the infrastructure requirements of firms and individuals between 2006 and 2020.

If the region aimed at closing the spending gap to a group of East Asian economies, annual spending would have to increase to 7.9 per cent of GDP. Most countries face large infrastructure requirements across a wide range of sectors on the one hand and resource constraints on the other hand. In view of this situation, investment could be allocated to targeted sectors and geographic regions based on its job creation potential.

One can draw on a recent study for the Asia-Pacific region by UN-ESCAP (2013) to highlight the role fiscal policy can play to support the financing of core development goals. The study finds a negative association between the tax ratio and inequality as well as between social spending and inequality. It stresses that inequality has been exacerbated by the lack of progressivity of tax systems and a low tax burden, which has reflected in a lack of public spending. UN-ESCAP also quantifies the fiscal implications of supporting core development goals. The study – influenced by similar exercises conducted by other UN agencies (such as ILO, 2010b) – specifies six elements of a policy package that cuts across the provision of job guarantee schemes, social protection and environmental sustainability. Developing countries in the Asia-Pacific region would need public expenditures ranging between 5 and 8 per cent of GDP to meet the resource requirements of such a policy package at the national level. How to implement such public expenditure programmes in an efficient and fiscally sustainable fashion through tax and other revenue mobilization measures then becomes a core issue for macroeconomic policy-makers.

Finally, the need for a stable macroeconomic environment to foster growth and job creation requires the adoption of counter-cyclical policies that can smooth out economic volatility. Counter-cyclical policies entail both automatic stabilizers and discretionary interventions. Automatic stabilizers can be linked to social protection, such as unemployment benefits. In the United States, for example, the unemployment insurance programme was estimated to have mitigated the loss in real GDP by 15 per cent during the five recessions that occurred between 1969 and the early 1990s (Chimerine et al., 1999). Yet, due to large informal sectors in the developing world, automatic stabilizers might not reach the poorest (Ocampo, 2011). Policy measures designed to suit developing country conditions, such as job guarantees and cash transfer programmes, might thus be useful to alleviate the employment consequences of economic downturns. The experiences of some Latin American countries, such as Brazil and Mexico with conditional cash transfers, and the case of India with the world's largest rural employment guarantee scheme, suggest that it is possible for developing countries to engage in policy innovations with respect to counter-cyclical measures.

Getting out of the pro-cyclical trap also requires an ability to build up fiscal space during boom periods and normal periods of growth. A dedicated 'stabilization fund' that is activated during recessions might be an instrument to achieve this (ibid., p. 15). There are successful examples of such initiatives. One can draw attention to Chile's experience with respect to the prudent and counter-cyclical management of revenues from natural resources.

3.8 CONCLUDING REMARKS

The chapter argued that there is a strong case for renewing the full employment compact. This means that governments across the world have a responsibility to ensure that all those willing and able to work have ample opportunities to do so at living wages and under safe and secure working conditions.

Reviving the full employment compact requires a commitment to a dual mandate for policy-makers in both developed and developing countries. In the case of developed countries, the single-minded pursuit of inflation targeting can impose significant losses on the real economy in terms of lost employment opportunities, as the experiences of Canada in the mid-1990s, the ECB and Sweden today have shown. In all cases, policy-makers disregarded the obligation to pursue both price stability and the promotion of employment.

The US Federal Reserve Board suggests how one can overcome the deleterious consequences of a single-minded pursuit of inflation targeting in developed countries by adopting a framework of 'forward guidance' that explicitly links changes to monetary policy to changes in the unemployment rate. Despite this innovation, the revival of the full employment compact faces major challenges when judged from the perspective of monetary policy ineffectiveness due to the ZLB. It appears that advanced country central banks have opted for too low an inflation target that is incompatible with the attainment of full employment. Furthermore, given that many developed economies, most notably those in the Euro area, are preoccupied with fiscal austerity, policy-makers seem unable to make a renewed commitment to expansionary policies to stimulate aggregate demand, despite the emergence of mass unemployment in a number of developed countries. The emphasis still seems to be on a combination of quantitative easing and structural reforms to promote economic and employment recovery. Unfortunately, this combination has, so far, not worked well enough to bring about a return to full employment in many developed countries.

In the case of developing economies, operationalizing the dual mandate requires a move away from a focus on unemployment, given the incidence of informal and low productivity employment. Instead, the dual mandate for low- and middle-income countries means that governments should seek to be (1) guardians of stability and (2) agents of inclusive development. Translated to specific policy actions, this means the use of exchange rate policy and prudent capital account management to promote an agenda of structural transformation, having the capacity to conduct counter-cyclical policies to smooth business cycles, promoting financial inclusion, and mobilizing domestic revenue to meet core development goals and attenuating infrastructure deficits.

NOTES

1. This is enshrined in the Employment Act of 1946. For a discussion, see Strayer et al. (1950). See also Palley (2007).
2. In a simulation undertaken by the ILO for a sample of 15 countries, the findings indicate that the impact of an exogenous 1 per cent decrease in the 'labour income share' in GDP on the *level* of aggregate demand is 'ambiguous', but the *composition* changes. Thus, in all cases private consumption decreases, but net exports increase in all cases, while investment increases in ten cases (ILO, 2012, Table 2, p. 54).
3. This is a revised version of an account in Islam and Chowdhury (2012).
4. See ILO's information system on international labour standards (Normlex), www.ilo.org/dyn/normlex/en/f?p=1000:12100:0::NO::P12100_INSTRUMENT_ID:312267; last accessed 25 August 2014.
5. One should not discount historically specific factors that enabled political commitment to full employment. These include the need to integrate returning soldiers into labour markets after the termination of World War II and the post-War reconstruction boom.
6. See OECD (2011, Table 1, p. 23). Palley (2007) offers a forceful exposition of these issues in the case of the United States.
7. For a sample of 32 European countries, during 2004–11, the employment-to-population ratio is negatively correlated with the share of people at risk of poverty or social exclusion (the estimated correlation coefficient is −0.54). Calculations are based on Eurostat (2013) for people at risk of poverty or social exclusion, and ILO (2011a) for employment-to-population ratio. It has to be conceded that correlation does not mean a robust affirmation of causality. Social exclusion and poverty are multifaceted in nature and also have deep institutional roots, such as discrimination against minorities. The correlation reported in the text will not pick up these deep institutional factors.
8. This is a revised version of an account in Islam and Chowdhury (2012).
9. See Rodgers et al. (2009).
10. Member states of the currency union should have low single-digit inflation rates, stick to a −3 per cent annual fiscal deficit and an annual 60 per cent debt-to-GDP ratio.
11. Article 105.1 as cited in Fitoussi and Saraceno (2013). The authors argue that the key pillars of European economic governance – the ECB and the fiscal compact – represent an institutionalization of the 'Berlin-Washington Consensus'. The reference to 'Berlin' is meant to highlight the influence of Germany on European economic governance, while the 'Washington Consensus' is, of course, widely attributed to Williamson (2002). The epithet stands for a policy framework that highlights the primacy of macroeconomic stability.
12. See www.federalreserve.gov/faqs/money_12848.htm; last accessed 25 August 2014.

13. Blanchard (2013).
14. There is a lively discussion in the professional literature on abandoning inflation targeting and moving to other targets, such as nominal GDP. See, for example, Woodford (2012).
15. For an overview on China's currency policy see Morrison and Labonte (2011).
16. Williamson et al. (2013) drawing on Jeanne et al. (2012).
17. In their survey on Africa for McKinsey, Fine et al. (2012) find that access to finance is among the top three barriers to private sector growth. In addition, the Asian Development Bank (ADB, 2012) points out that small and medium-sized enterprises frequently face constraints related to accessing finance in Asia.
18. In addition to these measures, modern technology can be harnessed to promote financial inclusion. The successful cases of M-PESA in Kenya and Easypaisa in Pakistan, among others, show how mobile phone technology can be deployed to reach the unbanked (for more information, see Safaricom, 2012 and Easypaisa, 2012).
19. It should be noted that the Nigerian case has not been evaluated in terms of its impact on employment.
20. It is noteworthy that Ecuador represents an example of a country that has combined conservative monetary policy (dollarization) that constrains policy autonomy with innovations in financial policy that enable the central bank to play a role beyond the traditional focus on stability.
21. Calculations based on OECD (2013).
22. Likewise, a survey across five African countries by Fine et al. (2012) identifies infrastructure shortcomings, including transport and electricity, among highly cited barriers to job growth.

REFERENCES

Abel-Smith, B. (1992), 'The Beveridge Report: its origins and outcomes', *International Social Security Review*, **45**(1–2), 5–16.

Agenor, P. and P. Montiel (2008), *Development Macroeconomics*, Princeton, NJ: Princeton University Press.

Akerlof, G. and R. Shiller (2009), *Animal Spirits: How Human Psychology Drives the Economy and Why It Matters for Global Capitalism*, Princeton, NJ: Princeton University Press.

Allen, F., A. Demirgüç-Kunt, L. Klapper and M.S. Martinez Peria (2012), 'The foundations of financial inclusion: understanding ownership and use of formal accounts', *Policy Research Working Paper No. 6290*, Washington, DC: World Bank.

ADB (2012), *Outlook 2012: Confronting Rising Inequality in Asia*, Mandaluyong City: Asian Development Bank.

Bahamani-Oskooee, M., I.A. Mirzaie and I. Miteza (2007), 'Sectoral employment, wages and the exchange rate', *Eastern Economic Journal*, **33**(1), 125–36.

Ball, L. (2013), 'The case for 4% inflation rate', 24 May, *Vox*, accessed 25 August 2014 at voxeu.org, http://www.voxeu.org/article/case-4-inflation.

Banco Central del Ecuador (2012), *De la Definición de la Política a la Práctica: Haciendo Inclusión Financiera* [Definition of Policy to Practice: Making Financial Conclusion], accessed 4 March 2014 at www.afi-global.org/library/publications/de-la-definicion-de-la-politica-la-practica-haciendo-inclusion-financiera.

Bastagli, F., D. Coady and S. Gupta (2012), 'Income inequality and fiscal policy', *Staff Discussion Notes Paper No. 12/08*, Washington, DC: IMF.

Blanchard, O. (2013), 'Monetary policy will never be the same', 19 November, *IMF Direct forum*, accessed 25 August 2014 at http://blog-imfdirect.imf.org/2013/11/19/monetary-policy-will-never-be-the-same/#more-6624.

Blanchard, O., J. Florence and P. Loungani (2013), 'Labour market policies and IMF advice in advanced economies during the Great Recession', *Staff Discussion Note No. 13/02*, Washington, DC: International Monetary Fund.

Bleakley, H. and K.N. Cowan (2002), 'Corporate dollar debt and depreciations: much ado about nothing?', *Working Paper No. 02-5*, Boston, MA: Federal Reserve Bank of Boston.

Burgess, S. and M.M. Knetter (1998), 'An international comparison of employment adjustment to exchange rate fluctuations', *NBER Working Paper No. 5861*, Cambridge, MA: National Bureau of Economic Research.

Campa, J.M. and L.S. Goldberg (2001), 'Employment versus wage adjustment and the U.S. dollar', *The Review of Economics and Statistics*, **83**(3), 477–89.

CEPAL (2011), 'The economic infrastructure gap in Latin America and the Caribbean', *Bulletin*, Issue No. 293, Number 1/2011, Santiago: United Nations Commission for Latin America and the Caribbean.

Chenery, H.B. (1974), *Redistribution with Growth: Policies to Improve Income Distribution in Developing Countries in the Context of Economic Growth*, New York: Oxford University Press.

Chimerine, L., T. Black and L. Coffey (1999), 'Unemployment insurance as an automatic stabilizer: evidence of effectiveness over three decades', *Occasional Paper No. 99-8*, Washington, DC: Department of Labor.

Chowdhury, A. and I. Islam (2012), 'The debate on expansionary fiscal consolidation: how robust is the evidence?', *The Economic and Labour Relations Review*, **23**(2), 13–38.

Demirgüç-Kunt, A. and L. Klapper (2012), 'Measuring financial inclusion: the Global Findex database', *Policy Research Working Paper No. 6025*, Washington, DC: World Bank.

Easterly, W. (2001), 'The lost decades: developing countries' stagnation in spite of policy reform 1980–1998', *Journal of Economic Growth*, **6**(2), 135–57.

Easypaisa (2012), 'Branchless banking: the Easypaisa way', accessed 25 August 2014 at http://www.slideshare.net/Tameerbankmarketing/branchless-banking-the-easypaisa-way.

Eichengreen, B. (2008), 'The real exchange rate and economic growth', *Commission on Growth and Development Working Paper, No. 4*, Washington, DC: International Bank for Reconstruction and Development/World Bank of behalf of the Commission on Growth and Development.

Epstein, G. (2007), 'Central banks as agents of employment creation', *DESA Working Paper No. 38*, Washington, DC: United Nations Department of Economic and Social Affairs.

Eurostat (2013), *Population and Social Conditions Database*, accessed 24 April 2013 at www.epp.eurostat.ec.europa.eu/portal/page/portal/statistics/themes.

Faria, J.R. and M.A. León-Ledesma (2005), 'Real exchange rate and employment performance in an open economy', *Research in Economics*, **59**(1), 67–80.

Filiztekin, A. (2004), 'Exchange rate and employment in Turkish manufacturing', Faculty of Arts and Social Sciences, Sabanci University, Istanbul.

Fine, D., A. van Wamelen and S. Lund et al. (2012), *Africa at Work: Job Creation and Inclusive Growth*, report for the McKinsey Global Institute, accessed 25 August 2014 at http://www.mckinsey.com/insights/africa/africa_at_work.

Fitoussi, J.-P. and F. Saraceno (2013), 'European economic governance: Berlin-Washington Consensus', *Cambridge Journal of Economics*, **37**(3), 479–96.
Frenkel, R. and J. Ros (2006), 'Unemployment and the real exchange rate in Latin America', *World Development*, **34**(4), 631–46.
Freund, C.L. and M.D. Pierola (2008), 'Export surges: the power of a competitive currency', *World Bank Policy Research Working Paper No. 4750*, Washington, DC: World Bank.
Galindo, A., A. Izquierdo and J.M. Montero (2006), 'Real exchange rates, dollar ization and industrial employment in Latin America', *Working Paper No. 575*, Washington, DC: Inter-American Development Bank.
Ghosh, A., J. Ostery and M.S. Qureshi (2013), 'Exchange rate management and crisis susceptibility: a reassessment', 14th Jacques Polak Annual Research Conference, 7–8 November, Washington, DC: International Monetary Fund.
Gourinchas, P. (1999), 'Exchange rates do matter: French job reallocation and exchange rate turbulence, 1984–1992', *European Economic Review*, **43**(7), 1279–316.
Harris, J. and M. Todaro (1970), 'Migration, unemployment and development: a two-sector analysis', *The American Economic Review*, **60**(1), 126–42.
Herndon, T., M. Ash and R. Pollin (2013), 'Does high public debt consistently stifle economic growth? A critique of Reinhart and Rogoff', 15 April 2013, Political Economy Research Institute, University of Massachusetts Amherst.
Hua, P. (2007), 'Real exchange rate and manufacturing employment in China', *China Economic Review*, **18**(3), 335–53.
ILO (2010a), *Global Wage Report 2010/11: Wage Policies in Times of Crisis*, Geneva: International Labour Office.
ILO (2010b), *World Social Security Report 2010/2011: Providing Coverage in Times of Crisis and Beyond*, Geneva: International Labour Office.
ILO (2011a), *Key Indicators of the Labour Market (KILM)*, 7th edition, Geneva: International Labour Office.
ILO (2011b), *Efficient Growth, Employment and Decent Work in Africa: Time for a New Vision*, Geneva: International Labour Office.
ILO (2012), *Global Wage Report 2012/2013*, Geneva: International Labour Office.
ILO/World Bank (2013), *Joint Synthesis Report: Inventory of Policy Responses to the Financial and Economic Crisis*, Geneva/Washington, DC: International Labour Organization/World Bank.
Ilzetski, E. and C. Veigh (2008), 'Procyclical fiscal policy in developing countries: truth or fiction?', *NBER Working Paper No. 14191*, Cambridge, MA: NBER.
IMF (2013), *Jobs and Growth: Analytical and Operational Considerations for the Fund*, Washington, DC: International Monetary Fund.
Islam, I. (2011), 'The perennial quest for fiscal and policy space in developing countries', in I. Islam and S. Verick (eds), *From the Great Recession to Labour Market Recovery: Issues, Evidence and Policy Options*, Basingstoke/Geneva: Palgrave Macmillan/International Labour Office.
Islam, I. and A. Chowdhury (2012), 'Full employment and the global development agenda: going beyond lip service', 19 January, *Vox*, accessed 25 August at www.voxeu.org/debates/commentaries/full-employment-and-global-development-agenda-going-beyond-lip-service.
Jeanne, O., J. Williamson and A. Subramanian (2012), *Who Needs to Open*

the Capital Account, Washington, DC: Peterson Institute for International Economics.

Jolly, R. (1991), 'Adjustment with a human face: a UNICEF record and perspective on the 1980s', *World Development*, **19**(12), 1807–21.

Kandil, M. and I.A. Mirzaie (2003), 'The effects of dollar appreciation on sectoral labour market adjustments: theory and evidence', *The Quarterly Review of Economics and Finance*, **43**(1), 89–117.

Klein, M.W., S. Schuh and R.K. Triest (2003), 'Job creation, job destruction, and the real exchange rate', *Journal of International Economics*, **59**(2), 239–65.

Lewis, W.A. (1979), 'The dual economy revisited', *The Manchester School of Economic and Social Studies*, **47**(3), 211–29.

Lin, J.Y. and D. Doemeland (2012), 'Beyond Keynesianism: global infrastructure investments in times of crisis', *Policy Research Working Paper No. 5940*, Washington, DC; World Bank.

Lobato, I., S. Pratap and A. Somuano (2003), 'Debt composition and balance sheet effects of exchange rates and interest rate volatility in Mexico: a firm level analysis', accessed 17 Aril 2013 at www.iadb.org/res/laresnetwork/projects/pr197finaldraft.pdf.

Luengnaruemitchai, P. (2003), 'The Asian crisis and the mystery of the missing balance sheet effect', Economics Department, University of California, Berkeley, accessed 25 August 2014 at http://eml.berkeley.edu/~webfac/gourinchas/e281_f03/pipat.pdf.

McMillan, M.S. and D. Rodrik (2011), 'Globalization, structural change and productivity growth', *NBER Working Paper No. 17143*, Cambridge, MA: National Bureau of Economic Research.

Morrison, W.M. and M. Labonte (2011), *China's Currency Policy: An Analysis of the Economic Issues*, Washington, DC: Congressional Research Service.

Ngandu, S.N. (2009), 'The impact of exchange rate movements on employment: the economy-wide effect of a rand appreciation', *Development Southern Africa*, **26**(1), 111–29.

Ocampo, J.A. (2011), 'Macroeconomy for development: counter-cyclical policies and production sector transformation', *CEPAL Review*, No. 104, August, 7–35.

OECD (1994), *The OECD Jobs Study: Facts, Analysis, Strategies*, Paris: Organisation for Economic Co-operation and Development.

OECD (1996), *Shaping the 21st Century: The Contribution of Development Co-operation*, Paris: Organisation for Economic Co-operation and Development.

OECD (2011), 'An overview of growing income inequalities in OECD countries: main findings', in *Divided We Stand: Why Inequality Keeps Rising*, Paris: Organisation for Economic Co-operation and Development.

OECD (2013), *OECD.StatExtracts*, accessed 28 May 2013 at http://stats.oecd.org/.

Ostry, J., A.R. Ghosh and K. Habermeier et al. (2011), 'Managing capital inflows: what tools to use?', *IMF Staff Discussion Note No. 11/06*, Washington, DC: International Monetary Fund.

Palley, T. (2007), 'Time for change: seeking full employment again', *Challenge*, **50**(6), 14–50.

Rodgers, G., L. Swepston, E. Lee and J. van Daele (2009), *The International Labour Organization and the Quest for Social Justice, 1919–2009*, Geneva/Ithaca: International Labour Office/ILR Press.

Rodrik, D. (2008), 'The real exchange rate and economic growth', John F. Kennedy School of Government, Harvard University, Cambridge MA.
Safaricom (2012), 'Celebrating 5 years of M-PESA', accessed 6 March 2013 at www.squaddigital.com/beta/safaricom/facebook/saftimelineiframe/pdf/infograph.pdf.
Steinberg, J. (2011), 'Real exchange rate undervaluation, financial development and growth', accessed 17 April 2013 at www.econ.umn.edu/~stein781/files/rerpaper.pdf.
Strayer, P.J., G. Leland Bach and R. Blough (1950), 'The Council of Economic Advisers: political economy on trial', *The American Economic Review, Papers and Proceedings of the American Economic Association*, **40**(2), 144–54.
Streeten, P. (1982), *First Things First: Meeting Basic Human Needs in Developing Countries*, New York: Oxford University Press.
Svensson, L. (2012), 'Differing views on monetary policy', speech delivered at SNS, Stockholm, 8 June, accessed 25 August 2014 at http://www.riksbank.se/en/Press-and-published/Speeches/2012/Svensson-Differing-views-on-monetary-policy/.
UN-ESCAP (2013), *Economic and Social Survey of Asia and the Pacific: Forward-looking Macroeconomic Policies for Inclusive and Sustainable Development*, Bangkok: United Nations Economic and Social Commission for Asia and the Pacific.
United Nations (1995), *World Summit for Social Development*, accessed 25 August 2014 at http://www.un.org/esa/socdev/wssd/text-version/.
van der Hoeven, R. (2010), 'Inequality and employment revisited: can one make sense of economic policy?', *Journal of Human Development and Capabilities*, **11**(1), 67–84.
Williamson, J. (2002), 'What Washington means by policy reform', Washington, DC: Peterson Institute for International Economics, accessed 25 August 2014 at http://www.iie.com/publications/papers/paper.cfm?researchid=486.
Williamson, J., O. Jeanne and A. Subramanian (2013), 'International rules for capital controls', *Vox*, 11 June, accessed 25 August 2014 at http://www.voxeu.org/article/international-rules-capital-controls.
Woodford, M. (2012), 'Methods of policy accommodation at the interest-rate lower bound', paper prepared for presentation at the Jackson Hole Symposium, 'The Changing Policy Landscape', 31 August–1 September, 2012.
World Bank (2012a), *Enterprise Surveys*, Washington, DC: World Bank, accessed 14 January 2013 at www.enterprisesurveys.org/.
World Bank (2012b), *The Little Data Book on Financial Inclusion*, Washington, DC: World Bank.
World Bank (2013), 'Three quarters of the world's poor are unbanked', Washington, DC: World Bank, accessed 24 April 2013 at www.econ.worldbank.org/WBSITE/EXTERNAL/EXTDEC/0,,contentMDK:23173842~pagePK:64165401~piPK:64165026~theSitePK:469372~isCURL:Y,00.html.
World Economic Forum (2012), *The Global Competitiveness Report 2012–2013*, Geneva: World Economic Forum.

PART II

Income from work

4. Unions and collective bargaining

Susan Hayter

4.1 INTRODUCTION

Trade unions have an important role to play in stemming the rising tide of inequality. As actors in political processes they can influence the direction of economic and social policy and shape the pattern of growth and the distribution of income. When it comes to income from work, unions can use collective bargaining to balance the unequal relationship between an employer and employee and negotiate a fair share of the gains. The results achieved through collective bargaining are more equitable than those arrived at through individual bargaining or unilateral contracting. There is also a greater likelihood that a jointly agreed 'common rule' will be complied with.[1]

Underpinning this system of social regulation are two fundamental workers' rights: freedom of association and the right to collective bargaining. The International Labour Organization's fundamental conventions that are the subject of these rights have been widely ratified by governments. Of the 185 member States, 152 have ratified the Freedom of Association and Protection of the Right to Organise Convention, 1948 (No. 87) and 163 have ratified the Right to Organise and Collective Bargaining Convention, 1949 (No. 98).[2] In 1998, the ILO adopted a Declaration on Fundamental Principles and Rights at Work that commits all member states to respect and promote principles and rights in four categories, whether or not they have ratified the relevant conventions. These are freedom of association and the effective recognition of the right to collective bargaining; the elimination of all forms of forced or compulsory labour; the effective abolition of child labour; and the elimination of discrimination in respect of employment and occupation. They provide the fundamental means with which to achieve social justice.

This chapter examines the role that trade unions and collective bargaining play in compressing wage structures and reducing inequality in earnings. While the international norms on freedom of association and the effective recognition of collective bargaining rights are universal, the collective bargaining arrangements that these rights give effect to vary across countries. Section 4.2 examines trends in union density and collective bargaining coverage. Section 4.3 discusses the role unions play in influencing income distribution. Given that the focus of this part of the volume is on earnings, the remainder of the chapter examines the relationship between trade unions, collective bargaining and wage inequality. Section 4.4 reviews the theoretical literature on the effect of unions and collective bargaining on wage inequality. Section 4.5 examines the empirical literature in both the developed and developing world. Section 4.6 considers whether the decline in trade union membership and erosion of collective bargaining institutions is a likely cause of the increase in wage inequality. Section 4.7 concludes with some remarks on the need to strengthen these institutions in order for them to take their rightful place in the political economy, defending the interests of workers and reducing wage and income inequality.

4.2 TRENDS IN UNIONS AND COLLECTIVE BARGAINING INSTITUTIONS

The structure of unions and nature of collective bargaining arrangements reflect a particular industrial relations system and historical context. As a result, the proportion of employees that are members of a trade union (trade union density) and the extent to which they are covered by a collective bargaining agreement varies significantly across countries. Collective bargaining can take place at the plant level, enterprise level, industry/branch level, municipal or regional level and inter-professional level. It can also take place at more than one level with varying degrees of bargaining coordination.

The regulatory effect of collective agreements tends to be more limited in industrial relations systems in which collective negotiations take place at the plant or enterprise level by a *single* employer. Collective bargaining patterns in these industrial relations systems have been characterized as exclusive, meaning that collective agreements only apply to members of the signatory parties or the bargaining unit (Traxler, 1996). As a result, the numbers of employees covered by collective agreements are relatively low and either equal to or less than union density. Collective negotiations may be coordinated, such as by a trade union, or remain uncoordinated. Countries in this group include the Republic of Korea, Japan, the United Kingdom, the United States and parts of Eastern Europe.

One can distinguish this from a second group of countries in which collective negotiations take place in *multi-employer* settings at the sectoral or central level. These collective agreements may be supplemented by plant or enterprise agreements. Collective agreements typically encompass a much higher proportion of employees and collective bargaining coverage is either equal to, or exceeds trade union density. They may also be extended to include non-party employers and their employees within a given industrial and territorial scope. Collective bargaining within these inclusive systems tends to be highly coordinated whether by peak organizations (employers' organizations and industry or national trade unions), as a result of pattern bargaining, tripartite social dialogue or some other form of government intervention (e.g., wage guidelines). The importance of such coordination in determining outcomes is discussed further in section 4.5 of the chapter.

When we examine data for the last ten years we see that trade union density has declined in many countries (Figure 4.1). While the proportion of employees who have their terms and conditions of employment

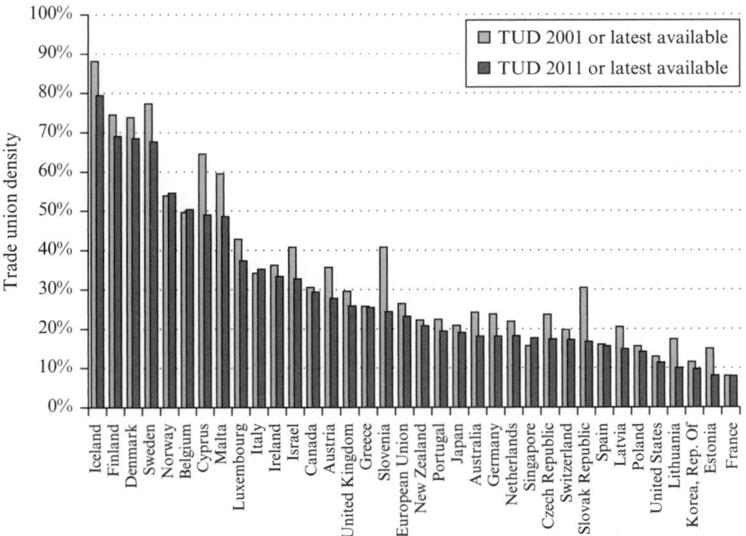

Note: Weighted average for European Union (excluding Croatia, data not available).

Source: ICTWSS Database (Version 4.0 – April 2013).

Figure 4.1 Trade union density (TUD) as a proportion of employees (developed economies – 2001 and 2011 or latest available data)

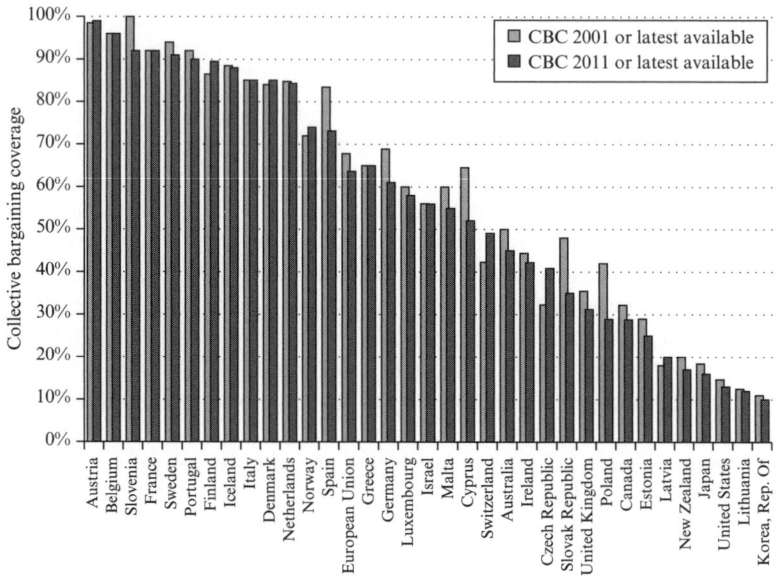

Note: Weighted average for European Union (excluding Croatia and Romania, data not available).

Source: ICTWSS Database (Version 4.0 – April 2013).

Figure 4.2 Collective bargaining coverage as a proportion of employees (developed economies 2001 and 2011 or latest available data)

regulated by a collective agreement (collective bargaining coverage) fell in some countries, it remained relatively stable in others (Figure 4.2). There are two reasons for the relative stability. The first is the predominant bargaining mode with multi-employer bargaining providing more stability (for example, in Austria, Belgium, Denmark, Finland and Norway). The second is the role that governments play in promoting collective bargaining as a cornerstone of wage policy, for example through the extension of collective agreements. However, just as public policies can help sustain coverage by collective agreements, discontinuous changes in public policy can erode collective wage setting.

Figures 4.1 and 4.2 present data available at the time of writing. They show a moderate decline in the weighted average of union density and collective bargaining coverage for European Union countries between 2001 and 2011. However, a number of governments in the region adopted austerity programmes in response to the Eurozone crisis that unfolded in 2010. These were often accompanied by reforms to labour law in 2012

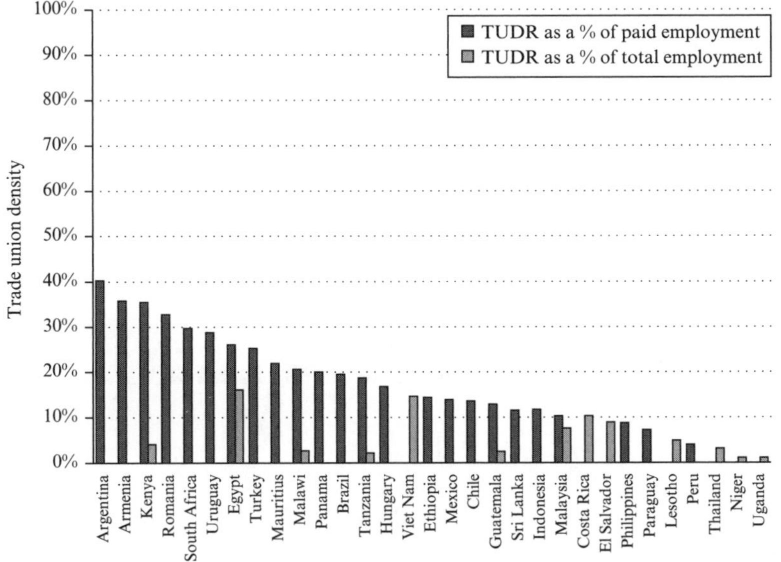

Sources: Hayter and Stoevska (2011) and ILOSTAT.

Figure 4.3 Trade union density rates (TUDR) in emerging and developing economies, 2010 or latest available data

and 2013 that altered systems for collective representation and bargaining. The result is a significant decline in coverage by collective bargaining in countries such as Bulgaria, Greece, Hungary, Italy, Portugal, Romania and Spain.

Available data for developing countries shows that trade union density and collective bargaining coverage are more limited with the exception of some emerging economies such as Argentina, Brazil and South Africa. We also see a significant difference in some countries between trade union membership or collective bargaining coverage (1) as a proportion of wage earners and (2) as proportion of total employment (Figures 4.3 and 4.4). This is because of the high proportion of own-account workers in many of these countries. Organizations representing own-account workers in the informal economy do exist but are often not 'counted' as trade unions.

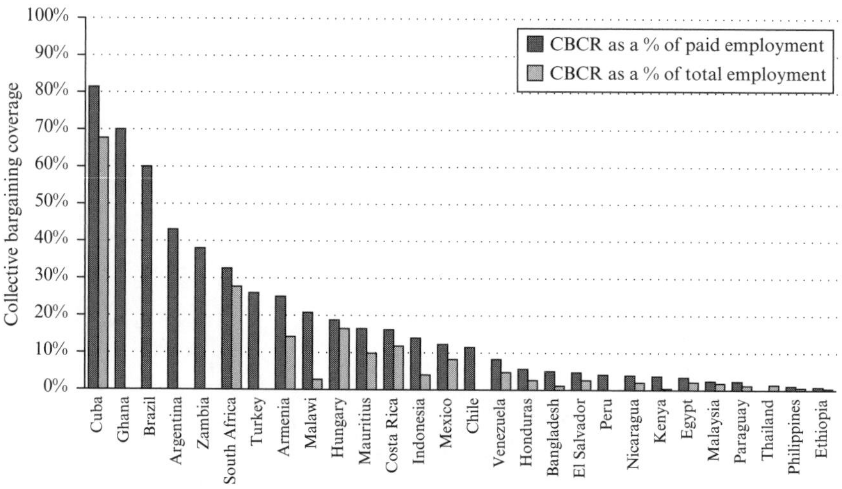

Sources: Hayter and Stoevska (2011) and ILOSTAT.

Figure 4.4 Collective bargaining coverage rates (CBCR) in emerging and developing economies, 2010 or latest available data

4.3 UNIONS AND INCOME DISTRIBUTION: NEGOTIATING FOR SOCIAL JUSTICE

Trade unions can affect the income distribution in different ways. First, they may provide 'countervailing power' to offset market dominance by a few large corporations and prevent a winner-take-all economy with its extreme concentrations of wealth. In *American Capitalism* (1952) John Kenneth Galbraith wrote: 'Not only has the strength of corporations [in these industries] made it necessary for workers to develop the protection of countervailing power, it has provided unions with the opportunity for getting something more as well' (p. 122).

Strong unions can insist on the necessary checks and balances that prevent the abuse of market power. In his analysis of the collapse of the financial sector in the United States in 2008–09, Freeman (2011) describes the regulatory capture of financial rules by the banking and financial sector and the cost to workers in income and employment when financial markets failed. He argues that modern economies need the countervailing power of labour institutions to develop and implement rules that make finance work for the real economy:

> The notion that unions and labour institutions are critical in providing a 'balance' or 'countervailing power' to the forces of capital and in determining the rules for capital markets is a radical one but I do not see another way that society can reform the Achilles heel of market capitalism . . . Moreover, I suspect that that countervailing power [between labour and capital] can produce economic outcomes closer to the free market ideal than outcomes generated by a system in which one side of the market – capital – writes its own rules. (Freeman, 2011, p. 270)

Second, trade unions may influence the direction of economic and social policies. The inclusion of labour in the political economy led to the progressive development of the welfare state in a number of countries, exemplary cases of which are the Nordic countries that adopted policies of full employment (Streek and Hassel, 2003). This contributed significantly to a reduction in income inequality. In the 2000s, trade unions in Brazil played a central role in the design of minimum wage policies. This, together with the Bolsa Família (Family Allowance) programme contributed to a decline in income inequality. It is thus not surprising that we see a strong association between union strength (union density) and higher levels of public expenditure on social protection, including unemployment benefits and active labour market policies (Traxler and Brandl, 2009).

Third, unions may affect the distribution of income through direct negotiations with employers and employers' organizations over wages and other aspects of income (e.g., provident funds, profit-sharing schemes etc.). This chapter focuses on the role of trade unions and collective bargaining in reducing inequality in earnings. Wage inequality is understood either as increasing differentials between high-, middle- and low-wage earners or as an increase in the variation of wages (wage dispersion).

A typical measure of wage inequality is to compare the wage level above which the top 10 per cent of workers are paid (commonly referred to as D9) with the wage level below which the bottom 10 per cent of workers are paid (commonly referred to as D1). We see a clear relationship between the proportion of wage earners covered by a collective bargaining agreement and the ratio of the D9 to the D1. Countries that have low collective bargaining coverage have higher D9/D1 ratios, whereas countries with a high coverage of collective bargaining agreements have more compressed wage distributions (Figure 4.5). We can also see that the manner in which trade unions influence the wage structure differs depending on whether the collective bargaining is narrow and exclusive or encompassing and inclusive.

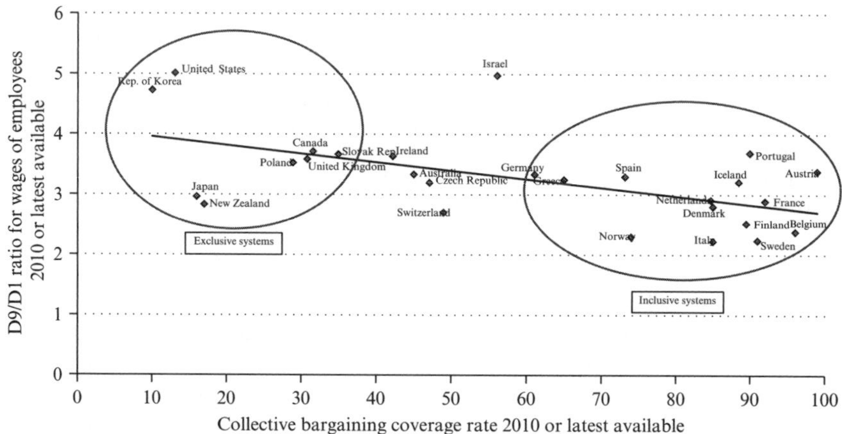

Sources: ICTWSS Database (Version 4.0 – April 2013) and OECD Stats.

Figure 4.5 D9/D1 ratio and collective bargaining in developed economies (2010 or latest available data)

4.4 UNIONS, COLLECTIVE BARGAINING AND WAGE EQUALITY: THE THEORY

Broadly speaking, we can distinguish between two schools of thought: those who view labour market institutions, such as unions and collective bargaining, as distorting the functioning of labour markets, and those who view unions as potentially contributing to equity and efficiency.

For 'distortionists', unions introduce a wedge between labour supply and demand. They interfere with labour market relocation, which impedes the functioning of labour markets. Unions use their monopoly power to raise wages above the competitive ideal. This mark-up or 'union premium' widens the gap between unionized and non-unionized workers, which reduces the efficiency of labour markets. This view is clearly articulated by the following quote from Milton Friedman (1962):

> If unions raise wage rates in a particular occupation or industry, they necessarily make the amount of employment available in that occupation or industry less than it otherwise would be – just as any higher price cuts down the amount purchased. The effect is an increased number of persons seeking other jobs, which forces down wages in other occupations. Since unions have generally been strongest among groups that would have been high-paid anyway, their effect has been to make high-paid workers higher paid at the expense of lower-paid workers. Unions have therefore not only harmed the public at large and

> workers as a whole by distorting the use of labor; they have also made the incomes of the working class more unequal by reducing the opportunities to the most disadvantaged workers. (Friedman, 1962, p. 124)

Neoclassical theories of unemployment, such as insider–outsider theory, also provide an account of how unions distort labour markets and contribute to inequality. Insider–outsider theory focuses on labour turnover costs: the cost of dismissal, of hiring and of training of new incumbents. It divides workers into three groups: insiders, who tend to be well paid; outsiders, who are either unemployed or work for much less pay in the informal economy; and entrants, who hold jobs that might result in insider status. The central tenet of the theory is that cost associated with hiring and firing protects insiders, to the detriment of outsiders (Lindbeck and Snower, 1989). As Lindbeck and Snower argue, union presence in workplaces raises labour turnover costs. Unions may lobby politicians to strengthen employment protection legislation, or they may augment labour turnover costs by coordinating activities among their members. These circumstances make employers much more likely to agree to wage increases, since the alternative entails the costly replacement of all unionized employees, rather than simply firing one or two employees. The turnover costs associated with unionized workplaces negatively affect the income and employment prospects of the (non-unionized) outsiders, who may be unemployed or in the informal economy.

A distortionary view of what unions do is also at the heart of 'unified theory', which links patterns of unemployment with earnings inequality (Howell, 2002). According to this line of reasoning, skills-biased technological change shifted the demand from low-skilled to high-skilled labour. Countries in which trade unions and collective bargaining play a significant role in wage formation, such as those in Europe, maintain higher wages for low-skilled workers and more equitable wage distributions but, it is argued, this comes at the cost of employment. In the United States where labour markets are less affected by these distortionary institutions, wages are more responsive to labour market conditions, adjusting downward and delivering better employment performance, albeit at the cost of greater inequality.

A second school of thought, the 'institutionalists', views trade unions as potentially contributing to both equity and efficiency.[3] While recognizing the 'monopoly face' of trade unions Freeman and Medoff (1984) argue that trade unions have a second face, which through the expression of 'voice' can contribute to efficiency and has a strong equalizing effect on the distribution of wages *within* the union sector. As democratic organizations, trade unions negotiate collective agreements that reflect the preferences of the median member – who is typically low skilled and earns less that the average worker. Collective agreements lift wage floors (where the majority of union members are located) and reduce the gap between low- and high-wage earners. Union wage policies are premised on equal pay for equal work and seek to standardize pay rates. Collective negotiations set wages according to objective rules that can be agreed upon, thus reducing discretionary wage-setting practices based on the subjective assessment of individual merit. In the interests of maintaining organizational solidarity, unions coordinate efforts and pursue these egalitarian wage policies both within a company and across firms in the same industry.

Unions and the expression of 'voice' can also encourage the exchange of information and foster cooperative behaviour. This can contribute to better decision-making and facilitate the introduction of technological improvements that improve productivity (Fakhfakh et al., 2011; see also Aidt and Tzannatos, 2002 for a review). Unionized firms are also more likely to invest in the training of their workforce (Heyes and Rainbird, 2011). Just as equity and efficiency can go hand in hand, rising wage inequality can also have a negative effect on worker satisfaction, collaboration and productivity.

Hayter and Weinberg (2011) suggest three possible channels through which unions might affect wage inequality: a 'within sector' effect, that is, on the wage structure within a unionized firm, bargaining unit or industry; a 'between sector' effect, that is, between unionized and non-unionized firms or industries; and a 'compositional' effect, that is, the effect of union wages on the relative share of employment in unionized and in non-unionized sectors.

4.5 UNIONS, COLLECTIVE BARGAINING AND WAGE INEQUALITY: THE EVIDENCE

There is a vast empirical literature on the relationship between trade unions, collective bargaining and wage inequality (see Hayter and Weinberg, 2011 for detailed review). Not surprisingly, the manner in which trade unions influence the wage structure differs depending on whether the collective bargaining system is exclusive or inclusive.

Trade Unions and Wage Inequality in Exclusive Systems

In systems in which the application of a collective bargaining agreement is limited to the parties or bargaining unit, trade unions reduce the gap between high- and low-wage earners and compress wage structures. Early empirical work by Freeman (1980 and 1982), examining micro-data from unionized and non-unionized sectors in the United States for the 1970s, found that wage dispersion is smaller *within* the unionized sector. Since the objective of union wage policy is to standardize wage rates, this reduces the impact of individual characteristics such as education, age and experience on the variance of wages among organized blue-collar workers. Thus, one finds smaller wage differentials between blue-collar and white-collar workers *within* the organized sector. Metcalf (1982) and Gosling and Machin (1995) find similar results for the United Kingdom: the dispersion of earnings is smaller *within* the union than the non-union sector. Hara and Kawaguchi (2008) examining micro-data for Japan also find less wage dispersion *within* the union than non-union sectors.

What if unionized workers are simply better skilled and thus more productive than their non-union counterparts? The compression of the wage structure in the union sector may thus be the result of consistently choosing more skilled workers rather than union wage policies. Freeman (1984) considers this possibility by examining longitudinal data and finds that wage differences increase for a worker moving from a union to a non-union job, compared with a worker who remains in employment in an organized establishment. Similarly, wage differences decrease for a worker moving from a non-union to a unionized establishment, compared with a worker remaining in an unorganized establishment. Lemieux (1998), in a study of Canada, also addresses the possibility that compressed wage structures in the union sector are the result of a selectivity bias. He corrects for unobservable skill differences and finds that union bargaining reduces returns to both observable and unobservable skill measures.

The distortionist's concern over the dis-equalizing effect of unions is based on the *between* sector effects, that is, the difference between unionized workers who benefit from a union mark-up and non-unionized workers who do not. Freeman (1980) shows that for the United States the *within* (union) sector equalizing effect offsets the *between* (union and non-union) sector dis-equalizing effects. The net effect of union wage policies is to reduce wage dispersion overall.

Recent studies that consider differences in union membership by sub-group (men, women, skill level etc.) continue to confirm the finding that unions reduce wage inequality.[4] Card et al. (2004) update and extend existing studies on the effect of unions on wage inequality in the United States, United Kingdom and Canada. Their results are remarkably consistent across countries and over time (from the 1970s to 2001). Wage dispersion is always smaller *within* the union than the non-union sector. For men, the *within* sector effect always dominates the *between* sector effect with the result that union wage policies have an equalizing effect on wage dispersion overall. This equalizing effect is much smaller for female earnings than it is for male earnings.

From this we can conclude that in exclusive systems, where the coverage of collectively negotiated agreements is limited to the parties or bargaining unit, the effect of unions on wage structures is likely to be an equalizing one. The negotiation of standardized wage rates within and across firms tempers discretionary wage-setting practices that might otherwise increase inequality among workers. Unions also increase the pay of lower-skilled, low-paid workers relative to higher-skilled workers, management and those typically at the top of the wage structure. This results in the compression of wage structures. Union wage policies reduce wage inequality *within* the unionized sector, the magnitude of which offsets the dis-equalizing effect *between* union and non-union workers and sectors. The net effect is an equalizing one, particularly for men.

Trade Unions and Wage Inequality in Inclusive Systems

Given the foregoing review, it is reasonable to expect that the greater the number of workers belonging to a trade union (as a proportion of all wage earners), the greater is the equalizing effect of unions on earnings in a given country. Indeed, cross-country studies that estimate the effects of trade union density on wage inequality find that higher trade union density is associated with lower differentials and less wage dispersion at a more aggregate level (for example, see Blau and Kahn, 1999; Rueda and Pontusson, 2000; Aidt and Tzannatos, 2002; OECD, 2004 and European Commission, 2009 for a review).

In more inclusive multi-employer bargaining settings the coverage of collective bargaining agreements tends to exceed trade union membership. In these institutional settings, measures such as the coverage of collective bargaining, the degree of coordination and extent of union centralization provide a more accurate indication of the influence of union power on wage formation than trade union density alone (Visser and Checchi, 2009). Industrial relations systems with higher levels of collective bargaining coverage that are more centralized with high degrees of coordination tend to have better outcomes in terms of wage inequality. These studies also show that greater equity in the wage distribution does not come at the cost of unemployment.

Wallerstein (1999) examines the effect of different features of collective bargaining institutions on wage differentials in 16 countries between 1980 and 1992. These include union density, collective bargaining coverage and the level at which bargaining takes place. The study controls for other variables that may affect the distribution of wages, such as the political orientation of government. The author finds that the degree of bargaining centralization is the most important determinant of differences in wage inequality between countries. Golden and Londregan (2006) reproduce the study and find a smaller but still statistically significant relationship between centralized collective bargaining and a reduction in the D9/D1 ratio.[5]

The equalizing effect of centralized bargaining is also confirmed by country-specific evidence involving a shift to a more centralized bargaining structure. Kahn (1998) examines micro-data for 1987 and 1991 for Norway to assess the impact of bargaining centralization on wage dispersion in the late 1980s. Following a period of decentralization from the early to mid-1980s, employers' organizations, trade unions and the government reasserted the primacy of centralized negotiations. The change in the bargaining regime and (re)centralization of collective bargaining resulted in the compression of the bottom half of the wage distribution between 1987 and 1991 and reduced wage inequality.

Inclusive collective bargaining systems are typically characterized by the extension of collective bargaining agreements. Evidence suggests that this administrative extension also has a moderating effect on wage inequality. In their comparison of the wage structure and wage-setting institutions in the United States to those in nine other high-income countries, Blau and Kahn (1996) find a correlation between the level of centralization and (lower) wage dispersion in the bottom half of the wage distribution. They also find that the practice of extension to the non-union firms has a significant compression effect on wage structures in these countries (relative to the United States). Western (1998) shows that countries that did not experience an increase in wage inequality between 1970 and 1990 (Germany, Italy and the Netherlands) all had a practice of extending collective agreements. Kahn (1997) also examines possible spillover effects and finds evidence that contract extension and voluntary imitation by firms of what they perceive to be a 'fair wage' (set by unionized firms) compresses wage structures at the bottom of the wage structure in Austria, West Germany, Norway and Sweden, again relative to the United States.

Another important consideration is the degree to which these inclusive collective bargaining institutions reduce the gender pay gap (see also Chapter 12 on gender equality). Blau and Kahn (2003) examine micro-data for 22 countries for the period from 1985 to 1994 and find a significant relationship between collective bargaining coverage and a reduced gender pay gap in each country. They conclude that by raising the wage floor, these inclusive bargaining arrangements also raise the relative pay of women who tend to be at the bottom of the wage distribution and reduce the gender pay gap. A study by the European Commission (2009) also finds that collective bargaining reduces the gender pay gap.

In recent years, we have seen an increased role in Western Europe for supplementary enterprise-level bargaining. In the past there was fear that wage rates and bonus payments (linked to performance) in enterprise-level agreements would exceed levels set in national and industry agreements and that this 'wage drift' would undo the equalizing effects of centralized bargaining. More recently there has been growing concern over the dis-equalizing effect of 'opt-out' clauses and other changes that enable enterprise agreements to derogate from the terms of agreements reached at a sectoral or inter-sectoral level.

What is the empirical evidence to date on the relationship between multi-level bargaining and wage inequality? Hibbs and Locking (1996) in their study of centralized bargaining in Sweden show that peak employers' organizations and trade unions anticipated the potential for wage drift in their central agreement. High degrees of coordination by the bargaining partners reinforced the overall compression effect of the central agreement. In their study of systems that combine multi-employer and single-employer bargaining Dell'Aringa and Pagani (2007) find that single-employer bargaining in the context of a multi-employer agreement led to greater wage dispersion in Spain. By contrast, higher degrees of coordination in Belgium and Italy, significant imitation by firms and actions by unions to compress wages even further at the firm level narrowed the dispersion of wages in those countries. These findings appear to contradict those of Plasman et al. (2007) who find that single-employer agreements in a multi-employer bargaining context increased wage dispersion in Belgium and in Denmark and reduced it in Spain. While there is clearly the need for more research on the issue, available evidence suggests that what is critical is the capacity of unions and employers' organizations to coordinate subsequent firm-level bargaining. Vernon (2011) in a cross-country comparison of joint regulation and pay inequality concludes that it is the strength of unions and employers' organizations and their role in bargaining structures not the anatomy of the body of joint regulation that makes the difference.

Turning to the 'compositional' effects, that is, whether or not collectively determined wages affect the relative share of employment in the unionized and non-unionized sectors, research examining the macroeconomic impact of collective bargaining institutions on aggregate economic outcomes such as unemployment and employment finds no robust evidence to suggest that institutionally shaped wages raise unemployment (see OECD, 2006 for a review, and Traxler and Brandl, 2009). OECD researchers Bassanini and Duvel (2006), examining the period from 1982 to 2003, find no statistically significant association between trade union density and unemployment. On the contrary, they find that highly centralized or coordinated systems reduce unemployment. Howell and Huebler (2005) review trends in earnings and employment outcomes and find no evidence in support of the 'unified theory', that inclusive collective bargaining arrangements and 'too much wage compression' come at the cost of increased unemployment in Europe.

Trade Unions, Collective Bargaining and Wage Inequality in Developing Countries

Separate consideration needs to be given to the relationship between trade unions, collective bargaining institutions and wage inequality in developing countries. Given the relatively high levels of informal employment, the context for determining the effects of trade unions is very different. Trade union membership as a proportion of total employment tends to be low and the coverage of collective agreements also tends to be low, suggesting that the role that collective bargaining plays in wage determination is fairly limited (see Figures 4.3 and 4.4). This raises two questions. First, do unions and collective bargaining have an equalizing effect on the wages of their members and those covered by collective agreements? Second, what is the impact of unions and collectively determined wages on those that fall outside of the coverage of these institutions and regulations?

Trade unions, collective bargaining and the 'insiders'

Given the paucity of data, there are fewer studies of the economic effects of these institutions in developing countries. Nevertheless existing studies show that similar inferences can be made about 'what unions do'. The union wage mark-up in studies of developing countries ranges between 3 and 17 per cent (Hayter and Weinberg, 2011). This does not differ that significantly from the range for higher-income countries, which is between 5 and 25 per cent (Aidt and Tzannatos, 2002). Findings on the *within-sector* effects are also very similar to those for higher-income countries. Unions compress wage structures and moderate returns to individual worker characteristics, thereby reducing the dispersion of wages. In countries with inclusive collective bargaining arrangements, union wage bargaining has an equalizing effect across all workers covered by the terms of a collective agreement.

It is important to understand the industrial relations context including the structure of trade unions in order to understand their effects. In Mexico, collective bargaining takes place at the level of the enterprise with the exception of a few sectors. Once concluded, a collective agreement applies to all workers in the particular enterprise (both union and non-union members). A number of researchers find that unions have an equalizing effect on wage structures analogous to the *within-sector* effect. Panagides and Patrinos (1994) find lower wage dispersion *within* the union sector than the non-union sector. Their results show that while discrimination against women and indigenous workers in the non-union sector is common, these differences are negligible in the unions sector. Fairris (2003 and 2005), using data from household and establishment surveys, finds that union wage policies reduce wage dispersion *within* the union sector (both within and across firms). Popli (2007), using similar data for an equivalent time period, also finds that the dispersion of wages is lower *within* the union sector, compared to the non-union sector.

In a study of Malaysia, Standing (1992) examines micro-data for manufacturing firms in 1988 to establish whether independent 'industrial' unions pursue more egalitarian agendas than 'house' unions, which are supported by government and/or management and operate in the interests of select groups. Standing finds that the wage ratios between skilled, semi-skilled and unskilled workers are smaller *within* industrial unions than house unions, which in turn are smaller than those in the non-union sector. The gender pay gap is also smaller *within* the union sector than the non-union sector.

For Korea, a study by Kim (1993) examines the historical development of unions between 1987 and 1989, during which there was an increase in trade union membership. The study analyses data from occupational wage surveys to examine gross and net wage differentials between production and non-production workers in both the union and non-union sectors. The author finds that wage differentials between production and non-production workers and the gender pay is smaller *within* the union setting than the non-union setting. Additional evidence of a *within-sector* equalizing effect of unions is found in studies of Ghana and Cameroon, which find a union wage mark-up for those at the bottom of the wage distribution (Blunch and Verner, 2004; Tsafack-Nanfosso, 2002).

A study of semi-skilled male workers in 22 manufacturing industries in Brazil provides somewhat mixed results. Of the industries examined, wage dispersion is higher in the union sector in 14, lower in the union sector in seven and equal to that of the non-union sector in one (the metallurgic sector) (Arbache, 1999). There is a negligible difference between the D9/D1 ratio for the union and non-union sector.[6] These results are most likely explained by the effect of the minimum wage on the wage distribution in Brazil, which raises the wage floor where most non-union workers are concentrated. It highlights two important points that deserve examination in developing country contexts. The first is the relationship between minimum wages and collective bargaining. The second is the effect of the union mark-up on the different deciles of the wage distribution in different industries.

Modalities for collective bargaining in South Africa differ from industry to industry. Employers' organizations and trade unions have established inclusive bargaining councils in some industries. The terms of the collective agreement may be extended by the Minister of Labour to non-parties, including those in informal employment. In other industries, such as mining and automotive manufacturing, collective agreements may be negotiated on a multi-employer basis and the terms apply to all in the bargaining unit. Collective bargaining can also take place on a single-employer basis such as in the banking and retail sectors. A study by Schultz and Mwabu (1998) examining data for 1994, prior to significant labour reforms, finds that unions have an equalizing effect *within* the union sector, raising wage floors and reducing interracial disparities and the gap between low and high earners. Butcher and Rouse (2001) in their study of the wage effects of unions and bargaining councils also find a larger union wage mark-up for those in the lower quintiles and a more compressed wage structure *within* unionized sectors. Bhorat et al. (2009) examine the effect of union membership and bargaining council coverage on wage formation. Their findings confirm those of previous studies. Union membership is associated with smaller D9/D1, D9/D5 and D5/D1 ratios. The impact is greatest at the bottom of the wage distribution where unions raise wage floors and compress wage structures. Coverage by a bargaining council agreement in both the public and private sector is associated with a smaller gap between the middle and top of the wage distribution (D9/D5 ratio).

In Argentina, collective agreements concluded by the most representative union are applied to all workers within the relevant sector or occupation. Trajtemberg (2008) finds that wage dispersion and differentials are greater for workers not covered by a collective agreement than those who are covered (both members and non-members). The study also finds that the wage mark-up would decrease and the dispersion of wage increase in the absence of unions.

Trade unions, collective bargaining and the 'outsiders'

The focus of much of the debate on the impact of unions and collective bargaining in developing countries is not on whether they advance goals of equity and social justice for members and workers covered by collective agreements, but the effect of these institutions on the income and employment prospects of those who do not belong to trade unions and may be working in the informal economy. Unions are portrayed as creating a 'labor aristocracy' that exacerbates the insider–outside divide, fuels informal employment and amplifies inequality.

This insider–outsider dichotomy is very pervasive in policy debates. Unions are blamed for the lack of decent jobs in these countries. 'Insider' privileges are amplified when the working conditions of 'outsiders' deteriorate because of labour market deregulation. The call for further deregulation – rather than more inclusive regulation – is then justified on equity grounds. Yet the dividing line between 'insiders' and 'outsiders' is seldom as stark as portrayed. The wages of 'insiders' often contributes to capital for the income-generating activities of 'outsiders' within a household or provides the necessary resources for their job searching and employment prospects (Devey et al., 2006). Rather than pitting 'insiders' against 'outsiders' policy-makers should aim at encouraging encompassing and inclusive forms of collective representation and wage bargaining.

As noted, unions in developing countries represent a very small percentage of those in total employment and the coverage of those in employment by collective agreements is also very limited (see Figures 4.3 and 4.4). Freeman in evaluating research on the impact of institutions in developing country labour markets, concludes that:

> Institutions are unlikely to affect aggregate outcomes unless they have very large effects on the formal sector, sizable spillovers to the informal sector, or are located in sectors that may be particularly important for economic development, for instance traded goods. (Freeman, 2009, p. 12)

What does the empirical evidence show on the impact of unions and collective bargaining on the 'outsiders'? For the Republic of Korea, Fields and Yoo (2000) find that despite an increase in the union wage mark-up (from 3.0 per cent to 5.8 per cent) between 1986 and 1993 unions had a negligible effect on inequality at the aggregate level over this period. For Mexico, Fairris (2003) finds that unions have an equalizing effect on wage inequality overall, including both formal and informal employment. For Argentina, Trajtemberg (2008) concludes that unions reduce the total variability of wages for all workers by 26 per cent. Standing (1992) finds evidence of positive spillover effects in Malaysia (benefits for casual workers).

Does the wage mark-up enjoyed by those who are members of a union come at the cost of greater informal employment? If this were the case, it would be reasonable to expect that countries with stronger civic rights including collective bargaining rights would have higher shares of informal employment. However, evidence from Latin America shows that on the contrary, countries with stronger civic rights have higher shares of formal employment and less informal employment than those with weaker civic rights (Galli and Kucera, 2004).

Maloney and Ribeiro (1999) in their study of Mexico find that not only do unions raise wages for low-paid unskilled workers, but they also raise the numbers of unskilled workers hired.[7] Rather than reducing the level of employment, displacing low-skilled workers into the informal economy, the authors find that unions are preserving low-skilled jobs. According to the authors, labour market segmentation would continue to be a feature of the labour markets in the absence of unions and wage policies. In their study of South Africa, Butcher and Rouse (2001) conclude that the share of union membership in total employment is too low to account for the country's high level of unemployment.

4.6 MIND THE GAP: THE EROSION OF COLLECTIVE WAGE SETTING

The fact that the rise in inequality has been accompanied by a decline in the strength and bargaining power of trade unions raises a question as to whether there is a link between these two phenomena. Is the shift from collective wage setting to market-determined pay one of the factors behind the rise in wage inequality?

There is a sizeable body of literature examining possible causes for the rise in wage inequality in recent years.[8] One view attributes the increase in wage inequality to rapid technological change, in particular computer technology, which raised the relative demand for high-skilled workers and led to widening wage gaps between low- and highly skilled workers (for example, Autor et al., 2008 and Beaudry and Green, 2005).[9] A second attributes the rise in inequality (in advanced countries) to international trade with low-wage countries (for example, Wood, 1994). A third focuses on the role that institutional factors play in explaining cross-country differences in changes in inequality (for example, Freeman and Katz, 1995).

We examine country-specific evidence of the effect of the fall in union membership and erosion of collective wage setting on wage inequality. In 1980, half of employees belonged to a union in the United Kingdom and around 20 per cent in the United States. By 2011 only 26 per cent of employees belonged to a trade union in the United Kingdom and 11 per cent in the United States (OECD, 2011). A growing number of studies attribute the rise in wage inequality in these countries to the decline in union density and influence.

After the election of a conservative government in the United Kingdom in 1979, a series of labour law reforms were enacted that weakened the protection of trade unions and collective action. They also eliminated wage councils that were responsible for setting minimum wages. Machin

(1997) finds that this weakening of trade unions and minimum wages played a major role in the rise in wage inequality in the 1980s. Bell and Pitt (1998) attribute approximately 20 per cent of the increase in the standard deviation, a measure of the degree of variation or dispersion of male wages during the 1980s to the decline in union density. Gosling and Lemieux (2001) evaluate developments in the United Kingdom and United States between 1979 and 1998, a period during which the pattern of inequality became increasingly similar in the two countries. The authors find that the steep decline in unionization in the United Kingdom explains the comparatively sharper rise in wage inequality in that country during this period.

In their study of the United States, DiNardo et al. (1996) find that while the decline in the real value of the minimum wage between 1979 and 1988 had a significant impact on inequality, the decline in unionization accounted for 14 per cent of the change in the standard deviation of wages for men during that period.[10] By contrast, between 1973 and 1979 increases in the real value of the minimum wage and the unionization rate were associated with a decline in wage inequality for both men and women (only the minimum wage affected the women's distribution). Card (2001) finds that the decline in union membership between 1973 and 1993 accounts for between 15 and 20 per cent of the rise in male wage inequality. Western and Rosenfeld (2011) attribute one-third of the rise in male wage inequality and a fifth of the rise in female wage inequality between 1973 and 2007 to declining unionization.

Outside the Anglo-Saxon context, a study of West Germany by Dustmann et al. (2009) finds that one-third of the increase in lower tail inequality in the 1990s was related to the decline in trade union density. A study by Antonczyk et al. (2010) examines the period between 2001 and 2006 during which coverage by collective agreements declined by 16.5 per cent for males and 19.1 per cent for females. Wage inequality rose over this period driven by real wage increases at the top and real wage losses at the bottom of the wage distribution. The study finds that the stark decline in collective bargaining coverage contributed to the strong rise in wage inequality.

For developing countries, a study by Fairris (2003) of Mexico finds that the decline in union density from 31 per cent in 1984 to less than 20 per cent in 2000 is associated with rising wage inequality. Had unions retained the same structural power that they had in 1984, overall wage inequality would have been 5.6 per cent lower in 1996. A study by Popli (2007) of Mexico examining the same period finds that the decline in unionization accounts for 28 per cent of the increase in wage inequality. The decline in the real value of the minimum wage and changes in the skill distribution also played a role in rising wage inequality.

The erosion of inclusive collective bargaining arrangements, either through deregulation or decentralization is also associated with a rise in wage inequality. In Sweden, wage dispersion decreased during a period of centralized bargaining (1960s to 1980). In 1983, employers withdrew from centralized bargaining. The decentralization of wage setting was accompanied by an increase in wage dispersion both within and across industries (Hibbs, 1990). Similarly, in Israel, the deregulation and decentralization of bargaining arrangements between 1970 and 2003, involving a decline in the use of extension orders and the proliferation of local agreements, resulted in a rise in wage inequality (Kristal and Cohen, 2007). Dahl et al. (2011) examine the effect of organized decentralization in the Danish labour market during the 1990s, a period in which wage setting shifted from national to sectoral-level bargaining and in which firm-level bargaining gained increasing significance. They find that wages became more dispersed under firm-level bargaining than centralized wage setting.

The increase in contingent work presents a number of challenges for union organization and collective forms of wage setting. There is evidence that it is being used to escape entitlements associated with an employment contract and undercut wages in collective agreements (Skinner and Valodia, 2002; Underhill and Rimmer, 2009). This not only contributes to growing gaps between workers with different types of contracts but also reduces the potential effect of collective wage setting on wage inequality.

4.7 CONCLUDING REMARKS

The notion that there may be a trade-off between equity and efficiency has been a central concern of neoclassical economics. This focus on how redistribution may affect growth and thus the size of the pie has distracted attention from one of the critical issues today – labour's income has been shrinking. Within this smaller slice of the pie, gaps between low and high earners have been growing. This has implications for workers, for enterprises and for the health of the economy.

Unions and collective bargaining institutions reduce wage inequality and disparities between different groups of workers. The evidence is well established for both exclusive and inclusive systems, and in both developed and developing countries. Abstract concerns over an equity–efficiency trade-off do not reflect reality. There is no robust evidence to support the contention that institutionally determined wages affect the employment prospects of the unemployed and come at the cost of those that fall outside of the reach of collective bargaining agreements.

The failure of the labour markets in developing countries to generate well-paying jobs in the formal sector seldom has anything to do with the institutions in the formal labour market. We should recall that what are now inclusive collective bargaining institutions in many countries today all started as small unions for 'insiders'. Rather than adopting a static, fatalistic view of the effects of 'insider' unions in developing countries there is a need to consider the evolution of these collective institutions over longer time periods. The transformation of emerging and small unions and weak collective bargaining structures into inclusive collective bargaining institutions requires public policies that support freedom of association and promote collective bargaining. They also need to address challenges in respect of coordination and ensuring the ongoing effectiveness of collective bargaining systems.

The strengthening of trade unions and collective bargaining in the period following the Great Depression was not a historical accident. It was the explicit intention of public policy.[11] Unfortunately it appears that the political tide has turned and collective bargaining institutions are being eroded at a point in time when they are most needed. Yet desire for collective representation and action remains, as evidenced by recent protests and collective gatherings in different parts of the world. It is important to consider ways to strengthen and extend the scope and inclusiveness of collective bargaining and enhance its equity-generating effects in all countries. The stakes are high. They require political commitment to social justice and sound policy choices that make that commitment a reality.

NOTES

1. The 'device of the common rule', first postulated by Sidney and Beatrice Webb, could be achieved through three methods: mutual insurance, collective bargaining and legal enactment (Webb and Webb, 1902).
2. Entered into force 1950 and 1951 respectively. See: http://www.ilo.org/dyn/normlex/en/f?p=NORMLEXPUB:12100:0::NO:12100:P12100_INSTRUMENT_ID:312232:NO and http://www.ilo.org/dyn/normlex/en/f?p=NORMLEXPUB:12100:0::NO:12100:P12100_INSTRUMENT_ID:312243:NO; last accessed 30 November 2013.
3. In efficient bargaining models firms and unions negotiate simultaneously over wages and employment to a Pareto-efficient contract 'leaving nothing on the table' (McDonald and Solow, 1981).
4. See, for example, DiNardo et al. (1996); Machin (1997); Bell and Pitt (1998); Gosling and Lemieux (2001); and Card et al. (2003) for a review of 'second-generation studies' including Lemieux (1993); Card (1996); and Metcalf et al. (2001).
5. They find that the switch from a plant-level system of bargaining to an industry-level system results in a 5 per cent rather than 30 per cent decrease in wage differentials as calculated by Wallerstein.
6. The D9/D1 ratio is 1.83 for the union sector and 1.80 for the non-union sector.
7. The authors attribute this to the role that collective bargaining plays in ensuring the

optimal allocation of resources – both wages and employment – as per efficient bargaining models (McDonald and Solow, 1981).

8. See Machin (2008) for an appraisal of literature.
9. A number of authors question this skills-biased technological change (SBTC) explanation. Card and DiNardo (2002) argue that the diffusion of information and communication technology in the 1990s is at odds with the slowdown in inequality in the United States during the same period. Howell (2002) notes that inequality by skill group remained stagnant and even decreased in many advanced countries, contrary to what the SBTC would predict. Lemieux (2007) argues that the growth in inequality since 1990 has been concentrated at the top end of the distribution, which is inconsistent with what standard models of SBTC would predict.
10. They find that the decline in the real value of the minimum wage explains 25 per cent and 30 per cent of changes in the standard deviation of log wages for men and women respectively.
11. John Maynard Keynes, in a letter to President Roosevelt on recovery policies from the Great Depression (1 February 1938) wrote: 'I regard the growth of wage bargaining as essential. I approve minimum wage and hours regulation'.

REFERENCES

Aidt, T. and Z. Tzannatos (2002), *Unions and Collective Bargaining: Economic Effects in a Global Environment*, Washington, DC: World Bank.

Antonczyk, D., F. Fitzenberger and K. Sommerfeld (2010), 'Rising wage inequality, the decline of collective bargaining, and the gender wage gap', *IZA Discussion Paper No. 4911*, Bonn: Forschungsinstitut zur Zukunft der Arbeit (IZA).

Arbache, J.S. (1999), 'Do unions always decrease wage dispersion? The case of Brazilian manufacturing', *Journal of Labor Research*, **20**(3), 425–36.

Autor, D., L.F. Katz and M.S. Kearney (2008), 'Trends in U.S. wage inequality. Revisiting the revisionists', *Review of Economics and Statistics*, **90**(2), 300–23.

Bassanini, A. and R. Duval (2006), 'Employment patterns in OECD countries: reassessing the role of policies and institutions', *Social, Employment and Migration Working Papers No. 35*, Paris: Organisation for Economic Co-operation and Development.

Beaudry, P. and D.A. Green (2005), 'Changes in U.S. wages, 1976–2000: ongoing skill bias or major technological change?', *Journal of Labor Economics*, **23**(3), 609–48.

Bell, D.B. and M.K. Pitt (1998), 'Trade union decline and the distribution of wages in the UK: evidence from kernel density estimation', *Oxford Bulletin of Economics and Statistics*, **60**(4), 509–28.

Bhorat, H., C. van der Westhuizen and S. Goga (2009), 'Analysing wage formation in the South African labour market: the role of bargaining councils', *Development Policy Research Unit Working Paper No. 09/135*, Rondebosch: Development Research Unit.

Blau, F.D. and L.M. Kahn (1996), 'International differences in male wage inequality: institutions versus market forces', *Journal of Political Economy*, **104**(4), 791–837.

Blau, F.D. and L.M. Kahn (1999), 'Institutions and laws in the labour market', in O. Ashenfelter and D. Card (eds), *Handbook of Labour Economics, Vol. 3*, Amsterdam: North-Holland, 1399–461.

Blau, F.D. and L.M. Kahn (2003), 'Understanding international differences in the gender pay gap', *Journal of Labor Economics*, **21**(1), 106–44.
Blunch, N. and D. Verner (2004), 'Asymmetries in the union wage premium in Ghana', *World Bank Economic Review*, **18**(2), 237–52.
Butcher, K.F. and C.E. Rouse (2001), 'Wage effects of unions and industrial councils in South Africa', *Industrial and Labor Relations Review*, **54**(2), 349–74.
Card, D. (1996), 'The effect of unions on the structure of wages: a longitudinal analysis', *Econometrica*, **64**(4), 957–79.
Card, D. (2001), 'The effect of unions on wage inequality in the U.S. labor market', *Industrial and Labor Relations Review*, **54**(2), 296–315.
Card, D. and J. DiNardo (2002), 'Skill-biased technological change and rising wage inequality: some problems and puzzles', *Journal of Labour Economics*, **20**(4), 733–83.
Card, D., T. Lemieux and W. Riddell (2003), 'Unions and the wage structure', in J.T. Addison and C. Schnabel (eds), *International Handbook of Trade Unions*, Cheltenham, UK and Northampton, MA, USA: Edward Elgar Publishing, pp. 246–92.
Card, D., T. Lemieux and W. Riddell (2004), 'Unions and wage inequality', *Journal of Labor Research*, **25**(4), 519–59.
Dahl, C., D. le Maire and J. Munch (2011),'Wage dispersion and decentralization of wage bargaining', *IZA Discussion Papers No. 6176*, Bonn: Forschungsinstitut zur Zukunft der Arbeit (IZA).
Dell'Aringa, C. and L. Pagani (2007), 'Collective bargaining and wage dispersion in Europe', *British Journal of Industrial Relations*, **45**(1), 29–54.
Devey, R., C. Skinner and I. Valodia (2006), 'The state of the informal economy', in S. Buhlungu, J. Daniel, R. Southall and J. Lutchman (eds), *State of the Nation: South Africa 2005–2006*, Cape Town: HSRC Press, pp. 223–46.
DiNardo, J., N.M. Fortin and T. Lemieux (1996), 'Labor market institutions and the distribution of wages, 1973–1992: a semiparametric approach', *Econometrica*, **64**(5), 1001–44.
Dustmann, C., J. Ludsteck and U. Schönberg (2009), 'Revisiting the German wage structure', *The Quarterly Journal of Economics*, **124**(2), 843–81.
European Commission, Directorate-General for Employment, Social Affairs and Equal Opportunities (2009), *Industrial Relations in Europe 2008*, Brussels: European Commission.
Fairris, D. (2003), 'Unions and wage inequality in Mexico', *Industrial and Labor Relations Review*, **56**(3), 481–97.
Fairris, D. (2005), 'What do unions do in Mexico?', *Working Paper*, July 2005, University of California Riverside, accessed 26 August 2014 at http://www.uia.mx/campus/publicaciones/IIDSES/pdf/investigacion/iidses14.pdf.
Fakhfakh, F., V. Pérotin and A. Robinson (2011), 'Workplace change and productivity: does employee voice make a difference?', in S. Hayter (ed.), *The Role of Collective Bargaining in the Global Economy*, Cheltenham, UK and Northampton, USA/Geneva: Edward Elgar Publishing/International Labour Office.
Fields, G. and G. Yoo (2000), 'Falling labour income inequality in Korea's economic growth: patterns and underlying causes', *Review of Income and Wealth*, **46**(2), 139–59.
Freeman, R.B. (1980), 'Unionism and the dispersion of wages', *Industrial and Labour Relations Review*, **34**(1), 3–23.

Freeman, R.B. (1982), 'Union wage practices and wage dispersion within establishments', *Industrial and Labour Relations Review*, **36**(1), 3–21.
Freeman, R.B. (1984), 'Longitudinal analysis of the effects of trade unions', *Journal of Labour Economics*, **2**(1), 1–26.
Freeman, R.B. (2009), 'Labor regulations, unions and social protection in developing countries: market distortions or efficient institutions?', *NBER Working Paper Series No. 14789*, Cambridge, MA: National Bureau of Economic Research.
Freeman, R.B. (2011), 'New roles for unions and collective bargaining post the implosion of Wall Street capitalism', in S. Hayter (ed.), *The Role of Collective Bargaining in the Global Economy*, Cheltenham, UK and Northampton MA, USA/Geneva, Edward Elgar Publishing/International Labour Office.
Freeman, R.B. and L.F. Katz (eds) (1995), *Differences and Changes in Wage Structures*, Chicago, IL: University of Chicago Press.
Freeman, R.B. and J.L. Medoff (1984), *What Do Unions Do?*, New York: Basic Books.
Friedman, M. (1962), *Capitalism and Freedom*, Chicago, IL: University of Chicago Press.
Galbraith, J.K. (1952), *American Capitalism: The Concept of Countervailing Power*, Cambridge, MA: Riverside Press.
Galli, R. and D. Kucera (2004), 'Labour standards and informal employment in Latin America', *World Development*, **32**(5), 809–28.
Golden, M.A. and J.B. Londregan (2006), 'Centralization of bargaining and wage inequality: a correction of Wallerstein', *American Journal of Political Science*, **50**(1), 208–13.
Gosling, A. and T. Lemieux (2001), 'Labour market reforms and changes in wage inequality in the United Kingdom and the United States', *NBER Working Paper Series No. 8413*, Cambridge, MA: National Bureau of Economic Research.
Gosling, A. and S. Machin (1995), 'Trade unions and the dispersion of earnings in British establishments, 1980–1990', *Oxford Bulletin of Economics and Statistics*, **57**(2), 167–84.
Hara, H. and D. Kawaguchi (2008), 'The union wage effect in Japan', *Industrial Relations: A Journal of Economy and Society*, **47**(4), 569–90.
Hayter, S. and V. Stoevska (2011), 'Social dialogue indicators: trade union density and collective bargaining coverage', Technical Brief, Industrial and Employment Relations Department, Geneva: International Labour Office.
Hayter, S. and B. Weinberg (2011), 'Mind the gap: collective bargaining and wage inequality', in S. Hayter (ed.), *The Role of Collective Bargaining in the Global Economy*, Cheltenham, UK and Northampton, MA, USA/Geneva: Edward Elgar Publishing/International Labour Office.
Heyes, J. and H. Rainbird (2011), 'Bargaining for training: converging or diverging interests?', in S. Hayter (ed.), *The Role of Collective Bargaining in the Global Economy*, Cheltenham, UK and Northampton, MA, USA/Geneva: Edward Elgar Publishing/International Labour Office.
Hibbs, D.A. (1990), 'Wage compression under solidarity bargaining in Sweden', *Economic Research Report No. 30*, Stockholm: Trade Union Institute for Economic Research.
Hibbs, D.A. and H. Locking (1996), 'Wage compression, wage drift and wage drift in Sweden', *Labour Economics*, **3**(2), 109–41.
Howell, D.R. (2002), 'Increasing earnings inequality and unemployment in

developed countries: markets, institutions, and the "unified theory"', *Politics and Society*, **30**(2), 193–243.

Howell, D.R. and F. Huebler (2005), 'Wage compression and the unemployment crisis: labour market institutions, skills and inequality–unemployment trade-offs', in Howell, D.R. (ed.), *Fighting Unemployment: The Limits of Free Market Orthodoxy*, New York: Oxford University Press.

ICTWSS (2013), *Database on Institutional Characteristics of Trade Unions, Wage Setting, State Intervention and Social Pacts in 34 Countries Between 1960 and 2007*, accessed 28 August 2014 at http://www.uva- aias.net/208.

Kahn, L.M. (1997), 'Collective bargaining and the inter-industry wage structure: international evidence', *Economica*, **65**(260), 507–34.

Kahn, L.M. (1998), 'Against the wind: bargaining recentralisation and wage inequality in Norway 1987–1991', *Economic Journal*, **108**(448), 603–45.

Kim, H. (1993), 'The Korean union movement in transition', in S. Frenkel (ed.), *Organized Labor in the Asia-Pacific Region*, Ithaca, NY: ILR Press, pp. 133–61.

Kristal, T. and Y. Cohen (2007), 'Decentralization of collective agreements and rising wage inequality in Israel', *Industrial Relations*, **46**(3), 613–35.

Lemieux, T. (1993), 'Unions and wage inequality in Canada and the United States', in D. Card and R. Freeman (eds), *Small Differences that Matter: Labour Markets and Income Maintenance in Canada and the United States*, Chicago, IL: University of Chicago Press, pp. 60–107.

Lemieux, T. (1998), 'Estimating the effects of unions on wage inequality in a panel data model with comparative advantage and non-random selection', *Journal of Labor Economics*, **16**(2), 261–91.

Lemieux, T. (2007), 'The changing nature of wage inequality', *NBER Working Paper Series No. 13523*, Cambridge, MA: National Bureau of Economic Research.

Lindbeck, A. and D.J. Snower (1989), *The Insider–Outsider Theory of Employment and Unemployment*, Cambridge, MA: MIT Press.

Machin, S. (1997), 'The decline of labour market institutions and the rise in wage inequality in Britain', *European Economic Review*, **41**(3–5), 647–57.

Machin, S. (2008), 'An appraisal of economic research on changes in wage inequality', *LABOUR*, **22**(S1), 7–26.

Maloney, W.F. and E.P. Ribeiro (1999), 'Efficiency wage and union effects in labour demand and wage structure in Mexico: an application of quantile analysis', *Policy Research Working Paper No. WPS2131*, Washington, DC: World Bank.

McDonald, I.M. and R.M. Solow (1981), 'Wage bargaining and employment', *American Economic Review*, **71**(5), 896–908.

Metcalf, D. (1982), 'Unions and the distribution of earnings', *British Journal of Industrial Relations*, **XX**(2), 163–9.

Metcalf, D., K. Hansen and A. Charlywood (2001), 'Unions and the sword of justice: unions and pay systems, pay inequality, pay discrimination and low pay', *National Institute Economic Review*, **176**(1), 61–75.

OECD (2004), *Employment Outlook*, Paris: Organisation for Economic Co-operation and Development.

OECD (2006), *Employment Outlook: Boosting Jobs and Incomes*, Paris: Organisation for Economic Co-operation and Development.

OECD (2011), *Trade Union Density in OECD Countries, 1960–2011*, Paris: Organisation for Economic Co-operation and Development.

Panagides, A. and H.A. Patrinos (1994), 'Union/non-union wage differentials in the developing world: a case study of Mexico', *Policy Research Working Paper No. 1269*, Washington, DC: World Bank.

Plasman, R., M. Rusinek and F. Rycx (2007), 'Wages and the bargaining regime under multi-level bargaining: Belgium, Denmark and Spain', *IZA Discussion Paper No. 1990*, Bonn: Forschungsinstitut zur Zukunft der Arbeit (IZA).

Popli, G.K. (2007), 'Rising wage inequality in Mexico, 1984–2000: a distributional analysis', *Journal of Income Distribution*, **16**(2), 49–67.

Rueda, D. and J. Pontusson (2000), 'Wage inequality and varieties of capitalism', *World Politics*, **52**(3), 350–83.

Schultz, T.P. and G. Mwabu (1998), 'Labor unions and the distribution of wages and employment in South Africa', *Industrial and Labor Relations Review*, **51**(4), 680–703.

Skinner, C. and I. Valodia (2002), 'Labour market policy, flexibility, and the future of labour relations: the case of KwaZulu-Natal clothing industry', *Transformation*, **50**, 56–76.

Standing, G. (1992), 'Do unions impede or accelerate structural adjustment? Industrial versus company unions in an industrialising labour market', *World Employment Programme Research Working Papers No. 47*, Geneva: International Labour Office.

Streek, S. and A. Hassel (2003), 'Trade unions as political actors', in J.T. Addison and C. Schnabel (eds), *International Handbook of Trade Unions*, Cheltenham, UK and Northampton, MA, USA: Edward Elgar Publishing.

Trajtemberg, D. (2008), 'El impacto de la determinación colectiva de salarios sobre la dispersión salarial' [The impact of collective wage determination on wage dispersion], *Trabajo, Ocupación y Empleo: Estudios Laborales 2008*, Buenos Aires: Ministerio de Trabajo.

Traxler, F. (1996), 'Collective bargaining and industrial change: a case of disorganization? A comparative analysis of eighteen OECD countries', *European Sociological Review*, **12**(3), 271–87.

Traxler, F. and B. Brandl (2009), 'The economic effects of collective bargaining coverage: a cross-national analysis', *Global Union Research Network (GURN) Working Paper*, Geneva: International Labour Office.

Tsafack-Nanfosso, R.A. (2002), 'Union wage differential: Cameroon', *Journal of Development Alternatives and Areas Studies*, **21**(3–4), 104–33.

Underhill, E. and M. Rimmer (2009), 'Rethinking employer responsibilities for temporary agency workers', paper presented at the ILO Regulating for Decent Work Conference, Geneva, 10 July.

Vernon, G. (2011), 'Still accounting for difference? Comparative joint regulation and pay inequality', *Economic and Industrial Democracy*, **32**(1), 29–46.

Visser, J. and D. Checchi (2009), 'Inequality and the labour market: unions', in W. Salverda, B. Nolan and T. Smeeding (eds), *The Oxford Handbook of Economic Inequality*, Oxford: Oxford University Press.

Wallerstein, M. (1999), 'Wage-setting institutions and pay inequality in advanced industrial societies', *American Journal of Political Science*, **43**(3), 649–80.

Webb, S. and B. Webb (1902), *Industrial Democracy*, London: Longmans, Green and Co.

Western, B. (1998), 'Institutions and the labour market', in M.C. Brinton and

V. Nee (eds), *The New Institutionalism in Sociology*, New York: Russell Sage Foundation.

Western, B. and J. Rosenfeld (2011), 'Unions, norms, and the rise in U.S. wage inequality', *American Sociological Review*, **76**(4), 513–37.

Wood, A. (1994), *North–South Trade, Employment and Inequality: Changing Fortunes in a Skill-driven World*, Oxford: Clarendon Press.

5. Minimum wages and inequality

Patrick Belser and Uma Rani*

5.1 INTRODUCTION

Throughout the world, millions of workers earn the minimum wage, making it a potentially powerful tool to reduce or contain inequality in the lower half of the wage distribution and to reduce gender pay gaps, as women tend to be over-represented among low-paid workers. The recent theoretical and empirical studies reviewed in our chapter support the idea that carefully designed minimum wage policies can reduce low pay, inequality, and the gender pay gap at little or no adverse cost to employment. While the earlier consensus held that minimum wages always involved trade-offs with employment levels, the new conventional wisdom is that employment effects are unpredictable, often small, and depend on a large number of country-specific factors. In general, the now prevailing view is that statutory minimum wages affect wage distribution but have 'at best second-order impacts on labour reallocation' (OECD, 2010, p. 197).

To fully exploit the potential of minimum wages requires careful policy design. One aspect concerns the extent of legal coverage. Although minimum wages are nearly universal, in many instances coverage is too weak and excludes those most in need of social protection, such as domestic workers or homeworkers, or those at the bottom of the subcontracting chain. A second aspect is the level at which minimum wages are set. To be effective, minimum wages must be set at a level that guarantees a minimum living wage to all employed and in need of protection, without jeopardizing employment. Although these objectives are not necessarily contradictory (as our chapter shows), it is clear that when minimum wages are set too low, as is the case in many countries, they fail to provide workers and their families with a decent standard of living. On the contrary, when they are set too high, employment trade-offs become inevitable. A third aspect is compliance. When labour inspection services are too weak and when there are no public employment guarantee programmes to compete for the workers of underpaying employers, non-compliance rates can be so high as to severely reduce the ability of minimum wages to reduce inequality.

In the next section, we provide a brief account of the history of minimum wages, which involves a movement from industry-specific systems with partial coverage towards national minimum wage systems. Section 5.3 discusses minimum wages from a theoretical perspective. Section 5.4 provides empirical evidence on minimum wages and employment, poverty and inequality and section 5.5 concludes.

5.2 WHAT ARE MINIMUM WAGES? AN ILO PERSPECTIVE

Although there are several International Labour Organization (ILO) legal instruments on minimum wages, none provide a definition of what a minimum wage is. The ILO's Committee of Experts, however, has defined the minimum wage as 'the minimum amount of remuneration that an employer is required to pay wage earners for the work performed during a given period, which cannot be reduced by collective agreement or an individual contract' (ILO, 2014, p.33). Earlier, the ILO's Committee of Experts had also defined the minimum wage as 'the wage which in each country has the force of law and which is enforceable under threat of penal or other appropriate sanctions' (ILO, 1967, p. 10). Relevant ILO instruments recognize that minimum wages can be set either by statute, decision of a competent authority, decisions of wage boards or councils, labour courts or tribunals, or by giving the force of law to provisions of collective agreements.[1] Hence, minimum wages fixed by collective agreements made binding by public authorities are included in the ILO definition of minimum wages.

By this relatively broad definition, we estimate that close to 90 per cent of ILO member States (164 out of 185 according to our count) have a system of minimum wages in place. This includes 159 countries with a statutory minimum wage that applies to the private sector, as well as five countries, including Nordic countries and Italy, that have minimum wages based on extensions of collective agreements. Hence, minimum wages are today a nearly universal policy instrument. For policy-makers in most countries the question is not so much whether to have it or not, but rather how to operate the system in order to maximize its potential benefits and minimize its potential costs.

Historically, minimum wages developed in New Zealand and Australia at the very end of the 19th century, and were adopted in the UK in 1909, where they initially covered only four industries. When, following a proposal of the British government in the 1920s, the ILO adopted for the first time the Minimum Wage-Fixing Machinery Convention, 1928 (No. 26), it reflected the fact that minimum wages existed in only a limited number of countries and covered few categories of workers. The convention encouraged countries to protect the pay of workers, but only in sectors and occupations with exceptionally low pay and where collective bargaining did not exist. In effect, ILO Convention No. 26 was limited to manufacture and commerce and excluded agriculture, which represented a significant share of the labour force at that time. The convention was ratified by numerous countries and with 108 ratifications it is still amongst the most widely ratified in the ILO; it is recognized as having played a substantial role in the spread of minimum wages in the 20th century.[2]

After World War II the idea of a *national* minimum wage took hold. In France, for example, the national minimum wage was introduced in 1950 – a period of great precariousness and rising prices that followed the unpopular 'wage controls' of World War II. Coverage also expanded progressively in the United States under the Fair Labor Standards Act of 1938, which increased coverage from about 20 per cent of the country's workforce to nearly 80 per cent in 1970 (Neumark and Wascher, 2008). In light of this evolution, it became clear that the scope of ILO Convention No. 26 was too limited, and the ILO successively adopted in 1951 the Minimum Wage-Fixing Machinery (Agriculture) Convention, No. 99, which complements Convention No. 26 to cover agriculture, and the Minimum Wage-Fixing Convention, 1970 (No. 131), which promotes national coverage.

While ratification was rapid in the first ten years and minimum wages were generally regarded favourably until the 1970s, the context changed after the oil shock in 1973, the debt crisis in developing countries in the 1980s and the implementation of structural adjustment policies in the 1980s and 1990s. The 'Washington Consensus' called for 'flexible' labour markets and was followed by calls for the elimination of all labour market 'distortions'. In the UK, the Wage Councils were progressively abolished over a period running from the 1980s up until 1993.

However, over the last decade and a half, minimum wages have staged a strong comeback. In light of increasing child poverty, the UK introduced a new minimum wage with national coverage in 1999, which has been identified in a survey of UK academics[3] as the most successful government policy of the past 30 years. Experiences of proactive minimum wage policies in middle-income countries such as Brazil, China and South Africa have also contributed to reviving the interest in minimum wages as a tool for social protection.

In spite of the global financial and economic crisis that started in 2008–09, or perhaps better said *because* of the crisis, many advanced countries have continued to make upward adjustments in their minimum wages, at least to compensate for increases in the cost of living. Among the emerging economies, both Brazil and China have continued with their strategies of reducing inequality and increasing the purchasing power of low-paid workers through minimum wages, although China temporarily froze its rates in 2009. In Brazil, between 1996 and 2009, the minimum wage increased by 83 per cent in real (inflation-adjusted) terms. At the same time, austerity policies have led to severe cuts in minimum wages in Greece, where the level has been cut by more than 20 per cent. Overall, however, deeper trends suggest that minimum wages are not just reclaiming their role as a central institution of labour and social policies in industrialized countries, but are also increasingly seen as a modern instrument of social cohesion and aggregate demand growth in emerging parts of the world.

Yet in spite of this movement towards strengthening the minimum wage as a policy tool, the minimum wage remains low in many countries, and there remain important gaps in legal coverage.[4] Among developing countries, a large proportion of countries use industry-specific minima rather than national minimum wages (see the review of minimum wage systems in the ILO *Working Conditions Laws Report 2012* in ILO, 2013). As a result, legal coverage can sometimes leave out around one-third of all wage earners, with women comprising a substantial proportion of those excluded. Figure 5.1 shows, for example, that in India and South Africa, although legal coverage of the minimum wage improved, it still

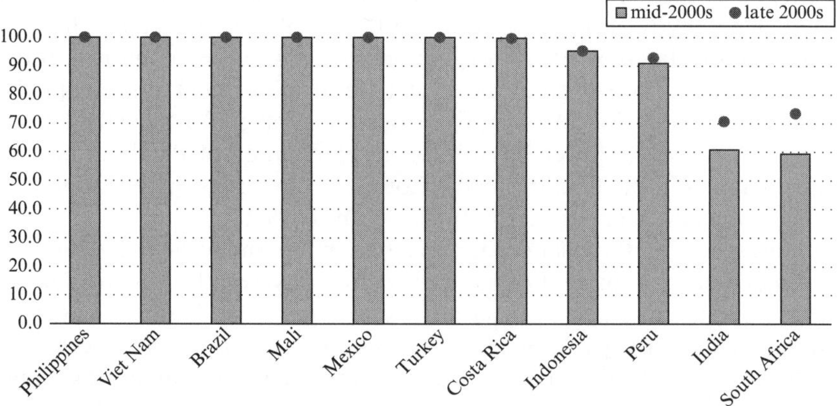

Source: Authors' calculations based on legal information and data from household and labour force surveys.

Figure 5.1 Legal coverage of minimum wage legislation in selected developing economies, %

only covered about 70 per cent of workers in the late 2000s. In Peru, like in many other countries in the world, domestic workers were excluded from the minimum wage.

5.3 THE THEORY OF MINIMUM WAGES

The Neoclassical Model

For many years, and particularly in the second half of the 20th century, the standard neoclassical model of labour demand and labour supply came to dominate perceptions about the effects of minimum wages. In the simple version of the model with an upward-sloping labour supply curve that intersects with a downward-sloping demand curve, any attempt to raise wages through legislation leads to the conclusion that the minimum wage decreases employment (unless the higher wage costs are passed on to workers through lower non-wage benefits). The argument being that, employers have no other choice but to raise prices, thereby losing customers (the 'scale effect'), and at the same time deciding to employ more machines and less humans (the 'substitution effects'). In Neumark's words 'a minimum wage mandates a movement up the labour demand curve, towards higher wages and lower employment. This policy clearly presents a trade-off between higher wages and lower employment, unless the labour demand curve is perfectly elastic' (2008, p. 41).

For developing countries, the theory of labour demand and minimum wages is often adjusted to make space for the 'informal sector' where minimum wage laws do not apply or – even if they apply in principle – they are weakly enforced. This variation leads to a multiplication of markets within the framework, from one to two. But ultimately the conclusion is only marginally different: by hurting employment in the formal sector, the minimum wage – instead of creating unemployment – redirects the excess labour supply towards the informal sector and depresses labour earnings there. Another part of excess labour supply, namely those whose 'reservation wage' is above the level of informal sector wages, are predicted to simply drop out of the labour force.

In a more sophisticated version of the neoclassical story, a distinction is made between skilled and unskilled labour: a higher minimum wage is then predicted to result in lower employment of unskilled labour, while the employment of skilled labour might actually increase if skills are complementary to capital equipment (the idea being that skilled workers are needed to operate machines and computers). Hence the predicted overall decline in employment will tend to be less than the decline in the employment of the group of low-skilled workers, but employment will nevertheless fall as long as unskilled workers can be replaced by machines. Because different industries operate with different levels of labour, skill and capital intensities, the minimum wage will tend to push up total costs and prices in different ways across industries. This can lead to cross-industry effects, whereby the minimum wage can hurt employment in labour-intensive industries, and increase employment in sectors that produce goods that are substitutes.

While the neoclassical model does not predict that the minimum wage will reduce employment in all industries (Neumark and Wascher, 2008), overall it states unambiguously that minimum wages hurt employment of at least some groups of workers. By how much does it hurt employment? The answer, in this framework, depends on the 'elasticity' of labour demand – the percentage change in employment that follows from a 1 per cent change in wages. This elasticity varies from industry to industry, depending on: (1) the share of labour costs in total production (the higher the share of labour in production costs, the more employers will have to raise prices for consumers); (2) the extent to which consumers will reduce their demand as a result of price increases (the so-called price elasticity of the product demand); and (3) the ease by which employers can replace workers with machines (Hammermesh, 1993).

The Real World of Imperfect Markets

Up to the mid-1990s, the neoclassical framework underpinned a large consensus among economists that minimum wages reduce employment. But, as pointed out by Card and Krueger (1995a) and by others since then, 'there is one problem: the evidence is not singularly agreed that increases in the minimum wage reduce employment' (p. 1). As our review of the evidence later in the chapter shows, some of the evidence points towards positive employment effects of minimum wages, while recent 'meta-studies' (statistical 'studies of studies') found that in advanced economies the weight of the evidence points towards no significant employment effects. Because empirical studies of minimum wages provide such a clear test of the neoclassical model, this recent evidence has contributed to undermining the general acceptance of the neoclassical framework.

Newer theoretical models have dropped some of the most unrealistic assumptions of the neoclassical model – in particular the assumption of 'perfect competition'. This assumption is itself at the origin of another extreme and unrealistic assumption, namely that any attempt by a firm to raise its wages above the wages paid by other firms means automatic bankruptcy, and that any attempt by a firm to press down wages below those paid by other firms means that the whole workforce immediately quits. In the real world, it is well observed that wages of apparently similar individuals differ sometimes substantially from one enterprise to the next. Such a fact is best understood in a context of 'imperfect markets' where firms make profits and where the labour market is replete with 'frictions', meaning that firms face difficulties and costs in hiring new workers.

Taking account of this reality implies that firms have some discretion in wage setting – a situation known as 'monopsony' power. This means that some firms will be able to attract more workers by paying higher wages, but others will be able to recruit some workers even if the pay is very low. And contrary to yet another unrealistic assumption of the neoclassical model, firms are not all disciplined by the market to pay workers the value of their marginal product. Under imperfect competition, firms can make profits by paying workers less than the value of marginal product. In such circumstances, minimum wages can have complex effects and firms have various possible channels to adjust to small increases in minimum wages (Schmitt, 2013). One possibility is that minimum wages might increase employment levels, by attracting people into the labour force and by allowing firms to fill their vacancies more quickly. Other possibilities are that the higher costs of minimum wages will be compensated through reductions in economic profits, wage compression within firms, reduced turnover rates, higher motivation and labour productivity, or even measures to increase efficiency at the firm level (which is impossible in the neoclassical framework where any less than perfectly efficient firm would go bust).

The net effects of minimum wages are thus ex ante uncertain and unpredictable. In a world where some firms have market power and others much less, a minimum wage might induce some firms to expand employment and others to cut back on their labour force, with no foreseeable net effect on overall employment levels. The imperfect nature of markets in which at least some firms have the ability to attract workers by increasing wages without going bankrupt, and the existence of frictions in the labour markets, explain why there may be what some earlier economists had called 'a range of indeterminacy' within which wages can vary with little aggregate effect on employment (see Card and Krueger, 1995a).

A View from Macroeconomics

The effects of minimum wages on individual firms should not be confused with their overall macroeconomic effects. It is always possible to find examples of firms that reduce employment or go bankrupt because of minimum wages. On the whole, however, such effects might be counterbalanced by higher aggregate demand resulting from a transfer of resources to low-paid workers and more employment in other firms. Keynes (1936) long ago criticized the classical model as 'a special case' whose assumed characteristics 'happen not to be those of the economic society in which we actually live, with the result that its teaching is misleading and disastrous if we attempt to apply it to the facts of experience' (p. 3). He considered that classical explanation of what determined employment levels included too many illegitimate assumptions and argued that this had contributed to a 'fundamental misunderstanding' of how 'the economy in which we live actually works' (p. 13).

In the *General Theory*, Keynes emphasized that the total economy-wide volume of employment is, in fact, determined by the overall volume of aggregate effective demand. While Keynes agreed that there probably exists a demand schedule for labour at the industry level, which inversely relates the quantity of employment with the level of wages, he considered it fallacious to transfer this reasoning without substantial modification to the economy as a whole (p. 259). The main reason is that industry-level demand can only be constructed on some assumptions about the nature of demand and supply in other industries, and that a simple transposition implicitly assumes that the aggregate effective demand is fixed and independent from the level of wages. Although he recognized that higher wages accompanied by the same aggregate effective demand as before would decrease employment, he asked whether an increase in wages would or would not be accompanied by the same aggregate effective demand as before.

Though he did not explicitly discuss minimum wages, Keynes made clear he believed that low wages would have a negative impact on aggregate demand. He considered that low wages were likely to transfer resources from wage earners to other factors of production, thereby reducing the community's propensity to consume, and that this fall in consumption would be unlikely to be offset by increasing investment.

In the same vein, post-Keynesian economics has continued to challenge the neoclassical model for its many unrealistic assumptions. In his short book, Lavoie (2009) makes clear that post-Keynesian economists view the neoclassical theory of firms operating under perfect competition and facing diminishing returns as a 'pure fiction' (p. 32) and considers that an increase in the minimum wage leads to an increase in consumption, which in turn increases the demand for labour and decreases unemployment. Similarly, Herr et al. (2009) point out that if minimum wages redistribute income from high- to low-wage earners, 'a positive demand effect can be expected as low-income households consume more out of their income' (p. 25).

Notwithstanding, the consensus in the 1980s was that policy-makers faced an inescapable trade-off as minimum wages would transfer overall resources to low-paid workers, but at the cost of some jobs for the young and low-educated workers. The new consensus that has emerged is that the impact of a minimum wage on employment is unpredictable and depends on country-specific factors like the overall macroeconomic context, the characteristics of the product and labour markets into which they are inserted, the different options available to firms for adjusting other variables, and – last but not least – the level at which they are set and measures that are taken to promote their enforcement. This new consensus challenges the neoclassical framework.

5.4 EMPIRICS ON MINIMUM WAGES

Effect of Minimum Wages on Employment

The empirical literature on minimum wages is a well-researched and controversial area especially from a policy perspective. As discussed earlier, much of the earlier empirics were grounded in neoclassical theory; as a result the empirical evidence often showed negative impacts on employment as a result of increase in minimum wages (Gramlich, 1976; Brown et al., 1982; Neumark and Wascher, 1992). Indeed, the minimum wage debates in the USA often cited the consensus view of 'a reduction of between one to three per cent in teenage employment as a result of a 10 per cent increase in federal minimum wage' (Brown et al., 1982, p. 508).

Research in the 1990s contested the conventional wisdom and argued that increases in minimum wages did not automatically lead to employment losses. The highly influential work by Card and Krueger (1994) on the fast food industry in the USA demonstrates that minimum wage increases employment contrary to the predictions of the perfectly competitive models. However, the most contested and controversial debate during the mid-1990s emerged in response to the study by Neumark and Wascher (1992) on the negative employment effects of the minimum wage on teenage employment in the USA. Card and Krueger (1995a) raise methodological concerns with the choice of the control variables and minimum wage measure, and the potential endogeneity of these variables. They show that when the control variable for schooling was dropped from the estimate then the parameter that is used to measure the impact of minimum wage is no longer significant. Their second concern with the measure of the minimum wage (the Kaitz index), which they argued is flawed, as adult wages were included in the denominator of the Kaitz index, which could actually be correlated with economic activity and subsequently with the teenage wage rate. Using the logarithm of minimum wage for either state or federal level, whichever was higher, they do not find any significant negative effect on teenage employment due to increase in minimum wages. The contradictory results using different specifications and variables provoked much debate. For example, Burkhauser et al. (2000) re-examine most of the studies including Card and Krueger's and conclude that if the individual year controls are dropped from the specification then minimum wage increases lead to significant negative employment effects for teenagers.

Despite the criticism from neoclassical researchers, there has been quite a bit of support towards Card and Krueger's findings. Dube et al. (2010) in their study on low-wage sectors in the USA, find that there are strong earnings effects and no employment effects of minimum wage increases in states where minimum wages were raised compared to the bordering areas where there were no mandated minimum wages. In Europe, the UK Low Pay Commission has commissioned research since 1999 on the effect of the minimum wage in the UK labour market; studies have found little impact of the minimum wage on employment (LPC, 2009, 2012). Even the case studies of firms across low-paying sectors show that firms 'tended to change their pay structures in response to minimum changes rather than adjust employment' (LPC, 2012, p. 59). Similarly, for Australia, Lee and Suardi (2010) analyse the impact of minimum wage increases on employment using a time series approach and conclude that the seven minimum wage increases from 1997 to 2003 do not appear to have had any significant negative employment effects on teenagers. One of the plausible explanations for this could be that the increases have generally been moderate and predictable, closely tracking the general rise in price levels. Even Neumark and Wascher's (2008) extensive review of literature on minimum wage effects on employment shows mixed results.

There is also evidence from two recent meta-studies on the minimum wage suggesting that in most cases there are either only small or no negative employment effects. In the review by Doucouliagos and Stanley (2009) of 64 recent studies published between 1972 and 2007 on the impacts of minimum wages on teenage employment in the United States, the authors are able to demonstrate statistically that there was a bias in publication in the academic literature towards studies that found negative employment effects. When this bias is corrected through filtering techniques, they find little or no evidence of adverse employment effects. These results corroborate the earlier meta-analysis conducted by Card and Krueger (1995b). Another meta-analysis of 55 studies in 15 industrial countries by Boockmann (2010) finds that the employment effects of minimum wages are heterogeneous across countries and to a large extent dependent on the institutional framework of the respective country. The author tries to capture how other regulations influence the estimated employment effects of minimum wages, and finds that benefit replacement ratio and coordinated bargaining reduce the employment effects on minimum wages, while stricter employment protection legislation appears to enhance the negative employment effect on minimum wages.

The diversity in empirical findings could be largely due to the use of different estimated parameters or methodologies, different types of data, indicators, age groups and macro indicators, which not only makes comparisons difficult, but also exacerbates the difficulty of pinpointing the net employment effects (Dolton et al., 2010). This is also very evident from Boockmann's (2010) meta-analysis where he shows that 'Both micro and panel data generate more negative (more significant) employment results than time-series data' (p. 12). Similarly, the specification of the models also predefines the negative or positive employment effects, which is very well documented by Allegretto et al. (2013) wherein two-way fixed effects models with further specifications show sizeable disemployment effects, while region-specific time effects, state-specific linear trends, lagged dependent variables and other specifications show smaller disemployment effects.[5]

A growing body of evidence has emerged for developing economies. At the outset it is important to specify that the labour markets in developing countries are quite distinct from the developed countries, due to the large size of the informal sector, as well as the difficulty in regulating and enforcing labour laws, including minimum wages. As in the studies of developed countries, it is also difficult to make comparisons across countries or within a country because of the different periods studied, the different data sources, different sectors, as well as different methodologies. As such, the empirical evidence on the impacts of employment remains quite inconclusive.

Bell (1997) finds that minimum wages had no impact on employment in Mexico in the 1990s, while it did have a negative effect on employment in Colombia. The contrasting results could be due to the level of minimum wages in these two countries: Mexico had a stagnant or declining real minimum wage during this period, which might not have affected employment at all, as the level of minimum wages was not sufficient even to maintain basic minimum living standards. Colombia on the other hand, had high levels of minimum wages, which may have hurt employment.

Despite regular increases in real minimum wages in Brazil, Lemos (2009) finds little evidence of adverse employment effects in both formal and informal sectors, either in the short run or in the long run for the period 1995 to 2004. Both the number of jobs and the number of hours worked in either sector remain unchanged following an increase in the

Table 5.1 Impact of minimum wages on employment

	Brazil	Costa Rica	India	Peru	Viet Nam
Log of minimum wages	1.720 (2.02)	1.983 (1.14)	−0.620 (0.58)	1.384* (0.64)	−0.144 (0.153)
R^2	0.011	0.158	0.076	0.261	0.031
No. of observations	54	359	140	1687	125

Note: This is an instrument variable (IV) regression and the dependent variable is the employment rate, and only the required coefficient estimates are presented. For details on the methodology, see Appendix D of 'Chapter 3: Role of minimum wages in rebalancing the economy' in *World of Work Report 2013: Repairing the Economic and Social Fabric*, Geneva: ILO. Standard errors are in parentheses: * $p < 0.05$; ** $p < 0.01$; *** $p < 0.001$.

Source: Authors' calculations based on data from household and labour force surveys.

minimum wage. It is possible that higher income from a minimum wage increase may have allowed low-wage workers to buy minimum wage products, which would attenuate the disemployment effect of minimum wages. In China, Ni et al. (2011), using data from 2000 to 2005, find that minimum wages had mixed effects on employment depending upon the region: the eastern region experienced slightly negative effects, while the western region experienced slightly positive effects. This could be due to the different levels of minimum wages, extent of enforcement and also the labour market conditions. Our own analysis for five developing countries for the period mid-2000s and late 2000s shows that the employment effects are statistically insignificant in most countries; only in Peru is there a statistically significant effect on employment, and it is positive (Table 5.1).

Other researchers have shown that the increase in the ratio of minimum to mean wages could actually be associated with a net increase in employment, attracting inactive workers into the labour market. In Indonesia, the ratio of minimum to mean wage increased during the period 1996 to 2005, but this had a positive net impact on employment. Although formal employment declined and informal employment increased, the rising wages in the formal sector were associated with higher pay in the informal sector, which attracted inactive workers into the labour market, creating more employment in the informal sector (Comola and de Mello, 2010).

There is also some evidence that minimum wage policies protect the interests of vulnerable groups or low-wage sectors without any adverse effects on employment, at least in the short run. The evidence in South Africa, for example, shows that in some of the low-wage sectors like domestic services, retail and security, there were positive employment effects after the introduction of a minimum wage, though there is also some indication of reductions in weekly hours worked in retail and security (Bhorat et al., 2012). And, even within a specific low-wage sector like the domestic worker industry, which is largely informal, it was found that the introduction of minimum wage laws in this sector actually led to a large increase in average wages despite the absence of enforcement, with no evidence of negative employment effects (Dinkelman and Ranchhod, 2010).

Effect of Minimum Wages on Poverty, Income and Distribution of Wages

From a policy perspective, the smaller the adverse employment effects, the more attractive are the distributional benefits of minimum wages. Minimum wages are a labour market instrument often introduced for equity reasons and with the clear welfare objective of improving the income distribution or reducing poverty by raising the wages of the low-paid workers above the poverty line and towards average wages. Despite this intuitive appeal, studies have questioned the ability of minimum wages to reduce poverty. There have been numerous and highly contentious debates on the ability of the minimum wage to reduce poverty in the United States (see, for example, Card and Krueger, 1995a; Neumark et al., 1998). In developing countries, the legal minimum wage is sometimes relatively high compared to average wages (Rani et al., 2013a), which could imply that minimum wages have the potential to affect a larger fraction of the population. Yet with large informal sectors and lax enforcement, it is not always the case that minimum wages will affect many in developing country labour markets.

Bird and Manning (2008) calculate that in Indonesia more than 45 per cent of low-wage workers lived in poor households (less than purchasing power parity [PPP] US$2 per day) or ultra-poor households (less than PPP US$1 per day). In their simulations, they find that an increase in the minimum wage would reduce the number of people living below PPP US$2 by 2.7 million out of a total of 90.4 million poor people. The authors, however, assume that the net gains in poverty reduction would be reduced because of higher prices, but they do not take into account the effect of wage increases on overall aggregate demand.

The potential of minimum wages to have a positive impact on poverty depends on how well enforced minimum wages are in any particular country. Gindling and Terrell (2010), in their study on Honduras for the period 2001 to 2004, show that minimum wages are quite well enforced in large firms; as a result, a minimum wage increase of 10 per cent is able to reduce extreme poverty by 1.8 per cent and overall poverty by 1 per cent. In Honduras, 71 per cent of minimum wage earners are in poor households, thus an increase helps to reduce poverty. In India, legal minimum wages apply to only around 70 per cent of the wage earners; 35 per cent of wage earners live in poor households, of whom 50 per cent earn below the minimum wage. Enforcement has been a major issue, which is further accentuated by the complex system of minimum wages, as wage rates are determined for 1679 job categories in the country. A simulation exercise undertaken for the year 2004–05 shows that if all wage earners had received the legal minimum wage, then poverty may have been reduced by up to seven percentage points (Belser and Rani, 2011).

Others have argued that the impact of minimum wages on poverty depends upon who in the household is affected by it. It is possible that if minimum wages were applied to the main earner of the family, then the probability to pull households out of poverty might be much higher than if applied to secondary earners. A partial equilibrium analysis[6] in Nicaragua shows that every 1 per cent increase in minimum wage reduces poverty by 0.12 percentage points, if the higher minimum wage is applied to the head of the household (Alaniz et al., 2011). When the impact of higher minimum wages is considered for secondary earners, the impact is found to be insignificant on the probability of the household getting out of poverty.

Minimum wages can shape the wage distribution by shifting the earnings distribution in favour of low-paid workers and shrinking the bottom tail of the income distribution. The available evidence in the literature shows that minimum wages reduce wage inequality in the lower tail of the earnings distribution in a number of advanced economies.[7] In the United Kingdom, for instance, minimum wage increases during the period 1999–2007 were associated with a systematic annual reduction in lower tail wage inequality (Dolton et al., 2010), while in the United States the erosion of minimum wages has resulted in a rise in inequality in the lower tail of the wage distribution (Autor et al., 2010).

The equality-enhancing role of minimum wages is also evident in developing economies. In Indonesia where real minimum wages have increased by roughly 50 per cent during 1993 to 2007, Chun and Khor (2010) find that wage inequality declined as minimum wages were more beneficial for those at the bottom end of the distribution. Moreover, a 10 per cent increase in real minimum wages increased real wages by 14 per cent among workers earning less than 90 per cent of the minimum wage.

Lemos (2007) explores the effects of changes in the minimum wage on the wage distribution for Brazil from 1982 to 2000. She found that the minimum wage strongly compressed the wage distribution in both the formal and informal sectors. The compression effect is at the bottom of the wage distribution in the formal sector, while it is towards the centre of the informal sector distribution. Thus, the minimum wage does not seem to benefit the lowest paid in the informal sector. Nonetheless, a 10 per cent increase in the minimum wage reduced the 90/10 wage gap by 1.25 per cent and the 75/25 wage gap by 2.14 per cent.

Some researchers have found that minimum wages could be regressive, as in the case of Colombia during 1984–2001, where it only improved the earnings of those in the middle and upper part of the income distribution (Arango and Pachón, 2004). This anomaly stems from the high value of the minimum wage. When the minimum wages were low during the 1980s and early 1990s, inequality had declined, while later when minimum wages were high, inequality increased. The high level of minimum wages led to non-compliance, such that low-paid workers did not benefit from the increases.

The above review of the evidence suggests that, despite less than perfect compliance, higher minimum wage levels and improved compliance have tended to boost the relative position of low-paid earners and have contributed to the reduction in inequality observed in various of the 11 countries in our sample. Reductions in inequality at the bottom end of the distribution have been observed in particular in India, Mali, the Philippines, South Africa, Turkey and Viet Nam (Table 5.2).

Minimum wages that lose their value will also affect the wage distribution. For example in Mexico, Bosch and Manacorda (2010) analyse the effect of minimum wage on inequality between 1989 and 2001, when the Mexican minimum wage declined by about 50 per cent relative to median

Table 5.2 Wage inequality indices, change in inequality between mid-2000s and late 2000s

Countries	P50/P10	P90/P50	P75/P25	Gini
Brazil	0.15	−0.37	−0.48	−0.02
Costa Rica	0.34	0.46	0.11	0.03
India	−0.13	0.25	−0.07	−0.01
Indonesia	0.15	0.76	0.34	0.06
Mali	−2.37	1.00	−2.83	0.10
Mexico	0.34	−0.22	−0.07	−0.02
Peru	0.11	−0.29	−0.66	−0.04
Philippines	−0.13	0.21	0.00	0.03
South Africa	−0.45	−0.90	−0.70	0.00
Turkey	−0.22	0.48	0.02	0.01
Viet Nam	−1.71	−0.53	−1.23	−0.15

Source: Authors' calculations based on data from household and labour force surveys.

earnings. Their analysis suggests that 'the decline in the real value of the minimum wage is responsible for the rise in the 50/10 percentile gap of 1.4 percentage point a year and rise in the 90/50 percentile gap of 1.8 percentage point' (p. 146). The erosion in the real value of minimum wages is 'fully responsible for the observed increase in inequality at the bottom end of the distribution' (pp. 143–4). Our own analysis for the period 2005 and 2010 in Mexico, shows that inequality has increased in the lower part of the wage distribution by 0.34 percentage points annually (Table 5.2).

The level at which the minimum wages is set is fundamental as it can potentially impact other sectors in the economy. There is some evidence that shows that minimum wages influence the wage distribution of workers in the informal sector. This has also led to a shift in understanding the potential impact of minimum wages on the informal sector, compared to the earlier notions where minimum wages were supposed to suppress the wages in the informal sector or increase employment as a result of losses in formal sector employment. Bird and Manning (2008) advance two channels through which minimum wages could actually be beneficial to the workers in the informal sector, even if they were not covered by minimum wage laws. The first channel is through the linkages of labour and goods market (Fiszbein, 1992) wherein rises in the minimum wage of the formal sector workers would lead to increase in demand for goods and services in the informal sector, and would eventually lead to a rise in informal wages. The second channel is through minimum wage, which is often used as a signal for wage bargaining and therefore plays a role as a coordinator of the wage policy – what is often referred to in the literature as the 'lighthouse' effect.[8]

There is growing empirical evidence that shows minimum wages to be effective in raising the average wages in the informal sector. Khamis (2008), using quasi-experiments for Argentina where minimum wages had increased in 1993 and 2004, finds a significant change in the informal wage distribution after the minimum wage changes as well as wage increases, which did not occur in the formal sector. Gindling and Terrell (2004) provide evidence for Costa Rica where legal minimum wages have a larger impact on the average wages of workers in rural and small enterprises, who are more likely to earn low wages or have market wages below the institutionally determined minimum wages. These findings support the view that minimum wages are often used as a benchmark for setting wages in this sector.The impact of minimum wages on improving wages in the informal sector is also consistent with our own analysis of ten developing countries, where the average wage earnings in the informal sector increased by between 0.33 per cent and 18 per cent per year depending upon the country (Figure 5.2). Countries that experienced

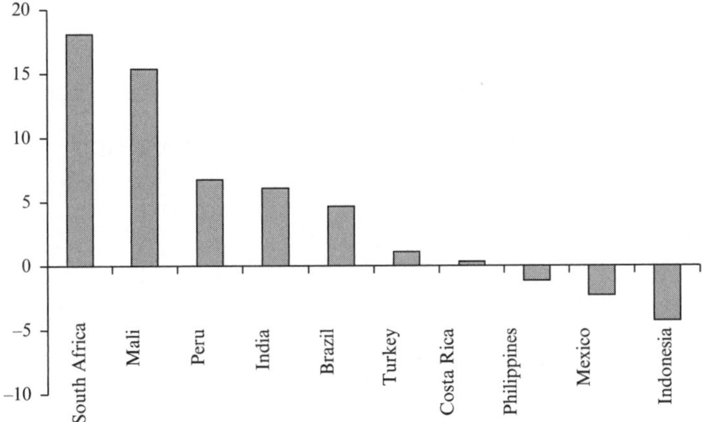

Source: Authors' calculations based on data from household and labour force surveys.

Figure 5.2 Annual percentage change in real wage earnings in the informal sector between the mid-2000s and the late 2000s

the greatest improvements in levels of compliance (India and Peru) were actually able to significantly increase their average real earnings in the informal sector. Of course, one needs to be cautious as this could also reflect the improved macroeconomic conditions and not just the spillover effects from minimum wages. However, there were some countries such as Indonesia, Mexico and the Philippines where the wage earnings in the informal sector declined.

Ensuring Compliance

For minimum wages to be effective, efforts need to be made to improve enforcement. If the compliance rate is too low then the ability of minimum wages to reduce inequality or to have spillover effects in other sectors is compromised. The fact remains that 'simply legislating a minimum wage will not make it happen' (Murgai and Ravallion, 2005, p. 2). In advanced economies, the proportion of workers paid less than the national minimum wages is often relatively low (Metcalf, 2008; Bureau of Labor Statistics, 2009). Ensuring compliance, as measured by the proportion of wage earners who receive minimum wages, however, is more problematic in developing economies. An analysis for 11 countries shows that the rate of compliance using this measure ranges between 95 per cent in Viet Nam to 49 per cent in Indonesia and Turkey (Figure 5.3). The compliance rate is relatively high in Brazil, Mali, Mexico and Viet Nam, while in all the

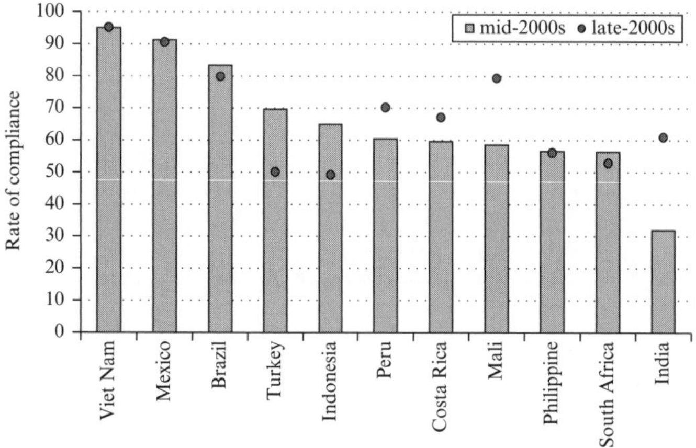

Source: Authors' calculations based on data from household and labour force surveys.

Figure 5.3 Estimated rate of compliance with minimum wage legislation in selected developing economies

other countries the rate of compliance hovers around 60 per cent. The high level of compliance in Brazil could be due in part to the simple national minimum wage system, which makes it easy to implement and administer. On the other hand, a relatively high degree of compliance, as in Mali, Mexico and Viet Nam could be associated with a low level of minimum wages.[9] Conversely, a higher level of minimum wages as observed in Costa Rica, India, Indonesia, Peru, the Philippines, South Africa and Turkey, tends to be associated with lower levels of compliance.

There is no doubt that the degree of compliance depends upon the complexity of the minimum wage system and the level at which the minimum wage is set, but it is also linked to the general institutional environment. A high rate of compliance requires effective labour inspection, a coherent strategy based on provision of information, and sanctions in the event of failure to comply with legal provisions. Social partners also play a key role in protecting workers against abuses. The regulatory structures in developing economies, including labour inspection services, are often under-resourced and under-staffed and penalties may be too weak to induce compliance (Ghosheh, 2013). For example, although Costa Rica and India have complex minimum wage systems, the two countries have successfully improved compliance rates, largely due to the strengthening of enforcement mechanisms. Costa Rica was able to improve compliance by 7.5 percentage points between 2005 and 2011. The improvement stemmed from an increase in the number of labour inspectors, allowing an increase in the proportion of firms inspected regularly. Further, in August 2010, a national campaign for Minimum Wages (Campaña Nacional de Salarios Mínimos) was launched, which combined sustained awareness raising, facilitation and encouragement of complaints, and increased the number of wage inspections with the aim of increasing compliance (Gindling et al., 2013). Workers were encouraged to report employers who paid less than the minimum wage. The programme also increased the capacity of the call centre to handle complaints, resulting in 77 816 calls in the first year alone, as well as an increase in joint inspections with the social security administration (Rani et al., 2013b).

Similarly, in India the Mahatma Gandhi National Rural Employment Guarantee Act 2005 (MGNREGA), which provides all households in rural areas with 100 days of employment per year, also paid wages at minimum wages and there was equal remuneration for both males and females. The act also relies on a legislated Right to Information and Social Audits, which provides an opportunity for civil society to ensure that the implementation of the programme is effective. This has not only provided a number of days of work at minimum wages to poor households but also improved the compliance rate with minimum wages in rural parts of India where the programme operates (see Rani and Belser, 2012 for more details). A high proportion of female workers have benefitted from the programme and the strategy has effectively redistributed resources to low-paid workers.

5.5 CONCLUSION

This chapter has discussed minimum wages from a theoretical perspective and provided empirical evidence on minimum wages and employment, and on inequality. We argue that the standard neoclassical model has over-emphasized the adverse consequences of minimum wages on employment, giving more prominence to the topic than is warranted. A new consensus is emerging, based on empirical evidence, which views that the impact of minimum wages on employment is unpredictable and dependent on country-specific factors, the level at which the minimum wage is set, the extent of enforcement, as well as the labour market peculiarities and institutions prevailing in each country. If the minimum wage is set at too low a level, it may be ineffective in ensuring a minimum living income to workers and their families and may fail to act as an automatic aggregate demand stabilizer in the face of shocks. If minimum wages are set too high or raised unexpectedly, they can hurt employment and lead to widespread non-compliance.

The empirical evidence also brings out the distributive role played by minimum wages, which by assuring a minimum income for those at the bottom of the pay scale can help in reducing inequality and poverty. The empirical evidence in the literature shows that minimum wages are effective in distribution, when they are well enforced, if the main earner in the households receives minimum wages and if they are set at the right level. So for minimum wages to be an effective redistributive tool, the level at which the minimum wage is set and the extent of enforcement are critical. Good policy design is what can transform a potentially powerful tool into an effective instrument whose benefits outweigh the costs, and which can improve the lives of millions of low-paid workers at the lower end of the wage distribution.

NOTES

* We would like to gratefully acknowledge Setareh Ranjbar and Laura Ravazzini for meticulously helping us with the statistical analysis.

1. Minimum Wage-Fixing Machinery Recommendation, 1970 (No. 135), IV.
2. See, for example, Sankaran (1997) for the case of India.
3. See http://www.instituteforgovernment.org.uk/sites/default/files/PSA_survey_results.pdf; see also http://www.bbc.co.uk/news/uk-politics-11896971?print=true; last accessed 29 August 2014.
4. The term 'legal coverage' refers to workers who have been included in the minimum wage legislation and who are therefore entitled to be paid at least the minimum wage.
5. For more details on the specification of the models see Allegretto et al. (2013, pp. 39–40).
6. This analysis tries to estimate the impact of minimum wages on the probability of a worker's family transitioning in and out of poverty, controlling for individual-level characteristics of the workers and the level of GDP of the sector where the worker is engaged. The analysis does not take into consideration the impact on household incomes, cost of living of workers and families, and the direct effect on employment.
7. See, for example, Lee (1999) for the United States; Dickens and Manning (2004), Dolton et al. (2010) and Butcher et al. (2012), for the United Kingdom; and Vaughan-Whitehead (2011) for other European countries.
8. The original reference is Souza and Baltar (1979). Studies that discuss the lighthouse effect include Fajnzylber (2001); Carneiro and Henley (2001); Lemos (2009) for Brazil; Gindling and Terrell (2004) for Costa Rica; Maloney and Núñez (2001) for Colombia; Chun and Khor (2010) for Indonesia.
9. In Mexico, fewer than 2 per cent of workers earn less than the minimum wage.

REFERENCES

Alaniz, E., T.H. Gindling and K. Terrell (2011), 'The impact of minimum wages on wages, work and poverty in Nicaragua', *Labour Economics*, **18**(S1), S54–S59.

Allegretto, S., A. Dube and M. Reich et al. (2013), 'Credible research designs for minimum wage studies', *IZA Discussion Paper No. 7638*, Bonn: Forschungsinstitut zur Zukunft der Arbeit (IZA).

Arango, C.A. and A. Pachón (2004), 'Minimum wages in Colombia: holding the middle with a bite on the poor', Bogota: Central Bank of Colombia, unpublished.

Autor, D.H., A. Manning and C.L. Smith (2010), 'The contribution of the minimum wage to U.S. wage inequality over three decades: a reassessment', *NBER Working Paper No. 16533*, Cambridge MA: National Bureau of Economic Research.

Bell, L.A. (1997), 'The impact of minimum wages in Mexico and Colombia', *Journal of Labor Economics*, **15**(3), S102–S135.

Belser, P. and U. Rani (2011), 'Extending the coverage of minimum wages in India: simulations from household data', *Economic and Political Weekly*, **56**(20), 47–55.

Bhorat, H., R. Kanbur and A. Mayet (2012), 'The impact of sectoral minimum wage laws on employment, wages, and hours of work in South Africa', *Working Papers No. 12154*, University of Cape Town, Development Policy Research Unit.

Bird, K. and C. Manning (2008), 'Minimum wages and poverty in a developing country: simulations from Indonesia's Household Survey', *World Development*, **36**(5), 916–33.

Boockmann, B. (2010), 'The combined employment effects of minimum wages and labour market regulation: a meta-analysis', *IZA Discussion Paper No. 4983*, Bonn: Forschungsinstitut zur Zukunft der Arbeit (IZA).

Bosch, M. and M. Manacorda (2010), 'Minimum wages and earnings inequality in Urban Mexico', *American Economic Journal: Applied Economics*, **2**(4), 128–49.

Brown, C., C. Gilroy and A. Kohen (1982), 'The effect of the minimum wage on employment and unemployment', *Journal of Economic Literature*, **20**(2), 487–528.

Bureau of Labor Statistics (2009), *Characteristics of Minimum Wage Workers: 2008*, Washington, DC: United States Department of Labor.

Burkhauser, R.V., K.A. Couch and D.C. Wittenburg (2000), 'A reassessment of the new economics of the minimum wage literature with monthly data from the current population survey', *Journal of Labor Economics*, **18**(4), 653–80.

Butcher, T., R. Dickens and A. Manning (2012), 'Minimum wages and wage inequality: some theory and an application to the UK', *CEP Discussion Paper No. 1177*, London: London School of Economics and Political Science.

Card, D. and A.B. Krueger (1994), 'Minimum wages and employment: a case study of the fast-food industry in New Jersey and Pennsylvania', *American Economic Review*, **84**(4), 772–93.

Card, D. and A.B. Krueger (1995a), *Myth and Measurement: The New Economics of the Minimum Wage*, Princeton, NJ: Princeton University Press.

Card, D. and A.B. Krueger (1995b), 'Time-series minimum-wage studies: a meta-analysis', *American Economic Review*, **85**(2), 38–43.

Carneiro, F.G. and A. Henley (2001), 'Modelling formal versus informal employment and earnings: microeconometric evidence for Brazil', *Working Paper No. 2001-15*, Aberystwyth: School of Management and Business, Aberystwyth University.

Chun, N. and N. Khor (2010), 'Minimum wages and changing wage inequality in Indonesia', *ADB Economics Working Paper Series No. 196*, Manila: Asian Development Bank.

Comola, M. and L. de Mello (2010), 'How does decentralised minimum-wage setting affect unemployment and informality? The case of Indonesia', *OECD Economics Department Working Paper No. 710*, Paris: Organisation for Economic Co-operation and Development.

Dickens, R. and A. Manning (2004), 'Has the national minimum wage reduced UK wage inequality?', *Journal of the Royal Statistical Society, Series A (Statistics in Society)*, **167**(4), 613–26.

Dinkelman, T. and V. Ranchhod (2010), 'Evidence on the impact of minimum wage laws in an informal sector: domestic workers in South Africa', *Working Paper*, accessed 9 September 2014 at http://ideas.repec.org/p/ldr/wpaper/44.html.

Dolton, P., C. Rosazza-Bondibene and J. Wadsworth (2010), 'Employment, inequality and the UK national minimum wage over the medium-term', *IZA Discussion Paper Series No. 5278*, Bonn: Forschungsinstitut zur Zukunft der Arbeit (IZA).

Doucouliagos, H. and T.D. Stanley (2009), 'Publication selection bias in minimum-wage research? A meta-regression analysis', *British Journal of Industrial Relations*, **47**(2) 406–28.

Dube, A., T.W. Lester and W. Reich (2010), 'Minimum wage effects across state borders: estimates using contiguous countries', *Review of Economics and Statistics*, **92**(4), 945–64.

Fajnzylber, P. (2001), 'Minimum wage effects throughout the wage distribution: evidence from Brazil's formal and informal sectors', paper provided by ANPEC – Associação Nacional dos Centros de Pósgraduação em Economia in its series *Anais do XXIX Encontro Nacional de Economia No. 98*.

Fiszbein, A. (1992), 'Do workers in the informal sector benefit from cuts in the minimum wage?', *World Bank Policy Research Working Paper No. 826*, Washington, DC: World Bank.

Ghosheh, N. (2013), 'Wage protection legislation in Africa', *Conditions of Work and Employment Series No. 38*, Geneva: International Labour Organization.

Gindling, T.H. and K. Terrell (2004), 'Legal minimum wages and the wages of formal and informal sector workers in Costa Rica', *IZA Discussion Paper No. 1018*, Bonn: Forschungsinstitut zur Zukunft der Arbeit (IZA).

Gindling, T.H. and K. Terrell (2010), 'Minimum wages, globalization and poverty in Honduras', *World Development*, **38**(6), 908–18.

Gindling, T.H., N. Mossaad and J.D. Trejos (2013), 'The consequences of increased enforcement of legal minimum wages in a developing country: an evaluation of the impact of the Campaña Nacional de Salarios Mínimos in Costa Rica', mimeo.

Gramlich, E.M. (1976), 'Impact of minimum wages on other wages, employment and family incomes', *Brookings Papers on Economic Activity, Vol. 2*, Washington, DC: Brookings Institution, pp. 409–51.

Hammermesh, D.S. (1993), *Labour Demand*, Princeton, NJ: Princeton University Press.

Herr, H., M. Kazandziska and S. Mahnkopf-Praprotnik (2009), 'The theoretical debate about minimum wages', *Global University Working Papers, Paper No. 6*, Kassel and Berlin: Global Labour University.

ILO (1967), *Report of the Meeting of Experts on Minimum Wage Fixing and Related Problems, with Special Reference to Developing Countries*, presented at the 170th session of the Governing Body of November 1967, Geneva: International Labour Office.

ILO (2013), *Working Conditions Laws Report*, Geneva: International Labour Office, accessed 27 August 2014 at http://www.ilo.org/wcmsp5/groups/public/---ed_protect/---protrav/---travail/documents/publication/wcms_235155.pdf.

ILO (2014), *Minimum wage systems*, General Survey of the reports on the Minimum Wage Fixing Convention, 1970 (No.131), and the Minimum Wage Fixing Recommendation, 1970 (No.135), Report of the Committee of Experts on the Application of Conventions and Recommendations, ILC, 103rd session, 2014, Report III (Part 1B), Geneva: International Labour Office.

Keynes, J.M. (1936), *The General Theory of Employment, Interest and Money*, London: Macmillan.

Khamis, M. (2008), 'Does the minimum wage have a higher impact on the informal than on the formal labour market? Evidence from quasi-experiments', *IZA Discussion Paper Series No. 3911*, Bonn: Forschungsinstitut zur Zukunft der Arbeit (IZA).

Lavoie, D. (2009), *Introduction to Post-Keynesian Economics*, London: Palgrave Macmillan.

Lee, D.S. (1999), 'Wage inequality in the United States during the 1980s: rising dispersion or falling minimum wage?', *The Quarterly Journal of Economics*, **114**(3), 977–1023.

Lee, W.-S. and S. Suardi (2010), 'Minimum wages and employment: reconsidering the use of a time-series approach as an evaluation tool', *IZA Discussion Paper Series No. 4748*, Bonn: Forschungsinstitut zur Zukunft der Arbeit (IZA).

Lemos, S. (2007), 'Minimum wage effects across the private and public sectors in Brazil', *Journal of Development Studies*, **43**(4), 700–720.

Lemos, S. (2009), 'Minimum wage effects in a developing country', *Labour Economics*, **16**(2), 224–37.

LPC (2009), *National Minimum Wage: Low Pay Commission Report 2009*, London: Low Pay Commission.

LPC (2012), *National Minimum Wage: Low Pay Commission Report 2012*, London: Low Pay Commission.

Maloney, W.F. and J. Nuñez (2001), 'Measuring the impact of minimum wages: evidence from Latin America', *Policy Research Working Paper No. 2597*, Washington, DC: The World Bank.

Metcalf, D. (2008), 'Why has the British national minimum wage had little or no impact on employment?', *Journal of Industrial Relations*, **50**(3), 489–512.

Murgai, R. and M. Ravallion (2005), 'Employment guarantee in rural India: what would it cost and how much would it reduce poverty?', *Economic and Political Weekly*, **40**(31), 3450–55.

Neumark, D. (2008), 'Alternative labor market policies to increase economic self-sufficiency: mandating higher wages, subsidizing employment, and raising productivity', *IZA Discussion Paper, No. 3355*, Bonn: Forschungsinstitut zur Zukunft der Arbeit (IZA).

Neumark, D. and W.L. Wascher (1992), 'Employment effects of minimum and subminimum wages: panel data on state minimum wage laws', *Industrial and Labour Relations Review*, **46**(1), 55–81.

Neumark, D. and W.L. Wascher (2008), *Minimum Wages*, Cambridge, MA: MIT Press.

Neumark, D., M. Schweitzer and W. Wascher (1998), 'The effects of minimum wages on the distribution of family incomes: a non-parametric analysis', *NBER*

Working Paper No. 6536, Cambridge, MA: National Bureau of Economic Research.
Ni, J., G. Wang and X. Yao (2011), 'Impact of minimum wages on employment', *Chinese Economy*, **44**(1), 18–38.
OECD (2010), *OECD Employment Outlook: Moving Beyond the Jobs Crisis*, Paris: Organisation for Economic Co-operation and Development.
Rani, U. and P. Belser (2012), 'The effectiveness of minimum wages in developing countries: the case of India', *International Journal of Labour Research*, **4**(1), 45–66.
Rani, U., P. Belser and S. Ranjbar (2013a), 'Role of minimum wages in rebalancing the economy', *World of Work Report 2013: Repairing the Economic and Social Fabric*, Geneva: International Institute for Labour Studies, International Labour Organization.
Rani, U., P. Belser and M. Oelz et al. (2013b), 'Minimum wage coverage and compliance in developing countries', *International Labour Review*, **152**(3–4), 381–410.
Sankaran, S.R. (1997), 'Minimum wage legislation', *The Indian Journal of Labour Economics*, **40**(4), 705–13.
Schmitt, J. (2013), *Why Does the Minimum Wage Have No Discernible Effect on Employment?*, Washington, DC: Center for Economic and Policy Research.
Souza, P. and P. Baltar (1979), 'Salário mínimo e taxa de salários no Brasil' [Minimum wage and the wage rate in Brazil], *Pesquisa e Planejamento Econômico*, **9**, 629–60.
Vaughan-Whitehead, D. (2011), *Work Inequalities in the Crisis: Evidence from Europe*, Cheltenham, UK and Northampton, MA, USA/Geneva: Edward Elgar Publishing/International Labour Organization.

6. Temporary contracts and wage inequality

Sandrine Cazes and Juan Ramón de Laiglesia

6.1 INTRODUCTION

One of the key features of labour market developments over the last 25 years has been the increase in the share of temporary employment in most advanced countries as well as in emerging countries. Temporary employment takes multiple forms across countries, the most common of which are fixed-term contracts – which have a definite duration – and temporary agency work.[1] The expansion of those temporary forms of employment has both social and economic implications: the extensive use of temporary contracts has been singled out as contributing to dysfunctions in labour market performance, notably in terms of labour market segmentation[2] (Doeringer and Piore, 1971; Reich et al., 1973). Segmented labour markets are characterized by inequalities in labour market outcomes across submarkets or segments, as well as low rates of transition of workers from one segment to another. Most of the time, having a temporary contract means having a job with lower quality, with reduced (if any) access to training and fringe benefits, such as paid sick leave, unemployment insurance and retirement pension, higher insecurity due to reduced protection in case of termination of the employment relationship and often lower pay and fewer prospects of upward mobility. Beyond equity concerns, segmented labour markets may also induce suboptimal outcomes from an efficiency viewpoint. Indeed, highly segmented labour markets are also associated with large adjustments in employment levels during recessions, increasing the volatility of labour markets with possible negative effects on productivity (Dolado et al., 2011).

This chapter addresses the relationship between the prevalence of temporary contracts and wage inequality. More specifically, it investigates how and to what extent the diffusion of temporary employment has contributed to wider individual wage dispersion. The existence of wage differentials between fixed-term and permanent jobs means that an increase in the share of temporary contracts will increase inequality due to the existence of inter-group inequality – inequality between holders of one and the other type of contract. However, the impact on overall wage inequality will also depend on intragroup inequality – in particular the dispersion of temporary job earnings, which differs across countries, and on the degree to which temporary contracts have facilitated entry in the labour market of hitherto excluded groups. Therefore, the overall effect of the expansion of temporary contracts on wage inequality among all workers is a priori ambiguous.

This chapter concentrates on temporary contracts rather than examining the role of non-standard forms of employment at large (which also include part-time, self-employment, or other forms of employment such as casual work). The main reason for concentrating on temporary contracts is that it allows us to analyse the link between this type of form of employment and inequality in the context of labour market segmentation and suggest fine-tuned policy recommendations. Moreover, among all flexible forms of employment, temporary contracts, and fixed-term contracts in particular, have been those which have grown most significantly in a number of countries among OECD members and beyond.

The objectives of this chapter are to provide an overview of the prevalence of temporary contracts in both developed and emerging economies (OECD and Latin America); to highlight the range of inequalities generated by the fact of having those contracts; and finally, to assess to what extent the expansion of such contracts has been a significant driver of wage inequality. To address this issue, this chapter relies largely on comparative empirical evidence and investigates whether countries with higher shares of temporary contracts exhibit more unequal wage distributions.

While largely comparable data on wage inequality are broadly available, the same is not true for data on the prevalence of temporary forms of employment or summary data on institutional determinants of both inequality and the prevalence of temporary work. This chapter therefore concentrates on OECD countries and selected Latin American countries. In both groups of countries, the prevalence of temporary work is an important policy issue from the social and economic viewpoints. Data are available for OECD countries from secondary sources and estimates were prepared for this chapter for Latin American countries based on available survey data.

The remainder of the chapter is structured as follows. Section 6.2 provides an overview of the diffusion of temporary contracts in total employment in both OECD and Latin American countries over the past two decades. The main characteristics of temporary jobs are then introduced in terms of statutory specificities and labour market inequalities such as wage gaps between workers on fixed-term contracts and open-ended contracts.

Section 6.3 then examines the link between the growing incidence of temporary contracts and wage inequality. Beyond the existence of a wage penalty (on average) for fixed-term contracts, the overall impact of an increase in the use of temporary contracts on inequality is a priori unclear, as it depends on how the prevalence of temporary contracts will affect the shape and symmetry of the wage distribution. After a short summary of the main trends and drivers of wage inequality over the past 20 years, we provide indicative evidence based on multivariate cross-country analysis for a set of OECD and emerging countries. Once institutional determinants of wage inequality are controlled for, we find a positive correlation between a higher share of fixed-term contracts and more unequal wage distributions. Since the relationship is driven by a group of countries with very high shares of fixed-term contracts, we examine in section 6.4 the impact of temporary contracts on wage distributions and compare wage profiles across countries. The wage distribution of temporary jobs is found to differ across countries, when compared to that for permanent jobs. We find that in countries with high shares of fixed-term contracts, the shape of the wage distribution is affected by those contracts that add mass at the bottom, but that the bottom of the wage distribution is ultimately shaped by other wage-setting institutions such as minimum wages and collective bargaining. We interpret these different patterns across countries to correspond to the differences in the roles and uses of temporary contracts in the different labour markets. We review in section 6.5 the regulation governing the use of temporary contracts and corresponding effective demand for this type of contract. Section 6.6 provides some concluding remarks.

6.2 TRENDS AND MAIN FEATURES OF TEMPORARY EMPLOYMENT

Temporary employment can take different forms, depending on the contractual forms available to employers and workers in the legislation of a given country. This chapter concentrates on the most widespread forms of temporary employment: fixed-term contracts and temporary agency work. Fixed-term contracts are employment contracts for a given duration, which may be formally recorded as a definite end date or as a definite task.[3] Work in a temporary work agency does not necessarily imply having a fixed-term contract, as it is common practice in a number of countries (such as Austria, Germany or Slovakia) for temporary work agencies to hire staff on permanent contracts, in which case they are also paid in between assignments. They are nevertheless treated jointly in this chapter for two reasons. First, aggregate data on temporary employment usually compound both forms of temporary employment. Second, temporary agency workers face similar penalties and obstacles in the labour market as workers on fixed-term contracts.

The prevalence of different types of temporary work depends on the specific country, given differences in law, practice and the composition of the economy. In European countries, temporary employment is dominated by fixed-term contracts: in 2010, about 12 per cent of employees were on fixed-term contracts while only 1.3 per cent were temporary agency workers.[4] In a small number of countries, however, temporary work agencies do employ sizeable shares of the temporary workforce (the highest shares are 32 per cent in Slovenia, 21 per cent in Slovakia and 20 per cent in Belgium; OECD, 2013a). Even in those countries, fixed-term contracts represent the majority of temporary work.

The Prevalence of Temporary Employment: Evolution Since the Mid-1980s

The use of flexible forms of employment such as fixed-term, temporary work agency or other atypical forms of employment with different employment status (e.g., independent contractors, dispatched workers, daily and on-call workers) has increased substantially over the past three decades throughout the world, but particularly in advanced and middle-income countries. This section documents the diffusion of temporary employment in both European and Latin American countries over the past decades. Figure 1 shows that the upward trend is not a new phenomenon and started back in the mid-1980s (see Figure 6.1). According to Eurostat data, the share of temporary workers[5] increased on average in the European Union from around 9 per cent in 1987 to 15.2 per cent in 2006, before the crisis hit particularly those workers; this resulted in a fall in their share at about 13.7 per cent in 2012.[6] In Spain the growth in the mid-1980s was dramatic as the share grew rapidly from 15.6 per cent in 1987 before reaching a peak of 35 per cent in 1995. As said before, due to the magnitude of the crisis in Spain, the share has fallen since 2008 to 23.7 per cent in 2012, indicating that labour market adjustment disproportionately took place among those on temporary contracts. While the patterns are less spectacular in other European countries, the proportion of temporary employees has been also increasing in countries such as Germany (from 11.6 per cent in 1987 to 14.8 per cent in 2008 and 13.9 in 2012), France and Italy.[7]

As already mentioned, this development has been partly driven in Europe by partial labour market reforms which sought to increase labour market flexibility by promoting the use of temporary employment. Typically, governments have focused on reforms at the margin in terms of deregulating the use of fixed-term contracts and agency work, leaving

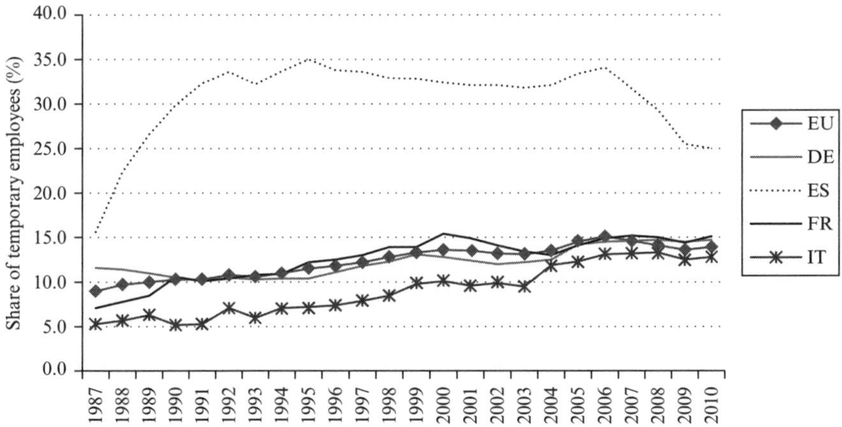

Note: Workers aged 15–64; EU resp. (EU-10, EU-12, EU-15, EU-25, and EU-27).

Source: Eurostat LFS database.

Figure 6.1 Share of temporary workers in total dependent employment (%) (1987–2011)

employment protection for workers on permanent contracts essentially unaltered. As argued by many labour economists, these partial (or two-tier) labour market reforms led firms to increasingly use workers on fixed-term positions, resulting in an increased duality in most European labour markets over the last two decades (Bentolila et al., 2010; Boeri, 2011; Eichhorst and Marx, 2011).

Temporary contracts are also widely used outside Europe: temporary work accounts, for example, for 24 per cent of dependent employment and 17 per cent of total employment in the Republic of Korea in 2011, making it the largest component of non-regular work;[8] this figure has been rather stable since 2005 when data became available. This is double the OECD-average incidence of temporary work (11.9 per cent). Overall, the share of temporary employment was particularly high vis-à-vis OECD countries, at above 20 per cent in Chile, Spain, Poland and Portugal in 2011. Data for other emerging countries, including Latin American countries, are neither systematically available nor comparable, but case studies suggest that temporary employment is widespread in Chile, Colombia and Peru, among others.[9] Moreover, according to Inter-American Development Bank data, of all 'new' jobs (e.g., jobs with less than one year of tenure), 32 per cent were fixed-term contracts in Chile, 21 per cent in Panama and 9 per cent in Colombia (Pagés-Serra, 2012).

The evolution of temporary employment in Latin America differs markedly across countries and is related to each country's path in labour market reforms over the past two decades. Indeed, a number of countries implemented reforms liberalizing the labour market to different degrees during the 1990s, and in particular liberalizing the use of temporary forms of employment (fixed-term contracts and temporary work agencies) (Vega Ruiz, 2005).

Figure 6.2 shows the evolution of temporary employment for selected Latin American countries and illustrates the different paths taken by different countries. Data are shown for countries where temporary employment shares can be estimated on the basis of available survey data.[10] While Brazil has maintained a low level of temporary employment throughout the period, Argentina liberalized the use of temporary employment contracts during the 1990s and re-regulated the labour market following the crisis of 2002. As a result, temporary employment is on a declining trend. The Chilean labour market was liberalized in 1979 and the labour code remains based on the reforms undertaken during the Pinochet regime, despite some re-regulation (in particular the regulation of fixed-term contracts in 1990). Temporary employment in Chile is high relative to international standards and has remained high despite a dip associated with the international financial crisis at the end of the 2000s. The Peruvian experience mirrors that of a number of European economies, in that labour regulation is protective of workers in open-ended contracts but has been liberalized at the margins, resulting in a dramatic increase of temporary employment in recent years.

Figure 6.2 shows temporary employment as a share of salaried employment, which also includes informal salaried workers. The impact of including informal workers differs across countries, although the trends are not modified in the four cases presented. In Argentina and Brazil, formal employees are more likely to be in permanent relationships, and both countries have seen a reduction in informality during the period, but in both cases, the trend of temporary employment is also decreasing when limited to formal employees. In Chile, the share of temporary employment is lower among formal employees than among all employees. Indeed, a significant share of temporary employment is in the form of triangular employment relationships[11] (temporary work agencies and subcontracting relationships), some of which are themselves informal. Finally, in Peru, most informal workers have no contract at all, so that the share of formal workers with temporary contracts is even higher than shown (indeed, over 50 per cent in 2010).

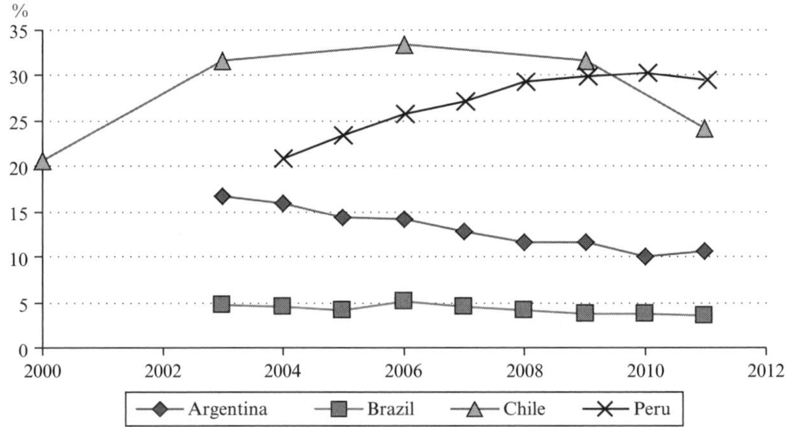

Sources: EPH (INEC) for Argentina (Q4 of each year), PME (IBGE) for Brazil (Q4), CASEN (MDS) for Chile, Jaramillo (2013) and ENAHO (INEI) for Peru.

Figure 6.2 Share of temporary employment for selected Latin American countries (2000–12, in %)

Characterization of Jobs on Temporary Contracts

Temporary workers face generally less favourable conditions. Having two types of contracts (temporary and permanent) creates a divide in the labour market between workers in the primary and secondary segment, as postulated in segmentation theory (Doeringer and Piore, 1971). Thus, workers with permanent contracts, like those in the primary segment of the labour market, typically enjoy better working conditions, have more opportunities for promotion, receive relatively higher wages and are better protected in the case of dismissals; on the other hand, workers with temporary contracts, like those in the secondary market, tend to have 'second-best jobs' both in terms of employment conditions and job stability, and to be paid less. Other theoretical arguments suggest that temporary workers may actually receive higher pay than they would otherwise to compensate for any less advantageous characteristics[12] which would be consistent with certain workers choosing such employment contracts. These compensating differentials do not seem empirically very important.

Those inequalities may arise from either statutory rules for entitlement to fringe benefits (e.g., temporary workers are *de jure* excluded) or from *de facto* conditions on entitlements, for example when those eligibility conditions are formulated in terms of earnings thresholds, minimum duration of employment or minimum contribution periods; as a result, those workers tend to have narrower (if at all) access to social protection, including in working conditions and pension schemes. Temporary workers are, for example, excluded from paid vacation in Mexico;[13] branch or company collective agreements do not extend to temporary agency workers in Portugal, Germany or Switzerland;[14] temporary workers in general have limited access to unemployment benefits.[15]

Another source of inequality relates to the legal gap in terms of job security since different employment protection legislation (EPL) rules govern the two different kinds of contracts as pointed out above. This EPL wedge triggers inequalities among workers regarding the dismissal probability, in particular in an economic downturn (Cahuc and Kramarz, 2004). Workers with a permanent contract, regardless of their individual characteristics and productivity levels, are more likely to remain in their position, as employers will first adjust their workforce simply by not renewing temporary contracts when facing an adverse shock. Another form of inequality is unequal access to training. Firms will invest in human capital if they expect to benefit from productivity gains which will not be fully compensated by wage increases. Hence the employment relationship between firm and worker should be long enough to compensate the costs of training (Wasmer, 2006). Evidence shows that temporary workers receive considerably less employer-funded training: according to an OECD study covering 12 European countries, holding a temporary job would reduce access to training by 6 percentage points relative to an average access to training of 18 per cent (OECD, 2002), and by 3.5 percentage points in Chile, a significant magnitude as only 7 per cent of temporary workers receive employer-sponsored training in Chile (Carpio et al., 2011). Those inequalities seem to be even more pronounced when contracts are of short duration. Additional ‘non-wage’ differences also include lower transitions from fixed-term to permanent jobs even if those mobility patterns vary considerably across countries: for EU countries, yearly transitions never exceed 55 per cent, with very low levels in Portugal, Spain and France at around 12 per cent versus 40–55 per cent in the United Kingdom, Ireland, Austria, Denmark or the Netherlands (OECD, 2006; Boeri, 2011). Figures for the Republic of Korea indicate that those yearly transitions are at about 15 per cent (Grubb et al., 2007) to 23 per cent (Lee, 2011).

As indicated before, the coexistence of different segments in the labour market implies wage differentials. While theoretical arguments are quite inconclusive regarding the impact of temporary employment on pay, empirical studies largely suggest that temporary workers are paid less than permanent ones on average, even when controlling for wage determinants such as education and tenure (Boeri, 2011). This is indeed the case in the

Table 6.1 *Wage premium for permanent contracts, selected European countries*

Country	Premium (%)	Country	Premium (%)
Austria	20.1***	Italy	24.1***
Belgium	13.9***	Luxembourg	27.6***
Denmark	17.7***	Netherlands	35.4***
Finland	19.0***	Portugal	15.8***
France	28.9***	Spain	16.9***
Germany	26.6***	Sweden	44.7***
Greece	20.2***	United Kingdom	6.5*
Ireland	17.8**		

Note: ***Significant at 99%; **significant at 95%; *significant at 90%.

Source: Boeri (2011).

majority of countries, as workers on temporary contracts earn less than comparable workers on open-ended contracts. Table 6.1 provides evidence on the wage penalty for fixed-term contracts. Using micro-data from the European Community Household Panel and from the European Union Statistics on Income and Living Conditions, Boeri estimates the monthly wage premium provided by permanent contracts vis-à-vis temporary contracts for 15 European countries. The wage regression is carried out over male dependent employment, controlling for education and tenure.[16]

The table indicates that in all the selected European countries, workers on permanent contracts are paid, other things being equal, substantially more than workers on temporary contracts. The estimated wage premia are always statistically significant and range from 6.5 per cent in the United Kingdom to almost 45 per cent in Sweden. In the majority of the countries, the premium is around 20–25 per cent.

The empirical evidence points to a substantial wage premium for permanent contracts even if the estimates may significantly differ from one study to the other. Dekker (2007) finds evidence of significant wage penalties for temporary workers in the Netherlands, Germany and the United Kingdom based on wage regressions estimated using national longitudinal data. Booth et al. (2002) find that temporary workers in Britain earn less then permanent workers, with a wage premium of about 8.9 per cent for men and 6 per cent for women. Blanchard and Landier (2001) conclude that workers on fixed-term contracts earned on average about 20 per cent less than permanent ones in France. Hagen (2003) finds an even larger gap of about 23 per cent in Germany, controlling for selection on unobservable characteristics, while, more recently, Pfeifer (2012) finds a smaller premium of about 10 per cent for Germany. Jahn and Pozzoli (2013) find wage penalties of 22 per cent for men and 14 per cent for women among temporary agency workers in Germany when controlling for self-selection into the sector. Finally, Houseman (1997) found that temporary workers (fixed-term contracts, on-call work, contracting out and seasonal workers) in the United States were paid significantly less than permanent ones.

6.3 WAGE INEQUALITY AND TEMPORARY CONTRACTS

This section briefly describes trends in wage inequality over the past two decades, focusing on the diverging experiences of OECD and Latin American countries, and goes on to examine the link between inequality and the prevalence of temporary contracts empirically across countries with the use of aggregate data.

Trends in Wage Inequality

Income inequality has increased in OECD countries over the past 25 years, reaching in some countries the levels seen just before the Great Depression of the 1930s. As documented in Chapter 1 of this volume, income inequality also increased in many developing countries between the early 1990s and the late 2000s. In regional terms, income inequality fell in most of Latin America during the same period, but it remains the most unequal region in the world.

According to OECD data, the increase in inequality in most OECD countries responds to changes in the extremes of the household income distribution, with earnings among the 10 per cent better-paid workers growing more rapidly than earnings among the bottom 10 per cent of workers, in some cases by a substantial margin.[17] This was, however, not the case in France and Spain, two countries of particular interest for this chapter and where incomes at the bottom grew more quickly than those at the top. Part of the increase in inequality is concentrated at the very top, as documented by the increase in the income shares of the richest 1 per cent, which in the United States grew from 9 per cent in 1976 to 20 per cent in 2011 (Alvaredo et al., 2013). This pattern is also found in other English-speaking countries such as Canada and the United Kingdom, but is much more muted in most of Continental Europe and absent in Japan (Atkinson et al., 2011).

As discussed in this volume, inequality in household incomes depends on a number of factors on top of wage inequality. First, working time and wages determine the distribution of income from employment for employees. Second, employment and unemployment levels combine with the distribution of income from employment and that of incomes from self-employment to determine the dispersion of individual labour earnings. Third, household composition determines how individual earnings translate into household earnings. Fourth, income from labour combines with income from other market sources (including capital income) to determine household market income. Finally, taxes and transfers determine the distribution of household disposable income.

In practice, changes in the distribution of labour earnings account for the lion's share of the trend in household income inequality, because labour earnings make up most of household income.[18] Wage inequality is the most important determinant of inequality in labour earnings. The relative impact of working time and self-employment differ across the main regions of interest and are discussed below.

Figures 6.3 and 6.4 present the evolution of wage inequality for a selection of OECD and Latin American countries, as measured by the ratio of wages between the upper bound of the ninth decile of the distribution of earnings and that of the first decile of the earnings distribution (the D9/D1 ratio).[19] OECD countries show a marked upward trend in wage inequality, with the exception of France, Germany and Spain in the years after

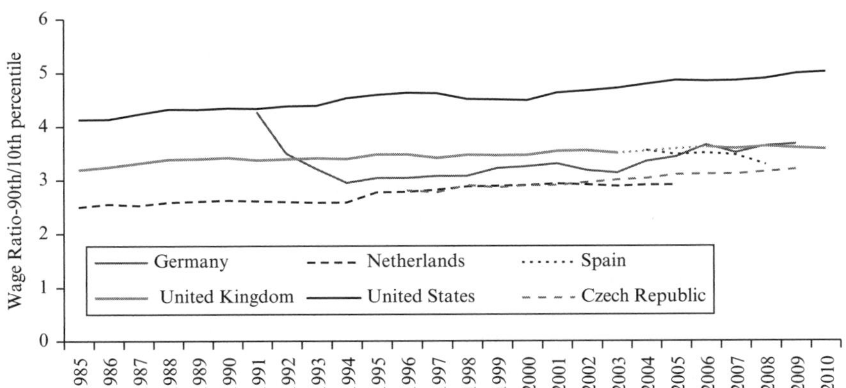

Note: Grey dotted line indicates use of different data series for the same country. For the United Kingdom, series are splined.

Sources: OECD (2012); OECD.stat, database.

Figure 6.3 Wage inequality in selected OECD countries, 1985–2010

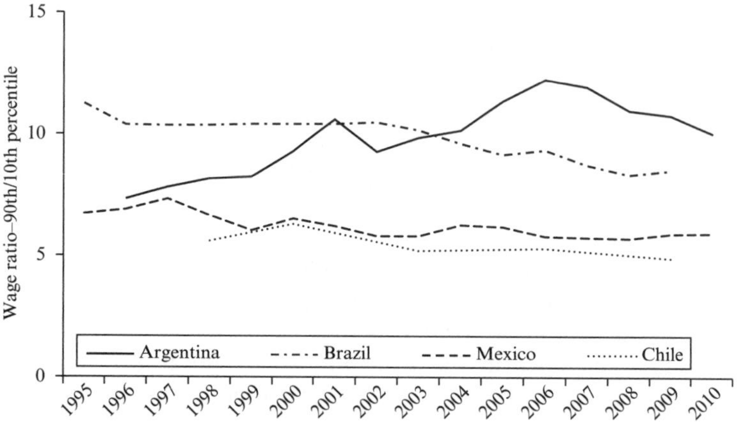

Source: ILO Global Wage Database.

Figure 6.4 Wage inequality in Latin America

reunification. This trend has been particularly strong in Eastern European countries undergoing market reform during the early 1990s (OECD, 2011). In general, in 23 OECD countries, inequality in labour earnings has followed the trend of wage inequality. Indeed, self-employment contributes between 3 per cent and 13 per cent of gross labour income, and has modest effects on overall inequality. On the other hand, hours worked have fallen on average more at the bottom of the income distribution than at the top in most OECD countries, so that changes in working hours tend to exacerbate the impact of growing inequality in wages (ibid.).

The declining trend of wage inequality in Latin America contrasts sharply with the experience of OECD countries. After increases in wage inequality during the 1990s in most of Latin America, wages have become more equal in the majority of Latin American countries during the 2000s, with the change concentrated in the latter part of the decade for some of the countries (Figure 6.4). The trend is the same if working hours are considered: the World Bank (2012) finds that inequality in labour earnings fell on average by 3.6 points for dependent employees for a set of 15 countries. Finally, in Latin American countries, self-employment is a more significant contributor to total income, contributing 21 per cent of labour income in Argentina and over 30 per cent in Brazil and Chile, for example. The fall in the share of self-employment has therefore contributed substantially to the fall in household income inequality (Keifman and Maurizio, 2012).

As discussed in Chapter 1, the fall in wage inequality in Latin America stems in part from the increased human capital in the workforce. The Latin American workforce became increasingly educated during the 2000s, with the share of the labour force with secondary education increasing by 7 percentage points. As a result, skills premia fell, driving wage inequality down (López-Calva and Lustig, 2010; World Bank, 2012). But the fall in inequality was also driven by the creation of formal jobs and the strengthening of labour market institutions in several countries in the region – in particular minimum wages (see Chapter 5) and collective bargaining (see Chapter 4).

Empirical Evidence

The summary of the available evidence on the determinants of wage inequality suggests that it is driven by a number of factors, including those determining relative demand and supply of workers of different skill levels – which are influenced by macroeconomic performance, international trade and technological progress – as well as by institutional factors that mediate or remediate labour market inequality.

Labour market institutions play important roles in determining levels and trends in wage inequality. Koeninger et al. (2007) find that in OECD countries factors like union density, employment protection legislation, unemployment benefits and the size of minimum wages were important determinants of changes in wage inequality.

The experience of a number of Latin American countries is consistent with labour market institutions having a significant impact on wage inequality. A number of countries in the region carried out liberalizing labour market reforms in the 1990s, particularly deep in Argentina and Peru, but also notable in Brazil, Colombia, Ecuador and Panama (Vega Ruiz, 2005), while policies to strengthen labour market institutions – by increasing the real value of minimum wages and supporting collective bargaining in particular – were implemented in the 2000s.[20]

Since workers on temporary contracts are on average paid less than workers on permanent contracts, institutional features allowing or even encouraging the use of temporary contracts will tend to generate wage distributions that exhibit more mass at the bottom and possibly a wider dispersion. The correlation between the share of temporary contracts and wage inequality supports a positive relationship between fixed-term contracts and inequality (Figure 6.5).[21] This simple exercise also shows that two groups of countries can be identified among OECD countries.

A first group includes countries with relatively low shares of temporary employment and the most unequal wage distributions among OECD

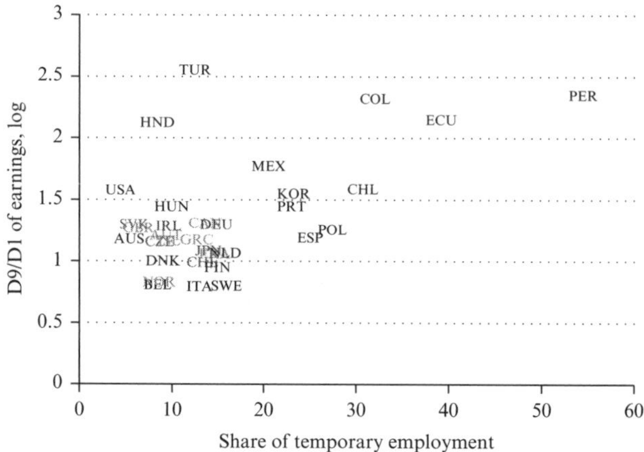

Sources: OECD Earnings Database for OECD countries except Mexico, Chile and Turkey; ILO Global Wage Database for non-OECD countries, Mexico, Chile, and Turkey. Calculations from national household surveys for Latin American countries.

Figure 6.5 Wage inequality and the prevalence of temporary employment

countries. This suggests that a high share of temporary contracts is not necessary for high inequality nor are contractual conditions determining length of employment so relevant for wage dispersion in some institutional contexts. This is clearly the case of the United States, given employment at will, but also of the United Kingdom, where individual dismissals are lightly regulated especially for employees with less than two years' tenure, and where dismissals based on economic grounds are not considered unfair dismissals.[22]

A second group of countries – which includes the Republic of Korea, Portugal, Spain and Poland – exhibits high shares of temporary employment and above-average inequality.[23] In these terms, Mexico and Chile are close to this group, although it should be noted that both countries also have large informal labour markets that are likely to lead to high wage inequality on top of that driven by contractual differences in the formal sector. The same is true, to an even greater extent, of Colombia, Ecuador and Peru.

The positive correlation between the prevalence of temporary employment and wage inequality is therefore driven by a relatively small group of OECD countries, although the addition of Latin American countries strengthens the result. Given the number of factors, including other institutional factors that can drive wage inequality, a multivariate framework is more appropriate to explore the relationship between the prevalence of fixed-term contracts and wage inequality.

Wage inequality is considered to be jointly determined by the relative supply and demand for skills and by institutional factors (Koeninger et al., 2007). Institutional characteristics are correlated across countries; in particular, Bertola and Rogerson (1997) argue that countries with strict dismissal regulations also have wage-compressing institutions.[24] A first concern is that the correlation between the prevalence of temporary contracts and wage inequality is spurious and driven by other institutions, in which case conditioning on such institutions should weaken the relationship between temporary employment and wage inequality.

Table 6.2 presents the results from a regression of wage inequality on a number of determinants to examine the robustness of the relationship between the share of temporary employment and wage inequality. A number of institutional factors are included that have been found to be related to wage inequality (Koeninger et al., 2007; OECD, 2011), as well as the skill endowment of the labour force. They include the existence and level of statutory minimum wages, the coverage of collective bargaining, the level of coordination of wage setting and the strictness of employment protection legislation. Detailed definitions and sources for correlates can be found in the Appendix.

The key result for the purposes of this chapter is the robustness of the relationship between wage inequality and the prevalence of temporary employment even when controlling for a series of other institutional determinants of wage inequality. The coefficient on the share of temporary contracts is quite stable and of the order of 1 per cent, implying a quantitatively important relationship. As would be expected, a higher share of the workforce with post-secondary education lowers inequality. Among other institutional determinants, greater coverage by collective bargaining and greater wage coordination are also associated with less unequal wage distributions. Minimum wage indicators behave as expected when they enter on their own (column 2) since countries with higher minimum wages have more equal distributions.[25] They have the reverse sign when all indicators are considered, however, suggesting that some countries without minimum wages have other mechanisms to reduce inequality. Finally, the chosen indicator for employment protection legislation (EPL) reflects the protection of regular contracts only, to avoid endogeneity with the share of temporary workers. However, similar exercises (OECD, 2011) have found the link between EPL and wage inequality to be driven mainly by the protection of temporary workers and its decrease during the 1980s and 1990s. The results are largely unchanged when time effects are included (column 8) but are not robust to the inclusion of country effects (not

Table 6.2 Institutional determinants of wage inequality

Panel Regression, OECD Countries, 2000–10 (Dependent Variable: Natural Log of D9/D1 of Earnings)								
	Pooled panel, OLS							Year fixed effects
	(1)	(2)	(3)	(4)	(5)	(6)	(7)	(8)
Share of temporary employment (%)	0.006 (2.25)**	0.002 (1.08)	0.006 (2.30)**	0.006 (2.16)**	0.007 (2.85)***	0.007 (2.39)**	0.009 (3.18)***	0.009 (2.94)***
Minimum wage (share of mean)		−1.011 (4.24)***					0.941 (2.54)**	1.013 (2.70)***
Country has minimum wage		0.64 (6.93)***					−0.294 (1.85)*	−0.321 (1.99)**
Workforce with post-secondary education (%)			−0.002 (1.42)				−0.004 (2.38)**	−0.005 (2.70)***
Coverage of collective bargaining				−0.005 (8.84)***			−0.005 (5.93)***	−0.005 (5.60)***
Wage coordination					−0.082 (6.76)***		−0.028 (1.81)*	−0.028 (1.79)*
EPL regular						−0.037 (1.45)	0.008 (0.33)	0.000 (0.00)
Observations	203	203	203	117	197	167	109	109
R-squared	0.02	0.42	0.03	0.41	0.21	0.04	0.57	0.61

Note: Absolute value of t statistics in brackets; *significant at 10%; **significant at 5%; ***significant at 1%.

shown). This is probably due to the small sample (only 19 countries are in the final sample for a given year) but also suggests that it is cross-country variation that drives the results.

An important limitation of the exercise presented in Table 6.2 is the potential endogeneity of the prevalence of temporary employment. Of particular concern would be the situation in which the wage distribution and the share of temporary contracts are jointly determined by relative demand and supply for skills but the share of temporary contracts has no bearing on wage inequality. This could be the case if workers with certain characteristics that determine their wages to be lower – for example, lower skills – are more likely to receive temporary contracts regardless of the wages they actually receive.

The share of the workforce with post-secondary education accounts for the supply of skills, but no control for the demand for labour with different skills is included. If the share of temporary employment and wage inequality were jointly driven by relative demand for skills with no further interaction, an increase in the demand for low-skilled labour would increase the share of temporary workers and the return to those workers, which would tend to *compress* the wage distribution, lowering inequality, contrary to what is shown in Table 6.2.

The results in Table 6.2 are consistent, however, with a situation in which low-wage workers receive temporary contracts and the share of temporary contracts and the wage distribution are jointly determined. In this case a causal interpretation of the coefficient on the share of temporary contracts is not warranted, but the association between the prevalence of temporary contracts and wage inequality is not spurious – even though this exercise cannot shed light on the direction of causality: whether workers receive lower wages because they are in temporary contracts or are more likely to be on temporary contracts because they receive lower wages.

Figure 6.5 suggests that the consideration of countries beyond advanced economies should strengthen the results. To this end, the sample is extended to include not only advanced OECD economies, but also Chile, Colombia, Ecuador, Honduras, Republic of Korea, Mexico, Peru and Turkey (Table 6.3). The extension of the sample is an innovation of this chapter relative to similar exercises in the literature (Koeninger et al., 2007; OECD, 2011).

The extension of the sample imposes significant constraints on the indicators used. The strictness of employment protection legislation is measured by the cost of severance pay only, following OECD methodology[26] (Venn, 2009). The coverage of collective bargaining emerges from multiple sources. Finally, the indicator for the degree of wage coordination is drawn from Visser (2011) and covers mostly OECD countries, which

Table 6.3 Institutional determinants of wage inequality

OLS Regression, Latest Available Year for Each Country (Dependent Variable: Natural Log of D9/D1 of Earnings)

	(1)	(2)	(3)	(4)	(5)	(6)
Share of temporary employment	0.02 (3.50)***	0.02 (4.23)***	0.02 (3.41)***	0.02 (2.19)**	0.01 (1.29)	0.00 (0.30)
Workforce with post-secondary education (%)		−0.01 (1.57)	−0.01 (1.55)	0.00 (0.68)	−0.01 (1.29)	0.00 (1.25)
Minimum wage (% mean)			0.09 (0.16)	−0.29 (0.32)	0.52 (0.61)	−0.02 (0.05)
Country has minimum wage			0.29 (1.05)	0.42 (0.95)	−0.19 (0.43)	0.11 (0.40)
EPL (cost of severance pay)				0.07 (0.81)	0.04 (0.51)	−0.02 (0.43)
Collective Bargaining coverage					−0.01 (3.05)***	−0.01 (3.13)***
Wage coordination						0.00 (0.11)
Observations	33	32	32	30	29	25
R-squared	0.28	0.41	0.51	0.49	0.61	0.66

Note: Absolute value of t statistics in brackets, *significant at 10%; **significant at 5%; ***significant at 1%.

explains the fall in the sample size in column 6. Moreover, the paucity of comparable data on the prevalence of temporary employment for Latin American countries means that the analysis is only cross-sectional.

Despite the limitations, the multivariate analysis confirms the observations made with respect to Figure 6.5. The relationship is stronger when non-OECD countries are included; the coefficient on the share of temporary employment is larger and stable, with the exception of the last specification, in which the addition of the wage coordination measure significantly reduces the sample size.

The empirical evidence therefore points to the existence of a relationship between the prevalence of temporary employment and wage inequality across countries. However, it also suggests that, while the relationship is positive when a wide set of countries is considered, it is negative among certain groups of countries (in particular those with relatively fewer short-term contracts). Moreover, while the relationship is empirically stable to the inclusion of a number of institutional determinants, it breaks down when certain elements of wage determination are included. Differences across countries in the role of temporary contracts and the wage penalty they command may be a possible explanation for these results, one that the data available across countries and the methods used in this section cannot resolve.

6.4 TEMPORARY CONTRACTS AND WAGE DISTRIBUTIONS

The analysis in section 6.3 suggests substantial heterogeneity across countries in the implications of the prevalence of temporary contracts for wage inequality. There is, of course, heterogeneity in the size of wage premia associated with permanent jobs (Table 6.1). However, the observed differences in average wage premia are positively correlated with the share of temporary work despite a few clear outliers (Figure 6.6).[27] This would tend to confirm a positive relationship between temporary contracts and inequality even at low levels of prevalence. Furthermore, differences also

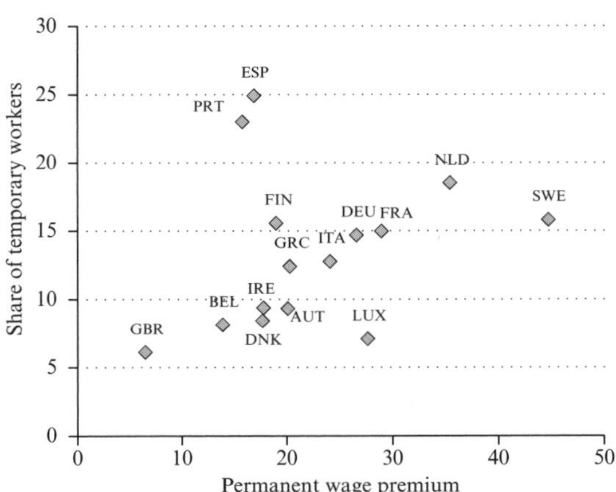

Sources: Boeri (2011) for wage premia and OECD for share of temporary workers.

Figure 6.6 Prevalence of temporary work and wage premium of permanent contracts, OECD countries, circa 2010

arise across countries in the way the expansion of fixed-term contracts may change wage distributions.

This section analyses the shape of the wage profiles within countries with the use of survey data from the Fifth European Working Conditions Survey (Eurofound, 2012). Wages among temporary workers are found to be both lower, on average, than those of permanent workers (consistent with the evidence summarized in section 6.2). They are also found to have lower dispersion in the majority of the countries studied. Scalar measures of inequality may therefore be limited in demonstrating the impact of fixed-term contracts on wage distributions, the shapes of which are then studied for selected countries.

Channels of Transmission and Inequality Decomposition

As stated earlier the implications of the prevalence of temporary employment for wage inequality depend on several factors: first, the existence of a wage gap between temporary and permanent contracts; second, whether wage gaps are constant across the wage distribution; third, whether a selection process exists by which the most productive or least productive workers receive temporary contracts which would determine whether most wage gaps are indeed large; fourth, whether the increase in temporary employment results from a substitution of temporary jobs for permanent jobs for workers with similar characteristics or from entry of hitherto excluded workers into employment – most likely towards the bottom of the distribution.

Regarding the first factor, section 6.2 has presented evidence of the existence of wage gaps in a large set of countries. This implies that wage distributions will differ for temporary workers. When most temporary contracts are substituting for open-ended contracts in the same jobs, the distribution of wages for temporary workers would be expected to resemble that of permanent workers shifted to the left to account for the wage penalty. However, evidence on wage gaps, including on the regressivity of wage gaps (see section 6.2 and Fournier and Koske, 2012), suggests that there is a selection mechanism at work in most countries by which lower-earnings workers are more likely to suffer a wage penalty – and possibly more likely to be in temporary contracts as well. This selection mechanism will lead to wage distributions for temporary contracts that have greater dispersion than those for permanent contracts. This finding also provides support to the existence of segmentation in labour markets: in the absence of labour market segmentation, the lower protection of fixed-term contracts would translate into *positive* wage gaps in favour of holders of fixed-term contracts, conditional on their skills and experience. Finally, the integration of otherwise excluded workers in labour markets would tend to increase the mass at the bottom of the earnings distribution – since it would be expected that workers were excluded due to their relatively low productivity and hence low earnings potential.

The decomposition of wage inequality by contractual status (Table 6.4) provides interesting information on the relative weight of the different effects on wage inequality, as measured by the mean log deviation (MLD) of monthly wages. The table presents the decomposition of the inequality into *between* and *within* components[28] for 13 selected countries out of the 34 available in the European Working Conditions Survey (EWCS) 2010. The MLD is chosen as the measure of inequality because it has the advantage of being additively separable into these two components, unlike other usual indices of inequality such as the Gini coefficient, which is presented for ease of reference.[29] The MLD is chosen over other indices with the same property because it is more sensitive to changes at the bottom of the distribution, where most of the differences are expected to take place.

The decomposition exercise confirms that the wage gap between temporary and permanent contracts plays a limited role in determining individual wage inequality. The wage gap is responsible for the between component, which is an order of magnitude smaller than the within component. A second result is that the relative dispersion of wages of fixed-term and permanent contracts differs across countries. The column displaying the MLD for fixed-term contracts highlights this, when compared to the within component for the whole distribution[30] (given the relatively low shares of fixed-term contracts and the very low contribution of the between component, the within component is dominated by inequality among permanent workers).

The results show that wage distributions for fixed-term contracts are particularly concentrated in Finland, Spain and especially Italy, while they are significantly wider than those of permanent contracts in Belgium, the Netherlands and Germany. In the remainder of countries, the differences are smaller. It should be noted that if two distributions have identical values for within-group MLD, the one with the lower mean will appear to be more concentrated in an absolute scale (such as a linear monetary scale), since the MLD is multiplicatively invariant. This means that the above analysis may in fact understate the high concentration of fixed-term wages in cases like Italy.

Finally, Table 6.4 presents gross wage gaps expressed in terms of the ratio between average wages among fixed-term workers and the whole sample. These data paint a picture that is consistent with the variation in wage gaps discussed in section 6.2. Interestingly wage gaps are very low in a number of countries where the dispersion of wages between the two

Table 6.4 Decomposition of inequality by contractual status – selected countries, 2010, male full-time workers

Country	Inequality as Measured by:		Mean Log Deviation Decomposition			Wages of Temporary Workers Relative to Permanent Employees	Share of Temporary Workers (%)
	Gini	Mean log deviation (MLD)	Between component	Within component	Within Temporary		
Belgium	0.18	0.06	0.001	0.06	0.07	0.88	9.3
Czech Republic	0.18	0.05	0.001	0.05	0.07	0.90	10.3
Denmark	0.26	0.12	0.010	0.11	0.06	0.67	9.1
Finland	0.18	0.05	0.001	0.05	0.04	0.86	7.6
France	0.22	0.08	0.004	0.07	0.08	0.81	11.1
Germany	0.22	0.09	0.019	0.07	0.10	0.70	9.1
Italy	0.15	0.04	0.004	0.04	0.01	0.80	9.0
Netherlands	0.19	0.06	0.002	0.06	0.09	0.89	8.3
Norway	0.16	0.04	0.003	0.04	0.04	0.95	7.9
Poland	0.22	0.09	0.006	0.08	0.08	0.86	20.0
Portugal	0.22	0.07	0.004	0.07	0.07	0.84	16.2
Spain	0.23	0.08	0.007	0.07	0.06	0.82	19.9
United Kingdom	0.27	0.13	0.000	0.13	0.11	1.07	7.1

Note: The share of temporary workers reported is that estimated on the basis of the EWCS 2010 data; relatively small samples imply rather large confidence intervals, which account for the difference between the estimates presented in Table 6.4 and values for the share of temporary workers presented in sections 6.2 and 6.3.

Source: Authors' estimates based on EWCS data.

groups is also similar, as in the case of Norway. In those cases contractual status seems *not* to matter for inequality. In other cases, like in Spain or Italy, significant wage gaps and a narrower distribution for fixed-term contracts suggest that they are concentrated at the bottom of the wage distribution. In a third set of countries, exemplified by Germany, wage gaps are small and the dispersion of wages among fixed-term contracts is high. As a result, the prevalence of fixed-term contracts is an important driver of inequality in the latter two groups of countries.

Beyond Wage Gaps: Distribution of Temporary Wages

The previous analysis confirms that the impact of temporary contracts on the shape of wage distributions differs across countries. Using monthly wage data from the European Working Conditions Survey, a visual analysis of distributions confirms the conclusions drawn from the inequality decomposition.

Figure 6.7 illustrates four cases found among the 34 countries covered in the EWCS data. Most other countries reviewed in Table 6.4 correspond to one of these cases, as do the majority of countries in the data. In a few cases the prevalence of fixed-term contracts is low and sample sizes are therefore insufficient for analysis of this kind (Austria, Sweden), while in a number of other cases, other non-standard forms of employment (apprenticeships, informal work) are more prevalent, so that the role of temporary contracts is less important (Greece, Ireland, Turkey). The figure shows kernel density estimates of (the logarithm) of monthly wages. The sample is restricted to male full-time workers so as to isolate the role of temporary contracts from that of other non-standard forms of employment (in particular part-time employment). Density plots are weighted by the share of the labour force they represent so as to provide a visual cue of their weight in the wage distribution.

In the first case, which is illustrated by Norway, wage gaps are very low (there is no gross wage gap in the data for Norway in this case) and the distribution of wages among temporary contracts mimics that of wages among permanent workers. The distribution in the United Kingdom (not shown in Figure 6.7) follows a similar pattern.

The second case is exemplified by Germany and includes Denmark. In this case, there is also a small average wage gap but a wider distribution of earnings among temporary workers. The absence of statutory minimum wages in both countries explains the wide variation in wages at the bottom.

The third case corresponds to Spain, Portugal and Poland, three countries with significant shares of temporary contracts. Temporary workers are concentrated towards the bottom of the distribution. This is due in

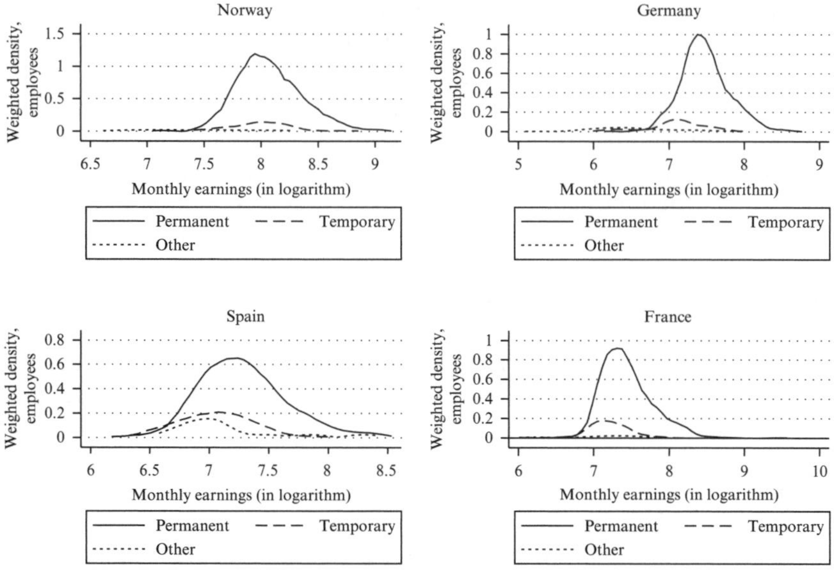

Source: Authors' estimates based on European Working Conditions Survey data.

Figure 6.7 Kernel density estimates of wage distributions, selected countries, 2010, male full-time workers

part to the absence of temporary workers at the top. A detailed analysis shows that the bottom of the distribution is largely made up of temporary workers in all three countries, so that the distribution of temporary wages is heavily skewed to the left, that is, concentrated at the bottom of the range. This behaviour is potentially driven by minimum wages being binding in particular for this category of workers, so that a substantial proportion of temporary workers earn wages at or close to the minimum wage, while they are not so important for permanent workers.

The fourth and final case is illustrated by France and also includes Italy. In these two countries, the wage distribution for permanent workers is also skewed to the left, compressed clearly in the case of France by relatively high minimum wages relative to the average wage.

Overall, the analysis of the shape of wage distributions shows that only in a few countries (e.g., those in the first group) fixed-term contracts *are not* systematically associated with low-paid work. In fact, the similarity between unconditional wage distributions suggests that fixed-term contracts do not play a screening role in those countries either, as otherwise, workers with less experience and tenure and therefore lower wages would tend to drag the distribution down. In other countries, temporary work is *largely* associated with low-paid work and the influence of fixed-term work in the wage distribution depends on the existence of other institutions that limit downwards wages adjustment. In their absence, such as in the German[31] or Danish cases, wage distributions are very wide for temporary workers.

6.5 USING TEMPORARY CONTRACTS: LEGAL FRAMEWORK AND EFFECTIVE DEMAND FOR TEMPORARY WORK

Regulation of Temporary Employment

The regulation of the working conditions of temporary workers is one possible policy instrument to rationalize the use of temporary contracts and prevent them driving wage inequality upwards. A glance at the intensity of regulation across different dimensions of the legislation governing fixed-term contracts, such as the valid reasons for using those contracts, the maximum number of their successive use, and so on, as summarized, for example, by the OECD EPL index does not help mapping out countries along the lines described above: Norway, France or Spain, which illustrated different cases, all have, for instance, very high (protective) legislation governing temporary contracts. In a scale from 0 (least protective) to 6 (most protective) Norway scores 3.42, France 3.75 and Spain 3.17, all of which are high against the OECD average of 2.08 (OECD, 2013a).

There are two reasons why such measures of the intensity of regulation are insufficient. First, because they do not take into account that different types of regulation seek to achieve different outcomes (for example, limiting the use of temporary contracts or protecting workers on temporary contracts). Second, because they cannot account for the impact of other labour market institutions, in particular wage-setting institutions.

Three policy orientations are particularly salient: regulation governing termination of employment, regulation concerning the uses of temporary contracts and the principle of equal pay for work of equal value. In what follows, key international instruments relative to these policy orientations are presented.[32]

The relevant international labour standard regarding termination of employment is the Termination of Employment Convention, 1982 (No. 158). Its scope is, however, limited by two factors: this convention has only been ratified by 36 countries and it provides for countries to exclude fixed-term and task-based contracts from the application of the provisions implementing the convention, a provision implemented by almost all countries.[33] Although national legislation typically provides protection against unfair dismissal and other forms of employment protection to fixed-term workers, the absence of international law on the subject permits national legislation to lower this protection substantially for workers on fixed-term contracts.

Regulation limiting the condition and purpose of use of temporary contracts is by far the most common. Convention No. 158 and the Termination of Employment Recommendation, 1982 (No. 166) do address the issue of fixed-term work in calling for safeguards to prevent fixed-term work from being used to go around the provisions of Convention 158.

The range of legally acceptable uses of fixed-term contracts varies substantially from country to country. In most countries fixed-term contracts can be used for temporarily replacing a worker on leave and for seasonal or time-bound tasks. In a number of countries, including Brazil, France, Mexico and Turkey, the use of a fixed-term contract is only possible when justified by such 'material' or 'objective' criteria, although the scope of the criteria and their application also vary. In contrast, other countries (including Germany, the Netherlands, the United Kingdom) allow hiring on fixed-term contracts with no restrictions of purpose. Likewise, the use of temporary agency workers is typically restricted to performing tasks outside the 'core' business of the user firm (OECD, 2013a). Other restrictions on use include limits on the number of renewals or the total length of employment under these contractual forms.

Comparatively, regulation on equal pay tends to be less clearly binding across contract types. Although they establish the principle of equal pay for work of equal value, international labour standards regarding equal pay do not explicitly require equal treatment or equal pay for equal work regardless of the contractual arrangement. The Equal Remuneration Convention, 1951 (No. 100) calls for rates of remuneration established without discrimination based on sex (Art. 1), while the Discrimination (Employment and Occupation) Recommendation, 1958 (No. 111) lists a number of dimensions of discrimination (race, colour, sex, religion, political opinion, national extraction, and social origin).

There exist examples of more direct approaches. EU Council Directives 1999/70/EC and 2008/104/EC, which govern fixed-term contracts and temporary work agencies (respectively), set out equality principles. Both directives introduce the principle of equal treatment, in one case of fixed-term workers with comparable permanent workers, in the other case of workers from temporary work agencies with the treatment they would receive had they been contracted directly by the user firm. However, in particular in the case of temporary agency work, there are a number of derogations, including when temporary workers have open-ended contracts with the temporary work agency[34] (a common practice in Austria and Germany; see OECD, 2013a), when collective bargaining sets out conditions of work for temporary agency workers, and when a national agreement with the social partners sets conditions for temporary workers (Petrylaite and Kuoras, 2012). Such derogations help explain the wide range of wages for temporary workers in Norway and Germany where they are extensively used. However, they apply to temporary work agencies only, and these still represent a small share of temporary workers.

Equal pay legislation appears however insufficient to tackle the inequality-increasing effect of temporary work. In the case of temporary agency work, the derogations have been extensively used in European countries. In the case of fixed-term work, the reasons are less clear. It should be noted that certain sectors and occupations (notably elementary occupations in agriculture, construction and certain services) have very high proportions of fixed-term workers, which is likely to make it difficult in practice to implement equality principles.

The Different Roles of Temporary Contracts Across Labour Markets

The different patterns of inequalities identified across countries in the previous sections are likely to reflect differences in the functions and uses of forms of temporary employment in labour markets. Overall, the uses of temporary contracts will depend on the legal circumstances for which such contracts are allowed as discussed above, as well as the functions they actually fulfil that are driven by either sector composition or screening process. There are multiple de facto business reasons for the use of both fixed-term and temporary agency work, and they are similar between the two types of temporary work. The analysis of Spermann (2011) for the reasons to use agency work (in Germany) and that of Portugal and Varejão (2009) for the use of fixed-term contracts in Portugal, largely overlap. On top of the response to short-term needs, they include lowering both non-wage and wage costs (the latter especially for temporary work agencies), avoiding dismissal protection and as screening devices for prospective permanent employees.

These motivations coexist in practice. Portugal and Varejão (2009) find evidence of screening behaviour but also that uncertainty and labour costs associated with permanent positions play an important role. Beckmann and Kuhn (2012) examine strategies directly for German firms using temporary work agencies and find that 19 per cent of firms using temporary work agencies did so in response to fluctuations in demand and that 14 per cent promoted at least one agency worker to a permanent position, showing the screening role of temporary work. The motivations for 74 per cent of firms are not explored, but the categorization above points to cost-saving measures.

The relative importance of reasons for using temporary work is a critical determinant of the link between temporary work and wage inequality. If used as a screening device, temporary workers will tend to have lower wages (because they tend to be younger and have less experience) but the gap need not grow over time. If used as a cost-reduction strategy, the use of temporary work is likely to result in labour market segmentation and to lead to inefficiently high turnover, with the ensuing shortfall in human capital and firm-specific knowledge accumulation.

What seems to matter to understand the relationship between temporary contracts and inequality is the existence of contractual segmentation between temporary and permanent contract labour markets. The presence of fixed-term workers relatively high in the wage distribution in the third group (Poland, Portugal and Spain) is at odds with fixed-term contracts playing a screening role, as is the persistence of wage gaps when experience and skills are controlled for (Boeri, 2011). Labour market segmentation is likely to increase the unequalizing effect of fixed-term contracts, especially if returns to experience are lower among fixed-term workers. Further research would be necessary (in particular a dynamic analysis of individual transitions on the labour market) to investigate the role of contractual segmentation on inequality.

6.6 CONCLUDING REMARKS

This chapter has shown how the holders of jobs that are governed under temporary contracts rather than standard open-ended contracts are disfavoured in terms of labour market outcomes in a number of ways, including sizeable wage penalties. Moreover, the prevalence of such contracts has increased in the past 25 years, not only in Southern Europe, where it has been the focus of much political and economic debate, but also in other OECD countries, and in a number of Latin American countries.

The cross-country evidence presented shows that countries with a greater share of temporary employment are also more likely to exhibit greater wage inequality, even when other institutional factors are considered. This is all the more true when data for a number of Latin American countries is included, a significant contribution of this chapter to existing analyses.

The increased use of fixed-term contracts over the last decades is not likely to be the main cause of rising wage inequality in OECD countries.

Indeed, wage inequality within jobs with either fixed term or open-ended contracts remains an order of magnitude larger than the inequality implied by the wage differentials observed between fixed-term and permanent contracts.

An examination of wage densities shows that the contribution of fixed-term contract prevalence to inequality takes different forms in different countries. With few exceptions, the distribution of wages for fixed-term contracts is more concentrated at the bottom. However, its shape and therefore its contribution to overall inequality depends critically on the role played by other labour market institutions, in particular wage-setting institutions such as collective bargaining and minimum wages. It also depends on whether the introduction of fixed-term contracts allowed the creation of more jobs for certain categories of workers.

Nevertheless, the differences in labour market outcomes for workers in fixed-term contracts relative to workers on regular contracts raise important fairness concerns. Even more so if there is labour market segmentation between these two groups. Such segmentation would imply a growing divide, as those in dead-end, fixed-term jobs are unable to reap the full benefits of on-the-job training, or receive the same returns to experience. Whether segmentation happens also along occupation or sectoral lines is particularly important to determine the applicability of equal pay for equal work principles and legislation, which will be more difficult to enforce if fixed-term jobs are concentrated in sectors or occupations where comparable tasks are not carried out by regular employees.

An analysis of the dynamic impact of labour market segmentation and in particular contractual segmentation on inequality is beyond the scope of this chapter, but would throw light on the degree of labour market segmentation. The results in this chapter have highlighted the heterogeneity in the role played by fixed-term contracts in determining wage distributions; a dynamic analysis would also help understand whether those patterns are stable and whether they are sustainable economically and socially.

ACKNOWLEDGEMENTS

The views expressed and arguments employed in this chapter are those of the authors and should not be reported as representing the official views of the OECD or of its member countries.

We extend our gratitude to the Instituto Brasileiro de Geografia e Estadística (IBGE) of Brazil, to the Ministerio de Desarrollo Social (MDS) of Chile, to the Departamento Administrativo Nacional de Estadística (DANE) of Colombia, and to Eurofound for providing access to microdata used in this chapter. We would also like to thank Roxana Maurizio for providing time series of temporary work for several Latin American countries as well as for feedback provided on earlier versions of this chapter and Mariya Aleksynska for providing data on labour market regulation for a number of countries. We also thank participants in the Workshop on Labour Market Institutions and Inequality (Geneva, February 7–8, 2013), in the Jornadas sobre Análisis de Mercado Laboral held in Buenos Aires in 25–26 September 2013 and in the 9th IZA/World Bank conference on Employment and Development and especially the editor of this volume for comments on earlier versions of this chapter.

NOTES

1. Throughout this chapter, 'temporary workers' refers to workers in temporary employment relationships and 'temporary contract' refers to the existence of a temporary contractual relationship between the worker and the ultimate user of labour (employer or client firm). Similarly, the term 'permanent worker' is used to refer to workers on open-ended contracts.
2. Labour market segmentation can occur across a number of dimensions. Typically here, the coexistence of two different types of contracts (namely fixed-term versus permanent ones) is identified as driving labour market differences between workers as well as preventing mobility from fixed-term towards permanent jobs.
3. This chapter uses the term fixed-term contracts for all contracts with an end date whether specified or implicit in the completion of a task.
4. Own calculations based on Eurofound (2012).
5. Defined as employees whose main job will terminate either after a period fixed in advance, or after a period not known in advance, but nevertheless defined by objective criteria, such as the completion of an assignment or the period of absence of an employee temporarily replaced (European Labour Force Survey – ELFS). Persons with a seasonal job, engaged by an employment agency with limited duration or with specific training contracts are included.
6. Figures respectively for EU-10, EU-25 and EU-28.
7. Careful comparative analysis based on data on temporary employment from the ELFS should take into account some limitations. For example, a large share of fixed-term contracts in German data are apprenticeship contracts; in France, about 500 000 people surveyed in the French LFS, not being civil servants (i.e., *fonctionnaires titulaires*) are classified as 'temporary' by Eurostat; this figure actually mixes a multitude of contract forms, some very 'precarious' and some not at all in practice.
8. In the Republic of Korea, self-employment still provides employment for a significant proportion of the labour force. While self-employment has fallen markedly since the turn of the century, from 37 per cent of employment in 2000 to 28 per cent in 2011, much of the new entry into dependent employment has been in the form of fixed-term contracts.
9. Temporary employment in Chile was 30 per cent of salaried employment in 2011 according to OECD data; similarly Peña (2013) reports that during the 2000s, 30 per cent of Colombian salaried workers reported having a fixed-term job. See Jaramillo (2013) for the Peruvian case.
10. Data are not strictly comparable: while data for Argentina and Brazil consider the

open-ended nature of the job, data for Peru and Chile consider the open-ended nature of the contract.

11. According to calculations based on CASEN (Ministerio de Desarrollo Social, 2009) data, in 2009 temporary employment in Chile amounted to 32 per cent of salaried employment, of which fixed-term employment and task-based contracts contributed 13 per cent each, with service contracts contributing 5 per cent. Durán (forthcoming) reports a surge in agency work from 11 per cent of employees in 2010 to 17 per cent in 2012.
12. Wage formation theories based on the hypothesis of compensating differentials predict thus that everything else controlled for and notably productivity, wages should be lower for permanent workers given greater employment stability.
13. The Mexican labour code (Ley Federal del Trabajo) grants paid vacation to workers with tenure of one year or more and to discontinuous and seasonal service providers (Arts. 76 and 77).
14. Temporary agency workers can be, however, covered by collective agreements if they apply to the agency or the temporary work sector. In Portugal, such agreements are rare, but equal pay provisions apply (Eurofound, 2009), in Germany, collective agreements cover the majority of staffing agencies, usually with less beneficial provisions than those of client companies (Spermann, 2011), in Switzerland, a cross-sectoral agreement was signed in 2011.
15. While entitlement to unemployment insurance is a statutory right in most OECD countries, the ability to draw benefits is actually subject to either long contribution periods or to a minimum earnings threshold or an hours threshold.
16. The following equation was estimated: $\log wi = \alpha + \beta 1 EDUi + \beta 2 EDUi^2 + \Upsilon 1 TENi + \Upsilon 2 TENi^2 + \mu PERMi + \varepsilon i$ where wi is monthly wage of individual *i*, *EDU* is years of schooling, *TEN* is years of tenure and *PERM* is the dummy taking the value one in case of permanent contracts and zero otherwise.
17. An example is the United Kingdom where real incomes of the top decile grew by 2.5 per cent per annum between the mid-1980s and the late 2000s, while those at the bottom grew at 0.9 per cent per annum (OECD, 2011).
18. In OECD countries, labour earnings make up over three quarters of household incomes (OECD, 2011). In fact, the increase in the incomes at the very top in the United States is not driven by capital income but by earned income, although the returns on capital are exacerbating the trend (Alvaredo et al., 2013). Labour earnings include total salaried income (wages multiplied by working time) and income from self-employment.
19. Wage inequalities are presented for full-time workers, to isolate movements in wages, which are the focus of this chapter, from changes in working hours or in the status composition of employment.
20. Argentina is a case in point: as a response to the 2001 crisis, a number of the liberal labour market reforms of the 1990s were repealed and labour market institutions strengthened, after which inequality fell considerably (see Gasparini and Cruces, 2010). The impact of the evolution of minimum wages in Brazil and other experiences in Latin America also concord with this view (Bertranou and Maurizio, 2011; Keifman and Maurizio, 2012).
21. Data for Latin American countries in Figure 6.5 represent the share of fixed-term contracts out of all employees with contracts, as data on agency work is not available for most countries (see the data Appendix below for details of sources). However, fixed-term contracts represent the great majority of temporary workers in those countries and the share of fixed-term contracts is therefore a reasonable proxy for the share of temporary employment in formal employment.
22. The Employment Rights Act, as amended in 2012, provides for a 'qualifying period of employment' of two years, during which employees are excluded from protection against unfair dismissal. Moreover, the notice period (one week) and severance pay (in the case of economic redundancy, two weeks) induce relatively small costs compared to other European countries (ILO, 2013a).

23. The average of the D9/D1 indicator for OECD countries in Figure 6.5 is 3.3; all four countries in this group have inequality above that level.
24. The association suggested by Bertola and Rogerson (1997) would imply negative correlation between the share of temporary contracts and inequality if the use of temporary contracts is more likely when employment protection is high, however.
25. Minimum wages enter the specification twice, once through their level and once through the existence of statutory minimum wages. This allows including countries that do not have minimum wages in the sample. To interpret the coefficients, consider the average of the minimum wage levels in the sample (0.35 of the mean).
26. The indicator used in the regression in Table 6.2 corresponds to the Level 3 indicator 'Notice and severance pay for no-fault dismissals' for regular contracts. The data are drawn from Aleksynska and Schindler (2011).
27. The correlation is 0.24 with the countries shown in the figure, but becomes 0.71 if Portugal and Spain are excluded.
28. The *between* component reflects the inequality that originates in differences between averages for permanent and temporary workers, while the *within* component reflects differences among (respectively) permanent and temporary workers.
29. The correlation between the two inequality indicators over all 34 countries is 0.97, so that the two scalar indicators summarize the same information.
30. Note that the 'within component' is the weighted sum of the MLD for the two groups where the weights are the proportions of each type of contract among dependent workers.
31. A statutory minimum wage is foreseen to be enforced on 1 January 2015 in Germany.
32. The analysis of the implementation of such policies in individual countries is beyond the scope of this chapter.
33. The two exceptions are Bosnia and Herzegovina and Cameroon.
34. This exception applies to pay only, not to other working conditions.

REFERENCES

Aleksynska, M. and M. Schindler (2011), 'Labor market regulations in low-middle- and high-income countries: a new panel database', *IMF Working Paper No. WP/11/154*, Washington, DC: International Monetary Fund.

Alvaredo, F., A.B. Atkinson and T. Piketty et al. (2013), 'The top 1 percent in international and historical perspective', *NBER Working Paper No. 19075*, Washington, DC: National Bureau of Economic Research.

Atkinson, A.B., T. Piketty and E. Saez (2011), 'Top incomes in the long run of history', *Journal of Economic Literature*, **49**(1), 3–71.

Beckmann, M. and D. Kuhn (2012), 'Flexibility vs. screening: the performance effects of temporary agency work strategies', *WWZ Discussion Paper No. 2012/03*, Wirtschaftswissenschaftliches Zentrum (WWZ), Basel University.

Bentolila, S., P. Cahuc and J.J. Dolado et al. (2010), 'Two-tier labor markets in the Great Recession: France vs. Spain', *IZA Discussion Papers No. 5340*, Bonn: Forschungsinstitut zur Zukunft der Arbeit (IZA).

Bertola, G. and R. Rogerson (1997), 'Institutions and labor reallocation', *European Economic Review*, **41**(6), 1147–71.

Bertranou, F. and R. Maurizio (2011), 'The role of labour market and social protection in reducing inequality and eradicating poverty in Latin America', MPRA paper, accessed 27 August 2014 at http://mpra.ub.uni-muenchen.de/39843/.

Blanchard, O. and A. Landier (2001), 'The perverse effect of partial labour market reform: fixed-term contracts in France', *The Economic Journal*, **112**(480), F214–F244.

Boeri, T. (2011), 'Institutional reforms and dualism in European labor markets', in D. Card and O. Ashenfelter (eds), *Handbook of Labor Economics, Vol 4B*, Amsterdam: Elsevier.

Booth, A., M. Francesconi and J. Frank (2002), 'Temporary jobs: stepping stones or dead ends?', *Economic Journal*, **112**(480), F189–F213.

Cahuc, P. and F. Kramarz (2004), *De la précarité à la mobilité: vers une sécurité sociale professionnelle* [From Insecurity to Mobility: Towards an Extended Social Security], Report for the French Ministry of the Economy, Finance and Employment, La Documentation Française.

Carpio, S., D. Giuliodori and G. Rucci et al. (2011), 'The effect of temporary contracts on human capital accumulation in Chile', *IDB Working Paper Series No. IDB-WP-253*, Washington, DC: Inter-American Development Bank.

Dekker, R. (2007), 'Non-standard employment and mobility in the Dutch, German and British labour market', PhD Dissertation, Tilburg University.

Departamento Administrativo Nacional de Estadística (DANE) (2012), *Gran Encuesta Integrada de Hogares, 2012* [Integrated Household Survey, 2012], DANE, accessed 29 August 2014 at www.dane.gov.co.

Doeringer, P. and M. Piore (1971), *Internal Labour Markets and Manpower Analysis*, Lexington, MA: Heath.

Dolado, J.J., S. Ortigueira and R. Stucchi (2012), 'Does dual Employment Protection affect TFP? Evidence from Spanish manufacturing firms', *CEPR Discussion Paper, No. 8763*, Washington, DC: Center for Economic and Policy Research.

Durán, G. (forthcoming), 'Does formal employment equal quality employment in Chile?', *Employment Working Paper*, Geneva: ILO Employment Sector.

Eichhorst, W. and P. Marx (2011), 'Reforming German labor market institutions: a dual path to flexibility', *Journal of European Social Policy*, **21**(1), 73–7.

Eurofound (2009), *Temporary Agency Work and Collective Bargaining in the EU*, Dublin: Eurofound.

Eurofound (2012), *Fifth European Working Conditions Survey*, Dublin: Eurofound.

Fournier, J.-M. and I. Koske (2012), 'Less income inequality and more growth – are they compatible? Part 7. The drivers of labour earnings inequality', *OECD Economics Department Working Papers, No. 930*, Paris: Organisation for Economic Co-operation and Development.

Gasparini, L. and G. Cruces (2010), 'A distribution in motion: the case of Argentina', in L.F. López-Calva and N. Lustig (eds), *Declining Inequality in Latin America: A Decade of Progress?*, Washington, DC: Brookings Institution Press.

Grubb, D., J.-K. Lee and P. Tergeist (2007), 'Addressing labour market duality in Korea', *OECD Social, Employment and Migration Working Papers No. 73*, Paris: OECD Publishing.

Hagen, T. (2003), 'Do fixed-term contracts increase the long-term employment opportunities of the unemployed?', *ZEW Discussion Paper, No. 03-49*, Mannheim: Zentrum für Europäische Wirtschaftsforschung.

Houseman, S. (1997), 'Temporary, part-time and contract employment in the United States: a report of the W.E. Upjohn Institute's Employer Survey on Staffing Policies', Kalamazoo, MI: W.E. Upjohn Institute for Employment Research.

Instituto Nacional de Estadística (INE) (2007), *Encuesta Permanente de Hogares de Propósitos Múltiples 2007* [Multiple Purpose Household Survey [2007], INE, Gobierno de Honduras.

Instituto Nacional de Estadística (INE) (2012), *Encuesta Nacional de Empleo e Ingresos – ENEI – 2012* [National Survey of Employment and Income], INE, Gobierno de Guatemala, Guatemala.

Instituto Nacional de Estadística y Censos (INEC) (2006), *Encuesta Condiciones de Vida – Quinta Ronda, Sistema Integrado de Encuestas de Hogares* [Living Conditions Survey – Fifth Round, Integrated System of Household Surveys] (SIEH), INEC, Gobierno de Ecuador.

Instituto Nacional de Estadística e Informática (INEI) (2011), *Encuesta Nacional de Hogares sobre Condiciones de Vida y Pobreza – ENAHO 2011* [National Household Survey on Living Conditions and Poverty], INEI, Gobierno de Peru.

ILO (2012), *ILO Global Wage Database 2012*, accessed 28 January 2013 at http://www.ilo.org/travail/areasofwork/WCMS_142568/lang–en/index.htm.

ILO (2013a), *Employment Protection Legislation Database – EPLex*, accessed 6 December 2013 at http://www.ilo.org/dyn/eplex/termmain.home.

ILO (2013b), *ILOSTAT Database*, accessed 6 June 2013 at http://www.ilo.org/ilostat/faces/home.

Jahn, E. and D. Pozzoli (2013), 'The pay gap of temporary agency workers – does the temp sector experience pay off?', *Labour Economics*, **24**(C), 48–57.

Jaramillo, M. (2013), 'Employment growth and segmentation in Peru, 2001–2011', *ILO Employment Working Paper No. 151*, Geneva: International Labour Organization.

Keifman, S.N. and R. Maurizio (2012), 'Changes in labour market conditions and policies: their impact on wage inequality during the last decade', *WIDER Working Paper No. WP/014*, Helsinki: UNU-WIDER.

Koeninger, W., M. Leonardi and L. Nunziata (2007), 'Labor market institutions and wage inequality', *Industrial and Labor Relations Review*, **60**(3), 340–56.

Kohl, R. (ed.) (2003), *Globalisation, Poverty and Inequality*, Development Centre Seminars, Paris: Organisation for Economic Co-operation and Development.

Lee, B. (2011), 'Labor-market characteristics and poverty dynamics of the working poor in Korea', *Labor Issues in Korea 2010*, Seoul: Korea Labor Institute.

López-Calva, L.F. and N. Lustig (eds) (2010), *Declining Inequality in Latin America: A Decade of Progress?*, Washington, DC: Brookings Institution Press.

Milkman, R., E. Reese and B. Roth (1998), 'The macrosociology of paid domestic labor', *Work and Occupations*, **25**(4), 483–510.

Ministerio de Desarrollo Social (MDS) (n.d.), *Encuesta de Caracterización Socioeconómica (CASEN)* [Socioeconomic Characterization Survey], MDS, Gobierno de Chile, accessed 27 August at http://observatorio.ministeriodesarrollosocial.gob.cl/casen_obj.php.

OECD (2002), *OECD Employment Outlook*, Paris: Organisation for Economic Co-operation and Development.

OECD (2006), *OECD Employment Outlook*, Paris: Organisation for Economic Co-operation and Development.

OECD (2011), *Divided We Stand: Why Inequality Keeps Rising*, Paris: Organisation for Economic Co-operation and Development.

OECD (2013a), *OECD Employment Outlook*, Paris: Organisation for Economic Co-operation and Development.

OECD (2013b), 'Labour force statistics in OECD countries: sources, coverage and definitions', accessed 29 August 2014 at www.oecd.org/els/emp/LFSNOTES_SOURCES.pdf, Paris: Organisation for Economic Co-operation and Development.

Pagés-Serra, C. (2012), 'La otra cara de la precariedad laboral en América Latina' [The flip side of job insecurity in Latin America], accessed 27 August 2014 at focoeconomico.org/2011/09/27/la-otra-cara-de-la-precariedad-laboral-en-america-latina.

Parreñas, R.S. (2001), *Servants of Globalization Women, Migration, and Domestic Work*, Stanford, CA: Stanford University Press.

Peña, X. (2013), 'The formal and informal sectors in Colombia: country case study on labour market segmentation', *Employment Working Paper No. 146*, Geneva: International Labour Office.

Petrylaite, D. and S. Kuoras (2012), 'Legal regulation of temporary agency employment in the European Union: from the beginning to modern interpretation', *Current Issues of Business and Law*, **7**, 233–47.

Pfeifer, C. (2012), 'Fixed-term contracts and wage revisited using linked employer-employee data', *Zeitschrift für Arbeitsmarktforschung*, **45**(2), 171–83.

Portugal, P. and J. Varejão (2009), 'Why do firms use fixed-term contracts?', *IZA Discussion Paper No. 4380*, Bonn: Forschungsinstitut zur Zukunft der Arbeit (IZA).

Reich, M., D.M. Gordon and R.C. Edwards (1973), 'A theory of labor market segmentation', *The American Economic Review*, **63**(2), 359–65.

Spermann, A. (2011), 'The new role of temporary agency work in Germany', *IZA Discussion Paper No. 6180*, Bonn: Forschungsinstitut zur Zukunft der Arbeit (IZA).

Vega Ruiz, M.L. (ed.) (2005), *La Reforma Laboral en América Latina: 15 años después* [The Labour Reform in Latin America: 15 Years Later: A Comparative Analysis], Lima: ILO Regional Office for Latin America and the Caribbean.

Venn, D. (2009), 'Legislation, collective bargaining and enforcement: updating the OECD employment protection indicators', *OECD Social, Employment and Migration Working Papers, No. 89*, Paris: Organisation for Economic Co-operation and Development.

Visser, J. (2011), *Database on Institutional Characteristics of Trade Unions, Wage Setting, State Intervention and Social Pacts, 1960–2010 (ICTWSS)*, Amsterdam Institute for Advanced Labour Studies, University of Amsterdam, May.

Wasmer, E. (2006), 'General versus specific skills in labor markets with search frictions and firing costs', *American Economic Review*, **96**(3), 811–31.

World Bank (2012), *The Labor Market Story Behind Latin America's Transformation*, Washington, DC: World Bank.

World Bank (2013), *World Development Indicators*, Washington, DC: World Bank.

APPENDIX

Data Sources

Wage inequality data used in section 6.3, including in the econometric exercises presented in Tables 6.2 and 6.3 are drawn from multiple sources. D9/D1 ratios for OECD countries are drawn from the OECD Income Distribution Database (OECD, 2013b) when available, as are data for China, India and South Africa. Data for non-OECD countries, Chile, Mexico and Turkey are drawn from the ILO Global Wage Database 2012 (ILO, 2012).

Wage inequality decompositions and kernel density estimates presented in section 6.4 are calculated by the authors on the basis of micro-data of the European Working Conditions Survey 2010 (Eurofound, 2012), made available through the UK Data Service. Access to the UK Data Service through the UK Data Archive is gratefully acknowledged. The corresponding question relates to net earnings, but only data on employees is used for the calculations shown in section 6.4.

Temporary employment prevalence data comes from multiple sources. Data for OECD countries comes from the OECD Labour Force Statistics. Definitions are homogeneous for most EU countries and the data sourced from the European Labour Force Survey. When data is presented only for EU countries, the original source (Eurostat) is cited, rather than the OECD Labour Force Statistics. Definitions for other countries vary as indicated by the dataset. Details are available in OECD (2013b).

Temporary employment prevalence data for countries not covered by the OECD Labour Force Statistics come from multiple sources. Data for Guatemala are drawn from the published results of the Encuesta Nacional del Empleo e Ingresos – ENEI – 2012 (INE, 2012). For the remaining Latin American countries, data used in section 6.3 are calculated by the authors on the basis of the following survey data: Gran Encuesta Integrada de Hogares 2012 (DANE, 2012) for Colombia; the Encuesta de Condiciones de Vida 2006 (INEC, 2006) for Ecuador; Encuesta Permanente de Hogares de Propósitos Múltiples 2007 (INE, 2007) for Honduras; the Encuesta Nacional de Hogares sobre Condiciones de Vida y Pobreza – ENAHO 2011 (INEI, 2011) for Peru. In all cases, the data represent workers in fixed-term contracts as a share of workers who have contracts and therefore do not include informal employment.

Trends shown in Figure 6.2 for Latin American countries are based on data calculated on the basis of multiple waves of household surveys: Encuesta Permanente de Hogares (EPH), for Argentina; Pesquisa Mensal de Emprego (PME) for Brazil; Encuesta de Caracterización

Socioeconómica (CASEN) for Chile and Encuesta Nacional de Hogares sobre Condiciones de Vida y Pobreza – ENAHO 2011 (INEI, 2011) for Peru.

Other Variables Used in the Multivariate Regressions Presented in Tables 6.2 and 6.3

Minimum wage data (both the existence of a statutory minimum wage and its level relative to mean wages) are drawn from the ILO Global Wage Database (ILO, 2012).

Skills in the workforce are measured by the share of the workforce with post-secondary education sourced from OECD for OECD countries and from the World Development Indicators (World Bank, 2013) for non-OECD countries (in Table 6.3).

Coverage of collective bargaining is drawn primarily from the ILO (ILO, 2013b) and completed by adjusted coverage (variable AdjCov) as found in the Database on Institutional Characteristics of Trade Unions, Wage Setting, State Intervention and Social Pacts (ICTWSS) Version 3.0 (Visser, 2011).

Wage coordination is variable WCOORD from the ICTWSS (Visser, 2011) and measures coordination in a five-point scale with higher figures representing higher levels of coordination in wage-setting.

Employment protection legislation is measured according to the OECD EPL database. The regression in Table 6.2 uses EPL for regular workers (Version 1.0). This is a summary indicator ranging from 0 (least) to 6 (most) regulated. The indicator combines data on layoff procedures, notices and severance pay and the difficulty of dismissals (see Venn, 2009 for details). Table 6.3 uses the sub-indicator for 'Notice and severance pay for no-fault dismissals' available for OECD countries in the OECD EPL database and extended by the authors for the remaining countries on the basis of data provided by Aleksynska and Schindler (2011).

7. The 'deconstruction' of part-time work

Jon C. Messenger and Nikhil Ray

7.1 INTRODUCTION TO THE ISSUE: WHAT IS PART-TIME WORK?

Part-time work has a complex relationship with inequality, as it can be both a source of discrimination and also a means for integrating certain disadvantaged groups into the labour force. While part-time work can give parents, older workers and youth job opportunities they might not otherwise enjoy, it is also associated with less favourable conditions regarding wages ('the part-time pay penalty') and other employment benefits, inferior job security, restricted social security coverage, and more limited career prospects.

Part-time work is of growing importance in many countries as a means for otherwise excluded groups to participate in the paid labour force, especially groups such as homemakers, students and retirees. Many authors (e.g., Fagan et al., 2012) highlight the link between part-time work and gender, especially as a means for women to reconcile family responsibilities with paid work, while also underlining how extended periods of part-time work can permanently relegate women to an inferior position in the professional world. In a number of developed countries (e.g., the Netherlands, Sweden), part-time work is encouraged by government policy as a means of access for women who might otherwise not have the opportunity to join the paid labour force (Anxo, 2007; Kjeldstad and Nymoen, 2012).

Part-time work is also frequently used as a means for companies to retain older, skilled workers, who might otherwise retire, or to attract and retain workers in difficult jobs, such as nursing (MacPhee and Svendsen Borra, 2012). This is especially important in view of population ageing and the demographic transition, whereby the size of the working-age population cohort in many countries will shrink relative to the size of the elderly population cohort (Beard et al., 2012). As such, many governments are seeking to encourage increased labour force participation through the use of part-time work, especially to attract under-participating groups, such as individuals with disabilities, for equity purposes and to allow workers with family responsibilities to balance paid work with their responsibilities in caring for children and the elderly.

However, as we will show, there are a number of inequalities associated with part-time work stemming from labour market institutions favouring working-age, male-dominated full-time professions. This chapter attempts to 'deconstruct', or unpack, the concept of part-time work by outlining how part-time work is structured in different countries, in order to identify the sources of these inequalities, and then briefly examine the various dimensions of inequality. Finally, it explores some potential remedies for these inequalities, with the objective of permitting part-time work to become 'normalized' along the lines of full-time work in a given country. This chapter examines the case of part-time work defined as 'shorter' (part-time) weekly hours, that is, those that are less than full-time hours according to national legislation and worker self-reporting, in the context of labour market inequality.

Definitions of Part-time Work

The International Labour Organization's Part-Time Work Convention, 1994 (No. 175) defines part-time work as those weekly working hours that are shorter than full-time; such a period is usually less than 40–48 hours per week, depending on the national legislation. Alternative (statistical) definitions describe work schedules with less than 35 hours or 30 hours a week as part-time work, while many labour surveys leave it up to the workers themselves to describe their position as 'part-time' or 'full-time'. However, certain countries, such as Japan, define part-time work as short-term contracted employees rather than employees working less than a certain number of hours per week (Mayne et al., 1996; Kalleberg, 2000). In Japan, part-time employment refers to the employment status within the firm (e.g., those employees working on a less than six-month contractual basis, irrespective of whether this contract is renewed continuously) and not to the number of hours worked (Kalleberg, 2006). Other authors (e.g., Yeraguntla and Bhat, 2005) include job sharing and 'moonlighting' – holding multiple jobs, some of which are usually worked on a part-time basis. There are also very short hours, usually defined as 15 hours a week or less, which are often referred to as 'marginal' part-time employment, such as 'mini-jobs' in Germany[1] (ILO, 2011).

Figures 7.1 and 7.2 illustrate the greater prevalence of part-time work in the high-income industrialized countries, with the Netherlands standing out as the leader in the practice, with 75.3 per cent of women and 18.8 per cent of men in part-time work. Part-time work has increased in

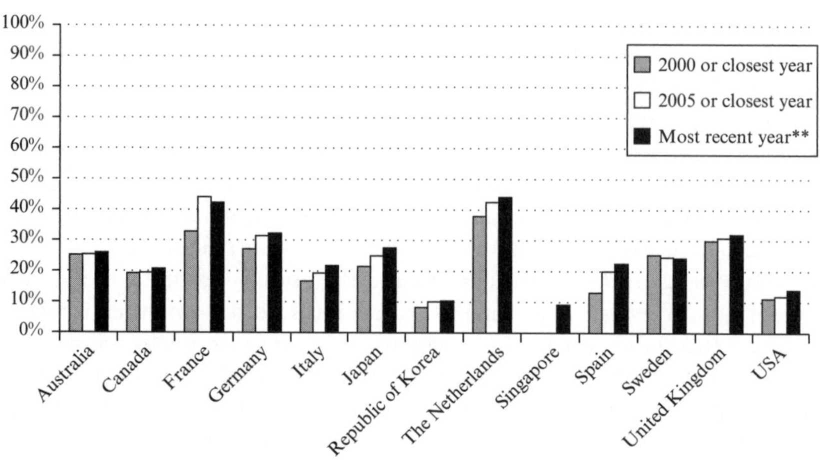

Notes:
Due to France having a legislated 35-hour workweek, Figure 7.1 overstates the percentage of French workers doing part-time work. In France, part-time workers are defined as those workers working fewer than 80% of the normal week, i.e., 28 hours a week or less.
** 2009 or 2010 (if this data was available), although for Brazil, Morocco, Peru and the Russian Federation, data from 2008 was used as this was the most recent year for which data was available when the figure was prepared.

Sources: Eurostat, ILO (2011), and the National Statistical Offices.

Figure 7.1 Percentage of persons working short hours in developed countries (total employment)

all the countries examined here, except for Singapore. With regard to the developing countries in Figure 7.2, Argentina and Peru exhibit the greatest prevalence of part-time workers among the countries shown here, although at a lower level, 30 to 35 per cent. Figure 7.3 demonstrates the greater incidence of women undertaking short-hours work, presumably due to the traditional family-responsibilities role ascribed to women by most societies (Lee, McCann and Messenger, 2007). Among the developed countries, the Netherlands is the leader in the proportion of men working short hours, while Argentina, Peru and the Philippines stand out in this regard in the group of developing countries.

An important issue is whether part-time work is voluntary or involuntary – that is, whether employees freely choose such work, rather than being effectively compelled to take it up for lack of a viable alternative. Another significant distinction is between regular and temporary part-time workers – the former are committed to part-time work for the long term, usually due to other priorities outside work or a limited skills set, while the latter

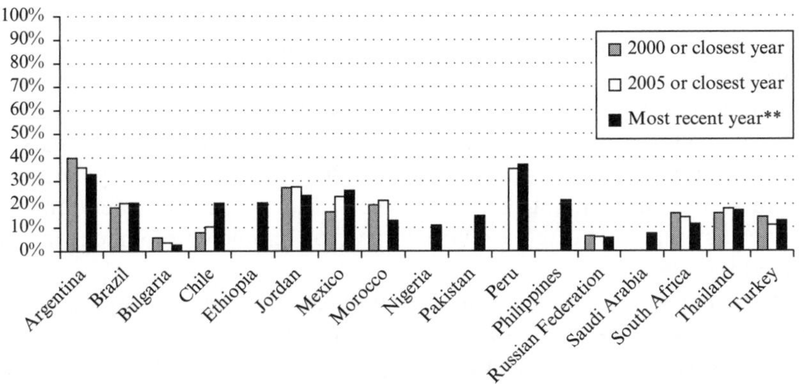

Note: **2009 or 2010 (if this data was available), although for Brazil, Morocco, Peru and the Russian Federation, data from 2008 was used as this was the most recent year for which data was available when the figure was prepared.

Sources: Eurostat, ILO (2011), and the National Statistical Offices.

Figure 7.2 Percentage of persons working short hours in developing countries (total employment)

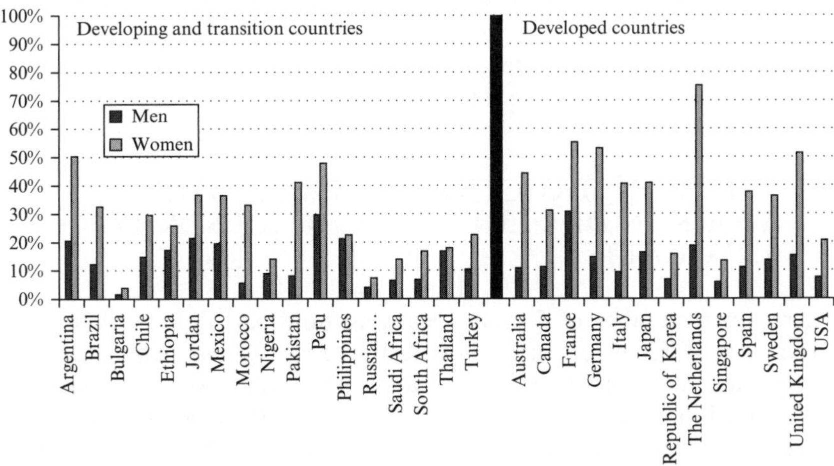

Note: Due to France having a legislated 35-hour workweek, Figure 7.3 overstates the percentage of French workers doing part-time work. In France, part-time workers are defined as those workers working fewer than 80% of the normal week, i.e., 28 hours a week or less.

Sources: Eurostat, ILO (2011), and the National Statistical Offices.

Figure 7.3 The percentage of workers working short hours by gender (2010 or most recent year)

are usually people in labour market transition, such as students or retirees. Kjeldstad and Nymoen (2012) find that voluntary short-term part-time work has the smallest gender difference in terms of labour force participation in Norway, possibly due to the fact that its short-term nature prevents it from having a major negative effect on workers' career prospects. In contrast, involuntary regular or long-term part-time employment is a major source of inequality, both relative to full-time employment and due to the fact that it is often a characteristic of female employment in low-skilled jobs (ibid.).

Part-time work also has a quality dimension, reflecting 'segmentation' in the labour market. This means that there are several labour markets present with limited crossover ability: workers in the part-time sector cannot easily switch to full-time work. A related issue is occupational segregation, a situation in which certain groups of workers are associated with certain types of occupations. For example, Sparreboom (2013) examines occupational segregation by gender in a number of European countries, finding high rates of such segregation in Estonia, Finland and Slovakia and the lowest rates in Austria, Cyprus and Greece.

While not the same as part-time work per se, 'time-related' underemployment is another issue frequently related to shorter working hours. Time-related underemployment reflects the same basic idea as involuntary part-time work: someone who would prefer to work longer hours, but cannot do so due to restricted job options. We will also briefly examine time-related underemployment in this chapter.

7.2 THE 'CONSTRUCTION' OF PART-TIME WORK IN DIFFERENT COUNTRIES: WHY INEQUALITY?

There are a number of factors regarding how part-time work is constructed in different countries that can give rise to inequality. First, in many countries, part-time work is associated with lower-paid and less-skilled positions, suggesting that segmentation in the labour market is an important source of inequality for part-time workers. Many higher-paid, higher-skilled jobs are simply unavailable on a part-time basis, and there are considerable barriers for moving from part-time to full-time jobs due to the related skills requirements. For instance, Manning and Petrongolo (2008) explain 13.4 per cent of the penalty for working part-time among women in the UK through occupational skills requirements, when compared with those women working full-time, whereas Jepsen et al. (2005) speculate that differences in human capital may account for as much as

68 per cent of the wage gap they observe between full-time and part-time workers in Belgium.

Second, as noted in the introduction, many research studies on part-time work (see Fagan et al., 2013 for a comprehensive synthesis of these studies) also distinguish between 'voluntary' and 'involuntary' part-time work. From the employer's perspective, voluntary part-time work – a part-time work arrangement chosen by the employee – is sometimes a 'retention strategy' (Tilly, 1996) by firms to retain skilled employees facing parental obligations or during an economic downturn. At other times, it reflects social attitudes and a desire to accommodate the employee (Kjeldstad and Nymoen, 2012). In contrast, involuntary part-time work often arises from the inability of workers to find work on a full-time basis due to economic difficulties, skills mismatches or institutional obstacles to full-time hiring.

An alternative view is held by some researchers such as Hakim (1997), who believe that the decision to take up part-time work is the result of the worker's choice for non-career-oriented priorities, such as more time for family responsibilities or a greater preference for leisure time. Manning and Petrongolo (2008) note that part-time status might reflect individuals' differing levels of 'commitment to the world of paid work' (p. 33), with those more committed to their careers making greater investments in their education and skills (and so are less likely to be in a part-time position). Indeed, Blau and Kahn (2012) associate the limited availability of certain 'family-friendly' policies, such as part-time work in the USA, with career advancement opportunities for women, given that, in 2010, US women tended to have higher-level positions than women in many other OECD countries. As a result, part-time positions are often directed at workers felt by management to be less 'committed' to career advancement due to other obligations or priorities, such as education (students), family (usually women with children) and retirement (older workers).

Yet, this apparent 'choice' for part-time work is often a highly constrained one: many part-time workers are obliged to opt for part-time work for some economic or social reasons, and thus have a limited ability to bargain with their employers for better working conditions (Jepsen et al., 2005; Hall and Krueger, 2012). Riley (1997) attributes this to lower union membership rates among part-time workers than among full-time ones, while Skåtun (1998) considers firms to have greater power in the individual bargaining process with part-time workers than with full-time ones. Ermisch and Wright (1991) view the limited geographical mobility of part-time workers, due to the length of their commuting time relative to their working day, as another major constraint on their bargaining power. Similarly, Badaoui et al. (2007) find many more part-time workers in South Africa's informal economy than in the formal one, and speculate as to whether this is due to a real choice or rather is the result of a lack of alternative opportunities. In Brazil, for example, 22.5 per cent of workers in the informal economy worked part-time, while only 5 per cent of formal economy employees worked part-time (de Azevedo and Fontes, 2010). Such perceptions impact upon societal and governmental attitudes towards part-time work, including the existence of anti-discrimination legislation (Visser et al., 2004).

Part-time work is more likely to result in labour market inequalities when it is designed to reduce employers' labour costs and/or to accommodate substantial fluctuations in market demand. This trend is noticeable in the retail trade sector in Canada and the USA; for example, retail consultant Burt P. Flickinger III cites the following figures on the growth of part-time work in that sector: 'Over the past two decades, many major retailers went from a quotient of 70 to 80 per cent full-time to at least 70 per cent part-time across the [retail] industry' (cited in Greenhouse, 2012). Carré and Tilly (2012) link this part-time expansion with a desire to cut costs, including reducing expenses linked to employees' social security. In addition, with the implementation of the US Patient Protection and Affordable Care Act 2010, there is a concern that some employers might push their full-time workers into part-time work under the Act's 30-hour threshold, so as to avoid paying healthcare-related benefits (Woodman, 2013). As such, this shift towards part-time work is strongly linked with inequalities relative to full-time work.

With many jobs increasingly requiring a variety of duties, some employers feel that part-time workers are not in a position to fulfil these duties adequately due to their more restricted working hours. Barzel (1973) and Gregory (2010) describe workers as having 'start-up costs' at the beginning of their shifts, with productivity increasing at a constant rate, so as to peak in the final hours of the shift; their argument is that part-time workers work fewer hours than full-time ones and so do not reach the same productivity levels at the end of their shifts. Moreover, researchers such as O'Dorchai et al. (2007) feel that part-time work is incompatible with these 'all-encompassing jobs'. Dubin (2012) and Moral Carcedo et al. (2012) also view the 'long hours work culture' prevalent in many professional firms (e.g., law firms) as reinforcing the association of part-time work with less-paid, less-skilled jobs: working normal or long hours is viewed as a signal of employee commitment to their profession and of the extent of their skill set. The inequality in part-time working conditions arises in part from these attitudes on the part of employers and many full-time employees, and precludes the 'balancing' role part-time work is intended to play between professional aspirations and the personal obligations or priorities mentioned earlier. These attitudes, in turn, contribute to part-time work being marginalized as a scheme for low-skilled, low-paid positions, in turn hindering the normalization of part-time work and its appeal to a wider section of the population.

Additionally, part-time work can also engender higher administrative costs (Rau Binder, 2010). Hiring two or more part-time employees in lieu of one full-time one imposes some additional administrative and supervision burdens on managers, including the need to match two or more compatible workers in a job-sharing arrangement. Jepsen et al. (2005) note that these administrative costs are usually associated with the worker's skills level, so higher-skilled part-time workers are likely to receive a higher wage penalty vis-à-vis their full-time counterparts – this might also explain why part-time work tends to cluster in the low-skilled professions category. Other costs may also work against part-time arrangements: for instance, Rau Binder (2010) states that a law requiring that firms with more than 19 employees provide childcare facilities discourages firms from using part-time workers in Chile, since they count as one of the 19 employees, yet work fewer hours. A related factor is that part-time workers tend to be employed by smaller firms, which are more sensitive to such costs: for example, Gallie and Zhou (2009) find that British women part-time workers are highly concentrated in firms with less than 24 employees. These costs, along with the potential additional social security contributions of employing two or more part-time workers, make firms reluctant to hire part-time workers on a pro-rata salary basis equivalent to the salary of full-time workers. This further contributes to the concentration of part-time work in the lower-paid spectrum of jobs, usually with lower skills requirements that cannot command a pro-rata wage that is comparable to that of full-time work.

Due to its strong association with female-dominated occupations, part-time work is potentially both a means for and an obstacle to increased female participation in the workforce. This stems from part-time work being a way to reconcile professional career aspirations with family obligations (e.g., care for children or elderly parents), whose care responsibilities frequently fall upon women – the so-called 'double shift' of paid work and unpaid family care work (see e.g., Fagan et al., 2013). Many women are reluctant to withdraw from the labour force completely owing to the need for an additional income, but the burden of unpaid care work and the limited availability of childcare and elder care services frequently restricts their ability to pursue full-time paid work (see, e.g., Chapter 12 by Gammage and Chapter 11 by Martínez Franzoni and Sánchez-Ancochea, in this volume). For instance, an estimated 7 million children accompanied their parents to building sites in India (ILO, 2004). The demographic transition from an extended to a nuclear family structure underway in many developing countries will exacerbate this shortage of care facilities even more.

One result of involuntary part-time work is time-related underemployment: workers who would prefer to work more hours to earn more, yet cannot obtain them. Time-related underemployment has been a growing problem in many developed countries since the onset of the global economic crisis in 2008. For instance, according to the findings from the 2010 Labour Force Survey in Spain, 56.2 per cent of men and 49.8 per cent of women are working part-time due to an inability to find a full-time job (see e.g., Fagan et al., 2013). In Norway, time-related underemployment appears to be prevalent in the health services sector, with a 2011 study claiming that one-sixth of all nurses would prefer to work longer hours (Kristiansen, 2011). Time-related underemployment also continues to be a problem in developing countries, for instance in Indonesia, where part-time work accounted for 19.4 per cent of the employed population in August 2012 (Allen, 2013). According to International Labour Organization (ILO) figures, 11.5 per cent of the Indonesian employed population was considered underemployed in August 2011, mainly women workers and workers in rural areas (ibid.). In the Philippines, approximately 20 per cent of the labour force (i.e., some 8 million workers) was underemployed in 2013 according to the National Statistics Office figures (ADB, 2013, p. 242). Such limitations in the availability of full-time jobs exacerbate job precariousness and make it difficult for these part-time workers to move into full-time employment at a later stage.

7.3 THE DIMENSIONS OF INEQUALITY IN PART-TIME WORK

Inequality in part-time work manifests itself in both the material and social conditions of employment. The material conditions relate to the reduced pro-rata wage rate (the 'part-time pay penalty'), diminished access to social security and benefits, fewer training and career advancement opportunities and unpredictable work schedules in certain occupations. The social conditions encompass the gender dimension of part-time work, as well as a lack of integration with full-timers in the workplace. The difficulty in moving from part-time to full-time work reflects the so-called 'part-time trap' and helps to sustain and reinforce the above-mentioned dimensions of inequality. Perhaps the most explicit form of inequality in part-time work is the lower hourly wage rate relative to a full-time worker in a comparable situation. Table 7.1 lists the average part-time wage

Table 7.1 Part-time wage penalty for selected countries

Country	Part-time Hourly Wage Penalty (%)	Data Year	Source and Year of Study
Australia	7*, 21**	2002	Rodgers (2004)
Belgium (women)	−2*	2009	Matteazzi et al. (2013)
Belgium (men)	24**	1995	O'Dorchai et al. (2007)
Belgium	13–14[a]	1995	Jepsen et al. (2005)
Canada (women)	11.7*	1994	Bardasi and Gornick (2007)
Chile	−61[b]	2006	Rau Binder (2010)
Denmark (men)	28**	1995	O'Dorchai et al. (2007)
Finland (women)	9.5*	2009	Matteazzi et al. (2013)
France (women)	11*	2009	Matteazzi et al. (2013)
Germany (women)	8.4*	2000	Bardasi and Gornick (2007)
Ireland (men)	149	1995	O'Dorchai et al. (2007)
Italy (women)	22.1*	1995	Bardasi and Gornick (2007)
Italy (men)	28*	1995	O'Dorchai et al. (2007)
Netherlands (women)	5*	2009	Matteazzi et al. (2013)
Norway	11	2000	Hardoy and Schøne (2004)
Poland (women)	15*	2009	Matteazzi et al. (2013)
South Africa (women)	7*	2003	Posel and Muller (2007)
Spain (women)	31*	2009	Matteazzi et al. (2013)
Spain (men)	16**	1995	O'Dorchai et al. (2007)
Sweden (women)	−1.1*	1995	Bardasi and Gornick (2007)
UK (women)	22–26*[c]	2001	Manning and Petrongolo (2008)
UK (men)	67**	1995	O'Dorchai et al. (2007)
US	19.7*, 37.1**	2002	Hirsch (2005)
US (women)	21.7*	1994	Bardasi and Gornick (2007)

Notes:
*Women; **men.
a. The 14% figure is the wage difference including bonus pay, while the 13% excludes bonus pay.
b. For salaried employees in a selected (non-representative) sample of Chilean private firms only.
c. The 22% figure is based Labour Force Survey figure, while the 26% comes from the National Earnings Survey.

penalty as a percentage of the average full-time wage for selected countries, along with the source of each figure.

Most of these studies find that the part-time pay penalty can be largely explained by differences in education level and labour market segmentation, with part-time jobs being at the lower end of the skills and prestige spectrum (e.g., Rodgers, 2004; Hirsch, 2005; Posel and Muller, 2007). Nonetheless, certain authors found part of the penalty to be unattributed: for instance, Manning and Petrongolo (2008) calculate that occupational skills requirements explain 13.4 per cent of the part-time wage penalty for women part-time workers in the UK on the basis of 2001 data, leaving 3–10 per cent as unexplained. Fernández Kranz and Rodríguez-Planas (2009) caution that the part-time wage penalty might be biased upwards due to firms systematically under-reporting the hours worked by part-time employees. In their study of part-time wages and productivity in Belgium, Garnero et al. (2014) found that 'long hours' part-time workers (defined as 30–35 hours a week) were more productive than both 'short hours' part-time workers (defined as less than 25 hours a week) and full-time workers (defined as more than 35 hours a week); yet, these long hours' part-time workers were probably underpaid relative to their productivity per hour.

On the other hand, in those cases where there is actually a part-time wage *premium* relative to the full-time wage, this might well reflect increased financial compensation for reduced benefits and wage security – as in the case of Australia, where part-time workers typically receive higher hourly wages than similar full-time workers due to the phenomenon of 'casual loading'[2] (Campbell et al., 2009). While not only applicable to part-time workers, such 'casual loading' applies to work that is temporary, has irregular hours and is not guaranteed to be ongoing (ACTU, 2013). Disadvantages in terms of contractual arrangements and social security coverage may explain the higher hourly wage of part-time workers in certain situations – for example, in the case of low-income professions, Posel and Muller (2007) find that part-time workers in South Africa command a higher premium to compensate for their lack of security and the reduced benefits vis-à-vis full-time workers.

Part-time workers are also frequently subject to contractual penalties that hinder their career advancement prospects and their ability to move into and out of part-time work. One major concern is their access to and level of social benefits, such as health insurance, pension schemes and unemployment benefits: part-time contracts often exclude these aspects of the social safety net in part or in whole. This is due primarily to the minimum threshold requirements imposed on workers in terms of hours worked, earnings and contributions, in order to receive social security benefits such as unemployment insurance. As these requirements are typically calculated on a full-time work basis, they hinder part-time workers' ability to meet the eligibility criteria. Klammer and Keuzenkamp et al. (2005) identify the strong equivalence principle underlying many pension system designs as a key problem: they are designed with full-time workers in mind, and so the minimum eligibility thresholds in terms of hours worked and obligatory social security contributions are very high for part-time workers. This makes it harder for part-time workers to qualify for such benefits later on. Moreover, part-time workers often forgo a large portion of their future pensions by not opting for full-time work, leaving them more vulnerable to poverty later in their lives. In addition, the low contractual and termination costs render part-time positions more vulnerable in the labour market, especially during an economic downturn or during firm restructuring (Saito, 2009). This combination of the precariousness of certain part-time positions and the lower pro-rata wage rate disadvantages part-time workers considerably and may even compel them to attempt to work longer work hours in order to earn a sufficiently large income to make ends meet, thus negating any work–life balance advantages (Fagan et al., 2013).

In addition, part-time working conditions are often less favourable than those in full-time employment, particularly in matters relating to occupational health and safety, paid sick leave and paid annual leave. Access to non-wage benefits, such as maternity protection, pension benefits and the various work-related insurance schemes are frequently absent entirely; health insurance is also an issue, notably in the USA (Kalleberg, 2006). A desire to cut down on social security expenses has been cited as a driving factor in certain firms' decisions to rely on part-time workers rather than full-time ones (see e.g., Greenhouse, 2012). In their study of working conditions in the retail sector in Canada, Mexico and the USA, Carré and Tilly (2012) find that American and Canadian store managers often resort to using part-time positions to reduce wage costs and to avoid social-security contributions.

Another significant consequence of working part-time is that such workers are often not selected for training opportunities, which limits both their ability to move into full-time work and their career advancement possibilities. Managers are reluctant to invest in part-time employees, whom they may perceive as contributing less to their firms, irrespective of the actual importance of their output. In addition, part-time workers' non-professional obligations can reduce their interest in pursuing such options. For example, Booth et al. (2002) found that non-regular workers, including part-time workers, are less proactive about skills development opportunities than regular staff in the UK. Russo and Hassink (2005) speak of career 'scarring' through missed promotional opportunities – this affects younger workers less as they start their careers, but can become a significant problem as their careers progress. Moreover, opting for part-time work frequently results in 'occupational downgrading' (Connolly and Gregory, 2008), in which workers' skills are underutilized and might even stagnate. In cases of involuntary part-time work, missing out on such training possibilities and not being able to develop their skill sets further often condemns workers to the 'part-time trap' and impedes their ability to advance within a firm or to specialize in a profession.

The unpredictability of certain work schedules is another dimension of inequality in part-time work. Many authors (e.g., Wallace, 2003) distinguish between fixed hours and 'employer-led' – as opposed to 'employee-led' – working time flexibility in the design of these work schedules. Fixed hours are rigid, yet offer a regularity that is often valued by part-time workers with domestic responsibilities, insofar as they can plan when they might need someone to look after their children or elderly relatives. With 'employer-led' working time flexibility, part-time workers may need to be available for work at any time depending on the employer's needs, which can lead to unpredictable work schedules and the attendant problems with planning domestic responsibilities and other activities. In sectors such as retail trade, store managers cannot always easily predict when customer traffic will be highest, and so have to resort to ad-hoc part-time schedules that can stretch much longer – frequently up to 40 hours – at short notice. Such unpredictability can impede part-time workers' ability to hold other part-time jobs, fulfil family obligations or attend college (ibid.). In contrast, 'employee-led' working time flexibility promises part-time workers 'time sovereignty' (i.e., a degree of choice or influence regarding their work schedules), but this can be impractical from a management perspective in all but larger enterprises and government institutions.

From a gender perspective, part-time work has been seen as a means to allow women to reconcile unpaid domestic work with their need to find paid employment. However, this situation can relegate women permanently to assuming the bulk of the domestic responsibilities, while curtailing their lifetime earnings and career potentials (see e.g., Fagan et al., 2013). In the majority of countries, men have been slow to assume a greater share of the domestic duties, leaving such tasks mostly up to women to handle, even if these women are also in paid employment (Gregory and Milner, 2009). Furthermore, there has been an increase in the number of single-parent (usually single mother) households, in which earnings from part-time work may be inadequate to meet household expenses (Fagan et al., 2012). The other consequence of the association of part-time work with women is gender segregation in the labour force (see e.g., Fagan et al., 2012), whereby certain occupations tend to become female-dominated. Sparreboom (2013) notes that employment policies directed at women may have had the unintended effect of reinforcing occupational segregation along gender lines. This situation can lead to a 'feminization' of these occupations and relegate women workers to less skilled and/or less prestigious jobs, including part-time positions. More often than not, these jobs are remunerated for less on a pro-rata basis than their male-dominated equivalents in terms of skill sets, leading to a 'gender gap' in wages as well (Matteazzi et al., 2013). For instance, teaching, nursing and secretarial work all exhibit a high degree of 'feminization', with all of the attendant risks of pay penalties and career limitations, linked with the higher perceived likelihood of women having family or other obligations outside of the workplace. Many authors highlight that such policies risk reinforcing the concentration – often called 'segregation' (see above) – of female employment in certain occupations, usually low-skilled ones, on a part-time basis (Uno, 1993; Fagan et al., 2012), thereby perpetuating existing inequalities between the sexes in terms of occupations and pro-rata remuneration, as well as in the distribution of domestic duties.

Another important dimension of inequality linked to part-time work is the poorer integration of part-time workers with their colleagues, and the resulting lack of consultation with them regarding important organizational planning decisions (Fagan et al., 2013). Part-time workers are usually less visible and have a lower profile in the firm hierarchy, so full-time staff and management tend to interact with them less often. In the worst cases, the existence of part-time possibilities can lead to resentment or jealousy between workers and weaken team morale. For similar reasons, part-time workers may even be seen as 'threats' by unionized full-time workers in certain sectors (Buckley, 1993), especially if they are not subject to the same employment standards, social security or pension regimes, or do not receive the same wage per unit of time. Conversely, unions can be reluctant to admit part-time workers for these reasons, which can further contribute to the precariousness of their working conditions (ibid.). The low profile of part-time work often attracts mainly unskilled workers, making it harder for part-time work to be accepted as a mainstream alternative for skilled workers. In fact, Hermosilla and Ortega (2003) find the inadequate skills set of the workers to be a significant hindrance to European metallurgy firms adopting more flexible working time arrangements, including part-time work. All this contributes further to a poorer visibility of part-time workers, reinforcing the likelihood that they will not be consulted on important firm decisions and will be overlooked for promotions (Lyonette et al., 2010). In jobs requiring 'face time', some studies suggest that the presence of workers in the evening tends to be more highly valued than the presence of those in the morning (Lewis and Humbert, 2010); yet, the morning shift is precisely the one part-time workers find most compatible with family care responsibilities.

The 'part-time trap' (Tilly, 1996), whereby part-time workers find themselves permanently unable to move into full-time positions, is a final major source of inequality. The decision to shift to a part-time work arrangement often limits career advancement opportunities and promotional possibilities; that is, it has a 'scarring effect' on their future career prospects (Francesconi and Gosling, 2005; Fagan et al., 2013). This is a significant issue for mothers (and fathers) returning from maternity leave or parental leave and seeking to reintegrate into their professional lives at a pace that is compatible with their new family responsibilities. In their study of part-time working women in the UK, Manning and Petrongolo (2008) highlight the problem of limited job mobility between part-time work and full-time work. Plantenga and Remery (2009) identify the 'marginal' part-time work phenomenon (e.g., 'mini-jobs' in Germany) – those jobs typically requiring less than 15 hours of work a week – as 'dead-end traps' with little prospect of career advancement or mobility. Likewise, in their study of the wage penalty in South Africa's informal economy, Badaoui et al. (2007) find that part-time status, along with a lower educational level, makes it less likely for a worker to move from the informal to the formal economy, and thereby benefit from social security coverage and reduced precariousness of employment. As a result of these factors, those workers opting for part-time work often find it difficult to resume their professional career paths due to barriers to moving back into full-time work.

7.4 WHAT CAN BE DONE? IMPROVING THE QUALITY OF PART-TIME WORK ARRANGEMENTS

In order to redress the inequalities mentioned above, policy-makers have a number of instruments at their disposal. Notably, the principle of equal treatment of part-time workers on a pro-rata wages and benefits basis is enshrined in the ILO Part-Time Work Convention, 1994 (No. 175) and in various national and supra-national laws, such as the EU Part-time Work Directive (Fagan et al., 2013). In fact, a number of national laws draw their inspiration from this ILO Convention, and governments are increasingly keen to establish viable part-time work schemes to encourage greater participation of women and older workers in the workforce. Fagan et al. (2013) see national minimum wage legislation as a potential device to create a pro-rata wage-floor and bring part-time and mini-jobs into the mainstream by reducing the systematic underpayment of wages in these positions. For instance, in 2003, the UK's Low Pay Commission reported that 53 per cent of the women beneficiaries of the national minimum wage were part-time workers, compared with 17 per cent of full-time workers. Posel and Muller (2007) posit that there is an unofficial 'wage floor' in South Africa beneath which part-time wages cannot fall: this is one interpretation of the part-time wage premium they find in their study. Nevertheless, minimum wage legislation mainly addresses those part-time work problems linked to lower-skilled occupations, that is, where the wage is close to a wage floor; it does not necessarily help with the problems linked with part-time positions requiring higher skill levels.

Effective equal treatment legislation is an important instrument for addressing the inequalities stemming from part-time work. In the Dutch case, the 1996 Equal Treatment (Working Hours) Act prohibits differences in treatment on the basis of the number of hours worked for many aspects of the employment relationship (see e.g., Visser et al., 2004; Bovenberg et al., 2008; Sloan Centre, 2009), with the pro-rata equivalence principle to full-time work being strictly applied to part-time work (Visser et al., 2004). Calculating social benefit contributions on a pro-rata basis can also help address some of the difficulties faced by part-time workers. In fact, the EU Part-Time Work Directive envisages equal access to pro-rata benefits, on a basis comparable to those enjoyed by full-time employees in the same firm. Other laws have also helped: Manning and Petrongolo (2008) note that the EU Working Time Directive, which prescribes a minimum of four weeks' paid vacation per annum, has reduced the gap in holiday entitlements between part-time and full-time workers in the United Kingdom.

Visser et al. (2004) associate the rise of part-time work in the Netherlands with the delayed, large-scale entry of women into the labour force, with government policy adapting to the situation. From the demand-side perspective, 'employers in services discovered the cheap and educated labour reservoir of married women' (Visser et al., 2004, p. 5), since married women, who had traditionally assumed most of the domestic duties in Dutch households, made up the bulk of the new part-time workers. Visser et al. (2004) observe that employers viewed part-time work as an extra pool of labour and a potential 'optimizing' tool, whereby they might match working hours and business hours, while limiting overtime costs. At the same time the Dutch government also saw part-time work as a means to increase women's participation rate in the labour force. Importantly, Visser et al. (2004) remark that the Netherlands benefitted from a 'latecomers' advantage' and that in other countries, such as Belgium or France, part-time work for women might be seen as a 'retrograde step', since they have a longer tradition of married women doing full-time paid work (p. 20). As such, changes in societal attitudes regarding the prestige of part-time work and gender roles in the household and in society at large will be crucial if part-time work is to be effective. Visser et al. (2004) believe that the adoption of 'the possibility to combine work with care' (p. 12) as a goal of Dutch labour law has been a major shift towards the strengthening of part-time workers' legal position. Equally significant, the Dutch trade unions switched from initially seeing part-time employment as weakening their attempts to secure a reduced workweek, to seeing it as a means to obtain that end (ibid.). The success of the Netherlands in promoting relatively good quality part-time work can be gauged by the prevalence of such work: in 2012, 49.8 per cent of the Dutch labour force worked part-time, compared to 19.9 per cent in the EU-28 member states as a whole (Eurostat, 2013). Of these figures, only 9.1 per cent of part-time workers in the Netherlands were working part-time involuntarily, compared with 27.6 per cent of workers in the EU-28 member states (ibid.)

Another major policy for promoting the reform of part-time work is to strengthen workers' rights to request changes in their working hours, and especially to be able to move back from part-time to full-time hours after having moved from full-time to part-time – the so-called 'reversibility' issue. This policy would ease the reinsertion of parents returning from maternity and parental leave into the paid labour force and help to avoid the 'part-time trap' in general. For example, France, Germany, the Netherlands and Poland have such a right of 'reversion to full-time' enshrined in their national laws for employees who have moved from full-time to part-time hours within the same enterprise, whereas Australia and New Zealand leave such an option up to the negotiated agreement between the employee making the request and their employer (OECD, 2011). In fact, Fouarge and Muffels (2009) underline the institutional support for childcare and better quality part-time work as important factors in reducing the 'scarring effect' of part-time work in Germany and the Netherlands, since these policies facilitate the transition from part-time to full-time work. The other major Dutch law applicable to part-time work is the 2000 Adjustment of Working Hours Act, which allows employees under certain conditions to change to their working time arrangements with their current employer. Visser et al. (2004) see this legislation as a means to encourage men to opt for part-time work, should they desire it; this law is also important for promoting gender equality insofar as men being able to negotiate shorter hours with their supervisors will strengthen the ability of women to negotiate a fairer sharing of domestic responsibilities in the household (ibid.).

In contrast, while Japan amended its ChildCare and Family Care Leave Act in 2009 to strengthen the rights of workers caring for young children or elderly relatives to request shorter hours (MHLW, 2012), there is no provision for a right of reversion to full-time hours afterwards. Similarly, Manning and Petrongolo (2008) observe that, while UK legislation gives workers with family obligations – recently expanded to cover all employees – the right to request flexible working arrangements (usually part-time work), it also gives employers many grounds for denying these requests. Intimately linked with any such institutional change would be the wider recognition of the skills part-time workers have to offer, including encouraging them to be provided with training opportunities and avoiding long-term occupational downgrading. Hermosilla and Ortega (2003) point out that EU policy focuses on flexibility in terms of work organization and training in order to create a more flexible labour market, in which job matching involves not only firms identifying the preferred skill sets for their potential employees, but also the worker's preferred working time arrangement, including part-time work.

Governments and firms should ideally also establish policies to expand part-time work arrangements into higher-skilled and higher-paid occupations. Even with regard to the case of the Netherlands, Bovenberg et al. (2008) and Sparreboom (2013) note that Dutch women in part-time work often face difficulties in obtaining top management and institutional positions, while continuing to face a gender-related gap vis-à-vis men. However, such an expansion of part-time work is already taking place in certain sectors, such as health services, where the shortage in nursing staff requires working time arrangements to be more compatible with family lives in order to improve recruitment; it could possibly be expanded into more technical positions in the health sector and other sectors as well. For example, the Brazilian government is examining proposals to allow doctors in the state-run Programa Saúde da Família to work 20–30 hours a week, in order to attract more physicians (Agência Estado, 2011). Moreover, part-time work can also be seen as a potential strategy for reducing absenteeism (Possenriede, 2012), and for promoting 'active ageing' (Beard et al., 2012; MacPhee and Svendsen Borra, 2012); that is, it can be used as a means to retain highly skilled staff nearing retirement in order to make up for shortages in personnel and to allow older workers to reduce their professional duties gradually.

By extension, policies should also be put into place to actively promote the use of part-time arrangements by men as well as women, especially to allow men to assume a greater share of the domestic duties. The Dutch experience has demonstrated that facilitating part-time work schemes encourages not only women, but also men, to work part-time, and that this practice seems well on the way to 'normalizing' part-time work as part of the accepted working time arrangements available to enterprises and workers in that country (see, e.g., Yerkes and Visser, 2006). As fathering appears to be an important component in male self-esteem (see, e.g., Fagan et al., 2012), one approach might be to appeal to fatherly duties in the home, in order to make male part-time work more socially acceptable – especially in more conservative societies. With increasing demands for varied skills in the workplace, allowing either one of two parents to work part-time might be most optimal for a firm's performance, let alone for the household's distribution of domestic tasks.

7.5 CONCLUSION: TOWARDS THE 'NORMALIZATION' OF PART-TIME WORK

Part-time work engenders many inequalities relative to full-time work, most notably in terms of the hourly wage and non-wage benefits, access to social security, job quality and career advancement opportunities. The disproportionate impact of these disadvantages on women, who assume the bulk of the family care responsibilities in most countries, is even more striking, given that part-time work is often viewed as a means to allow women with such obligations to participate in the paid labour force. Nevertheless, improvements in legal instruments and the quality of job opportunities in part-time work stand to reduce these inequalities vis-à-vis full-time employment; workers, households, enterprises and society all stand to gain from such improvements. Furthermore, a change in social attitudes regarding the distribution of domestic responsibilities should both improve the career prospects of women and allow them to engage in better-quality part-time work. Ultimately, part-time work should become 'normalized', as households can more easily select which parent should work full-time or part-time, and firms and society as a whole can benefit from the wider array of skills offered by such improved flexibility.

NOTES

1. 'Mini-jobs' are defined as jobs that pay under EUR400 per week (Plantenga and Remery, 2009).
2. The term 'casual loading' refers to the practice of providing part-time workers, most of whom are so-called 'casual workers' without employment contracts, with a higher hourly wage to compensate them for the fact that they do not receive non-wage benefits, such as paid annual leave.

REFERENCES

ACTU (2013), *Factsheets: Casual Workers*, Melbourne: Australian Council of Trade Unions, accessed 12 November 2013 at http://www.actu.org.au/HelpDesk/YourRightsfactsheets/CasualWorkers.aspx.

ADB (2013), *Asian Development Outlook 2013: Asia's Energy Challenge*, Mandaluyong City, Philippines: Asian Development Bank.

Agência Estado (2011), 'Saúde da família reduz jornada de trabalho para não perder medicos' [Family Health Programme reduces the working day in order not to lose doctors], accessed 8 October 2012 at http://ultimosegundo.ig.com.br/brasil/saude+da+familia+reduz+jornada+de+trabalho+para+nao+perder+medicos/n1597156515570.html.

Allen, E. (2013), *Working Time in Indonesia: Recent Trends and Developments*, Jakarta: ILO Country Office for Indonesia and Timor-Leste.

Anxo, D. (2007), 'Working time patterns among industrialized countries: a household perspective', in J.C. Messenger (ed.), *Working Time and Workers' Preferences in Industrialized Countries: Finding the Balance*, Geneva: International Labour Office.

Badaoui, E., E. Strobl and F. Walsh (2007), *Is There an Informal Economy Wage Penalty? Evidence from South Africa, Discussion Paper No. 3151*, Bonn: Forschungsinstitut zur Zukunft der Arbeit (IZA).

Bardasi, E. and J.C. Gornick (2007), 'Women's part-time wage penalties across countries', *Luxembourg Income Study Working Paper Series No. 467*, Luxembourg: Luxembourg Income Study.

Barzel, Y. (1973), 'The determination of daily hours and wages', *Quarterly Journal of Economics*, **87**(2), 220–38.

Beard, J.R., S. Biggs and D.E. Bloom et al. (eds) (2012), *Global Population Ageing: Peril or Promise*, Geneva: World Economic Forum.

Blau, F.D. and L.M. Kahn (2012), 'Female labor supply: why is the US falling behind?', *Discussion Paper No. 7140*, Bonn: Forschungsinstitut zur Zukunft der Arbeit (IZA).

Booth, A., M. Francesconi and J. Frank (2002), 'Temporary jobs: stepping stones or dead ends?', *Economic Journal*, **112**(480), 189–213.

Bovenberg, L., T. Wilthagen and S. Bekker (2008), 'Flexicurity: lessons and proposals from the Netherlands', *Journal for Institutional Comparisons*, **6**(4), 9–14.

Buckley, S. (1993), 'Altered states: the body politics of "being-woman"', in A. Gordon (ed.), *Postwar Japan as History*, Berkeley, CA: University of California Press.

Campbell, I., G. Whitehouse and J. Baxter (2009), 'Australia: casual employment, part-time employment and the resilience of the male-breadwinner model', in L.F. Vosko, M. Macdonald and I. Campbell (eds), *Gender and the Contours of Precarious Employment*, Abingdon, UK: Routledge, pp. 60–75.

Carré, F. and C. Tilly (2012), 'Part-time and short hours in retail in the United States, Canada, and Mexico: how institutions matter', *Employment Research*, **19**(4), 4–6.

Connolly, S. and M. Gregory (2008), 'Moving down: women's part-time work and occupational change in Britain 1991–2001', *The Economic Journal*, **118**(526), 52–76.

de Azevedo, L. and A. Fontes (2010), 'Brazil: mind the gap – employee perspectives',

Boston, MA: Sloan Center on Aging and Work, Boston College, accessed 10 May 2013 at http://www.bc.edu/content/dam/files/research_sites/agingand-work/pdf/publications/MTG_Brazil_Employee.pdf.

Dubin, K.A. (2012), 'Adjusting the law: the role of beliefs in firms' responses to regulations', *Politics & Society*, **40**(3), 389–424.

Ermisch, J.F. and R.E. Wright (1991), 'Wage offers and full-time and part-time employment by British women', *Journal of Human Resources*, **25**(1), 111–33.

Eurostat (2013), 'Persons employed part-time – total', Luxembourg: Eurostat, accessed 8 November 2013 at http://epp.eurostat.ec.europa.eu/tgm/table.do?tab=table&plugin=1&language=en&pcode=tps00159.

Fagan, C., C. Lyonette, M. Smith and A. Saldaña-Tejeda (2012), 'The influence of working time arrangements on work–life 'integration' or 'balance': a review of the international evidence', *Conditions of Work and Employment Series No. 32*, Geneva: International Labour Office.

Fagan, C., H. Norman and M. Smith et al. (2013), 'In search of good quality part-time employment', *Conditions of Work and Employment Series No. 43*, Geneva: Conditions of Work and Equality Unit, International Labour Organization.

Fernández Kranz, D. and N. Rodríguez-Planas (2009), 'The part-time pay penalty in a segmented labour market', *Discussion Paper No. 4342*, Bonn: Forschungsinstitut zur Zukunft der Arbeit (IZA).

Fouarge, D. and R. Muffels (2009), 'Working part-time in the British, German and Dutch labour market: scarring for the wage career?', *Schmollers Jahrbuch: Journal of Applied Social Science Studies/Zeitschrift für Wirtschafts- und Sozialwissenschaften*, **129**(2), 217–26.

Francesconi, M. and A. Gosling (2005), 'Career paths of part-time workers', *Working Paper Series No. 19*, Manchester, UK: Equal Opportunities Commission.

Gallie, D. and Y. Zhou (2009), 'Part-time work in Britain 1992–2006: from periphery to core?', *SKOPE Research Paper No. 83*, Centre on Skills, Knowledge and Organisational Performance, Universities of Cardiff and Oxford.

Garnero, A., S. Kampelmann and F. Rycx (2014), 'Part-time work, wages and productivity: evidence from Belgian matched panel data', *Industrial and Labor Relations Review*, **67**(3), 926–54.

Greenhouse, S. (2012), 'A part-time life, as hours shrink and shift', *The New York Times*, accessed 29 October 2012 at http://www.nytimes.com/2012/10/28/business/a-part-time-life-as-hours-shrink-and-shift-for-american-workers.html?pagewanted=all&_r=0.

Gregory, A. and S. Milner (2009), 'Trade unions and work–life balance: changing times in France and the UK?', *British Journal of Industrial Relations*, **47**(1), 122–46.

Gregory, M. (2010), 'Assessing unequal treatment: gender and pay', in L. Bond, F. McGinnity and H. Russell (eds), *Making Equality Count: Irish and International Research Measuring Equality and Discrimination*, Dublin: The Liffey Press.

Hakim, C. (1997), 'A sociological perspective on part-time work', in H.-P. Blossfeld and C. Hakim (eds), *Between Equalization and Marginalization: Women Working Part-time in Europe and the United States of America*, Oxford: Oxford University Press.

Hall, R.E. and A.B. Krueger (2012), 'Evidence on the incidence of wage posting, wage bargaining, and on-the-job search', *American Economic Journal: Macroeconomics*, **4**(4), 56–67.

Hardoy, I. and P. Schøne (2004), 'The part-time wage gap: how large is it really?', mimeo, Oslo; Institute for Social Research.

Hermosilla, A.P. and N. Ortega (2003), 'Training and flexible work organisation in the European metal industry – Spain, France, Italy and Portugal', *European Journal of Vocational Training*, **28**, Thessaloniki: European Centre for the Development of Vocational Training.

Hirsch, B.T. (2005), 'Why do part-time workers earn less? The role of worker and job skills', *Industrial and Labor Relations Review*, **58**(4), 525–51.

ILO (2004), 'Work and family responsibilities: what are the problems?', *Information Sheet No. WF-1*, Geneva: International Labour Office.

ILO (2011), *Working Time in the Twenty-first Century: Report for Discussion at the Tripartite Meeting of Experts on Working Time Arrangements*, Geneva: International Labour Office.

Jepsen, M., S. O'Dorchai and R. Plasman et al. (2005), 'The wage penalty induced by part-time work: the case of Belgium', *Brussels Economic Review/Cahiers Economiques de Bruxelles*, **48**(1/2), 73–94.

Kalleberg A. (2000), 'Nonstandard employment relations: part-time, temporary and contract work', *Annual Review of Sociology*, **26**, 341–65.

Kalleberg, A. (2006), 'Non-standard employment relations and labour market inequality: cross-national patterns', in G. Therborn (ed.), *Inequalities of the World*, London: Verso, pp. 136–61.

Kjeldstad, R. and E.H. Nymoen (2012), 'Part-time work and gender: worker versus job explanations', *International Labour Review*, **151**(1–2), 85–107.

Klammer, U. and S. Keuzenkamp in collaboration with I. Cebrián et al. (2005), *Working Time Options Over the Life Course: Changing Social Security Structures*, Dublin: Eurofound.

Kristiansen, N. (2013), 'What research says about part-time work', *ScienceNordic*, accessed 17 November 2013 at http://sciencenordic.com/what-research-says-about-part-time-work.

Lee S., D. McCann and J.C. Messenger (2007), *Working Time Around the World: Trends in Working Hours, Laws and Policies in a Global Comparative Perspective*, London/Geneva: Routledge/International Labour Office.

Lewis, S. and L. Humbert (2010), 'Discourse or reality? "Work–life balance", flexible working policies and the gendered organization', *Equality, Diversity and Inclusion: An International Journal*, **29**(3), 239–54.

Lyonette, C., B. Baldauf and H. Behle (2010), 'Quality part-time work: a review of the evidence', *Research Findings No. 2010/5*, London: Government Equalities Office.

MacPhee, M. and L. Svendsen Borra (2012), 'Flexible work practices in nursing', Geneva: International Centre for Human Resources in Nursing.

Manning, A. and B. Petrongolo (2008), 'The part-time pay penalty for women in Britain', *The Economic Journal*, **118**(526), 28–51.

Matteazzi, E., A. Pailhé and A. Solaz (2013), 'Does part-time employment widen the gender wage gap? Evidence from twelve European countries', *Working Paper No. 2013-293*, Verona: Society for the Study of Economic Equality (ECINEQ).

Mayne, L., O. Trgaskis and C. Brewster (1996), 'A comparative analysis of the link between flexibility and HRM strategy', *Employee Relations*, **18**(3), 5–24.

MHLW (2012 July), *Full Application of the Reformed ChildCare and Care Work Leave Law!!*, Tokyo: Ministry of Health, Labour and Welfare [in Japanese].

Moral Carcedo, J., F. García-Belenguer Campos and V. Bote Alvarez-Carrasco (2012), 'Flexibilidad del tiempo de trabajo en España – ¿Ha alterado la crisis el comportamiento del empleo a tiempo parcial?' [Flexibility of working time in Spain – has the crisis altered the behavior of the part-timer?], *Estudios de economía aplicada*, **30**(1), 209–36.

O'Dorchai, S., R. Plasman and F. Rycx (2007), 'The part-time wage penalty in European countries: how large is it for men?', *International Journal of Manpower*, **28**(7), 571–603.

OECD (2011), *Doing Better for Families*, Paris: Organisation for Economic Co-operation and Development.

Plantenga, J. and C. Remery (2009), *Flexible Working Time Arrangements and Gender Equality: A Comparative Review of 30 European Countries*, Brussels: European Commission.

Posel, D. and C. Muller (2007), 'Is there evidence of a wage penalty to female part-time employment in South Africa?', *Working Paper No. 061*, Durban: School of Economics and Finance, University of Kwa Zulu Natal.

Possenriede, D. (2012), 'The temporal and locational flexibility of work and absenteeism', paper prepared for the Forschungsinstitut zur Zukunft der Arbeit (IZA) Summer School 2012, Bonn: Forschungsinstitut zur Zukunft der Arbeit (IZA).

Rau Binder, T. (2010), 'El trabajo a tiempo parcial en Chile' [Part-time work in Chile], *Economía Chilena*, **10**(1), 39–59.

Riley N.-M. (1997), 'Determinants of union membership: a review', *Labour*, **11**(2), 265–301.

Rodgers, J.R. (2004), 'Hourly wages of full-time and part-time employees in Australia', *Australian Journal of Labour Economics*, **7**(2), 215–38.

Russo, G. and W. Hassink (2005), 'The part-time wage penalty: a career perspective', *Discussion Paper No. 1468*, Bonn: Forschungsinstitut zur Zukunft der Arbeit (IZA).

Saito, T. (2009), 'How the rapid growth of non-regular employees will impact on next round of employment adjustment', Tokyo: Economic Research Group, NLI Research, accessed 15 January 2013 at http://www.nli-research.co.jp/english/economics/2009/eco090325.pdf.

Skåtun, J.D. (1998), 'Divide the hours and conquer the surplus: part-time workers and pay', *Economics Letters*, **61**(2), 235–42.

Sloan Center on Aging and Work (2009 April), 'Measures that affect the quality of part-time or reduced-hour work', Boston, MA: Sloan Center on Aging and Work, Boston College, accessed 14 April 2013 at http://www.bc.edu/content/dam/files/research_sites/agingandwork/pdf/publications/GPS02_Quality_of_PTorRH.pdf.

Sparreboom, T. (2013), *Gender Equality, Part-time Work and Segregation*, Geneva: Research and Statistics Department, International Labour Organization.

Tilly, C. (1996), *Half a Job: Bad and Good Part-time Jobs in a Changing Labor Market*, Philadelphia, PA: Temple University Press.

Uno, K. (1993), 'The death of "good wife, wise mother"?', in A. Gordon (ed.), *Postwar Japan as History*, Berkeley, CA: University of California Press.

Visser, J., T. Wilthagen and R. Beltzer et al. (2004), 'Part-time employment in the Netherlands: from atypicality to a typicality', in S. Sciarra, P. Davies and M. Freedland (eds), *Employment Policy and the Regulation of Part-time Work in the European Union: A Comparative Analysis*, Cambridge, UK: Cambridge University Press.

Wallace, C.D. (2003),'Work flexibility in eight European countries: a cross-national comparison', *Czech Sociological Review*, **39**(6), 773–94.

Woodman, S. (2013), 'Obamacare prompts fear for low-wage workers as employers exploit the rules', *The Guardian*, accessed 8 May 2013 at http://www.guardian.co.uk/world/2013/mar/29/obamacare-employers-costs-full-time-workers.

Yeraguntla, A. and C.A. Bhat (2005), 'A classification taxonomy and empirical analysis of work arrangements', *Paper No. 05-1522*, Austin, TX: University of Texas at Austin.

Yerkes, M. and J. Visser (2006), 'Women's preference or delineated policy? The development of part-time work in the Netherlands, Germany and the United Kingdom', in J.-Y. Boulin, M. Lallement, J.C. Messenger et al. (eds), *Decent Working Time: New Trends, New Issues*, Geneva: International Labour Office.

PART III

Social transfers and income redistribution

8. Redistribution policies

Malte Luebker

8.1 INTRODUCTION

As the preceding chapters in Part I and II of this volume have documented, labour markets are central to understanding the evolution of income inequality (see also ILO/IILS, 2008 and UNRISD, 2011, Ch. 1). Labour market institutions and the bargaining power of workers and their trade unions help to shape the functional distribution of income and hence how much of the value-added in an economy finds its way into the pockets of workers in the form of wages. Workers will generally be in a weaker position to demand pay rises in the face of high unemployment, which also leaves the jobless without any wage income. As Islam and Hengge have argued in Chapter 3, full employment policies are therefore equity enhancing in multiple ways. Labour market institutions also shape inequality between wage earners. By setting a floor to the wage distribution, minimum wages can contain wage inequality (Chapter 5 by Belser and Rani). Likewise, strong trade unions and collective bargaining institutions usually benefit workers at the bottom end of the pay scale more than those near the top (Chapter 4 by Hayter).

Policy-makers are rediscovering the role of sound labour market institutions in protecting the weak. However, while institutions can make societies more equitable, achieving true equality of opportunity often remains an elusive goal. Further, levelling the playing field does not address other sources of inequality, such as the – sometimes grotesquely uneven – distribution of initial wealth. Institutions often fail to eliminate discrimination along the lines of sex and race and they cannot prevent some workers from losing their jobs. Governments across the world hence routinely intervene in the income distribution that emerges from the market. The intention is often not outright redistribution in a 'Robin Hood' sense, but takes the form of social security transfers such as old-age pensions for those who no longer work (see Chapter 9 by Behrendt and Woodall) or income support to the unemployed and those in need (see Chapter 10 by Berg). However, the combined effect of these transfers and the taxes that are levied to finance them (as well as general public expenditure) is that inequality of disposable incomes can be much lower than the initial inequality of market incomes.

The global financial and economic crisis – and the excess income inequality that preceded it during the bubble years – has brought the role of fiscal redistribution further into the public debate. In the immediate aftermath of the crisis, many countries responded to rising unemployment by expanding existing security schemes or, to a lesser extent, creating new programmes. Such counter-cyclical, expansionary measures were taken by 69 out of the 77 countries surveyed by the International Labour Organization (ILO) and World Bank (ILO/World Bank, 2012) in an inventory of policy responses to the crisis. Combined with the automatic stabilization effect of existing social security schemes, this explains why, across the European Union, social benefits paid to households increased sharply from 2007 to 2010. However, some of the temporary measures have since expired, and many countries have come under intense fiscal pressure (often after taking on the debt of their failing banking sector) and adopted austerity measures. Hence, the crisis has brought into the spotlight both the scope and constraints of fiscal redistribution.

As this chapter will show, the redistributive impact of tax and transfer systems (as well as their overall size) varies widely between countries. The principal aim of the chapter is to provide an overview of the tools available to policy-makers in shaping the secondary distribution of incomes, and to map the extent to which they have been used to address inequities produced by the market. The chapter starts by defining some basic concepts – what is meant by the terms primary, secondary and tertiary distribution, as well as redistribution itself – before discussing how redistribution is commonly measured. It then documents trends in redistribution over time and differences across countries, and asks how these differences can be explained (devoting some attention to two of the principal answers given in the literature). In its conclusion, the chapter argues that tax and transfer systems can have a significant effect on inequality. Inequality is therefore not an unavoidable outcome of market forces, but – to some degree – a matter of political choice. While some cases might entail trade-offs between equity and efficiency, the question whether a more equitable development path can also be good for growth is addressed elsewhere in this volume (see Chapter 2 by Lee and Gerecke).

8.2 SOME BASIC CONCEPTS: PRIMARY, SECONDARY AND TERTIARY DISTRIBUTION

When analysing the distribution of incomes among households and individuals (the so-called 'size distribution'), it is helpful to distinguish between different stages in the distribution process. The 'primary distribution of incomes' is what emerges from the market, that is, before direct taxes are levied and transfers are disbursed. The primary distribution of incomes is sometimes portrayed as an 'apolitical' outcome of market forces that has some inherent fairness, as long as everybody had a fair chance to emerge as a winner. Inequality in primary incomes can then be justified as a result of differences in skills and individual efforts that lead to unequal rewards. However, markets themselves require institutions, and institutional choices have implications for distributive outcomes (see Part II of this volume). Moreover, people enter life from such vastly different starting points that equality of opportunity itself is often no more than an illusion.

Governments across the world have therefore – albeit to different degrees – introduced institutions and programmes that alter the initial income distribution. Tax systems are usually progressive in design, requiring those with higher incomes (or greater wealth) to contribute a greater share of their incomes to general government revenues.[1] Conversely, transfer payments often target those who are in need due to unemployment, old age or invalidity, so that they often disproportionately benefit those with lower incomes. The term 'secondary distribution of incomes' refers to incomes after this process has taken place; or in other words, to disposable incomes after taxes and mandatory social security contributions have been deducted and transfer payments have been added.

Both the primary and secondary distributions of incomes are concerned with incomes in money terms. However, money is not an end in itself, but only a means to meeting human needs. In some countries, people have to pay (and sometimes cannot pay) considerable amounts to satisfy needs such as healthcare or quality education, while governments in other countries provide these services free of charge. Cash incomes are therefore only a partial proxy for individual welfare or – to use Amartya Sen's (2005) term – human capabilities, and comparisons of cash incomes can be misleading. The concept of a 'tertiary distribution of incomes' aims at addressing this shortcoming by adding in-kind benefits and entitlements to disposable incomes. However, while the analytical validity of the concept is apparent, the tertiary distribution is notoriously difficult to measure and the present chapter will leave the provision of public social services to Chapter 11 (by Martínez Franzoni and Sánchez-Ancochea).

The primary and secondary distributions are usually discussed from the standpoint of households, often by analysing the distribution of the different income components and how taxes and transfers alter the personal distribution of incomes. However, the distribution of income accounts under the System of National Accounts (SNA, 2008, para. 2.90ff.) describes the same process from an aggregate perspective, using a similar terminology. Here, the 'primary distribution of income account' shows the functional distribution of gross value-added between labour and capital (and government, which receives taxes on production and imports at this stage of the distribution process). The 'secondary distribution of income account' starts from the balance of primary incomes and records current transfers, current taxes on income and wealth, net social contributions, and social benefits to arrive at disposable incomes. Finally, in order to map the tertiary distribution of incomes, the 'redistribution of income in kind account' captures the provision of goods and services to individual households by governments.

8.3 DEFINING REDISTRIBUTION

In dictionaries, redistribution is defined as 'altering the distribution' of something.[2] This is a useful starting point: what follows is that income redistribution policies encompass all government interventions that alter the distribution of incomes, including those that affect the primary distribution of incomes. As argued in Part II of this volume, granting collective bargaining rights (or denying them) has consequences for the functional distribution of incomes and for wage inequality, as do minimum wages. However, governments alter the primary distribution of incomes in other, often even less visible ways. For instance, the liberalization of financial markets since the 1980s is widely believed to have contributed to a concentration of incomes at the top, and to a shift away from wages and towards profits (see ILO, 2012; Stiglitz, 2012). Likewise, trade liberalization has differential impacts on the incomes of various groups in society (see Jansen and Lee, 2007).

Such a broad definition of redistribution underlines the fact that most government action has redistributive consequences. To gain support for unpopular decisions such as the opening of trade, governments sometimes try to compensate the losers and impose a corresponding tax on the winners (ibid.). At this stage, redistribution becomes more apparent since it directly alters the primary distribution of incomes. This direct intervention in the form of taxes and transfers is commonly at the heart of public debates over redistribution, simply because it is more visible, even though the impact can be minuscule when compared with the original policy decision. For example, trade compensation schemes are commonly thought to redistribute less than 5 per cent of the gains from trade (ibid., p. 75).

The concept of 'fiscal redistribution' captures these direct interventions that governments make through taxes and transfers. A key policy concern is often their net effect on income inequality, usually expressed as the change in a summary measure such as the Gini coefficient between the primary and secondary distribution. The impact can be further disaggregated into the direct effect of taxes and mandatory social contributions and the contribution of transfers (see section 8.6).

Tax policies play a crucial role for both aspects: they determine how many resources are at the disposal of governments for social policies, but the structure of the tax code by itself has an impact on inequality. At one extreme, income taxes can be regressive, that is, the tax rates are higher for those with lower incomes. An example for a tax that widens inequality is the 'poll tax', an equal lump sum paid by every resident. However, although the top marginal tax rates have fallen substantially across the industrialized world since the 1970s, modern tax systems are still typically progressive and tax rates increase with incomes.[3] The result is that the rich pay (or are expected to pay) a greater share of their income as taxes, and that inequality after taxes is lower than before taxes. Between these two models lie distribution-neutral regimes with flat tax rates, where everybody pays the same proportion of his or her income in tax.

However, the structure of tax rates often gives an incomplete picture of their redistributive impact since the rich, in particular, often take advantage of tax exemptions or find other ways to avoid paying taxes in full. This practice, euphemistically known as 'tax optimization' or 'aggressive tax planning', can undermine the intended redistributive effects of the tax code – and has reignited the public debate about the fairness of tax systems in many countries.[4] Another facet of tax codes is that income from capital (be it in the form of interest, dividends or realized capital gains) is often taxed at a different, generally lower rate than income from labour (or is exempt from taxation altogether).[5] To the extent that the capital incomes accrue to those at the top of the income pyramid, this further undermines the progressiveness of taxation (see also Atkinson et al., 2011).

On the whole, the redistributive impact of direct taxes on income and wealth is relatively well understood, based on the analysis of household survey datasets or national accounts (see section 8.4 below).[6] However, countries have increasingly shifted towards indirect taxes such as a general sales tax (GST) or a value-added tax (VAT).[7] By taxing general consumption, these taxes have a bigger relative impact on those who consume a larger part of their incomes – generally the poor – and are hence often regressive (see Emran and Stiglitz, 2007). However, while households effectively pay these taxes, they affect prices (and not income) and their impact on income inequality is more difficult to assess than in the case of direct taxes.[8]

While the conventional analysis of fiscal redistribution has important insights to offer, it has some conceptual shortcomings. One important concern is that a snapshot taken at a single point in time (usually for a given year) focuses only on inter-personal redistribution, ignoring 'life-cycle redistribution'. For instance, old-age pensions appear as if they were a transfer from the young (who pay contributions and/or taxes to fund them) to the old (who receive pensions). In reality, the young and the old are not two distinct groups, but young workers will grow old over time so that today's contributors are tomorrow's beneficiaries. There is, of course, no guarantee that an individual's benefits will be equal to her or his contributions (those who die young will not receive anything in return, and those who are blessed with longevity will generally gain more). Pension systems therefore remain redistributive – albeit to different degrees, depending on their design (see Chapter 9 by Behrendt and Woodall).

A related criticism of the snapshot approach is that it focuses on outcomes (i.e., it measures redistribution after the event, or *a posteriori* redistribution), rather than the expected, *a priori* redistributive effect. Take the example of occupational accident insurance, where all workers must pay a small premium α_1 and those who suffer an accident are paid a benefit α_2 (which partly compensates for their lost income d). At the end of the year, we can see that those who had no accident have a lower income Y than their initial market income W, while the disposable income Y' of those who suffered an accident is amended by the insurance benefit:

$$\text{No accident:} \quad Y = W - \alpha_1 \tag{8.1}$$

$$\text{Accident:} \quad Y' = W - d - \alpha_1 + \alpha_2 \tag{8.2}$$

Under the conventional, a posteriori approach, this insurance arrangement appears as a redistributive transfer. However, at the beginning of the year, individuals do not yet know into which of the two groups they will fall, and their expected income $\hat{Y}$ depends on the probability p of having an accident:

$$\hat{Y} = (1 - p)(W - \alpha_1) + p(W - d - \alpha_1 + \alpha_2) \tag{8.3}$$

Since some individuals (say, bricklayers) are more likely to suffer an accident than others (say, office workers), their expected income gain or loss from the insurance will differ. However, from an *a priori* perspective, the redistributive impact of social insurance is usually much milder since all contributors are also potential beneficiaries. When approached from behind a Rawlsian 'veil of ignorance' (see below) about future events, most office workers would still opt for protection against the potentially disastrous income loss as a consequence of an occupational accident (even if their expected income from the scheme is negative). The same distinction between the *a priori* and the *a posteriori* effect applies to other social insurance schemes.[9]

8.4 MEASUREMENT ISSUES AND DATA SOURCES

A large number of academic studies have looked into fiscal redistribution, and many of them have sought to quantify its impact on income inequality. The most common approach is to make use of the Gini coefficient, which provides a convenient summary measure of inequality (ranging from zero for perfect equality to one, when all incomes accrue to a single individual). One can compare the Gini coefficient for the primary distribution of incomes, $G_{primary}$, to the Gini coefficient that emerges after taxes and transfers, $G_{secondary}$. This allows calculating the absolute differences, ΔG^{abs}, between the two coefficients:

$$\Delta G^{abs} = G_{primary} - G_{secondary} \tag{8.4}$$

or, alternatively, the reduction in inequality relative to its initial level, ΔG^{rel}:

$$\Delta G^{rel} = (G_{primary} - G_{secondary})/G_{primary} \tag{8.5}$$

Both the absolute and relative measures for redistribution are frequently used, depending on the research context.[10]

Although this approach is straightforward in principle, it poses a number of practical and conceptual challenges. One obvious requirement is to have sufficient data on the distribution of incomes among households, both before and after taxes and transfers. Tax records often provide some information on this – sometimes going back for many decades – though an obvious limitation is that not all residents of a country submit tax returns and some might do so in a less than fully honest manner (see the data collected by Atkinson et al., 2011).

Household survey data are therefore often the preferred source, especially since the Luxembourg Income Study has made them widely accessible to researchers in standardized format (Atkinson, 2004). However, data users have to make a number of methodological decisions. For example, a common assumption is that all members of a household pool their incomes, which ignores unequal access to resources between different household members (and hence intra-household inequality). Further, when household income per person is calculated, researchers need to take into account the fact that children need fewer resources than adults, and that households realize economies of scale (since, for instance, several household members can share a single fridge). A number of equivalence scales have been developed to address this issue.[11] In sum, these methodological decisions mean that the comparison of Gini coefficients is often difficult and that the small print needs careful attention.[12]

An alternative, less common measurement approach is based on national accounts, namely the secondary distribution of income accounts (SNA, 2008, 2.90; see also above). They provide information on how much of households' primary incomes were collected by the state and social security institutions in the form of taxes and contributions, and how much of their total disposable incomes stems from current transfer payments. While this offers insights into the size of the welfare state, it cannot illuminate how far these interventions are effective in reducing income inequality between households (or whether they increase it). Other studies have drawn on public social expenditure data to estimate the extent of redistribution (Bassett et al., 1999; Hicks, 1999; Huber and Stephens, 2001).

8.5 MOTIVATIONS FOR FISCAL REDISTRIBUTION

While virtually all government action has redistributive implications, some government interventions explicitly aim at redistribution. This gives rise to the question of why governments pursue redistribution policies? Boadway and Keen (2000) have suggested a broad typology of three principal objectives behind fiscal redistribution, namely (1) the pursuit of social justice, (2) achieving efficiency gains, and (3) that they reflect the self-interested use of the coercive power of the state. Although the distinction is not always sharp, it is nonetheless a useful framework for organizing a complex academic literature with very different views on the subject.[13]

The idea that the state has an obligation to promote 'social justice' has a long tradition. For instance, the social teachings of the Catholic Church argue that the state has a moral obligation to 'provide for the welfare and the comfort of the working classes' and to ensure distributive justice (Rerum Novarum, 1891, para. 33). Likewise, the ILO was founded on the principle that 'universal and lasting peace can be established only if it is based on social justice' (Preamble of the ILO Constitution).[14, 15] While labour market institutions can help to achieve greater equality of opportunity, initial conditions are sometimes so unequal – or markets so dysfunctional – that the outcomes are seen as ethically unacceptable or unfair. Without intervention, the market will deny some members of society basic capabilities and ultimately their rights as human beings (see also Sen, 2005). Hence, the state has a role to correct the outcomes of the primary distribution of income by transferring resources to facilitate all citizens to a meaningful participation in society.

Such transfers can increase aggregate utility and hence overall welfare when analysed with the tools of welfare economics. If the utility functions of all individuals are identical and depend on the available resources, and marginal utility of resources is decreasing, then the utility gain of poor transfer recipients is greater than the loss faced by richer contributors. An individual who does not yet know which position he or she will take in society therefore has a greater *expected* utility when income distribution is more equitable (see the summary in Boadway and Keen, 2000, p. 680).[16]

From a very different starting point, Rawlsian theories of justice make a related argument. They try to determine the kind of society that an individual would choose from behind a 'veil of ignorance', arguing that people will be averse to being born into a society where they face the risk of living in deprivation (Rawls, 1971). However, while it may be an insightful thought experiment to discuss the hypothetical preferences of individuals under conditions of ignorance, pursuing arguments for fiscal redistribution on the grounds of social justice is ultimately driven by value judgements – which, as will be discussed later, differ between people.

Interestingly, one argument in favour of redistribution on the grounds of efficiency also relates to values, namely altruism. From the fact that some people give (voluntarily) to others, economists have deduced that they must derive a utility from the welfare of their fellow citizens. However, any individual's gift to the poor has only a small impact unless other rich persons join in. In other words, the rich face a collective action problem, and private transfers will remain at a suboptimal level. This problem can be solved through compulsory redistribution that benefits everyone: the poor, who receive transfers, and the rich, who live in a more equitable society (Boadway and Keen, 2000, p. 684). One can therefore construct an argument that redistribution improves the welfare of everyone and is hence Pareto efficient. Although expressed in a highly formalistic terminology, this argument essentially boils down to an admission by economists that humans have a heart.

From a more conventional perspective, efficiency gains can be achieved by social security institutions (which carry out most of the redistribution in welfare states). In particular, they address market failures where private insurance markets fail to provide individuals with affordable insurance against some of the basic risks of life, such as ill health, old age, occupational accidents or unemployment (see Chapter 9 by Behrendt and Woodall and Chapter 10 by Berg). Insurance companies are likely to have less information on the risks faced by individuals than the individuals themselves. Any product they offer is thus likely to be bought primarily by those who face a higher risk, driving up insurance premiums – further disadvantaging those who face low risks, but nonetheless want to buy insurance.

As Rothschild and Stiglitz (1976) have shown, such information asymmetries mean that competition in insurance markets need not lead to an equilibrium, and that a number of responses by providers (such as rationing or the exclusion of bad risks from revealed buying protection) mean that market outcomes are not Pareto-optimal. The inefficiency that results from adverse self-selection can be overcome through the compulsory public provision of social insurance. Intriguingly, the pooling of high- and low-risk individuals under the same contract also leaves low-risk individuals better off since they obtain insurance at lower cost than they could buy in a competitive market.

Going back to these first principles provides a helpful perspective to the debate on the sustainability of welfare states, which have come under pressure in much of the developed world due to ageing populations, the rising relative cost of social services (known as Baumol's cost disease) and increased global competition due to trade and capital mobility. Arguably, institutions that increase efficiency by addressing market failures or that raise a country's human capital stock do not undermine a country's global competitiveness. Healthcare provision is a case in point. As a share of GDP, the United States spends twice as much on health as Finland (which has a largely state-controlled health system),[17] yet Finland outperforms the United States on almost every health indicator compiled by the World Health Organization (WHO, 2013), be it treatment success rate for smear-positive tuberculosis or immunization coverage for measles among one-year-olds. While the Affordable Care Act (better known as 'Obamacare') has sought to address failures in the private insurance market, businesses frequently cite the high cost of the United States' inefficient health system as a drag on competitiveness.

A less benign view of redistribution has emerged from the public choice literature, namely that it reflects the self-interested use of the coercive power of the state. In a paper that has influenced much of the subsequent debate on redistribution, Meltzer and Richard (1981) presented a model in which the state imposes a (linear) tax on all incomes and then redistributes the proceeds in the form of lump-sum benefits. While those at the top of the income distribution pay more in taxes than they receive in return in the form of benefits, citizens with low incomes will gain from the process – and therefore have an inherent interest in redistribution. Based on the notion of rational individuals who maximize their utility, Meltzer and Richard assume that the prospect of material gain shapes individuals' preferences for redistribution and leads them to demand redistribution at the ballot box. In the tradition of Schumpeter (1942) and Downs (1957), they then argue that the median voter will cast the decisive ballot and that his or her preferences will be decisive (at least under conditions of majority rule and universal suffrage).

These three perspectives differ sharply in how they conceptualize redistribution: on the first account, the moral imperative of social justice demands bettering the lot of the deprived, while the second viewpoint casts redistribution as efficiency-enhancing government interventions into failing markets that are in the interest of all. The third perspective brushes these considerations aside and portrays redistribution as driven by individual greed – it is the result of the tyranny of the majority that appropriates for itself what rightly belongs to the rich. This summary is, of course, a slight exaggeration made for the sake of clarity. Further, there are many other, often very practical, justifications for redistribution – for instance, from a broader perspective of macroeconomic performance or development policy.

8.6 TRENDS AND CROSS-COUNTRY DIFFERENCES IN REDISTRIBUTION

Tax systems and social security systems – the two main vehicles for fiscal redistribution – differ greatly in their scope and size across countries (see ILO, 2010). It is therefore not surprising that their redistributive impact varies significantly. This section provides some illustrative evidence for variation between countries and across time. It presents data both on (1) the overall redistributive impact of taxes and transfer (based on household survey data) and (2) the size of redistribution (based on national accounts). Common to both sources is poor data availability for developing countries.

In line with the approach discussed in section 8.4, Figures 8.1 to 8.3 provide an overview of the reduction in the Gini coefficient as a result of fiscal redistribution.[18] The total height of the bars in each figure corresponds to the Gini coefficients for the primary distribution of incomes,[19]

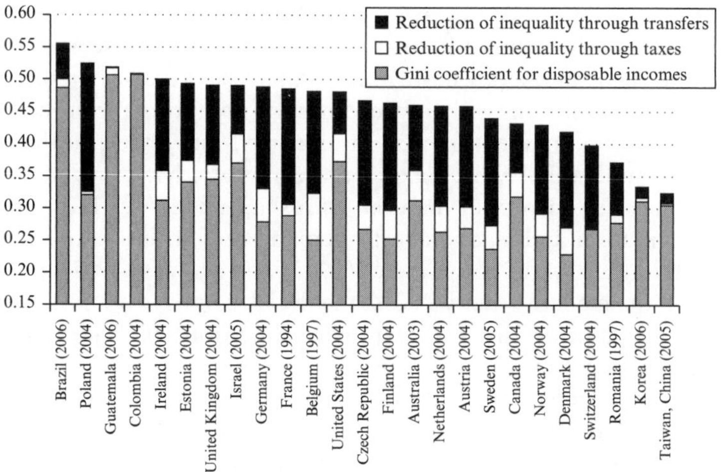

Note: The total height of the column corresponds to the Gini coefficient for market incomes (i.e., before taxes and transfers).

Source: Luxembourg Income Study Database (LIS); www.lisdatacenter.org (multiple countries; analysis of micro-data completed between February and May 2011). Luxembourg: LIS.

Figure 8.1 The impact of taxes and transfers on inequality, Gini coefficients (ca. 2000s)

whereas the grey sections at the bottom correspond to the Gini coefficients in the secondary distribution (i.e., for disposable incomes). The gap in between is the measure for absolute redistribution introduced in equation (8.4). It can be decomposed into the reduction in the Gini coefficient achieved through transfer receipts (top black bar) and through taxes and mandatory social security contributions (middle white bar).

The cross-section of 25 countries presented in Figure 8.1 shows remarkable differences in redistribution between countries. While countries such as Belgium (1997), the Czech Republic (2004), Finland (2004), Germany (2004), Poland (2004) and Sweden (2005) all achieved a reduction in the Gini coefficient of 0.20 or more, fiscal redistribution is much more limited outside Europe. In fact, one striking finding is that differences in the Gini coefficient for disposable incomes are, to a significant extent, driven by the magnitude of redistribution – and are not fully determined by inequality in the primary distribution. In technical terms, the simple correlation between Gini coefficients for the primary and secondary distribution is only $r = 0.499$ (p value: 0.011). This means that initial inequality matters, but can explain only about a quarter of the variation in the Gini coefficients for disposable incomes.[20] Political choice, rather than market forces, are therefore a substantial factor behind distributive outcomes.

Take the example of the Nordic countries and Belgium, which achieved a fairly equitable secondary distribution of incomes (Gini coefficients of roughly 0.25 or less). Yet, their underlying distribution of private sector incomes ranges from high inequality (as in Belgium, with a Gini of 0.481) to a more egalitarian distribution (as in Denmark, with a Gini of 0.418). Somewhat surprisingly, the United States and Belgium share the same Gini coefficient for the primary distribution of incomes (0.481). Hence, markets produce very similar outcomes in both countries. But whereas Belgium corrects these outcomes, the United States is left with the highest inequality of disposable incomes among the industrialized countries in the sample. Here, the decisive factor is not what happens in the primary distribution, but that taxes and transfers are far less redistributive in the United States.

The three Latin American countries in the sample – Brazil, Colombia and Guatemala – all share extremely high levels of inequality, with Gini coefficients for the primary distribution above 0.50. In Guatemala, the tax and transfer systems lead only to a negligible reduction in inequality, while they actually marginally increase inequality in Colombia. Here, transfers disproportionately benefit the richer segments of society and taxes impose only a very light burden on those with high incomes (see Alvaredo and Londoño Vélez, 2013). In line with these findings, a World Bank study on Latin America concludes that 'a good deal of Latin America's excess inequality over international levels reflects the failure of the region's fiscal systems to perform their redistributive functions' (Goñi et al., 2008, p. 22).

Three features of Latin America's tax and transfer systems account for much of this failure. First, the tax base of Latin American countries has historically been much narrower than in developed countries and declined further during the neoliberal reforms of the 1980s. In 1990, countries in the regions on average collected only 13.7 per cent of GDP in taxes (see Cornia et al., 2011, p. 20). Second, taxation relies heavily on value-added tax (VAT) and other indirect taxes, which – unlike direct taxes on incomes – target poor and rich alike and are therefore often regressive in their impact (ibid.). For instance, Chile and Mexico derive half of their total tax revenue from consumption taxes (compared to less than a third in the OECD as a whole; see OECD, 2012, Table 26). Third, social security entitlements are often tied to previous contributions and expenditure hence favour workers with formal sector jobs, making it highly regressive in many countries (see ECLAC, 2008, pp. 104ff.).

As López and Miller (2008) argue for the case of Chile, tax loopholes have strongly favoured the elites and – despite relatively high nominal tax rates – undermined the tax base, leaving government with insufficient sources to address the country's sky-high inequality. However, some countries in the region have begun to address these shortcomings. Led by Argentina and Brazil (where the tax take now approaches the OECD average), the region's tax ratio increased to 18.5 per cent of GDP by 2009 (see Cornia et al., 2011, p. 20). This created the fiscal space for social transfer programmes targeted at the poorest, such as the 'Bolsa Família' (Family Allowance) programme in Brazil (see Chapter 10 by Berg). The data presented in Figure 8.1 show that transfers indeed reduce Brazil's Gini coefficient by 0.055, while the redistributive impact of taxation remains small.

Compared to Latin America, countries in East Asia have managed to achieve lower private sector inequality. The literature attributes this success to heavy investment into broad-based education and lower levels of asset inequality (see, e.g., Birdsall et al., 1995). Crucially, land reforms – largely absent in Latin America – levelled entrenched rural inequality and enhanced agricultural productivity (see Chaudhry, 2003). The two East Asian economies with available data – the Republic of Korea and Taiwan, Province of China – have in fact by far the lowest pre-tax, pre-transfer inequality among all 25 countries in the sample. This reduces the need for redistribution, and despite only mildly redistributive tax and transfer systems, inequality of disposable incomes is relatively moderate (see also Jacobs, 2000). However, the low incidence of taxation and transfers also means that the automatic stabilizers of the developed countries are absent, and rising market inequality feeds directly through into rising inequality of disposable incomes. In response, regional agencies such as the Asian Development Bank (ADB, 2012) now advocate 'efficient fiscal policies' to address rising inequality, including by greater and more equitable revenue mobilization and more expenditure on social protection schemes (see also UN-ESCAP, 2013, pp. 50f.).

For Sub-Saharan Africa, no data were available from the Luxembourg Income Study at the time of data extraction. However, with the partial exception of Southern Africa, fiscal redistribution is extremely limited across the continent. First, taxation as a share of GDP is low compared to other regions and income taxes play a relatively minor role (see Bird and Zolt, 2005). Instead, countries rely on taxing trade and natural resources – and increasingly on value-added taxes, which are often regressive in their impact (see Riswold, 2004; Emran and Stiglitz, 2007). Second, the reach of contributory social security schemes is limited due to widespread informality. For instance, in the United Republic of Tanzania less than 1 per cent of the entire population is covered by one of the country's seven social security funds (see ILO, 2008). Third, non-contributory social assistance programmes are still in their infancy. The major exception is South Africa, where the child support grant, the older persons grant and other social grants now reach 16 million persons, almost one-third of the country's population (see National Treasury, 2013, p. 85). Although other countries have set up similar programmes, such as the Cash Transfer for Orphans and Vulnerable Children programme in Kenya, their reach is still far more limited (see Asfaw et al., 2012).

The different regional patterns are summarized in Figure 8.2. Whereas both the Latin American and East Asian countries have only mildly redistributive transfer systems, the gap between high and low inequality of private sector incomes means that the Gini for disposable incomes is much higher in Latin America (0.500) than in East Asia (0.308). By contrast, Europe and a group of mostly Anglo-Saxon OECD countries (Australia, Canada, Israel and the United States) start from very similar initial income distributions. However, the income transfers in European countries – which have well-developed social security systems – reduce

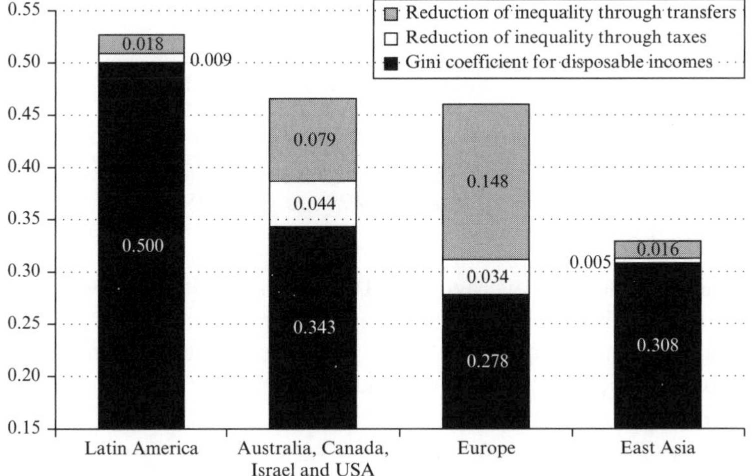

Note: The total height of the column corresponds to the Gini coefficient for market incomes (i.e., before taxes and transfers).

Source: Luxembourg Income Study Database (LIS); www.lisdatacenter.org (multiple countries; analysis of micro-data completed between February and May 2011). Luxembourg: LIS.

Figure 8.2 The impact of taxes and transfers on income inequality, regional averages of Gini coefficients (ca. 2000s)

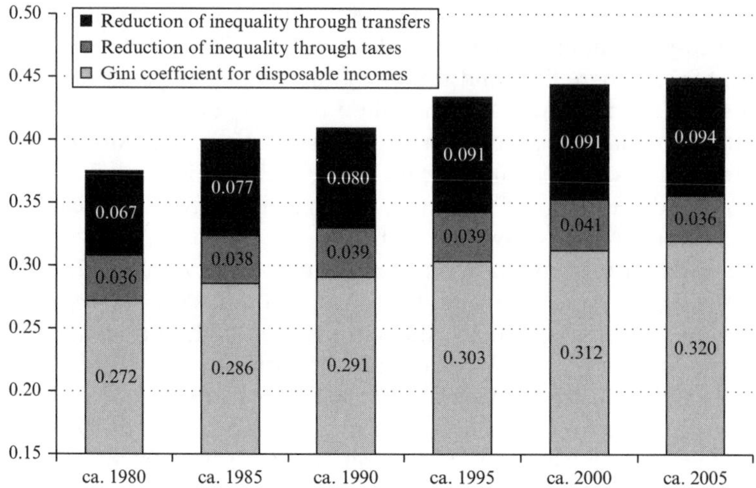

Note: Based on a stable sample of eight industrialized economies (Australia, Canada, Germany, Israel, Norway, Taiwan [Province of China], United Kingdom, United States). The total height of the column corresponds to the Gini coefficient for private sector incomes (i.e., before taxes and transfers).

Source: Luxembourg Income Study Database (LIS); www.lisdatacenter.org (multiple countries; analysis of micro-data completed between February and May 2011). Luxembourg: LIS.

Figure 8.3 The impact of taxes and transfers on inequality, trends in Gini coefficients from ca. 1980 to ca. 2005

the Gini coefficient on average by 0.148 points, while the more restricted welfare state in the latter group has a far smaller impact (–0.079). Australia, Canada, the United States and Israel thus have noticeably higher inequality of disposable incomes (0.343) than Europe (0.278), despite starting from a similar underlying distribution.

Looking at trends over time, data for eight countries with a consistent time series show a continued increase in inequality of disposable incomes: the Gini rose from an average of 0.272 in ca. 1980 to 0.320 in ca. 2005 (see Figure 8.3). The rise in inequality over the past decades was driven by a greater dispersion of market incomes; taxes and especially transfers slowed the rise in inequality. Using the absolute measure introduced in equation (8.4), redistribution increased from 0.103 (the sum of the black and dark grey bars) in 1980 to 0.130 in 2005. However, redistribution increased far more modestly under the relative measure for redistribution (from 0.275 to 0.289; not tabulated). While this finding is at odds with the thesis of widespread welfare state retrenchment, it does not imply that rules and entitlements have become more generous over the past decades. Rather, what seems to be at work here is a process of 'automatic stabilization', where the welfare state partially compensates for the surging market inequality (see Kenworthy and Pontusson, 2005). Moreover, there are substantial differences between individual countries – the United Kingdom and the United States, for instance, both saw declining relative redistribution.[21]

Where household survey data can map the effect of fiscal redistribution on personal income inequality, national accounts data can give some insights into the overall extent of fiscal redistribution. Figure 8.4 presents a summary of changes to the aggregate incomes of the household sector for 25 countries of the European Union, mainly for 1995 and 2009. On the left, the figure shows payments made by households in the form of direct taxes, social security contributions[22] and (a minor category) other current transfers.[23] They are expressed as a percentage of primary incomes, and reduce the market incomes that remain at the disposal of households, which are plotted on the right side of the chart.[24] However, households are also major recipients of social security benefits and, to a lesser degree, of other transfers. The total size of the bars on the right corresponds to the household sector's disposable incomes after redistribution, again expressed as a percentage of primary incomes.

Households' aggregate disposable income is usually lower than its balance of primary incomes. This reflects the fact that the household sector (as well as the corporate sector) finances general government expenditure through taxes. There are only a few exceptions to this rule, such as Greece and a few countries in Eastern Europe, where the household sector is a net recipient of resources in the redistribution process.[25] At the opposite extreme, the disposable income of households is only about 72 per cent of primary incomes in Denmark and the Netherlands, and about 82 per cent in Sweden and Belgium. This is due to the high incidence of taxes (Denmark and Sweden) or social contributions (Netherlands and Belgium). Although the household sector appears to be a net loser from redistribution, the four countries cited provide a broad range of public services to their citizens, which are not captured in the secondary distribution of income account (but in the redistribution of income in kind account; see Chapter 11 by Martínez Franzoni and Sánchez-Ancochea).

On average, households across the 25 European countries received 27.5 per cent of primary incomes in the form of social transfers, although there is a wide range from less than 21 per cent in Lithuania to almost 35 per cent in Denmark. Between 1995 and 2010, some of the Eastern European countries (Czech Republic, Estonia, Hungary, Romania and

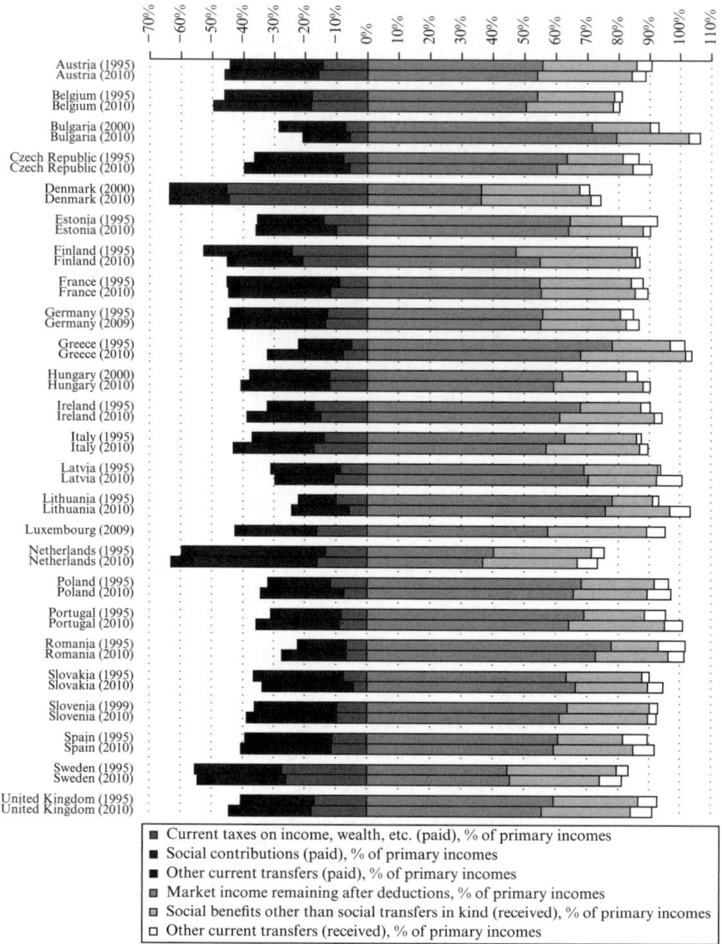

Note: The secondary distribution of income account for the household sector shows how the balance of the primary income is allocated by redistribution. Current taxes on income, wealth and so on, social contributions and other current transfers paid by households are deducted from the primary incomes, while benefits (excluding social transfers in kind) and other current transfers are added. Since all transactions are expressed in percentage of primary incomes, the total length of the bars on the right-hand side of the chart shows households' disposable incomes as a percentage of primary incomes. No data are available for Cyprus and Malta.

Source: Eurostat (series: nama_r_ehh2s; updated: 28 October 2013; last accessed 22 November 2013).

Figure 8.4 Changes to aggregate incomes of the household sector under the secondary distribution of income account in 25 EU countries, 1995 and 2010

Lithuania) have expanded the size of social benefits by 6.5 percentage points or more. This partly reflects a catch-up with the standard in old EU member countries, and partly a cyclical increase due to the economic crisis. Likewise, the substantial expansions of benefits in Ireland (+11.0 percentage points), Portugal (+11.5 percentage points) and Greece (+15.1 percentage points) are due both to the particularly severe impact of the crisis in all three countries, and to a starting position in the mid-1990s well below the EU average.

Large-scale welfare state retrenchments in the period before the crisis (1995 to 2007) can be seen in traditional welfare states such as Finland (–10.0 percentage points), Sweden (–7.7 percentage points) and the Netherlands (–5.2 percentage points) as well as in Latvia (–11.1 percentage points; not tabulated). However, this decline is partly offset by the expansion of benefits during the economic crisis so that the scale of retrenchment does not become as apparent in Figure 8.4. Overall, no clear trend towards welfare state expansion or retrenchment can be detected across the EU: in the pre-crisis period, the level of social benefits changed little from 23.7 per cent of household's primary incomes in the first year (generally 1995) to 23.1 per cent in 2007. Hence, the aggregate increase in benefit intensity (+3.7 percentage points) is entirely due to cyclical factors, and not due to a general policy shift towards greater redistribution.[26]

Do the two approaches to measuring fiscal redistribution show similar patterns? To answer this question, Figure 8.5 combines the data from both sources (using the latest available matching observations). From Figure 8.5a, the wide range in the share of taxes and social contributions – from 16.7 per cent in Romania (1997) to 59.2 per cent in Denmark (2004) – becomes once more apparent. While there is a positive association to the redistributive impact of taxes, the range of outcomes is fairly narrow and the slope of the regression line is relatively flat (0.081). By contrast, benefits translate more directly into a reduction in inequality through the transfer channel, as can be seen from the slope of the regression line (0.335) in Figure 8.5b. Finally, Figure 8.5c presents a summary measure of the size of fiscal redistribution (obtained by summing the two previous measures) and relates it to its overall redistributive impact. The figure shows that the size of the welfare state indeed matters for redistributive outcomes, though the simple measure used can account for only a third of the overall variation in redistributive impacts (R^2 = 0.340). This highlights the importance of the design of tax and transfer systems.

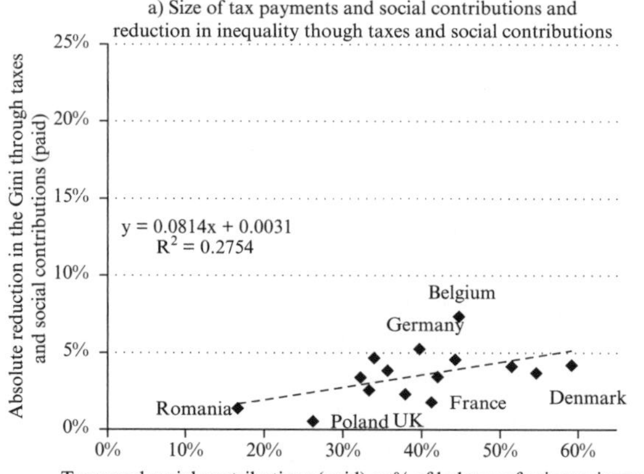

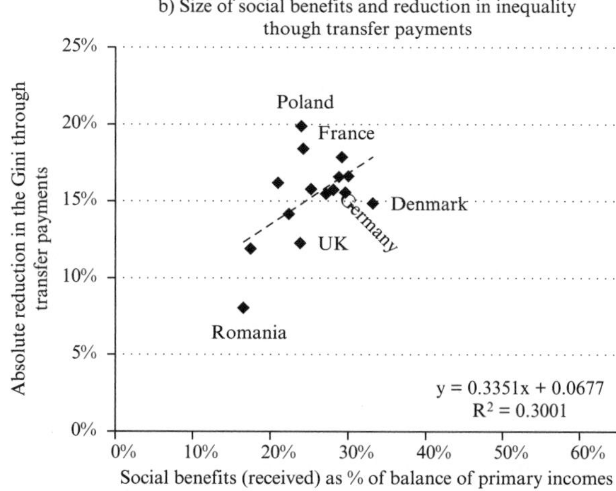

Note: The composite measure is calculated as the sum of benefits received and the absolute values of taxes paid and social contributions paid, all expressed as a percentage of the balance of primary incomes for the household sector. For further details, see notes to Figures 8.1 and 8.4. The country observations and years are: Austria (2004), Belgium (1997), Czech Republic (2004), Denmark (2004), Estonia (2004), Finland (2004), France (1994/95), Germany (2004), Ireland (2004), Netherlands (2004), Poland (2004), Romania (1997), Slovakia (1992/95), Sweden (2005) and the United Kingdom (2004).

Sources: Luxembourg Income Study Database (LIS); www.lisdatacenter.org (multiple countries; analysis of micro-data completed between February and May 2011); Eurostat (series: nama_r_ehh2s; updated: 5 July 2012; last accessed 29 January 2013).

Figure 8.5a–c The size of fiscal redistribution and reduction in inequality through fiscal redistribution in 15 European countries, late 1990s and 2000s

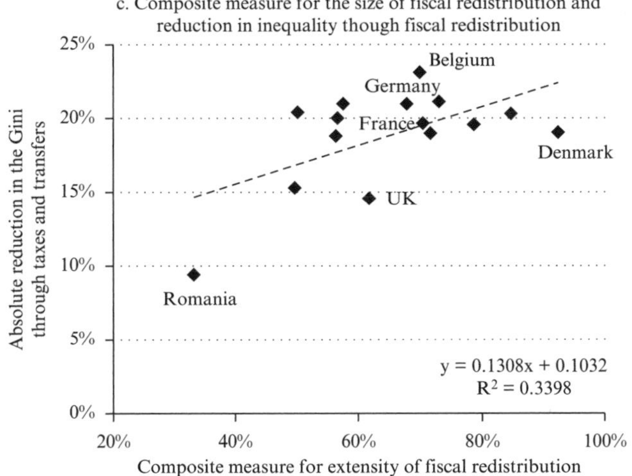

Figure 8.5a–c (continued)

8.7 WHAT EXPLAINS DIFFERENCES IN REDISTRIBUTION?

What explains the large differences in redistribution between countries that have been documented in the previous section? A vibrant literature has discussed this question, with contributions from the economics discipline, and – given that decisions about redistribution are ultimately political in nature – also from political sociology and political science. A helpful way to systematize some of the literature is to refer back to the motivations for redistribution, in particular the opposing view that it reflects the pursuit of social justice or individual utility maximization (see section 8.5).

The latter approach, which is placed in the broader tradition of rational choice, models the process of tax payments and transfer receipts discussed in the previous section from the perspective of individual households. In their previously cited paper, Meltzer and Richard (1981) show how much each household will gain in the process, and which tax rate maximizes the utility of the median voter (who, in their model, casts the deciding vote). There is, of course, some truth in this assumption: people with low incomes tend to view redistribution more favourably than those who occupy the top echelons of society (see, e.g., Guillaud, 2013). However, Meltzer and Richard do not confine their argument to the level of individuals and draw a conclusion at the macro level, namely that fiscal redistribution should rise in line with inequality of primary incomes. While

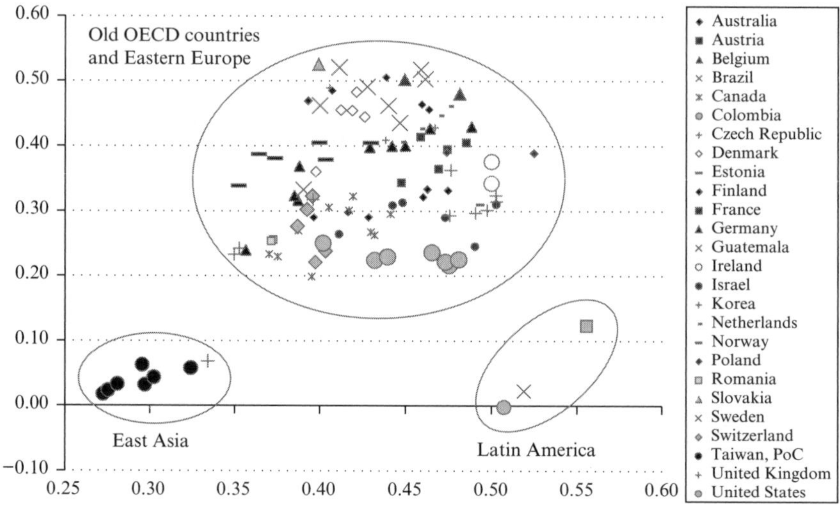

Source: Luxembourg Income Study Database (LIS); www.lisdatacenter.org (multiple countries; analysis of micro-data completed between February and May 2011). Luxembourg: LIS.

Figure 8.6 Gini for private sector income and relative redistribution in 26 countries and territories, 1990s and 2000s (latest available)

there has been some debate on whether the extent of redistribution should be measured in *absolute* or *relative* terms (see section 8.4), it is clear from the model specifications that higher inequality should give rise to greater relative redistribution.[27]

For those concerned with greater equity, this would be good news – redistribution would be in greater supply precisely where it is needed most. However, a range of studies has found no empirical confirmation that relative redistribution systematically rises with greater initial inequality, no matter whether they look at a cross-section of countries (see, e.g., de Mello and Tiongson, 2006; Lupu and Pontusson, 2011) or at trends over time within countries (Kenworthy and McCall, 2008). Likewise, Figure 8.6 with 110 observations from 26 countries shows little evidence for a correlation between the two variables. Two groups of outliers are immediately apparent: East Asia (with low inequality and low redistribution) and Latin America (with high inequality and low redistribution). Even for the old OECD countries and Eastern Europe no strong pattern emerges, though the hypothesis seems to have some validity for repeated observations from the same country. In a regression, initial inequality indeed becomes a significant explanatory variable for within-country changes in relative redistribution. However, the regression coefficient loses its significance when the unemployment rate and the share of the population aged 65 years and above are added as control variables (see Luebker, 2014).

There is thus little evidence to suggest that the simple mechanism of individual utility maximization proposed by the rational choice literature is sufficient to explain why some countries redistribute more than others. One body of literature, with many contributions from political science, has sought the explanation in the properties of different political systems and argued that they differ in how they translate voters' preferences into policy outcomes. For instance, proportional representation and majority voting, voter turnout and the structure of inequality could all influence the final outcome (see, e.g., Bassett et al., 1999; Tanninen, 1999; Austen-Smith, 2000; Cukierman and Spiegel, 2003; Iversen and Soskice, 2006; Borck, 2007; Solt, 2008; Mahler, 2008; Lupu and Pontusson, 2011). Others have drawn on the second school of thought – redistribution as social insurance (see section 8.5) – to argue that social security systems have unclear a priori distributive outcomes (Moene and Wallerstein, 2003). Therefore, greater risk exposure should increase support for these schemes (see Cusack et al., 2006).

An alternative strand of literature relates to the view that redistribution aims at greater social justice where markets fail to produce equitable outcomes. Hence, people's conceptions about what is just and fair should matter – in other words, values and value orientations become important (rather than economic utility). As Amartya Sen has argued:

> People's attitudes towards, or reactions to, actual income distributions can be significantly influenced by the correspondence – or the lack thereof – between (1) their ideas of what is normatively tolerable, and (2) what they actually see in the society around them. Ideas of social justice can sway actual behaviour and actions. (Sen, 2000, p. 60)

Relating income redistribution to the sphere of ideas and value orientations provides a fresh starting point. If different societies have different conceptions about what can be considered just, societies should indeed evaluate identical levels of inequality differently. Data from opinion surveys show that this is in fact the case: for instance, people from Eastern Europe, who were socialized in a (at least nominally) socialist system, are far more adverse to inequality than those from Western Europe. At the other extreme, citizens from the Anglo-Saxon countries, and especially the United States, are found to be far more tolerant of inequality (see Luebker, 2007). Interestingly, the evaluation of inequality as 'too large' translates into greater support for fiscal redistribution among the electorate – an effect that is independent of the actual level of inequality (ibid.).

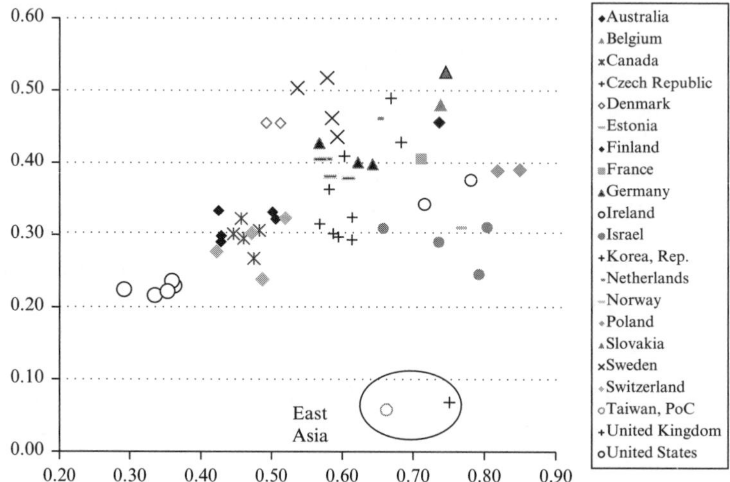

Sources: Luxembourg Income Study Database (LIS); www.lisdatacenter.org (multiple countries; analysis of micro-data completed between February and May 2011); International Social Survey Programme (ISSP, 2011a–f), modules on Role of Government II and III, and Social Inequality I to IV; see Luebker (2014) for details.

Figure 8.7 Support for redistribution and relative redistribution in 22 countries and territories

Do these differences in public support for redistribution matter for policy outcomes? Figure 8.7 plots the share of respondents from a large-scale public opinion survey who agree that it is the government's role to reduce income differences (on the horizontal axis) against actual redistribution (on the vertical axis). The fit is much better than in the previous figure, although East Asia remains an outlier (there are no matching observations from Latin America). When the East Asian outliers are excluded, a multivariate regression model shows that public support for redistribution indeed turns out to be a highly significant explanatory variable for the variation in actual redistribution (using the relative measure; see ibid.).[28] This suggests that voters hold sway over what welfare states do, and that the sphere of ideas and values matters in the electorate's decision-making process.

However, this finding needs to be qualified with at least two caveats. First, it is not entirely clear in which direction the causality runs: while it is likely that voters' demand for redistribution matter for policy (i.e., that they serve as an input into the political system, to use David Easton's terminology), it is equally plausible that voters' conceptions of what is just and fair are partly shaped by their socialization in a particular welfare state regime. Hence, they serve as 'feedback' that is generated by previous policy (see also Easton, 1965). Second, even if there is some evidence for policy responsiveness, it would be naive to assume that favourable public opinion is all that it takes to make governments more (or less) redistributive. The lack of any large-scale redistribution in Latin America has little to do with unsupportive public opinion (there is overwhelming support in Chile and Argentina, the two countries for which ISSP data are available). Rather, history and an entrenched power structure offer a better explanation for why the welfare state is so underdeveloped in Latin America (though this is beginning to change). Power resource theory has looked into this aspect of political decision-making (see e.g., Korpi and Palme, 1998).

8.8 CONCLUSIONS

When designing and reforming labour market institutions, policy-makers can ensure that they not only promote an efficient framework for markets to operate, but also enhance equity. However, providing a level playing field and protecting those who have weak individual bargaining power will not always achieve the desired outcomes – and developments in financial markets and trade policies can have effects that run counter to the objective of greater equity. As this chapter has shown, all countries therefore intervene into the primary distribution of incomes that emerges from the market through their tax and transfer systems. Justifications for this include the pursuit of social justice, a mission at the heart of the ILO's mandate, and the search for greater efficiency – though opponents of redistribution have argued that it is primarily driven by the selfish motives of the beneficiaries.

The extent of fiscal redistribution varies substantially between countries, both in terms of its impact on income inequality and the size of taxes and transfers involved. While a larger size of transfers and taxes (relative to primary incomes) usually entails a greater reduction in inequality, the size alone explains only about a third of the variation in redistributive impact. The repressiveness of taxes and the design of social security systems is therefore at least of equal importance – a topic that is taken up by Behrendt and Woodall in Chapter 9 (pension systems) and by Berg in Chapter 10 (income support for the unemployed and the poor). Likewise, the present chapter has only considered the primary and secondary distribution of incomes, but neglected the tertiary distribution – an aspect that Martínez Franzoni and Sánchez-Ancochea discuss in Chapter 11 on the provision of public goods.

What these chapters show is that inequality is not an unavoidable outcome of market forces, but – to some degree – a matter of political choice and institutional design. While policy-makers face objective constraints (and the paths taken in some countries are clearly not sustainable), they need to keep an open ear towards public opinion to remain responsive to public demand for an equitable society. What is needed is an informed debate on how labour market governance and social security and tax policies can become part of a more balanced development path that can combine equity with growth.

NOTES

1. Note, however, that 'quirks' in the tax code and 'tax optimization' strategies sometimes mean that the very rich can evade high taxes.
2. See, for example, the Merriam-Webster online dictionary at http://www.merriam-webster.com/dictionary/redistribute; last accessed 30 August 2014.
3. Note, however, that the marginal tax rates have declined significantly since the 1970s in many advanced countries, making the tax code less progressive than it used to be (see Alvaredo et al., 2013).
4. The debate on the fairness of tax systems itself has, of course, a long heritage. A frequently cited contribution was made by Adam Smith who argued in the *Wealth of Nations* that '[t]he subjects of every state ought to contribute towards the support of the government, as nearly as possible, in proportion to their respective abilities; that is, in proportion to the revenue which they respectively enjoy under the protection of the state' (Smith [1776] 1904: Book V, Chapter II, para. 25). This has sometimes been read to imply that Smith advocated flat tax regimes (and opposed fiscal redistribution through the tax system). In fact, he invocated the maxim to condemn regressive taxes, such as the 'poll-tax upon freemen', which in his view was 'either altogether arbitrary or altogether unequal, and in most cases is both the one and the other' (ibid., para. 110). By contrast, he was sympathetic to a 'tax upon house-rents', which 'would in general fall heaviest upon the rich' and argued that 'in this sort of inequality there would not, perhaps, be any thing very unreasonable' (ibid., para. 71). Smith extended this argument to conclude that '[i]t is not very unreasonable that the rich should contribute to the public expence [sic], not only in proportion to their revenue, but something more than in that proportion' (ibid.). Although not entirely consistent with his previously stated maxim, this sentence is, of course, a neat summary of the rationale for progressive taxation.
5. More specifically, tax on capital incomes is often flat rate and lower than the top marginal income tax rate. For example, since 2009 Germany levies a flat 25 per cent tax on capital incomes (deducted at source), which is substantially lower than the top marginal income tax rate 42 per cent.
6. The analysis of tax records has some additional insights to offer; see, in particular, the work carried out by Alvaredo et al. (2013) for the World Top Incomes Database.
7. Across the Organisation for Economic Co-operation and Development (OECD) countries, taxes on general consumption accounted for 13.4 per cent of total tax revenues in 1975, which rose to 20.5 per cent by 2010 (see OECD, 2012, Table 28). Over the same period, the share of taxes on personal incomes in total tax revenue declined from 29.8 per cent to 23.9 per cent (ibid., Table 10).
8. Household surveys do not typically capture indirect taxes paid by households and the national accounts (SNA, 2008) capture them in the distribution of income account (and the production account).

9. Note that in the case of maternity cash benefits, male contributors have a probability of zero to receive benefits. Social insurance schemes that fund maternity cash benefits are therefore redistributive a priori from a gender perspective. There is, however, a strong rationale to collect insurance contributions from both men and women workers (and their employers) in order not to establish a disincentive to hire women.
10. For studies that use the absolute measure for redistribution, see, for example, Kenworthy and Pontusson (2005) or Mahler and Jesuit (2006); some examples for studies based on the relative measure of inequality are Korpi and Palme (1998); Bradley et al. (2003); Mahler (2004); Iversen and Soskice (2006); or Luebker (2014).
11. The two most frequently used scales are: (1) the so-called 'modified OECD equivalence scale', which was first proposed by Hagenaars et al. (1994) and assigns a value of 1 to the household head, 0.5 to other adults and 0.3 to each child; and (2) the square root scale that divides household income by the square root of household size (see the short note by the OECD titled 'What are equivalence scales?', available at http://www.oecd.org/eco/growth/OECD-Note-EquivalenceScales.pdf; last accessed 30 August 2014).
12. One of the most comprehensive documentations can be found in the user guide to the World Income Inequality Database by the United Nations University World Institute for Development Economics Research (UNU-WIDER) (available at http://website1.wider.unu.edu/wiid/WIID2c.pdf; last accessed 30 August 2014).
13. Some of the discussion in this section follows the useful structure in Boadway and Keen (2000), in which a more detailed list of sources can be found.
14. See http://www.ilo.org/global/about-the-ilo/history/lang--en/index.htm; last accessed 30 August 2014.
15. The idea of social justice as an overarching policy objective is very much alive today. For a recent policy document that makes explicit reference to social justice, see the *ILO Declaration on Social Justice for a Fair Globalization*, adopted by the International Labour Conference at its 97th Session (Geneva, 10 June 2008); last accessed 30 August 2014 at http://www.ilo.org/wcmsp5/groups/public/---dgreports/---cabinet/documents/genericdocument/wcms_099766.pdf.
16. Sen (2000, p. 63) points to some obvious shortcomings of the welfarist analysis, namely the assumption that people derive identical utilities from the same basket of commodities (that may or may not enable them to exercise some capabilities) and that the summation of utilities across persons is blind to distribution. See Sen (ibid.) for a more nuanced discussion of social justice and the distribution of income.
17. According to the World Bank's *World Development Indicators*, health expenditure accounted for 17.9 per cent of GDP in the United States and for 8.9 per cent of GDP in Finland (data for 2011).
18. The results were previously published in Luebker (2011), on which the following discussion draws.
19. Under the definition used here, private sector incomes include all pre-tax incomes that derive from the private sector (such as income from employment, property income and private transfers). Unfortunately, no comparable data are available for developing countries.
20. The coefficient of determination, R^2, is equivalent to the squared correlation coefficient.
21. The measures for relative redistribution for the United Kingdom are United Kingdom 0.318 (1979) and 0.297 (2004) and for the United States 0.250 (1979) and 0.225 (2004).
22. Note that the black bars and the total size of the bars on the left add up to 100 per cent. For national accounts purposes, primary incomes include social contributions made by employers on behalf of their employees (in addition to those paid by employees themselves, which are often directly deducted from wages and salaries). Employers' social contributions are part of the compensation of employees, which is attributed to households in its entirety (SNA, 2008, para. 8.16). This is a difference to an analysis based on household survey data, where employers' social contributions are usually not classified as household income.
23. The residual category of other current transfers includes 'net premiums and claims

under non-life insurance policies . . . as well as current transfers to and from NPISHs [non-profit institutions serving households] and between resident and non-resident households' (see SNA, 2008, para. 8.19). The latter includes, for instance, alimony payments.
24. For presentational purposes, it is assumed that taxes and social contributions are paid out of primary incomes. In reality, some social benefits (and pensions in particular) are taxed. National accounts therefore first add benefits and other transfers to primary incomes, and then subtract taxes and contributions.
25. This means that the general government sector must finance itself by taxing corporations or generate its own primary income – or take on debt to finance the deficit.
26. Refers to the unweighted average of national figures for the 24 countries where data were available for 2010 and 1995 (or, in some cases, another base year; compare Figure 8.4). The averages exclude Cyprus, Luxembourg and Malta.
27. For further details, see Luebker (2014) on which this section draws heavily.
28. The model controls for the unemployment rate, the share of the population aged 65 years and above and the initial level of inequality; see Luebker (2014).

REFERENCES

ADB (2012), *Asian Development Outlook 2012. Confronting Rising Inequality in Asia*, Mandaluyong City: Asian Development Bank.

Alvaredo, F. and J. Londoño Vélez (2013), 'High incomes and personal taxation in a developing economy: Colombia 1993–2010', *CEQ Working Paper No. 12*, New Orleans and Washington, DC: Commitment to Equity.

Alvaredo, F., A.B. Atkinson, T. Piketty and E. Saez (2013), 'The top 1 percent in international and historical perspective', *NBER Working Paper No. 19075*, Cambridge, MA: National Bureau of Economic Research.

Asfaw, S., B. Davis and J. Dewbre et al. (2012), 'The impact of the Kenya CT-OVC programme on productive activities and labour allocation', mimeo, Rome: Food and Agriculture Organization.

Atkinson, A.B. (2004), 'The Luxembourg Income Study (LIS): past, present and future', *Socio-Economic Review*, **2**(2), 165–90.

Atkinson, A.B., T. Piketty and E. Saez (2011), 'Top incomes in the long run of history', *Journal of Economic Literature*, **49**(1), 3–71.

Austen-Smith, D. (2000), 'Redistributing income under proportional representation', *Journal of Political Economy*, **108**(6), 1235–69.

Bassett, W.F., J.P. Burkett and L. Putterman (1999), 'Income distribution, government transfers, and the problem of unequal influence', *European Journal of Political Economy*, **15**(2), 207–28.

Bird, R.M. and E.M. Zolt (2005), 'Redistribution via taxation: the limited role of the personal income tax in developing countries', *Research Paper No. 05-22*, Los Angeles, CA: University of California.

Birdsall, N., D. Ross and R. Sabot (1995), 'Inequality and growth reconsidered: lessons from East Asia', *World Bank Economic Review*, **9**(3), 477–508.

Boadway, R. and M. Keen (2000), 'Redistribution', in A.B. Atkinson and F. Bourguignon (eds), *Handbook of Income Distribution*, Amsterdam: Elsevier, pp. 677–789.

Borck, R. (2007), 'Voting, inequality and redistribution', *Journal of Economic Surveys*, **21**(1), 90–109.

Bradley, D., E. Huber and S. Moller et al. (2003), 'Distribution and redistribution in postindustrial democracies', *World Politics*, **55**(2), 193–228.

Chaudhry, M.G. (ed.) (2003), *Agrarian Reforms and Agricultural Productivity*, Tokyo: Asian Productivity Organization.

Cornia, A.C., J.C. Gómez-Sabaini and B. Martorano (2011), 'A new fiscal pact, tax policy changes and income inequality. Latin America during the last decade', *Working Paper No. 2011/70*, Helsinki: United Nations University World Institute for Development Economics Research (UNU-WIDER).

Cukierman, A. and Y. Spiegel (2003), 'When is the median voter paradigm a reasonable guide for policy choices in a representative democracy?', *Economics and Politics*, **15**(3), 247–84.

Cusack, T., T. Iversen and P. Rehm (2006), 'Risks at work: the demand and supply sides of government redistribution', *Oxford Review of Economic Policy*, **23**(3), 365–89.

de Mello, L. and E.R. Tiongson (2006), 'Income inequality and redistributive government spending', *Public Finance Review*, **34**(3), 282–305.

Downs, A. (1957), *An Economic Theory of Democracy*, New York: Harper.

Easton, D. (1965), *A Systems Analysis of Political Life*, New York: Wiley.

ECLAC (2008), *Social Panorama of Latin America 2007*, Santiago: Economic Commission for Latin America and the Caribbean.

Emran, M.S. and J.E. Stiglitz (2007), *Equity and Efficiency in Tax Reform in Developing Countries*, mimeo, Washington, DC/New York: George Washington University/Columbia University.

Goñi, E., J.H. López and L. Servén (2008), 'Fiscal redistribution and income inequality in Latin America', *Policy Research Working Paper No. 4487*, Washington, DC: World Bank.

Guillaud, E. (2013), 'Preferences for redistribution: an empirical analysis over 33 countries', *Journal of Economic Inequality*, **11**(1), 57–78.

Hagenaars, A., K. de Vos and M.A. Zaidi (1994), *Poverty Statistics in the Late 1980s: Research Based on Micro-data*, Luxembourg: Office for Official Publications of the European Communities.

Hicks, A. (1999), *Social Democracy and Welfare Capitalism: A Century of Income Security Policies*, Ithaca: Cornell University Press.

Huber, E. and J.D. Stephens (2001), *Development and Crisis of the Welfare State: Parties and Policies in Global Markets*, Chicago, IL: University of Chicago Press.

ILO/IILS (2008), *World of Work Report 2008: Income Inequalities in the Age of Financial Globalization*, Geneva: International Labour Office/International Institute of Labour Studies.

ILO (2010), *World Social Security Report 2010/11: Providing Coverage in Times of Crisis and Beyond*, Geneva: International Labour Office.

ILO (2012), *Global Wage Report 2012/13: Wages and Equitable Growth*, Geneva: International Labour Office.

ILO/World Bank (2012), *Inventory of Policy Responses to the Financial and Economic Crisis. Joint Synthesis Report*, Geneva/Washington, DC: International Labour Organization/World Bank.

ISSP (2011a), *Role of Government II, 1990*, Cologne, GESIS, ZA1950 [2 Aug. 2011], International Social Survey Programme.

ISSP (2011b), *Role of Government III, 1996*, Cologne, GESIS, ZA3430 [2 Aug. 2011], International Social Survey Programme.

ISSP (2011c), *Social Inequality I, 1987*, Cologne, GESIS, ZA1680 [2 Aug. 2011], International Social Survey Programme.

ISSP (2011d), *Social Inequality II, 1992*, Cologne, GESIS, ZA2310 [2 Aug. 2011], International Social Survey Programme.

ISSP (2011e), *Social Inequality III, 1999*, Cologne, GESIS, ZA3430 [2 Aug. 2011], International Social Survey Programme.

ISSP (2011f), *Social Inequality IV, 2009*, Cologne, GESIS, ZA5400 [2 Aug. 2011], International Social Survey Programme.

Iversen, T. and T. Soskice (2006), 'Electoral institutions and the politics of coalitions: why some democracies redistribute more than others', *American Political Science Review*, **100**(2), 161–81.

Jacobs, D. (2000), 'Low inequality with low redistribution? An analysis of income distribution in Japan, South Korea and Taiwan compared to Britain', *CASE Paper No. 33*, London: London School of Economics.

Jansen, M. and E. Lee (2007), *Trade and Employment: Challenges for Policy Research*, Geneva: World Trade and Organization and International Labour Organization.

Kenworthy, L. and L. McCall (2008), 'Inequality, public opinion, and redistribution', *Socio-Economic Review*, **46**(1), 35–68.

Kenworthy, L. and J. Pontusson (2005), 'Rising inequality and the politics of redistribution in affluent countries', *Perspectives on Politics*, **3**(3), 449–71.

Korpi, W. and J. Palme (1998), 'The paradox of redistribution and strategies of equality: welfare state institutions, inequality, and poverty in the Western countries', *American Sociological Review*, **63**(5), 661–87.

López, R. and S.J. Miller (2008), 'Chile: the unbearable burden of inequality', *World Development*, **36**(12), 2679–95.

Luebker, M. (2007), 'Inequality and the demand for redistribution: are the assumptions of the new growth theory valid?', *Socio-Economic Review*, **5**(1), 117–48.

Luebker, M. (2011), *The Impact of Taxes and Transfers on Inequality, TRAVAIL Policy Brief No. 4*, Geneva: International Labour Organization.

Luebker, M. (2014), 'Income inequality, redistribution and poverty: contrasting rational choice and behavioural perspectives', *Review of Income and Wealth*, **60**(1), 131–54.

Lupu, N. and J. Pontusson (2011), 'The structure of inequality and the politics of redistribution', *American Political Science Review*, **105**(2), 316–36.

Mahler, V.A. (2004), 'Economic globalization, domestic politics, and income inequality in the developed countries: a cross-national study', *Comparative Political Studies*, **37**(9), 1025–53.

Mahler, V.A. (2008), 'Electoral turnout and income redistribution by the state: a cross-national analysis of the developed democracies', *European Journal of Political Research*, **47**(2), 161–83.

Mahler, V.A. and D.K. Jesuit (2006), 'Fiscal redistribution in the developed countries: new insights from the Luxembourg Income Study', *Socio-Economic Review*, **4**(3), 483–511.

Meltzer, A.H. and S.F. Richard (1981), 'A rational theory of the size of government', *Journal of Political Economy*, **89**(5), 914–27.

Moene, K.O. and M. Wallerstein (2003), 'Earnings inequality and welfare spending: a disaggregated analysis', *World Politics*, **55**(4), 485–516.

National Treasury (2013), *National Budget Review*, Pretoria: National Treasury, accessed 30 August at http://www.treasury.gov.za/documents/national%20 budget/2013/review/.

OECD (2012),'Tax levels and tax structures, 1965–2011', *Revenue Statistics 2012*, Paris: Organisation for Economic Co-operation and Development.

Rawls, J. (1971), *A Theory of Justice*, Cambridge, MA: Harvard University Press.

Riswold, S. (2004), 'VAT in Sub-Saharan Africa – a critique of IMF VAT policy', *VAT Monitor*, **15**(2), 97–110.

Rothschild, M. and J.E. Stiglitz (1976), 'Equilibrium in competitive insurance markets: an essay on the economics of imperfect information', *Quarterly Journal of Economics*, **90**(4), 629–49.

Schumpeter, J.A. (1942), *Capitalism, Socialism and Democracy*, London and New York: Harper.

Sen, A. (2000), 'Social justice and the distribution of income', in A.B. Atkinson and F. Bourguignon (eds), *Handbook of Income Distribution, Vol. 1*, Amsterdam: Elsevier, pp. 59–85.

Sen, A. (2005), 'Human rights and capabilities', *Journal of Human Development*, **6**(2), 151–66.

Smith, A. ([1776] 1904), *An Inquiry into the Nature and Causes of the Wealth of Nations*, London: Methuen.

SNA (2008), *System of National Accounts 2008*, accessed 30 August 2014 at un.org/unsd/nationalaccount/sna2008.asp.

Solt, F. (2008), 'Economic inequality and democratic political engagement', *American Journal of Political Science*, **52**(1), 48–60.

Stiglitz, J.E. (2012), *The Price of Inequality: How Today's Divided Society Endangers Our Future*, New York, W.W. Norton and Company.

Tanninen, H. (1999), 'Income inequality, government expenditures and growth', *Applied Economics*, **31**(9), 1109–17.

UN-ESCAP (2013), *Economic and Social Survey of Asia and the Pacific 2013. Forward-looking Macroeconomic Policies for Inclusive and Sustainable Development*, Bangkok: United Nations Economic Commission for Asia and the Pacific.

UNRISD (2011), *Combatting Poverty and Inequality: Structural Change, Social Policy and Politics*, Geneva: United Nations Research Institute for Social Development.

WHO (2013), *World Health Statistics 2013. Part III: Global Health Indicators*, Geneva: World Health Organization.

9. Pensions and other social security income transfers

Christina Behrendt and John Woodall*

9.1 INTRODUCTION

Rising levels of inequality have been acknowledged as a major concern by various international organizations and other observers over recent years (ILO, 2000, 2008; World Bank, 2006; OECD, 2008, 2011a; UNRISD, 2010; IMF, 2012). As a consequence, many of these observers have called for a greater emphasis on policies that can contain inequality and foster more inclusive growth, with a view to promoting not only sustainability but also, importantly, social cohesion. However, much of the debate around institutional responses to inequality has been limited to policies aiming at the reduction of poverty in a narrow sense, while policy approaches that could address inequality more broadly have not yet been explored to a full extent. One such area is that of pension systems, which play a major role in preventing poverty and vulnerability for large groups of the population, and thus reach far beyond poverty reduction in a narrow sense.

Inequality has many dimensions, and, to the extent that the different dimensions call for a variety of labour market solutions and institutions, these are explored throughout this book. Certain dimensions have particular relevance to the design of social security systems. Along one such dimension, we may note that differences in the levels of income received by individuals give rise to issues of poverty, either actual or potential, in which case our concern is with the relative status of individuals and groups who are vulnerable to this condition. Along another dimension, we see individuals who are 'unlucky' enough to suffer the effects of some *contingency*, such as the occurrence of a disabling accident; others are 'lucky' in that they avoid such an eventuality, and, in particular, its consequences. This conceptualization of possible dimensions is by no means exhaustive. Inequality may be seen, for example, in inter-temporal terms – an individual may be relatively well-off now, but relatively poor at some time in the future. Or it may be seen in inter-generational terms – when the relationship between generations, of, say, younger as compared with older workers may be inequitable for various reasons. Important issues arise of inequality as between women and men, and, although a full study is far beyond the scope of this chapter, some discussion will be found below.

To address, and, it is hoped, correct, inequality as represented along any of these dimensions, is necessarily and inescapably a matter of *redistribution* of resources. In as far as that may be done at the level of 'society' (referring here, to the national level in general, or at least a high level of subnational grouping) and so reflect a concept of solidarity within that society, this is the proper scope of *social security* or *social protection*.

For the designers and administrators of social security schemes and systems – in general, 'practitioners' – it is likely to be a significant objective to address as great a quantum of poverty and vulnerability as is practically possible in any given, national setting. In many countries, schemes have been designed to meet the needs of workers – and their families – in the formal labour market, and these have typically focused on a certain set of closely defined 'contingencies',[1] most, if not all of which can be analysed as 'insurable risks' and which can be addressed very effectively (assuming that circumstances allow for efficient administration) through the mechanism of social insurance.[2] In many countries, these schemes are complemented by non-contributory schemes, largely financed out of general taxation. The International Labour Organization (ILO) has been influential in the design of such schemes in the majority of the countries of the world ever since its creation in 1919.

Over several decades the recognition has grown that, in many countries, labour markets are characterized by a dichotomy between 'formal' and 'informal'. In many cases, in particular but not exclusively in Africa and Asia, the informal predominates. This has resulted in some reassessment of the general framework of social protection – and may indeed be seen as the main driver of the concept of the *social protection floor*, the central aim of which is to guarantee at least a minimum level of social security for all.[3] The power of a national social security system to alleviate poverty and inequality is greatly undermined if the system cannot address the needs of the majority, either because of their inability to participate in the system at all, or because the factors that drive them towards vulnerability and into poverty differ qualitatively from those that have been covered traditionally (Townsend, 2009; ILO, 2010a, 2010b, 2011; UNRISD, 2010). Most plainly and most often, this means simply their lack of adequate income, which is the main focus of this chapter.

To begin, we look at the scope of social security schemes in which income transfers are aimed at replacing income from labour in situations where persons are unable – for shorter or longer periods, temporarily or permanently – to earn sufficient income in situations of unemployment, sickness, maternity and parenthood, disability or old age, and for a (limited) set of other reasons. Social security systems include *social insurance*, where entitlement to benefits depends on payment of contributions by insured persons for at least a certain minimum period and the benefit amounts are usually related to previous earnings of the beneficiary or the amount of contribution paid. Social security systems also usually include non-contributory components, which may include *universal benefits*, to which all residents in certain categories will be entitled, and non-contributory *social assistance* benefits where typically an income or *means test* decides the entitlements of a person or household.

Any income transfers modify of course – although in various ways – overall income distribution in its different dimensions. Since the main focus of this chapter is on the impact of pensions, we will look in more detail at the following selected aspects of impacts of pension systems on income inequality and directions of income redistribution:

- How do different pension systems impact overall income inequality and poverty?
- How do different pension systems interact with the income situations of those with differing labour market statuses (formal/informal economy, decent/precarious employment, high/low earnings)?
- In particular, what impact do different pension systems have on the relative income situation of women as compared with men?
- To what extent are different pension systems seen to provide equitably across different generations, now and in the future?

Pensions represent so-called long-term social security benefits, as they are paid over prolonged periods in situations of old age (retirement pensions), disability (disability pensions) and loss of the breadwinner (survivors' pensions). Pensions can be contributory, or non-contributory, and in the latter case universal or means-tested. Virtually every country has a pension system, sometimes of rather limited scope, and these exhibit various mixes of contributory benefits with benefits and interventions of a non-contributory character. National pension systems often include, in addition to public provision, private (occupational or personal) pension schemes, which may be mandatory or voluntary.

Pension policies form an important part of a national portfolio of redistributive policies, within a wider set of social protection policies. Together with expenditure on health, pensions often constitute the biggest item of expenditure in national social security budgets, and have a strong impact on redistribution. It is for this reason that we focus here on pensions in particular, but where appropriate we do refer also to other components of social security systems that have important implications for the relationship between labour market institutions and inequality.

Thus, we discuss first the relationship between pension systems and inequality by highlighting some of the key (re-)distributive channels (section 9.2). We then discuss the ways in which inequalities in the labour market can be perpetuated, attenuated or amplified in pension systems (section 9.3). These are particularly visible when comparing gender differences with respect to pension coverage and pension levels (section 9.4); moreover the extent to which inter-generational equality is or is not served represents a matter of significant topical concern (section 9.5). We conclude with some observations that summarize, and emphasize the importance of an environment in which social dialogue contributes to the search for productive and decent employment and social justice.

9.2 PENSION SYSTEMS, INCOME INEQUALITY AND POVERTY

Pension systems have a strong impact on inequality. In many countries, public pensions constitute the main channel of income redistribution through taxes and transfers (see Luebker, Chapter 8 in this volume). According to a recent study on income redistribution in 28 OECD countries around 2004, about half of total redistribution was channelled through the public pension system, yet with a wide variation between 20 and 83 per cent of total redistribution (Caminada et al., 2012; Wang et al., 2012). Figure 9.1 demonstrates the large variation of the role of public old-age and survivor pensions for redistributive policies in a larger group of countries. While public pensions play an important role in overall redistribution in Hungary, Italy and Poland, the Scandinavian countries achieve a relatively equal distribution of disposable incomes through the combined effect of pensions and other social transfers, despite a relatively unequal distribution of market incomes. At the other end of the spectrum, the redistributive impact of pensions and other social transfers tends to be relatively small across a range of countries in Latin America, as can be seen in the examples of Colombia, Guatemala, Mexico and Peru, yet Brazil and Uruguay achieve a marked reduction in inequality through pensions and other social transfers.

This variation is partly influenced by demographic factors, notably the share of the elderly population in the total population, in view of the dominance of old-age pensioners in the total number of pension beneficiaries.[4] However, Figure 9.2 suggests that redistributive outcomes also reflect other factors, which are more closely related to the structure of the pension system,

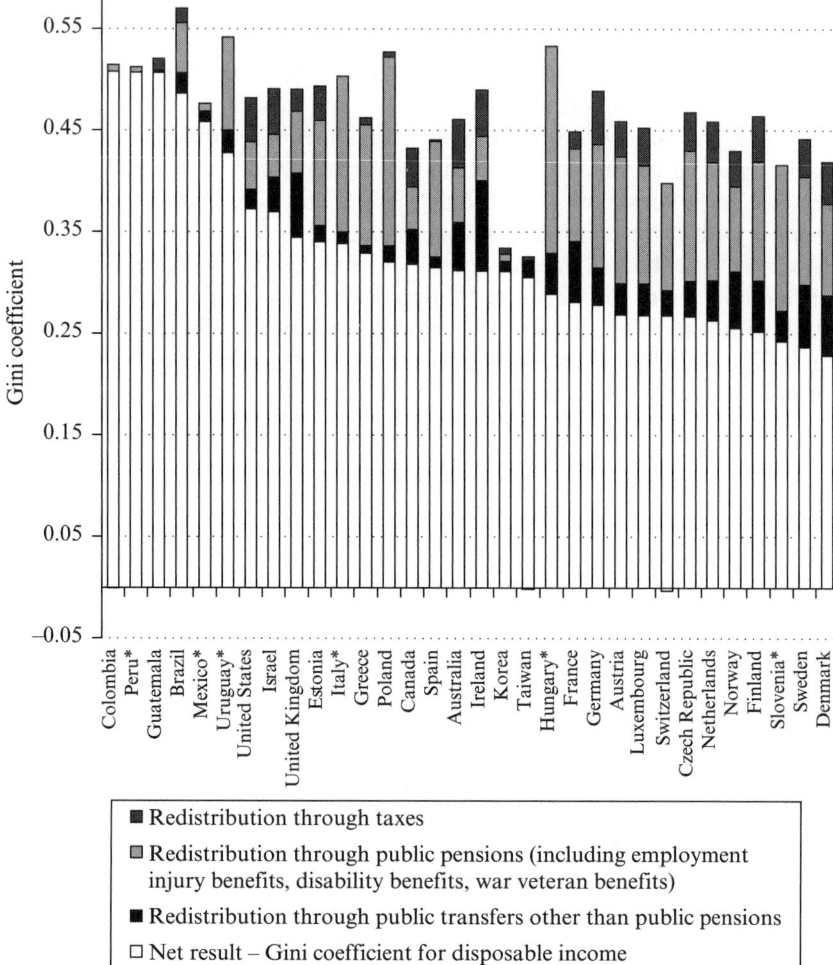

Notes:
Public pensions include contributory or non-contributory pensions for old age, survivorship, employment injury, disability as well as war veteran benefits.
* Data on taxes are not available.

Source: Own calculations from data provided in the Budget Incidence Financial Distribution Database (Wang and Caminada, 2011a, 2011b), which is based on household income survey datasets from the Luxembourg Income Study.

Figure 9.1 Income inequality and redistribution through public pensions, other social transfers and taxes (Gini coefficients), around 2004

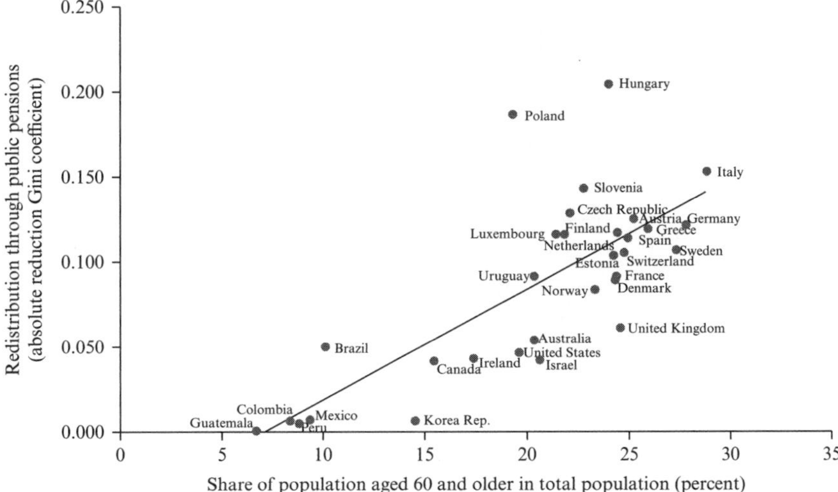

Source: Own calculations from data provided in the Budget Incidence Financial Distribution Database (Wang and Caminada, 2011a, 2011b), which are based on household datasets from the Luxembourg Income Study; UN World Population Prospects: the 2010 Revision.

Figure 9.2 Share of the elderly population and redistribution through public pensions, other social transfers and taxes (Gini coefficients), around 2004/05

including the combination of contributory and non-contributory benefits, as well as the respective roles of public and private provision in pension policy. For example, while Poland and the United States have a similar share of older persons in the total population, public pensions in Poland display a much stronger redistributive effect than those in the United States.

Nevertheless, the part played by pension systems in the reduction of inequality and income insecurity in many parts of the world is limited. This is largely due to the limited coverage of pension systems, in particular in low- and middle-income countries. Regional variations are also significant, and Figure 9.3 displays variant indicators. It can be seen from these ILO estimates that, first, only one in two older persons worldwide receives any kind of old-age pension and thus enjoys at least a minimum level of income security (ILO, 2010a). While the large majority of older persons in Europe and North America receive an old-age pension, this is the case for less than one in two older persons in Asia and the Pacific, the Middle East and North Africa, and only one in six in Sub-Saharan Africa (see Figure 9.3). Second, it is evident that the proportion of those contributing to a pension scheme does not correlate closely with the proportion,

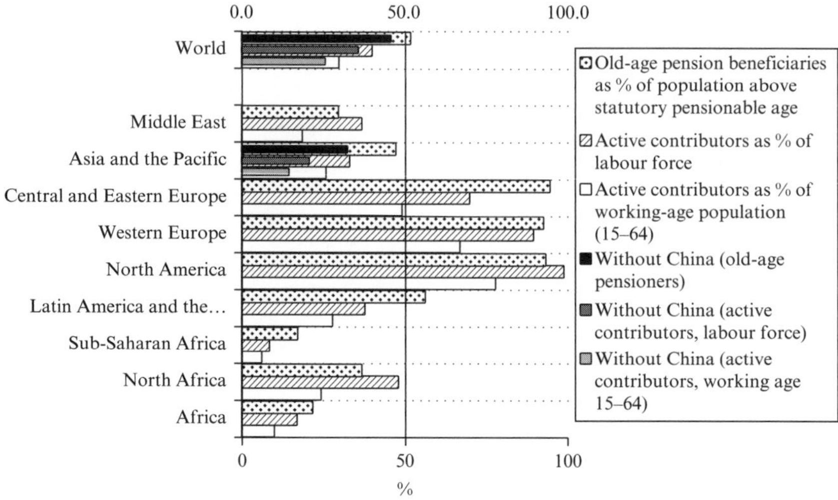

Source: ILO (2014), *World Social Protection Report*, Figure 4.8 and Annex Tables B.8 and B.9.

Figure 9.3 Proportion of working-age people contributing to a pension scheme and proportion of elderly people benefitting from an old-age pension

currently at least, in receipt of a pension. The share of the current working-age population actively contributing to a public pension scheme does, however, represent a broader indicator for the level of protection with regard to major social risks and contingencies in the present (employment injury, disability and survivorship) and in the future (old age). Where only a small share of the working-age population actively contributes to pension schemes, the conclusion is that the level of overall protection is low, unless non-contributory benefits are available to provide at least a basic level of protection against those risks and contingencies.

Recalling that, as depicted in Figure 9.1, a large proportion of the effective redistribution of income effected by social security systems is in fact channelled through pension systems, this represents a transfer from economically active to economically inactive groups of the population. Such redistribution helps to smooth income and consumption across the life course but contributes little to the redistribution of resources between richer and poorer groups of the population. A large proportion of social security schemes, particularly those providing pensions, are contributory in form, and provide for time-shifting ('inter-temporal' shifting) of consumption, resulting in patterns of redistribution that are both complex and subtle. However, an important aspect of the total redistribution through pension systems, to which some further attention is devoted in section 9.5, is of an inter-temporal (or inter-generational) nature, in the sense that people pay contributions into the system and earn entitlements that they can draw on in case they are affected by the risks of employment injury, disability or the death of the breadwinner, and/or once they have reached pensionable age. In the case of old-age pensions, inter-generational redistribution is obvious in the case of schemes financed on a pay-as-you-go (PAYG) basis, but is largely true even in the case of schemes financed partially or fully from the returns on invested funds.

Different tiers of public pension systems usually also include elements of direct redistribution of current income. The impact is strongest in the case of non-contributory pensions, whether these are universal or means-tested.[5] Such schemes, usually financed from taxes rather than social security contributions, play a critical role in providing a minimum level of income security to those who have not been able to accumulate sufficient pension entitlements in contributory schemes (see below). However, these schemes usually provide modest benefit levels that aim at preventing poverty, while the wider function of maintaining a certain level of income (smoothing consumption over the life course) is usually fulfilled by contributory schemes.

The contributory tiers of pension systems usually do, nevertheless, include some redistributive elements, such as benefit formulas with a flat rate component, minimum pension guarantees, or the continued (imputed or subsidized) payment of contributions through periods of education, unemployment, maternity or child care. The overall redistributive impact may differ depending on whether such a non-contributory element is financed within the scheme from its contribution revenue (redistribution taking place between members of the scheme) or is financed from general tax revenue (redistribution thus may involve financing at least indirectly by those who are not members of the scheme). The most important aspect to take into account in analysing patterns of such redistribution will be the extent of coverage by the scheme.

Many pension systems are fragmented and include separate pension schemes for specific groups of the workforce. For example, in many countries, civil servants are covered by a specific pension scheme. Such fragmentation constitutes particular challenges with regard to the redistributive effects of pension systems (and indeed the public perceptions of the overall 'fairness' of pension systems), particularly where such special schemes are not financed by employee and employer contributions but directly out of the state budget.

Distributive outcomes also depend on the interplay of public pension schemes (contributory or non-contributory) with private provision, which may be publicly mandated or voluntary. This interplay, which is also referred to as the 'public–private mix' in pension provision, contributes to shaping distribution outcomes (e.g., Rein and Behrendt, 2004).

Private pensions (occupational or personal pensions) are often assumed to include fewer redistributive elements (other than inter-temporal redistribution) than public pensions. However, they have distinctive redistributive outcomes, which tend to be less obvious than for public pension schemes. Measures to encourage contributions to private pension programmes for low-income earners by matching (subsidizing) contributions (Hinz et al., 2013) transfer public resources to low-income workers, which may result in a progressive effect, yet they often fail to reach the most vulnerable groups of workers. On the other hand, tax incentives for private provision (tax treatment of contributions and pension income) tend to benefit high-income groups disproportionately and may actually have regressive effects, that is, they redistribute resources from poorer groups to richer groups of the population.

9.3 DIFFERENT COMPOSITIONS OF PENSION SYSTEMS AND INCOME SITUATIONS OF PERSONS WITH DIFFERENT LABOUR MARKET STATUSES DURING THEIR WORKING CAREERS

Pension systems reflect and influence inequitable features of the labour market and employment in a variety of ways, and may aggravate or attenuate such inequalities. The distributive impact of pension systems depends in particular on the design of contributory pension schemes, the public–private mix, the interplay of contributory and non-contributory elements of protection, and the availability of non-contributory pensions and minimum pension provisions for those who are unable to build up sufficient pension entitlements during their working lifetimes.

Pension entitlements are closely associated with the nature of (previous) employment, not least because membership of a scheme is usually linked to participation in employment and employment status, and where the right to benefits depends on contributions paid, these are – at least loosely – calculated proportionately to earnings. While salaried employees usually constitute the core group of workers covered by public pension schemes, other categories of workers, such as self-employed workers or supporting family members, may also be covered on a mandatory or voluntary basis according to national legislation. In some cases, scheme

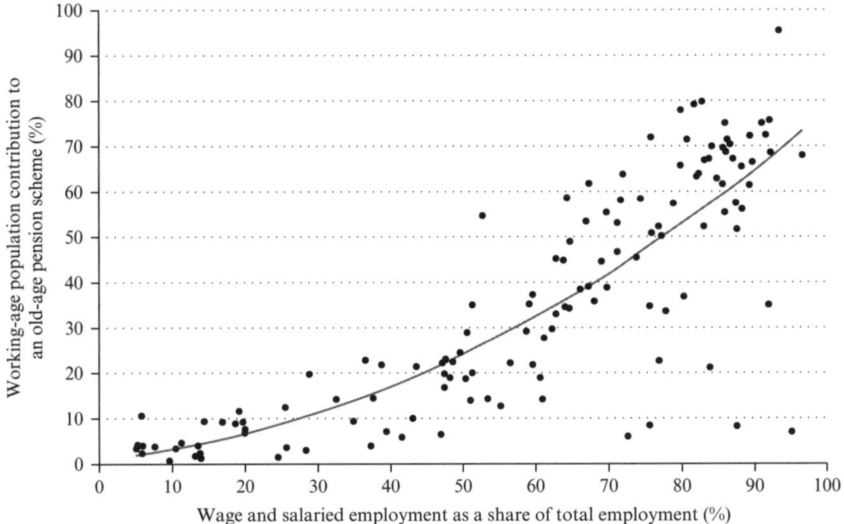

Source: ILO (2010a, Figure 4.4).

Figure 9.4 Wage and salaried employment and active contributors to public pension schemes as a share of total employment, latest available year (percentage of working-age population)

membership may not be explicitly linked to an employment contract, yet depends on a sufficient and regular stream of income, and so constitutes an indirect link to employment.

As a result, coverage by contributory pension schemes (both public and private) is – directly or indirectly – associated with the level of employment, particularly formal employment. Figure 9.4 shows for a sample of 130 countries that the percentage of contributors to public pension schemes is strongly correlated with wage employment. Low rates of wage employment – often reflecting the prevalence of precarious or informal employment – are found alongside low pension coverage rates.

For example, experience from Latin America demonstrates that this link between employment and social protection is present even in labour markets where a large part of the population is not (or only weakly) attached to formal employment. The hopes in some quarters that the privatization of pension schemes and the stronger emphasis on individual accounts would contribute to the extension of pension coverage have been disappointed. In fact, in response to shrinking coverage rates and inadequate benefit levels, some of the reforms have been, at one stage or another, reversed, and complemented by a stronger emphasis on the non-contributory elements of pension systems, aiming at a better balance of the contributory and non-contributory components (Bertranou and Maurizio, 2011).

The relationship between inequality in the labour market and in pensions reflects choices in policy design. Pension schemes may be designed in a way that amplifies existing inequalities, for example, by excluding certain categories of workers, or by having excessively long vesting periods. On the other hand, pension schemes may include provisions that compensate for such inequalities, for example, through pension credits accounting for care-related interruptions of employment careers, or subsidized contributions for low-income workers. In addition, combining different contributory or non-contributory pension schemes (often referred to as 'pillars' or 'tiers' of a pension system) may further help to attenuate inequalities. Such measures will be illustrated in section 9.4, looking in particular at inequality from a gender perspective.

9.4 HOW DIFFERENT PENSION SYSTEMS IMPACT THE INCOME SITUATION OF WOMEN AS COMPARED WITH MEN

In most parts of the world, women are less likely to be covered by pension systems, and if they are, they tend to receive lower pension benefits than men. These gender inequalities result from a combination of two factors. First, pension systems themselves may treat women and men in a different way. Second, and more importantly, existing gender inequalities in employment and the labour market are reflected in – and perpetuated by – pension systems, particularly in contributory pension schemes (see Gammage, Chapter 12 in this volume).

While, under the rules of many pension schemes, women and men may be treated by and large in an equal way, there are some exceptions. These concern in particular different pensionable ages for women and men (see Ginn et al., 2001; Marin and Zólyomi, 2010; ILO, 2013a). In many countries, women are eligible for a pension earlier than men (e.g., women at age 60 and men at age 65), which a priori limits women's possibilities to accumulate pension entitlements in contributory pension schemes, and may lead to lower pension benefits. Recent pension reforms in many countries have included measures to equalize pensionable ages between women and men, and gradually increasing pensionable ages for women, which should have an equalizing effect. The greater longevity of women in most countries means that, in the absence of specific equalizing legislation, the conversion of individual account balances to periodical pensions ('annuitization') results, other factors being equal, in lower pensions for women.[6] Other examples of unequal treatment include rules that encourage or force women to withdraw their contributions upon marriage, or different rules for survivor benefits for widows and widowers.

However, even pension systems that treat women and men on terms that 'on paper' may be 'perfectly' equal can produce highly unequal outcomes in terms of income inequality and poverty in old age. As discussed in the previous section, pension systems inevitably reflect deeper inequalities in employment and the labour market, and can perpetuate them into later life. In many countries, women tend to have lower levels of labour market participation than men, have shorter and more often interrupted careers, are more likely to work in precarious or informal employment, are more likely to work part-time and earn lower wages on average (see ILO, 2012b; 2013b). As a result, they face greater difficulties in accumulating contribution periods and entitlements in contributory pension schemes.

An issue of particular importance is the way in which gendered employment patterns reflect the unequal sharing of family and care responsibilities between women and men. Some countries have adopted specific measures to recognize periods of time spent outside work due to maternity or childcare as contribution periods in their pension schemes or providing specific pension credits for raising children or caring for relatives. Given women's higher involvement in care responsibilities, such measures benefit mostly women and help to attenuate gender inequalities. In addition, the provision of public social services (see Martínez Franzoni and Sánchez-Ancochea, Chapter 11 in this volume) can also play an important role in this respect.

Pension reforms over recent decades have often included elements that strengthen the link between contributions and benefits (defined contribution approach; individual accounts); extended vesting periods and reliance on sex-differentiated mortality tables for the calculation of annuities tend to aggravate gender inequalities over both the short and longer term.[7] As a result, private pensions, which inevitably exhibit these features more prominently than public pension schemes, tend to display particularly strong gender disparities, with women being less likely to be covered and receiving lower benefit levels, thus resulting in a marked gender gap in private pensions (e.g., Behrendt, 2000; Bardasi and Jenkins, 2010).

Strengthening the redistributive elements in public pension schemes, including a greater recognition of care work and emphasizing non-contributory pension components,[8] may partly compensate for these outcomes, yet such efforts will only be successful if accompanied by a more equal sharing of care responsibilities between women and men and higher women's participation in decent employment.

The extent to which pension schemes combat, perpetuate or even aggravate gender inequalities in the labour market and employment depends on the design and structure of the pension system as a whole. Minimum pensions and non-contributory pension schemes ('social pensions') and minimum benefit levels in contributory pension schemes can play a critical role in guaranteeing at least a minimum degree of income security to women and men alike and thus contain income inequality and poverty risks in old age.[9] In fact, the majority of recipients of non-contributory pension benefits are women (ILO, 2013a, 2014). However, as non-contributory pension schemes usually provide lower benefits than contributory schemes and are often subject to a means test, their potential for providing adequate levels of protection is limited. Achieving gender equality with regard to pension systems therefore requires adequate attention to both contributory and non-contributory elements of social protection systems.

9.5 HOW DIFFERENT PENSION SYSTEMS IMPACT THE INCOME SITUATION ACROSS DIFFERENT GENERATIONS NOW AND IN THE FUTURE

In this section we address our subject from a particular perspective – the distribution of financial resources within a country between the economically active population and the pensioners – which has become the subject of an intense debate. This discussion is important in its own right, but also serves to highlight certain critical principles relating to distributional aspects of equity. Various studies have sought to quantify the extent of redistribution by identifying the 'winners' and 'losers' of intergenerational redistribution through public transfers and taxes and arguing that differences in 'rates of return' among generations were unfair (e.g., Auerbach et al., 1999). Some proponents of this view also argued that the ageing of the population in many countries would lead to a fierce conflict over resources between generations (e.g., Johnson et al., 1989). However, other studies point to the balanced nature of inter-generational relations and the complex nature of inter-generational solidarity, which includes not only the transfer of resources, as well as aspects of care, social coherence and wider solidarity (Arber and Attias-Donfut, 2000; Albertini et al., 2007; OECD, 2011c; UNFPA and HelpAge International, 2012). In fact, in a survey covering 27 EU member countries, 85 per cent of respondents on average rejected the proposition that 'older people were a burden for society'[10] and 51 per cent agreed with the statement that the risk of a conflict between generations was exaggerated by the media.[11]

This question may be approached on a basis that is either qualitative or quantitative. In the former case, a notable reference is that to be found in the work of Rawls ([1971] 1998) on a theory of justice, in which 'the problem of justice between generations' is discussed in the light of a 'just savings principle'. In Rawls's work, the focus is on the transfer of wealth between generations, in particular as mediated through the mechanism of savings, which may, of course, vary in their relative volume, and the need to ensure that, within the overall framework of societal justice, the result is perceived by the different participants to reflect 'fairness' amongst them.

A more quantitative approach to the question of generational accounting is seen in the international project to develop National Transfer Accounts (NTAs),[12] which is presently active in about 40 countries globally. The NTAs, although perhaps still rather experimental in nature, are designed to integrate with and enhance the information provided by the longer-established System of National Accounts. The starting point is the observation that, while in the mid-life 'productive' age range, most individuals produce a greater quantum of wealth than they consume in a given period, at both the beginning and end of the usual span of human life, essentially all are 'dependent', consuming a greater quantum of resources than they produce. For example, the country analysis for Taiwan (1998 figures) shows that over all ages labour income suffices to meet 77 per cent of consumption, the balance being provided by asset-based reallocations. However, for the age range 0–19, labour income provides less than 4 per cent of consumption needs, while for the age range 20–64 the figure is 121 per cent, and above age 65, less than 11 per cent. The balance of consumption is met by private transfers (40 per cent), public transfers (24 per cent) and dissaving (25 per cent). For the USA (2003 figures), the general magnitudes are similar, although the needs of those over age 65 are met more substantially (58 per cent) by dissaving. In a country such as Sweden (2003 figures), the patterns are, again, similar, although the level of labour income over the age range 20 to 65 is higher, at 167 per cent of consumption, and this enables a much higher level of support (essentially 100 per cent) to the over-65s through public transfers.

From a technical perspective, it is worth noting that such a quantitative assessment may be made on either a 'cohort' or a 'period' basis. The former looks at the lifetime experience, comparing one year of age against another, of a group of individuals born within the same year; the latter compares individuals of different ages at the present time. The results can be significantly different, and the tendency for the debate on inter-generational equity to be conducted on the basis of selectively mixed evidence from the two sets of analysis may lead to unreliable 'conclusions'. From a cohort perspective, equity may be reflected in the capacity of individuals to 'save' resources for their own retirement years. However, the need to complement this by a 'period' view can be seen in the fact that the day-to-day needs of individuals mean that a large part, at least, of resources consumed by the elderly are, in fact, drawn from current production.

We conclude – taking these perspectives together – that effective retirement provision can be made only on the basis of redistribution of resources, that in bringing about such redistribution it is inescapable that there will be large-scale inter-generational – and inter-temporal – effects, and hence that solutions can be found that are seen to be 'fair' between generations, whether or not calculations show them to be equitable in a technical sense, only when they reflect the principle of solidarity between generations.

9.6 CONCLUDING OBSERVATIONS

The aim of this chapter has been to provide an overview, necessarily on a rather selective basis, of those aspects of broad inequality that are mediated by pensions and other social security schemes, as well as social security systems as a whole, within the wider class of labour market institutions. The links between social security and the kinds of inequality manifested, specifically, but not only, within the workplace and the labour market, are intimate, as the evidence presented in section 9.1 makes clear. It is also, to some degree, bi-directional – while social security systems can and do play a strong role in counteracting inequality, certain aspects of the design of some schemes, even in modern times, tend to reflect former social norms that are now understood to be inequitable. One obvious example is the prevalence of pension schemes with differential retirement ages for women and men.

If social security schemes are to fully realize their capacity to address the issue of inequality – and in more specific terms to combat poverty and vulnerability – their scope of action must be multi-dimensional. The policy approach of the ILO (ILO, 2012a) to this need is expressed, at the first level, in terms of a horizontal dimension, through national social protection floors, in which the objective is to ensure coverage of all members of society, so that the power of social protection to overcome poverty and vulnerability can be brought into play, and a vertical dimension in which the emphasis is on the provision of higher levels of social security, including income maintenance and consumption smoothing. Both dimensions play an important role in ensuring social security at the individual level, as well as at the societal level, providing an 'automatic stabilizer' function in times of economic instability.

National social protection floors (SPFs), as guided by the ILO's Social Protection Floors Recommendation, 2012 (No. 202), are conceived in terms of the provision to all individuals in a society/population of an appropriate set of income guarantees and basic services, meeting essential needs at all periods of life. The SPF concept therefore represents the core of the framework within which social security systems address the issues of poverty and vulnerability – the 'horizontal' aspect of the two-dimensional strategy. While the present discussion focuses in particular on the role of social security in old-age income security, and indeed reflects the importance of long-term vision, this should not obscure the need for a balanced and as far as possible comprehensive approach to social protection. It is expected that the global SPF approach will be given appropriate operational expression at the national level in each country. In particular, as shown in section 9.2, the phenomenon of population ageing is almost universal, meaning that there is a significant role to be played by pension systems, together with other elements of social security systems, in preventing poverty and containing inequality within countries.

Sections 9.3 and 9.4 have looked more closely at specific forms and aspects of inequality that are reflected in social security systems broadly and pensions schemes specifically, and that are amenable to being addressed through their multi-dimensional and redistributive character. Those that impact inequitably on women as compared to men are of particular significance, and – while this topic merits extensive treatment in its own right – one issue to be highlighted is that of the constraint on the ability of many women to accumulate adequate pension rights by reason of their greater involvement in care responsibilities and unpaid work, as well as persistent gender wage gaps. In an environment of an accelerating trend towards pension accumulation on the basis of individual accounts (in defined-contribution schemes), inequitable treatment can arise in many ways, one example being through annuitization rules. These issues stand to be solved in a more fully socially informed perspective. There is an urgent role to be taken up in relation to social protection for the application of the key ILO tool of social dialogue amongst the wide range of stakeholders in its schemes and institutions (Ghellab et al., 2011; Sarfati and Ghellab, 2012).

Section 9.5 introduced the topical issue of income redistribution and the question of how equitable this can be, from an inter-generational perspective. Whether such redistribution is mandated on a direct basis (typically in PAYG pension systems) or takes place on an indirect, and perhaps less obvious, basis (as is effectively the case in schemes relying on invested funds), the impact cannot be ignored. Almost everywhere, this topic has been afforded only the most limited degree of informed public discussion (as opposed to rhetoric), and deserves a much stronger focus in the political economy of most countries.

NOTES

* The authors wish to acknowledge substantial inputs from Krzysztof Hagemejer and three anonymous reviewers.

1. These contingencies, as defined in the ILO Social Security (Minimum Standards) Convention, 1952 (No. 102) are the following: need for medical care, sickness, unemployment, old age, employment injury, family needs, maternity, invalidity and survivorship (loss of a breadwinner).
2. In many countries, these contingencies are the subject of social security schemes, organized through the vehicle of social insurance for that part of the workforce that is formally employed and able to pay regular contributions to a scheme; this level of provision is usually complemented (or, if necessary, replaced) by a corresponding set of provisions under so-called 'social assistance' for those who are unable to participate fully in an organized contributory scheme.
3. The social protection floor is a global social policy approach promoting integrated strategies for ensuring access to essential social services and income security for all, as a first step toward the implementation of comprehensive social security systems. This approach is being promoted by an international coalition of major international organizations and development partners, under a mandate of the UN Chief Executives Board and the leadership of the ILO and the World Health Organization (WHO). A recently adopted international labour standard, the ILO Social Protection Floors Recommendation, 2012 (No. 202), guides the implementation of national social protection floors worldwide. See ILO (2012a) and Social Protection Floor Advisory Group (2011).
4. In fact, many studies assessing the redistribution through taxes and transfers limit themselves to households headed by people in working age, excluding households headed by pensioners, in order to avoid the confounding effect on their conclusions (e.g., OECD, 2011a).
5. In the case of tax-financed non-contributory pensions, redistribution reflects a range of factors, including the degree of progressiveness in the tax system.
6. Differential mortality rates, as between different population groups, not only women as compared with men, can lead to complex and diverse forms of inequity. Equalizing measures, such as the requirement that uniform mortality tables be applied in the annuitization of pensions, therefore play an important role in ensuring equitable outcomes.
7. See, for example, Ginn (2001); Ginn et al. (2001); Dion (2008); Fornero and Monticone (2010); as well as Fultz et al. (2003) and Fultz (2006) for Eastern Europe, and Bertranou (2006) and Arza (2012a) for Latin America.
8. This has been the case, for example, in some recent pension reforms, such as the ones in Argentina and Chile, which partly revoked earlier measures in order to achieve more equitable results (see Mesa-Lago, 2008, 2012; Arza, 2012a, 2012b).
9. See, for example, Barrientos et al. (2003); Barrientos (2004); Hagemejer and Schmitt (2012); UNFPA and HelpAge International (2012).
10. Average proportion of the population of the 27 member states of the European Union who indicated that they 'strongly disagreed' (62 per cent) or 'somewhat disagreed' (23 per cent) with this statement. See European Commission (2009).
11. Average level of disagreement ('strongly disagree': 26 per cent; 'somewhat disagree': 34 per cent) in the 27 member states of the European Union. See European Commission (2009).

12. See National Transfer Accounts Project website: http://www.ntaccounts.org/web/nta/show/; last accessed 4 September 2014.

REFERENCES

Albertini, M., M. Kohli and C. Vogel (2007), 'Intergenerational transfers of time and money in European families: common patterns – different regimes?', *Journal of European Social Policy*, 17(4), 319–34.

Arber, S. and C. Attias-Donfut (eds) (2000), *The Myth of Generational Conflict: The Family and State in Ageing Societies*, London: Routledge.

Arza, C. (2012a), 'Pension reforms and gender equality in Latin America', *UNRISD Gender and Development Programme Paper*, Geneva: United Nations Research Institute for Social Development, accessed 30 August 2014 at http://www.unrisd.org/80256B3C005BCCF9/%28httpAuxPages%29/3513162DF26920D5C12579CF0053534B/$file/Arza%20paper.pdf.

Arza, C. (2012b), 'Extending coverage under the Argentinian pension system: distribution of access and prospects for universal coverage', *International Social Security Review*, 65(2), 29–49, accessed 30 August 2014 at http://onlinelibrary.wiley.com/doi/10.1111/j.1468-246X.2011.01427.x/pdf.

Auerbach, A.J., L.J. Kotlikoff and W. Leibfritz (eds) (1999), *Generational Accounting Around the World*, Chicago, IL: University of Chicago Press.

Bardasi, E. and S.P. Jenkins (2010), 'The gender gap in private pensions', *Bulletin of Economic Research*, 62(4), 343–63.

Barrientos, A. (2004), 'Cash transfers for older people reduce poverty and inequality', *WDR Background Paper*, Manchester: IDPM/Chronic Poverty Research Centre, accessed 30 August 2013 at http://siteresources.worldbank.org/INTRANETSOCIALDEVELOPMENT/Resources/Pensions_Brazil_Bangladesh_SouthAfrica_Barrientos.pdf.

Barrientos, A., M. Gorman and A. Heslop (2003), 'Old age poverty in developing countries: contributions and dependence in later life', *World Development*, 31(3), 555–70, accessed 30 August 2014 at http://www.sciencedirect.com/science/article/B6VC6-480CHY3-8/2/83967e1e362f64f51ba74a6fc1082c53.

Behrendt, C. (2000), 'Private pensions – a viable alternative? Their distributive effects in a comparative perspective', *International Social Security Review*, 53(3), 3–26, accessed 30 August 2014 at http://onlinelibrary.wiley.com/doi/10.1111/1468-246X.00075/abstract.

Bertranou, F.M. (2006), 'Pensions and gender in Latin American social protection systems: where do we stand in the Southern Cone', *Gender Issues*, 23(1), 6–31, accessed 30 August 2014 at http://link.springer.com/article/10.1007%2Fs12147-006-0002-1?LI=true.

Bertranou, F.M. and R. Maurizio (2011), 'The role of labour market and social protection in reducing inequality and eradicating poverty in Latin America', *MPRA Paper No. 39843*, University of Munich, accessed 30 August 2014 at http://mpra.ub.uni-muenchen.de/39843/.

Caminada, K.C.L.J., K.P. Goudswaard and C. Wang (2012), 'Disentangling income inequality and the redistributive effect of taxes and transfers in 20 LIS countries over time', *Luxembourg Income Study Working Paper Series*, accessed 30 August 2014 at http://www.lisdatacenter.org/wps/liswps/581.pdf.

Dion, M. (2008), 'Pension reform and gender inequality', in S.J. Kay and T. Sinha (eds), *Lessons from Pension Reform in the Americas*, Oxford: Oxford University Press, pp. 134–63.

European Commission (2009), *Intergenerational Solidarity: Analytical Report, Flash Eurobarometer No. 269*, Brussels: European Commission, accessed 9 September 2014 at http://ec.europa.eu/public_opinion/flash/fl_269_en.pdf.

Fornero, E. and C. Monticone (2010), 'Women and pensions. Effects of pension reforms on women's retirement security', in B. Marin and E. Zólyomi (eds), *Women's Work and Pensions: What is Good, What is Best? Designing Gender-sensitive Arrangements*, Aldershot, UK: Ashgate, pp. 77–96.

Fultz, E. (ed.) (2006), *The Gender Dimensions of Social Security Reform: Vol. 2: Case Studies of Romania and Slovenia*, Budapest: ILO Country Office for Central and Eastern Europe, accessed 30 August 2014 at http://www.social-protection.org/gimi/gess/RessourcePDF.action;jsessionid=e666a8b86c230b4b9938e219905ce25bcc3df494bf37ace973cbbaeab5fbf671.e3aTbhuLbNmSe34MchaRah8TbNn0?ressource.ressourceId=8988.

Fultz, E., M. Ruck and S. Steinhilber (eds) (2003), *The Gender Dimensions of Social Security Reform: Case Studies of the Czech Republic, Hungary and Poland*, Budapest: ILO Country Office for Central and Eastern Europe, accessed 30 August 2014 at http://library.fes.de/pdf-files/gurn/00051.pdf.

Ghellab, Y., N. Varela and J. Woodall (2011), 'Social dialogue and social security governance: a topical ILO perspective', *International Social Security Review*, 64(4), 39–56.

Ginn, J. (2001), 'From security to risk: pension privatisation and gender inequality', *Catalyst Working Paper No. 3*, London: Catalyst.

Ginn, J., D. Street and S. Arber (eds) (2001), *Women, Work and Pensions: International Prospects*, Milton Keynes, UK: Open University Press.

Hagemejer, K. and V. Schmitt (2012), 'Providing social security in old age: the International Labour Organization view', in ADB (ed.), *Social Protection for Older Persons: Social Pensions in Asia, Manila*: Asian Development Bank, pp. 137–52, accessed 30 August 2014 at http://www.adb.org/sites/default/files/pub/2012/social-protection-older-persons.pdf.

Hinz, R., R. Holzmann and D. Tuesta et al. (eds) (2013), *Matching Contributions for Pensions: A Review of International Experience*, Washington DC: World Bank, accessed 30 August 2014 at https://openknowledge.worldbank.org/bitstream/handle/10986/11968/735130PUB0EPI001070120date010025012.pdf?sequence=1.

ILO (2000), *World Labour Report – Income Security and Social Protection in a Changing World*, Geneva: International Labour Office.

ILO (2010a), *World Social Security Report 2010/11: Providing Coverage in the Time of Crisis and Beyond*, Geneva: International Labour Office.

ILO (2010b), *Extending Social Security to All. A Guide Through Challenges and Options*, Geneva: International Labour Office.

ILO (2011), *Social Security for Social Justice and a Fair Globalization: Recurrent Discussion on Social Protection (Social Security) under the ILO Declaration on Social Justice for a Fair Globalization*, Geneva: International Labour Office.

ILO (2012a), *Social Security for All – Building Social Protection Floors and Social Security Systems: The Strategy of the International Labour Organization*, Geneva: International Labour Office.

ILO (2012b), *Global Employment Trends for Women 2012*, Geneva: International Labour Office.

ILO (2013a), *Employment and Social Protection in the New Demographic Context*, report submitted to the 102nd Session of the International Labour Conference, Geneva: International Labour Office.

ILO (2013b), *Global Wage Report 2012/13: Wages and Equitable Growth*, Geneva: International Labour Office.

ILO (2014), *World Social Protection Report 2014/15: Building Economic Recovery, Inclusive Development and Social Justice*, Geneva: International Labour Office.

ILO/IILS (2008), *World of Work Report 2008: Income Inequalities in the Age of Financial Globalization*, Geneva: International Labour Office/International Institute for Labour Studies.

IMF (2012), *World Economic Outlook: Coping with High Debt and Sluggish Growth*, Washington, DC: accessed 30 August 2014 at http://www.imf.org/external/pubs/ft/weo/2012/02/pdf/text.pdf.

Johnson, P., C.A. Conrad and D. Thompson (eds) (1989), *Workers Versus Pensioners: Inter-generational Justice in an Ageing World*, Manchester, UK: Manchester University Press.

Marin, B. and E. Zólyomi (eds) (2010), *Women's Work and Pensions: What is Good, What is Best? Designing Gender-sensitive Arrangements*, Aldershot, UK: Ashgate.

Mesa-Lago, C. (2008), 'Social protection in Chile: reforms to improve social equity', *International Labour Review*, 147(4), 377–402.

Mesa-Lago, C. (2012), 'The performance of social security contributory and tax-financed pensions in Central America, and the effects of the global crisis', *International Social Security Review*, 65(1), 1–27.

OECD (2008), *Growing Unequal? Income Distribution and Poverty in OECD Countries*, Paris: Organisation for Economic Co-operation and Development, accessed 30 August 2014 at http://www.oecd.org/els/soc/41527936.pdf.

OECD (2011a), *Divided We Stand: Why Inequality Keeps Rising*, Paris: Organisation for Economic Co-operation and Development.

OECD (2011b), *Pensions at a Glance: Retirement-income Systems in OECD and G20 Countries*, Paris: Organisation for Economic Co-operation and Development.

OECD (2011c), *Paying for the Past, Preparing for the Future: Inter-generational Solidarity in an Ageing World*, Paris: Organisation for Economic Co-operation and Development, accessed 30 August 2014 at http://www.oecd.org/els/pensionsystems/47712019.pdf.

Rawls, J. ([1971] 1998), *A Theory of Justice*, revised edition, Cambridge, MA: Harvard University Press.

Rein, M. and C. Behrendt (2004), 'The relationship of the public/private mix with poverty and inequality', in E. Overbye and P.A. Kemp (eds), *Pensions: Challenges and Reform*, Aldershot, UK: Ashgate, pp. 187–210.

Sarfati, H. and Y. Ghellab (2012), 'The political economy of pension reforms in times of global crisis: state unilateralism or social dialogue?', Geneva: International Labour Office.

Social Protection Floor Advisory Group (2011), *Social Protection Floor for a Fair and Inclusive Globalization*, Geneva: International Labour Office.

Townsend, P. (ed.) (2009), *Building Decent Societies: Rethinking the Role of Social Security in State Building*, Basingstoke/Geneva: Palgrave Macmillan/International Labour Office.

UNFPA and HelpAge International (2012), *Ageing in the Twenty-first Century: A Celebration and A Challenge*, New York/London: United Nations Population Fund/HelpAge International, accessed 30 August 2014 http://www.helpage.org/download/5059f6a23af15.

UNRISD (2010), *Combating Poverty and Inequality: Structural Change, Social Policy and Politics*, Geneva: United Nations Research Institute for Social Development, accessed 30 August at http://www.unrisd.org/publications/cpi.

Wang, C. and K.C.L.J. Caminada (2011a), Budget Incidence Fiscal Redistribution *Database*, accessed 30 August 2014 at http://www.lisdatacenter.org/resources/other-databases/ and http://www.lisdatacenter.org/wp-content/uploads/2011-Fiscal-Redistribution-Doc.pdf.

Wang, C. and K.C.L.J. Caminada (2011b), 'Disentangling income inequality and the redistributive effect of social transfers and taxes in 36 LIS countries', Department of Economics Research Memorandum No. 65, Leiden: University of Leiden, pp. 27–48, accessed 30 August 2014 at http://media.leidenuniv.nl/legacy/kc-2011-04.pdf.

Wang, C., K.C.L.J. Caminada and K.P. Goudswaard (2012), 'The redistributive effect of social transfer programmes and taxes: a decomposition across countries', *International Social Security Review*, 65(3) 27–48.

World Bank (2006), *Equity and Development – World Development Report 2006*, Washington DC: World Bank, accessed 30 August 2014 at http://www-wds.worldbank.org/external/default/WDSContentServer/IW3P/IB/2005/09/20/000112742_20050920110826/Rendered/PDF/322040World0Development0Report02006.pdf.

10. Income support for the unemployed and the poor

Janine Berg*

10.1 INTRODUCTION

Income support for the unemployed and the poor, which includes the different types of unemployment benefit systems as well as a myriad of policies to support the poor, is controversial, with debates on design and impact as great today as when the programmes were first instituted over a century ago. The policies are pillars of a social protection system as they mitigate the risk of job loss – an endemic feature of capitalist society – as well as attend to the unmet basic needs of households who are unable to find work or who do not earn enough from work to support themselves and their families.

As the focus of this chapter is on social protection policies for 'able-bodied' persons, it differs from the previous chapter, which analysed social protection policies for persons who were no longer working, either as a result of retirement, disability or illness. Providing income support to the 'able-bodied' is a much more contentious issue than providing for those who are no longer able to work. It was typically the last of social policies to be adopted and continues to be the source of debate, with great effort and funds spent on monitoring the unemployed to ensure that they are looking for work, and for the poor, on ensuring that they are both without means and deserving.

Today, most societies recognize the need to protect workers who lose their jobs and are without work or income or do not earn enough from work to escape poverty. Yet industrialized countries and some developing countries have struggled with designing unemployment benefit programmes that can provide sufficient protection for workers during labour market transitions, particularly in the face of important changes in the labour market that have eroded the standard employment relationship, as well as, for some countries, the continued presence of large informal economies. Like pension systems discussed in the previous chapter, unemployment benefit programmes can reflect the inequitable features of the labour market, and may even aggravate inequalities between workers.

Nevertheless, income support policies are central components of any effort to reduce poverty and inequality. Perhaps for the first time in history, the world and the international community are mobilized and committed to eradicating extreme poverty. Social assistance programmes have become increasingly central to national efforts and have allowed many countries to achieve the first Millennium Development Goal of halving extreme poverty by 2015. Furthermore, it has become apparent that high levels of inequality are an obstacle to poverty reduction and that a greater emphasis on redistributive policies can help to further success. In this chapter, we attempt to reflect not just on how the programmes affect the poor and the unemployed, but also on how these programmes can be part of a multi-pronged approach of constructing a more equitable society.

10.2 INCOME SUPPORT FOR THE UNEMPLOYED

Income support for the unemployed is an important source of protection for workers who suffer job loss. As unemployment rises during recessionary times, it is also an important counter-cyclical policy that helps to mitigate the impact of a recession. Compensation for the unemployed can take various forms – unemployment insurance, a contributory social insurance scheme that is usually funded through employers, workers and sometimes by government; unemployment assistance, which is financed through general taxes and is often means-tested; severance pay, which is not a programme per se, but a statutory benefit paid by employers to workers upon redundancy; and, more recently, unemployment insurance savings accounts, which are portable, individual savings accounts that workers can draw from in case of job loss.

Unemployment benefit programmes are limited in altering overall income inequality in a country because they are only directed at a small part of the labour force – the unemployed, which in in most countries, in normal periods, is around 5 to 10 per cent of the labour force. Thus, unlike pensions, which constitute the main channel of income redistribution through taxes and transfers (see previous chapter), unemployment benefit programmes have a much smaller overall impact on redistribution. Indeed, a study on income redistribution in 28 OECD countries found that benefits from unemployment insurance programmes accounted for 4 per cent of overall income redistribution through taxes and transfers. Social assistance benefits, including unemployment assistance, accounted for 8 per cent of overall redistribution, whereas pension benefits accounted for 50 per cent of total redistribution (Wang et al., 2012).

Nevertheless, unemployment benefits can provide an important source of support to workers who lose their job, and are therefore an important component of social protection policies. Though the first unemployment insurance programmes were instituted over a century ago, many countries in the developing world do not have unemployment insurance systems in place and only limited programmes of unemployment compensation. Indeed, of 184 countries studied in the *World Social Security Report 2010/2011* (ILO, 2010), only 78 countries (42 per cent) had statutory unemployment benefit schemes, though sometimes only covering a minority of the labour force, whereas 106 countries had no such scheme. Unemployment benefit systems are much less prevalent in low- and lower-middle-income countries; where they do exist, the legal entitlement covers only a small share of the labour force, due to the structure of the labour market (Table 10.1). Rather, income support for the unemployed is often in the form of severance pay, work programmes and cash transfers. Most high-income countries, on the other hand, use unemployment insurance to compensate the unemployed, with a smaller number favouring unemployment assistance programmes.

Table 10.1 Unemployment protection: extent of legal coverage, countries grouped by income level, late 2000s

	Low Income	Lower-middle Income	Upper-middle Income	High Income	Total
Legal coverage					
Existence of a statutory programme, number of countries (% of countries)	5 (8%)	17 (35%)	20 (54%)	36 (80%)	78 (42%)
Contributory and non-contributory schemes (% of EAP)	2.9	18.1	38.4	69.2	30.6
Mandatory contributory schemes (% of EAP)	2.9	15.4	30.3	58.9	25.7

Note: Excludes severance pay.

Source: ILO (2010).

Unemployment benefit systems differ regarding their coverage, their benefits, as well as how they are financed and operate. Depending on the profile of the employer, worker, or government, there are distinct advantages and disadvantages to the different forms of unemployment support. Firms and workers in industries that employ highly skilled workers prefer contributory insurance programmes that pool risk but preserve existing wage and skill hierarchies (Mares, 2001). The practice of tying benefit levels to past earnings reflects a principal objective of unemployment insurance – to improve labour force matching by ensuring that workers have sufficient time to find a job that better matches their skill level.[1] Doing so, firms that employ more skilled workers can more easily re-hire the workers when economic conditions improve, potentially improving the overall productivity of the economy. On the other hand, firms and workers in industries employing mostly low-skilled workers prefer tax-financed programmes that pay flat-rate benefits, as they are more likely to be covered by the programme.[2]

For governments, the main considerations when designing an unemployment benefit system are the policy objectives as well as the cost of the programme, both financial as well as administrative. Severance pay, for example, imposes no costs on governments and thus is attractive to countries with limited social spending and low administrative capacity. Although some unemployment insurance systems developed through private initiatives by trade unions, mutual aid societies or private firms, most contemporary unemployment insurance systems are government administered, even if financing is contributory, though decisions regarding eligibility and benefits are sometimes made by tripartite or bipartite boards. With contributory systems, the financial burden is not completely assumed by the state, which allows a greater justification of the programme's existence and its graduated benefit levels. This model differs from a basic income security model, whereby funding tends to be public, benefit levels are usually flat, and fewer distinctions are made regarding labour force attachment.

Because of competing objectives, unemployment benefit programmes will differ with respect to their generosity (the level and duration of benefits), their coverage, and the degree of controls – specifically, the monitoring, means-testing, job search and work requirements associated with the programme. Conditions for receipt of benefits include waiting periods, qualification periods (contingent on time in job and contributions into the system), qualifying conditions (must be actively looking for work), disqualifications (dismissal for misconduct or voluntary leaving); as well as different types of financing and calculation of contributions (flat or earnings related) (Alber, 1981). As a result, unemployment benefit systems, by

Table 10.2 Unemployment protection: effective coverage of unemployed, countries grouped by income level, 2012

Effective Coverage of Unemployed (% of all Unemployed)	Low Income	Lower-middle Income	Upper-middle Income	High Income	Total
Total receiving benefits	0.1	3.0	9.8	39.5	11.7
Receiving benefits from contributory schemes	0.1	3.0	9.8	30.9	10.2
Receiving benefits from non-contributory schemes	0.0	0.0	0.0	8.6	1.5
Not receiving unemployment benefit	99.9	97.0	90.2	60.5	88.3

Note: Excludes severance pay.

Source: ILO (2014).

design, typically perpetuate existing differences in the labour market and thus have a limited scope for narrowing inequalities. Thus, even among countries that have unemployment insurance programmes, many workers do not receive benefits upon becoming unemployed because they work in sectors or occupations that are not covered by the law or they do not fulfil certain eligibility requirements, such as length of service prior to dismissal.

Table 10.2 gives information on the effective coverage of unemployed workers; as can be seen, 88 per cent of the unemployed do not receive unemployment benefits and even in high-income countries, 61 per cent of the unemployed do not receive benefits. In poorer countries, the low effective coverage rates are due to the lack of an unemployment benefit scheme. In high-income countries, lack of coverage is the result of not qualifying for the existing programmes, reflecting differences in the programme design. As a result, coverage rates differ among high-income countries. In Western Europe, 45 per cent of the unemployed are covered through contributory unemployment insurance systems and 19 per cent are covered through non-contributory schemes, such that 64 per cent of the unemployed do receive some form of unemployment support (ILO, 2014). In Denmark, 85 per cent of the unemployed received unemployment insurance benefits in 2004, compared with 47 per cent in Germany, though 56 per cent of German unemployed were covered by unemployment assistance (Clasen and Clegg, 2006). In the United States and Canada, on the other hand, only 37 per cent of the unemployed received unemployment benefits and non-contributory systems do not exist.

The low effective coverage of unemployment insurance systems is partly attributable to their historical origins, particularly if the programmes evolved from union-run programmes that were limited to specific occupational groups. But even among programmes developed and administered by the state, the programmes were designed with a full-time, long-tenured (male) industrial worker in mind. Indeed, the International Labour Organization's first convention on unemployment compensation, the Unemployment Provision Convention, 1934 (No. 44)[3] mandated that countries establish and maintain benefits and allowances to unemployed workers, but exempted domestic servants, employees in public services, youths, agricultural workers and fishers, reflecting the common practice in national law (Alcock, 1971). Moreover, first-time job seekers are rarely eligible for unemployment benefits, even though they are, by definition, unemployed.

Unemployment insurance programmes are, as a result, typically biased against workers who have weaker attachment to the labour market, either because of restrictions on their participation due to caring obligations, or because there are fewer, stable jobs available to them. Low-skilled workers typically work in industries that are more prone to lay-off, in firms that invest little in their skills and thus can afford higher staff turnover rates. They are also more likely to be found in part-time work or temporary jobs. Moreover, unemployment rates among poorer, less-skilled workers are higher than amongst skilled workers but it is the poorer workers that are least likely to benefit from unemployment insurance, because the requirements imposed for participation are too stringent given their more erratic labour force attachment.

Adapting Unemployment Support to Changes in the World of Work

Changes in the world of work, including the growth in non-standard forms of employment, but also changing patterns of labour force participation, have contributed to lowering coverage rates of unemployment insurance programmes. As Chapter 7 on part-time work discussed, part-time workers are sometimes not eligible for unemployment insurance systems as benefit entitlements are based on full-time work, making it more difficult for them to qualify. Other forms of extreme part-time work, such as mini-jobs in Germany, are excluded explicitly from social security benefits, including unemployment insurance. As a result, coverage rates of unemployment benefits are much lower among part-time workers when compared with full-time workers, with differences ranging from 7 percentage points in Denmark, 9 percentage points in Germany and Spain, and 13 percentage points in the United Kingdom (Leschke, 2006). Chapter 6 in this volume documents the rising trend in temporary work in Europe, which increased from 9 per cent in 1987 to 15 per cent in 2006; in Spain, one-third of all jobs were temporary prior to the onset of the Great Recession. In Chile, Poland and Portugal, temporary jobs account for more than one-fifth of jobs. Although temporary workers may contribute to unemployment insurance programmes – depending on the design of the particular system – the higher rates of job rotation and greater likelihood of unemployment spells due to non-renewal, makes them less likely to be eligible for benefits. Indeed, Leschke (2006) shows that in Denmark, Germany and Spain, temporary employees who lose their jobs have coverage rates that are 10 percentage points below that of unemployed workers who were previously on permanent contracts. Finally, the rise of other forms of non-standard employment, such as dependent self-employment, whereby a worker provides services to a business under a commercial contract, including hiring workers through a third party, has also contributed to reducing the percentage of workers who are eligible for unemployment insurance, as well as harming the financial sustainability of contributory insurance systems (Advisory Council on Unemployment Compensation, 1996).

As a result of these trends, some researchers have questioned whether unemployment insurance is suited for the post-industrial age (Grimshaw and Rubery, 1997; Clasen and Clegg, 2006; Vosko, 2011). Clasen and Clegg (2006) argue that unemployment insurance was originally designed for industrial societies, with the objective of stabilizing employment relationships and maintaining consumption during short-lived, cyclical downturns in economic activity, but that today's labour market, characterized by heavy churning at the bottom end, the growth in atypical work, and the more irregular employment trajectories of women, makes unemployment insurance schemes that grant 'rewards in accordance with traditional status and skill differentials, i.e., status conforming . . . poorly equipped to provide protection and incentives which are congruent with a flexible, post-industrial economy' (Clasen and Clegg, 2006, p. 533). Grimshaw and Rubery (1997) maintain that unemployment benefit systems in Europe, and the reforms undertaken in the 1990s, have failed to take into account the increasing heterogeneity of the labour market, which has particularly hurt women, given their over-representation in low-paid and atypical employment.

Ironically, despite the need to make unemployment systems more encompassing as a result of the emergence of new forms of work, many European countries tightened eligibility requirements in the 1990s (Venn, 2012).[4] However, by the mid-2000s, there seemed to be growing recognition of the need to expand coverage of the programmes. For example, the reforms to the French unemployment insurance programme in the 1980s and 1990s focused on tightening eligibility criteria for the insured, as well as creating a separate, tax-financed system with modest flat-rate benefits for workers who were ineligible for the insurance programme (Clasen and Clegg, 2006).[5] In the 2000s, however, the system was once again reformed but this time by improving access to insurance benefits for workers with more limited contribution histories, as well as better integration of active labour market policies with benefit receipt, including for workers on social assistance (Clasen et al., 2012). In Germany, Clasen and Goerne (2011) argue that the Hartz reforms lessened dualism in social policies, through the merger of the means-tested unemployment assistance programme with the social assistance programme. Although access to the unemployment insurance system was not broadened, they argue that the merger of the two means-tested programmes gave social assistance beneficiaries who were out of the labour market greater access to training programmes and job placement services.

Denmark's unemployment insurance system has traditionally been more encompassing, with fewer distinctions between wage earners, and benefit thresholds and ceilings that are generous, but which resemble more of a flat-rate system. Qualification has also been less stringent, with workers needing to demonstrate that they worked 52 weeks in the previous three years (although this is stricter than in the pre-reform period when only 26 weeks of contribution over three years was required). Furthermore, there is less of a distinction in benefit rates between assistance and insurance beneficiaries, resulting in high coverage rates (85 per cent of unemployed, as mentioned earlier). Reforms to the system in the mid-1990s focused on reducing the length of benefit entitlement from seven to four years, as opposed to reducing benefit levels, as well as strengthening activation policies, with a particular emphasis on training and life-long learning (Madsen, 2002; Clasen and Clegg, 2006).[6]

Unemployment benefits in the United Kingdom have also become more homogenized, but mainly because unemployment insurance benefits are largely irrelevant – only 16 per cent of the unemployed qualified for insurance-based benefits in 2001 compared with 50 per cent in 1980, largely as a result of the tightening of eligibility criteria. Instead, the unemployed have recourse to a means-tested, job-seekers allowance. According to Leschke (2006), 32 per cent of unemployed were in receipt of benefits. Coverage is therefore narrow and because spending on the programme is so low – 0.3 per cent of GDP compared with 2.7 per cent of GDP in Denmark and 2.4 in Germany[7] – the benefits only provide modest support to families. Indeed, an analysis by Fernández Salgado et al. (2013) on benefit coverage of the unemployed in the Great Recession revealed the low replacement levels of the British system, with the contributory benefit accounting for just 11 per cent of post-unemployment household income and social assistance for 24 per cent. As a result, British households in the middle and upper end of the income distribution do not consider unemployment benefits as a source of income protection in case of job loss. Instead, they protect themselves through private savings and expectations about redundancy pay and individual employability (Clasen and Koslowski, 2013). As a result, the British model, while seemingly fairer because benefit rates are the same for all, provides only very modest protection and only to those at the bottom of the income distribution.

Severance Pay and Unemployment Insurance Savings Accounts (UISAs)

Unemployment insurance can be found in some developing countries though the programmes are less comprehensive than those of the industrialized countries, usually with shorter benefit periods and lower replacement rates. Moreover, because of the presence of large numbers of informally employed workers, far fewer workers are eligible for benefits in case of job loss. Instead, what is more typically found in developing countries is mandated severance pay. The amount of benefits covered by severance pay differs across countries and will also vary depending on tenure of the worker, with greater tenure associated with greater severance payments. Workers on probationary periods, or with short tenure (less than one year of service), typically do not qualify for severance pay. Also, many countries, particularly in Europe, exempt small businesses from severance pay as well as other laws concerning employment protection, including notice requirements and redress.

Firms subject to severance pay laws are presumed to invest more in their workforce, because of their greater labour force attachment, though critics contend that the policy infringes mobility and reduces hiring.[8] Moreover, severance pay can worsen a firm's financial condition if it is forced to pay benefits during an economic recession. Workers also risk losing their benefits if a firm declares bankruptcy or closes, negating the security that it is supposed to bring. Nevertheless, severance pay is attractive to governments because it imposes no direct costs as it is an obligation paid by employers. For this reason, many countries, particularly developing countries, have legislated severance pay. Of the 93 countries covered in the ILO's Employment Protection Legislation database (EPLex), 79 had legislation authorizing severance pay under specific conditions, 46 of which were in developing countries (including 20 in Africa, eight in the Americas, five in the Arab States and 13 in Asia).[9] Yet because severance pay is typically not paid to workers on short-term contracts and generally begins to accrue after one year of service, it is workers in more established employment relationships that are eligible for severance. As a result, it covers few of the unemployed. For example, MacIsaac and Rama (2001), in a study of severance pay in Peru in the mid- to late 1990s, found that although one-third of private sector wage earners was legally entitled to severance pay (or 20 per cent of private-sector workers), only 3.6 per cent of the unemployed received severance.[10] The low coverage is partly because of the high rates of job rotation, and thus lower percentage of workers with sufficient years of tenure, but also as a result of the high incidence of informality in Peru, including the large number of unregistered workers employed in micro-enterprises. Moreover, the study finds that workers covered by severance are less likely to become unemployed, though it is not clear whether this is because severance pay acts as a deterrent to firing, or because of the attributes of the firm and the worker, which make a stable employment relationship more likely (MacIsaac and Rama, 2001).

Rising unemployment and informality in Latin America during the 1990s led to debates on the effect of labour regulations on employment (see, for example, Heckman and Pagés, 2004 and Berg and Kucera, 2008, for a contrary view), with regulations on employee dismissal and severance pay blamed for raising the cost of labour and discouraging hiring. Coupled with arguments about the moral hazard problems associated with unemployment insurance (Feldstein and Altman, 1998), it was argued that developing countries should reform their severance pay systems into unemployment insurance savings accounts (UISAs) as opposed to adopting traditional contributory insurance programmes, which were felt to be ill-suited for developing countries as a result of the large informal economies, and the subsequent difficulty that they imposed for monitoring. UISAs are private savings accounts that workers can draw from in the case of job loss, retirement or death (in which case the heirs receive the funds). Because the accounts are individual, Feldstein and Altman (1998) argue that the worker internalizes the cost of the benefits and thus does not have the incentive to prolong unemployment. But UISAs are also associated with their own form of negative incentives, such as encouraging workers to quit their jobs in order to access the funds. Also, as UISAs are forced savings rather than insurance, risk is not pooled. As such, they can only play a limited role in protecting against contingency as unemployment can occur before sufficient funds are accumulated – particularly in developing countries where job tenure is much lower and turnover much greater – or unemployment may simply outlast the funds.

In 2002, Chile adopted a UISA to provide unemployment benefits based on individual savings, accumulated in private and portable accounts.[11] Contribution rates were set low (1.6 per cent of monthly wages by employers and 0.6 per cent on behalf of workers), which over the course of a year amounts to one-quarter of a month's wage. A supplementary solidarity fund was also set up to provide a top up to low-wage earners who had accumulated less than two months' wages in their account, although this was restricted to employees on open-ended contracts. Sehnbruch (2006), in an analysis of the Chilean system, argued that, like severance and contributory insurance programmes, the Chilean programme would also fail to provide sufficient coverage to the unemployed, who were more likely to be on atypical contracts or informal, to be low-wage earners, and to have had insufficient tenure in their previous job to qualify for benefits. She criticized the programme for having been sold as an 'insurance' that would 'protect the most vulnerable workers and those who are unemployed' (p. 41), when in fact it would 'protect the most precarious jobs the least' (p. 42). She argued that it was better described as an 'individual savings scheme' (p. 43).

Supporting the Unemployed through Other Measures

When coverage of unemployment insurance is inadequate, then the unemployed are likely to need other income support. As mentioned earlier, some unemployment assistance programmes, such as the German and British programmes, have been merged with social assistance programmes. Although in principle there is not much of a distinction between unemployment assistance and social assistance, in that both programmes are targeted at poorer households and thus means-tested, in practice it means that labour market integration measures have become a more integral component of social assistance programmes. These integration – or 'activation' – measures typically require participation in training or work programmes. They are sometimes targeted at specific groups facing particular labour market integration difficulties, such as younger and older people, the long-term unemployed and those who are hard to place, such as the disabled. In part, activation measures are an answer to the criticism that pure income replacement policies might entail disincentives to work once unemployment is of longer duration (ILO, 2003). In the next section, we turn to an analysis of social assistance programmes as well as other transfers, in order to assess the level of protection they provide and their redistributive effect.

10.3 INCOME SUPPORT FOR THE ABLE-BODIED POOR

There continues to be much debate regarding the type and extent of income support that societies should provide to 'able-bodied' individuals.

Countries differ on how they view this issue, and for those that have chosen to introduce some programmes, there exist substantial differences in the design, as well as the spending, on income support policies, with implications on overall equity. In general, we can divide the terrain of income support programmes into two main groups: social assistance programmes that are means-tested versus programmes that are universal. Within means-tested programmes, there are some programmes whose sole requirement is to be under a specific income threshold, but most programmes impose additional conditions on benefit receipt. This includes conditional-cash-transfer programmes (CCTs), which typically impose requirements regarding children's educational attendance and medical care; public employment programmes, which require that beneficiaries work in exchange for benefits; as well as employment subsidies that aim to 'make work pay' by providing extra income to the working poor, often in the form of a negative tax. These programmes contrast with universal programmes such as certain family and child allowances, which provide benefits to all, usually in an attempt to enhance equity between households with and without children, but also as an instrument to equalize wage rates in the labour market, by detaching wage setting from family status.

The Redistributive Impact of Different Welfare Models

As social assistance programmes are directed at the poorest segments of society, they are typically effective at reducing poverty, provided that coverage and benefit levels are sufficiently high. In countries that have more encompassing social protection systems, individuals and families receive benefits through other programmes, thus social assistance makes up a smaller percentage of social expenditures. These countries have programmes that not only provide traditional social security coverage to workers in retirement, but will also cover contingencies, such as illness, disability, maternity and unemployment. In addition, equity is enhanced through child and family grants that are provided to all families regardless of income, as well as more extensive public social services (see discussion in Chapter 11). As a result of these programmes (as well as institutions that support distribution in the labour market, as discussed in Part II of this volume), the incidence of relative and absolute poverty is lower and there is less of a need for social assistance.

In the European Union, for example, spending on means-tested benefits does not exceed 3 per cent of GDP, while total social expenditure is above 25 per cent on average (ILO, 2010). Nevertheless, within the European Union, and indeed between industrialized countries, there are differences in the importance of social assistance programmes. In the liberal,

Anglo-Saxon countries,[12] the welfare state has historically been conceived as based on 'need' as opposed to an explicit goal of universality, embraced by the Northern European countries. As a result, a greater percentage of social spending in the Anglo-Saxon countries is means-tested social assistance. In the United Kingdom, for example, as the social protection system is less developed, social assistance plays a more important policy role, accounting for 24 per cent of overall redistribution (Wang et al., 2012). The country is effective at reducing headcount poverty through social assistance, but nonetheless faces the highest poverty rate in Northern Europe and high poverty gaps, due to the low level of benefits provided (de Neubourg et al., 2007). In Sweden and Norway, on the other hand, with more encompassing 'social-democratic' welfare states, spending on social assistance cash benefits accounted for just 3 per cent of overall redistribution, less than the 4 per cent accounted for by maternal and other family leave benefits (Wang et al., 2012).

Although means-tested social assistance programmes may be more effective at redistributing income, per unit of money spent, overall levels of poverty and inequality are higher in the 'liberal' welfare regimes that emphasize this form of social assistance (see Figure 8.1, Chapter 8, this volume), precisely because benefits are only directed at lower-income groups. Korpi and Palme (1998) refer to this as the 'paradox of redistribution'. This finding is also implicit in the work of Esping-Andersen (1990), which demonstrated that the objective of needs-based social protection systems is not to alter 'the stratification outcomes produced in the marketplace' (p. 62). Rather, he argued that liberal welfare systems purposefully keep benefit levels low in order to promote private protection, through thrift and market-based solutions, for the more fortunate (ibid.).

While the equality of more encompassing welfare states, as exemplified in the 'social-democratic' welfare states of the Nordic countries, is clear, it is also true that few countries outside of Northern Europe fit this model. Among developing countries, social protection systems are underdeveloped, or unevenly developed, with many middle-income countries having programmes that are fragmented along occupational lines. These countries already had in place some elements of the welfare state in the post-war period, yet the programmes were limited to formal workers, typically employed in industry or the civil service. In many Latin American countries, for example, there exists a relatively well-developed pension system for public sector workers, parastatal works and workers in large, private firms, but with benefits limited to formal workers large sections of the labour market have been excluded from social protection. It is thus a welcome development that many developing countries have, over the past 15 years, introduced social assistance programmes targeted at the poor, aimed at guaranteeing at least a minimum level of social security for all, and in the process, moving towards the establishment of a social protection floor.[13]

Extending Social Assistance to Developing Countries through Cash Transfer Programmes

Part of the success in expanding social assistance into developing countries in the 2000s has been due to the advent of cash transfer programmes, which provide limited social benefits to poor families. Cash transfer programmes can be unconditional or conditional (CCTs), in which case benefits are provided on the condition that the families fulfil certain requirements, such as having their children attend school and receive vaccines. CCTs were first instituted in Mexico and in two Brazilian municipalities (the Federal District and Campinas) in the late 1990s, but have since been replicated throughout Latin America. By the end of the 2000s, over 30 countries had CCT programmes, including 17 in Latin America.[14] In Africa, cash transfer programmes also began to be widely implemented in the 2000s, but the region has favoured unconditional programmes (Garcia and Moore, 2012); Asia has seen a mix of unconditional (e.g., Indonesia) and conditional programmes (e.g., Bangladesh, Pakistan, Philippines).[15] The spread of cash transfer programmes throughout the developing world, and the support they have received from the International Financial Institutions is a remarkable policy shift, as previous social assistance policies were viewed with suspicion, as populist and ineffective, but also as potentially discouraging work.[16] Still, these concerns abound, which is partly why CCTs have often been sold as programmes 'to upgrade the productive capacities of younger generations' (Barrientos, 2011, p. 7).

An important characteristic of cash transfers is that the benefits paid are modest, with the objective of eliminating extreme poverty and reducing absolute poverty without discouraging work. For example, benefits from Brazil's Bolsa Família (Family Allowance) programme average approximately 120 reais (US$60) per month per household (benefits will vary depending on the size and income of the family).[17] Despite being the largest existing conditional-cash-transfer programme with approximately 13 million beneficiary households in 2012, just over one-quarter of the country's population, total spending on the programme was approximately 0.4 per cent of GDP, due to the low level of benefits. Still, the programme has contributed to reducing the percentage of families living in absolute poverty, which has fallen by more than half, from 13.2 per cent in 2001 to 6.1 per cent in 2011.

Cash transfers, in many countries, have also contributed to lowering inequality, particularly in Latin America, the region with the highest inequality in the world (Esquivel et al., 2010; Keifman and Maurizio, 2012).[18] Nevertheless, because of the modest benefits, there are limits to how much income inequality can be reduced through these programmes, though it is important to keep in mind that their objective is not inequality reduction, but rather poverty reduction. Nonetheless, the programmes can be instrumental for improving 'equality of opportunity', by allowing households to invest in their health through improved nutrition and access to health care, schooling for children, and other basic needs. These investments are particularly important for children who, upon reaching working age, will be better positioned in the labour market.

The ability of these programmes to upgrade capacities, however, is dependent on government provision of basic services, including schools and health clinics, but also sanitation, access to water, and transport services. Thus, conditionalities, when they are imposed, place an equal – if not more important – responsibility on governments to provide necessary services. Governments must ensure that there are enough schools and medical providers to attend to the needs of the poor, even if they live in remote areas. Governments that embark on more sophisticated means-testing – beyond geographical targeting – also need to have the administrative capacity to minimize errors of exclusion. In addition, governments need to have sufficient resources to cover the poor at a large scale and to sustain the programmes, as receiving benefits for a short time period is unlikely to break the inter-generational transmission of poverty – an explicit goal of CCTs.[19]

The Risks and Costs Inherent in Targeting and Monitoring

When compared with universal benefits, targeted systems may seem cheaper and better value, but there are greater administrative costs and a greater likelihood of leaving people out of the programme who need the benefits ('exclusion errors'). Programme administration can be costly, particularly if more sophisticated means-testing is involved and if programme rules are stricter. Mexico's Oportunidades programme works similarly to the Bolsa Família programme, though it has a much stricter conditionality programme and as a result incurs higher administrative costs, spending 9 per cent of its budget on administration compared with 4 per cent for Brazil's Bolsa Família programme (UNRISD, 2010). Under the Oportunidades programme, non-compliance with the conditionalities of children's school attendance, regular health check-ups and attendance at monthly health lectures, leads to an immediate reduction of payments. A 2012 study analysing drop-outs of the Oportunidades programme in urban areas of Mexico during 2002–07 found that 7–8 per cent of beneficiaries left the programme each year, which resulted in a 43 per cent turnover during the period under study. Three-quarters of the drop-outs left the programme because of failure to meet the conditionalities.[20] More troubling is that poorer and less-educated households were more likely to drop out; similarly, men, younger beneficiaries and the indigenous were also more likely to be excluded for non-compliance (González-Flores et al., 2012). Participants with full-time jobs were also more likely to drop out, suggesting the cost of the conditionalities in terms of time may have been too high.

Means-testing can also have the disadvantage of creating incentives for families to under-report income. Beneficiaries may erroneously believe that they will be better off if they limit work to informal activities, thereby avoiding the benefit cut-off.[21] But doing so would lower their earnings, given the significant wage penalties associated with informal work (Maurizio, 2014). Moreover, this practice is costly to the government as it becomes more difficult for countries to collect revenues and finance their programmes. Policies can be put in place to lessen the disincentives – for example, tax credits for work – but this further increases costs and administrative complexity and is not always a viable alternative for developing countries with underdeveloped tax systems. A critical distinguishing feature of universalism is that households do not lose benefits if their income rises. Although they may not 'need' the benefit as much as a poorer family, part of the benefit can be recovered through the tax system. Indeed, in Sweden, universal social assistance policies are efficiently combined with consumption taxes, which are simpler to administer and, overall, less distorting (Lindert, 2004).

Another disadvantage of targeting is that it can lead to stigmatization, resulting in higher non-take-up rates, thereby decreasing the effectiveness of the programme (de Neubourg et al., 2007). More problematic is that the poverty line can create a political divide, with middle-class households resenting and eventually opposing needs-based social assistance programmes (Korpi and Palme, 1998). The debate, and ultimate demise, of the US social assistance programme, Aid to Families with Dependent Children (AFDC), during the 1990s is a telling example. The negative effects of replacing that policy with a temporary assistance programme (Temporary Assistance for Needy Families, TANF) were not so apparent during the relatively prosperous years of the late 1990s and early 2000s, but with the global financial crisis of the late 2000s and early 2010s the negative consequences have become increasingly apparent as worsened labour market conditions and short-term support have been insufficient to stave off large increases in the poverty rate and the poverty gap (Pavetti et al., 2013).

Working for Benefits

A central concern of means-tested social assistance programmes is that it can create disincentives to work, as workers may not seek out employment for fear of losing benefits, or by encouraging unreported work, therefore contributing to informality. Policy-makers have responded to these concerns by either adopting benefit programmes that require work, such as public employment programmes or employment guarantee schemes, or by adopting in-work benefits that are targeted at low-wage workers, but that provide financial incentives for working.

Public works programmes have long been in existence, in both developed and developing countries, instituted during periods of high unemployment in response to specific crises, either economic or as a result of natural disasters. As such, they are usually of limited duration and sometimes restricted to specific regions within a country. They differ from employment guarantee schemes, which constitute a right to work, and thus provide a regular source of support for poor families, even in cases when there is no work available. Thus, as a social assistance programme, employment guarantee schemes (also known as employer-of-last-resort programmes) are preferable to public works programmes because, in principle, all who want to work will be able to (or be compensated with an income). And as they are not a response to cyclical fluctuations in employment, there is a guaranteed minimum benefit provided to citizens. As with cash transfers, having a reliable source of income is important for enabling families to make investments in their well-being through improved nutrition, access to healthcare and education and asset accumulation. Moreover, employment guarantee schemes, when permanent, can act as an effective wage floor that will influence private sector wages as well as minimum wage compliance. Indeed, Belser and Rani (Chapter 5 in this volume), find that minimum wage compliance increased in India as a result of the country's employment guarantee scheme.

The main disadvantage of public employment programmes is the higher cost as a result of the need to organize work and buy materials, which in many cases amounts to about 30–35 per cent of programme costs. These investments are necessary, however, to ensure that the programmes are not just 'make work' programmes, but that they lead to improvements in the community that promote economic development. Nevertheless, the programmes do save on the administrative costs of targeting as the work requirement encourages only those who need the income to present themselves. Yet there is an opportunity cost for these individuals who otherwise may have devoted their time to job search, self-employment or care responsibilities. Particularly for women, the burden of care responsibilities means that participation in the programme is likely to increase their working hours (both paid and unpaid), exacerbating problems of time poverty.[22] Furthermore, critics of public works programmes argue that there is little evidence that the programmes have a sustained impact on poverty reduction, economic growth or employment, typically due to the low wages paid, the short-term provision of employment, and the lack of training and therefore creation of poor quality assets (McCord, 2012).

In-work benefits or policies 'to make work pay' have become common in industrialized countries, with over half of OECD countries having such policies (Immervol and Pearson, 2009). Although the policies are less common in developing countries, they exist there as well.[23] The main objective of in-work benefits is to increase employment levels and improve incomes of the targeted population. The benefits usually take the form of tax credits (a 'negative' income tax), or wage-related transfers; a key distinguishing feature is that the benefit is paid to the worker, and not to the employer as a wage subsidy. Well-known policies include the Earned Income Tax Credit in the United States and the UK Working Families' Tax Credit. In these, and in most other programmes, benefits are usually financed through general taxes. Although the programmes have been shown to be largely effective in achieving their goals (see Immervol and Pearson, 2009, for a review) concerns remain as to whether the programmes subsidize low-wage work, thereby allowing employers to keep wages low, and thus of the need for effective minimum wage floors in countries where in-work benefits are applied.

10.4 CONCLUSION

This chapter has provided a selective overview of some of the different types of income support policies that exist for the unemployed and the poor, their effectiveness as well as their potential for improving equity. Unlike pensions programmes that have a significant impact on overall income inequality, unemployment benefit systems and social assistance programmes have a more limited redistributive effect. This reflects their comparatively smaller scope, due in part to the requirements imposed on accessing benefits, which is in turn a reflection of the political and societal debates on need and concerns over discouraging work.

Income support programmes for the unemployed and the poor cannot, on their own, tackle income inequality in a country, but rather are important pillars of social protection systems, aimed at addressing the contingency of job loss and mitigating poverty. Unemployment insurance gives workers the income, and thus the time necessary to search for employment that better matches their skill, allowing workers to safeguard their level of earnings, and for societies to benefit from the retention of the individual's skills. Yet because of changes in the world of work, a smaller proportion of the labour force qualifies for unemployment insurance upon job loss, such that the inequalities that exist in the labour market are replicated at the time of job loss. As a result, there is a need to make programmes more encompassing, so that workers with less stable employment histories can also have access to jobless benefits. These policies are important for preventing displaced workers from falling into poverty.

A pervasive feature of social policy design has been the concern that benefits to able-bodied persons lessen incentives to work. This belief has dominated policy debates and influenced policy design, regardless of the level of economic development of the country. It explains why benefits are often low and why conditions are placed on beneficiaries. But unfortunately this has resulted in higher administrative costs, people in need who have been excluded from benefits, and the need to introduce other programmes, such as in-work benefits, to reduce disincentives caused by income thresholds. Yet despite these shortcomings, there has been over the past 15 years a significant expansion of social assistance programmes in developing countries that have contributed substantially to poverty as well as inequality reduction. In developing countries, this has helped to bridge the gap in social protection coverage that has existed due to the occupationally segmented nature of programmes, helping to establish a minimum floor of protection to persons at the bottom of the income distribution.

Debates on the merits of programme design – who benefits and under what conditions – can become endless. The more important policy lesson is the need for all countries, regardless of their income, to develop – as well as adapt – social protection policies, including income support for the unemployed and the poor. Only then can we be assured of more just societies, free of want.

NOTES

* I am grateful to Christina Behrendt, Sarah Gammage, as well as four anonymous referees for helpful comments on an earlier draft.

1. For example, the Advisory Council on Unemployment Compensation in the United States reiterated in a 1996 report that 'the most important objective of the US system of Unemployment Insurance is the provision of temporary, partial wage replacement as a matter of right to involuntarily employed individuals who have demonstrated a prior attachment to the labour force. This support should help meet the necessary expenses of these workers as they search for employment that takes advantage of their skills and experience' (Advisory Council on Unemployment Compensation, 1996, p. 10).

2. See Mares (2001) for a discussion of the origins of unemployment insurance in Europe and the competing interests of high- and low-skilled industries.
3. Since 1934, the ILO has promulgated two more conventions concerning benefits to the unemployed: the Social Security (Minimum Standards) Convention, 1952 (No. 102) and the Employment Promotion and Protection Against Unemployment Convention, 1988 (No. 168). Convention No. 102 set forth specific standards on eligibility and benefits. Convention No. 168, passed in 1988 and considered up to date by the ILO's Governing Body, highlights the contribution that social security can make to employment promotion and strengthens the recommendation on unemployment benefits given in Convention No. 102, as this level had been surpassed by most industrialized countries.
4. For those qualifying for benefits, rules were also made more stringent with regard to job search and what jobs unemployed workers were allowed to refuse (Venn, 2012).
5. Decisions regarding adjustments to benefits and contributions are made through collective agreements, and then validated by the state and generalized across all firms. As a result, the French system, in general, strongly reflects previous labour market status with high ceiling benefits (Clasen and Clegg, 2006).
6. Nevertheless, as a result of the crisis in Europe and the rise in unemployment in Denmark, the unemployment benefit system has come under strain and as of 2013 benefits will be limited to two years. See 'Danish fairy tale loses the plot', *Financial Review*, 3 May 2011, accessed 30 August at http://www.afr.com/p/national/work_space/danish_fairy_tale_loses_the_plot_5r5Ocux1ADJcBSRWXHOAII.
7. Data from OECD, cited in Leschke (2006).
8. The empirical evidence on the effect of severance pay on employment is mixed (see, for example, World Bank, 2012; Cazes, 2013).
9. Data on coverage is limited to the 93 countries included in the database. See http://www.ilo.org/dyn/eplex/termdisplay.severancePay?p_lang=en; last accessed 30 August 2014.
10. Broken down by quintile, 5.6 per cent of unemployed in the top quintile received severance pay compared with 1.3 per cent in the bottom quintile (MacIsaac and Rama, 2001).
11. Despite the introduction of this programme, severance pay continues to exist, providing one month's salary per year of service, with a maximum of 11 years. According to Sehnbruch (2006), the funds accumulated in the individual savings accounts will be deducted from the full amount of severance pay due upon redundancy.
12. Based on the typology of welfare states developed in Esping-Andersen (1990).
13. In June 2012, the International Labour Conference adopted a new international social security standard, the Social Protection Floors Recommendation, 2012 (No. 202). The Recommendation complements the existing ILO social security standards by promoting national strategies to extend social security through universal, minimum coverage as well as to progressively build these systems up over time. It calls for access to essential health care and to basic income security that allows 'life in dignity'.
14. See http://web.worldbank.org/WBSITE/EXTERNAL/TOPICS/EXTSOCIALPROTECTION/EXTSAFETYNETSANDTRANSFERS/0,,contentMDK:20615138~menuPK:282766~pagePK:148956~piPK:216618~theSitePK:282761,00.html; last accessed 16 April 2013.
15. See http://www.ipc-undp.org/PageNewSiteb.do?id=121&active=3 for additional details of cash transfer programmes instituted in Asia.
16. There is still much debate on whether the programmes cause work disincentives. A study by Machado et al. (2011) found that beneficiaries of Bolsa Família (Family Allowance programme) had a higher probability of being economically active than non-beneficiaries. Rather the programme was important for reducing labour supply among children and the elderly.
17. In comparison, the minimum wage in Brazil in 2013 was 678 reais per month.
18. Between 2000 and 2008, the Bolsa Família programme is estimated to have been

responsible for 12 per cent of the reduction in income inequality, with job growth, minimum wage increases and the other programmes of the social security system responsible for the rest of the reduction (Soares, 2010).

19. In Paraguay, the Programa Tekoporã has faced problems in rural and outlying areas, as the government has been unable to provide the necessary public services to ensure that the conditionalities could be upheld. As a result, the programme collapsed to a simple transfer – which was frequently only given once a year – contributing to financial uncertainty for the families and political capture (UNDP-ILO, 2013). Indeed, a grave risk of the programmes is that they be manipulated for political gain. Having the first lady give out benefits, as was the case in Guatemala, is not the best approach for ensuring programme longevity (Cecchini et al., 2009).
20. The remainder were excluded because their income surpassed the threshold or they did not meet other administrative criteria. Every three years there is an automatic reassessment of recipients' eligibility.
21. In developing countries, family income is sometimes assessed using proxies that are based on the assets of the family; sometimes specific localities are targeted for receiving benefits (geographic targeting).
22. See Chapter 12 by Gammage for a discussion of time poverty.
23. The Abono Salarial, an extra month's salary paid to low-wage workers with families in Brazil, is an example of an in-work benefit in a developing country.

REFERENCES

Advisory Council on Unemployment Compensation (1996), *Collected Findings and Recommendations 1994–1996*, Washington, DC, accessed 30 August 2014 at http://www.ows.doleta.gov/dmstree/misc_papers/advisory/acuc/collected_findings/adv_council_94-96.pdf.

Alber, J. (1981), 'Government responses to the challenge of unemployment: the development of unemployment insurance in Western Europe', in P. Flora and A. Heidenheimer (eds), *The Development of Welfare States in Europe and America*, New Brunswick: Transaction Books.

Alcock, A. (1971), *History of the International Labour Organization*, London: Macmillan.

Barrientos, A. (2011), 'On the distributional implications of social protection reforms in Latin America', *UNU-WIDER Working Paper 2011/69*, Helsinki: United Nations University World Institute for Development Economics Research.

Berg, J. and D. Kucera (2008), *In Defence of Labour Market Institutions: Cultivating Justice in the Developing World*, Basingstoke, UK/Geneva: Palgrave Macmillan/International Labour Office.

Cazes, S. (2013), 'Labour market institutions', in S. Cazes and S. Verick (eds), *Perspectives on Labour Economics for Development*, Geneva: International Labour Office.

Cecchini, S., A. Leiva and A. Madariaga et al. (2009), *Desafíos de los programas de transferencias con corresponsabilidad: Los casos de Guatemala, Honduras y Nicaragua* [Challenges of responsibility transfer programmes: the case of Guatemala, Honduras and Nicaragua], Santiago: United Nations Commission for Latin America and the Caribbean.

Clasen, J. and D. Clegg (2006), 'Beyond activation: reforming European unemployment protection systems in post-industrial labour markets', *European Societies*, **84**(2), 527–53.

Clasen, J. and A. Goerne (2011), 'Exit Bismarck, enter dualism? Assessing contemporary German labour market policy', *Journal of Social Policy*, **40**(4), 795–810.
Clasen, J. and A. Koslowski (2013), 'Unemployment and income protection: how do better-earning households expect to manage financially?', *Journal of Social Policy*, **42**(3), 1–17.
Clasen, J., D. Clegg and J. Kvist (2012), 'European labour market policies in (the) crisis', *ETUI Working Paper No. 2012.1*, Brussels: European Trade Union Institute.
de Neubourg, C., J. Castonguay and K. Roelen (2007), 'Social safety nets and targeted social assistance: lessons from the European experience', *SP Discussion Paper No. 0718*, Washington, DC: World Bank.
Esping-Andersen, G. (1990), *Three Worlds of Welfare Capitalism*, Cambridge, UK: Polity Press.
Esquivel, G., N. Lustig and J. Scott (2010), 'A decade of falling inequality in Mexico: market forces or state action?', in L.F. López-Calva and N. Lustig, *Declining Inequality in Latin America: A Decade of Progress?*, Washington, DC: Brookings Institution Press.
Feldstein, M. and D. Altman (1998), 'Unemployment insurance savings accounts', *NBER Working Paper No. 6860*, Cambridge, MA: National Bureau of Economic Research.
Fernández Salgado, M., F. Figan and H. Sutherland et al. (2013), 'Welfare compensation for unemployment in the great recession', *Review of Income and Wealth*, **60**(S1), S177–S204.
Garcia, M. and C. Moore (2012), *The Cash Dividend: The Rise of Cash Transfer Programmes in Sub-Saharan Africa*, Washington, DC: World Bank.
González-Flores, M., M. Heracleous and P. Winters (2012), 'Leaving the safety net: an analysis of the dropouts in an urban conditional cash transfer program', *World Development*, **40**(12), 2505–21.
Grimshaw, D. and J. Rubery (1997), 'Workforce heterogeneity and unemployment benefits: the need for policy reassessment in the European Union', *Journal of European Social Policy*, **7**(4), 291–318.
ILO (2003), 'Active labour market policies', paper presented at the 288th session of the Governing Body, No. GB.288/ESP/2, Geneva: International Labour Office, accessed 30 August 2014 at http://www.ilo.org/public/english/standards/relm/gb/docs/gb288/pdf/esp-2.pdf.
ILO (2010), *World Social Security Report 2010/2011: Providing Coverage in Times of Crisis and Beyond*, Geneva: International Labour Office.
ILO (2014) *World Social Protection Report 2014/2015: Building economic recovery, inclusive development and social justice*, Geneva: International Labour Office.
Heckman, J. and C. Pagés (2004), *Law and Employment: Lessons from Latin America*, Cambridge, MA: National Bureau of Economic Research.
Immervoll, H. and M. Pearson (2009), 'A good time for making work pay? Taking stock of in-work benefits and related measures across the OECD', *IZA Policy Paper No. 3*, Bonn: Forschungsintitut zur Zukunft der Arbeit (IZA).
Keifman, S. and R. Maurizio (2012), 'Changes in labour market conditions and policies: the impact on wage inequality during the last decade', *UNU-WIDER Working Paper No. 2012/14*, Helsinki: United Nations University World Institute for Development Economics Research.
Korpi, W and J. Palme (1998), 'The paradox of redistribution and strategies

of equality: welfare state institutions, inequality and poverty in the Western Countries', *American Sociological Review*, **63**(5), 661–87.

Leschke, J. (2006), 'Are unemployment insurance systems in Europe adapting to new risks arising from non-standard employment?', *Working Paper No. 07-05. RS*, Brussels: DULBEA – Brussels Free University.

Lindert, P. (2004), *Going Public: Social Spending and Economic Growth Since the Eighteenth Century*, New York: Cambridge University Press.

Machado, A.F., G. Geaquinto Fontes and M. Furlan Antigo et al. (2011), 'Bolsa Família as seen through the lens of the Decent Work Agenda', *IPC-IG Working Paper No. 85*, Brasilia: International Policy Centre for Inclusive Growth of the UN Development Programme.

MacIsaac, D. and M. Rama (2001), 'Mandatory severance pay: its coverage and effects in Peru', Washington, DC: World Bank. accessed 30 August 2014 at http://elibrary.worldbank.org/doi/pdf/10.1596/1813-9450-2626.

Madsen, P.K. (2002), '"Flexicurity" through labour market policies and institutions in Denmark', in P. Auer and S. Cazes (eds), *Employment Stability in an Age of Flexibility: Evidence from Industrialized Countries*, Geneva: International Labour Office.

Mares, I. (2001), 'Firms and the welfare state: when, why and how does social policy matter to employers?', in P.A. Hall and D. Soskice (eds), *Varieties of Capitalism: The Institutional Foundations of Comparative Advantage*, Oxford: Oxford University Press.

Maurizio, R. (2014), 'Labour formalization and declining inequality in Argentina and Brazil in 2000s: a dynamic approach', *ILO Research Paper No. 9*, Geneva: International Labour Office.

McCord, A. (2012), 'The politics of social protection: why are public works programmes so popular with governments and donors?', *Overseas Development Institute Background Note*, September.

Pavetti, L., I. Finch and L. Schott (2013), 'TANF emerging from the downturn a weaker safety net', *Center on Budget and Policy Priorities Policy Brief*, accessed 6 November 2013 at http://www.cbpp.org/cms/?fa=view&id=3915.

Sehnbruch, K. (2006), 'Unemployment insurance or individual savings accounts: can Chile's new scheme serve as a model for other developing countries?', *International Social Security Review*, **59**(1), 27–48.

Soares, S. (2010), 'A distribuição dos rendimentos do trabalho e a queda da desigualdade de 1995 a 2009' [The distribution of labor income and the fall in inequality from 1995 to 2009], *Boletim Mercado de Trabalho – Conjuntura e análise*, No. 45, Nov., pp. 35–40.

UNDP-ILO (2013), *Human Development and Decent Work in Paraguay*, Geneva: United Nations Development Programme/International Labour Organization.

UNRISD (2010), *Combating Poverty and Inequality: Structural Change, Social Policy and Politics*, Geneva: United Nations Research Institute for Social Development.

Venn, D. (2012), 'Eligibility criteria for unemployment benefits: quantitative indicators for OECD and EU countries', *OECD Social, Employment and Migration Working Papers, No. 131*, Paris: Organisation for Economic Co-operation and Development.

Vosko, L. (2011), 'Precarious employment and the problem of SER-centrism in regulating for decent work', in S. Lee and D. McCann (eds), *Regulating for*

Decent Work: New Directions in Labour Market Regulation, Basingstoke, UK/ Geneva: Palgrave Macmillan/International Labour Office.

Wang, C., K.C.L.J. Caminada and K.P. Goudswaard (2012), 'The redistributive effect of social transfer programmes and taxes: a decomposition across countries', *International Social Security Review*, **65**(3), 27–48.

World Bank (2012), *World Development Report: Jobs*, Washington, DC: World Bank.

11. Public social services and income inequality

Juliana Martínez Franzoni and Diego Sánchez-Ancochea*

11.1 INTRODUCTION

In any market economy, inequality reflects the primary distribution of income between profits and various types of wages. It also reflects the state's capacity to redistribute resources through taxes and public spending, whether the latter is in the form of transfers, goods or services. Sustained reductions of inequality will involve some combination of 'market and social incorporation' (Martínez Franzoni and Sánchez-Ancochea, 2012).

Market incorporation refers to people's participation in remunerated work in stable and rewarding conditions. This requires the creation of a sufficient number of formal, well-paying private and public jobs. Even if successful, market incorporation is not a sufficient condition for the reduction of inequality. We can easily envision scenarios under which new formal jobs expand rapidly but wages of skilled workers and profits grow as fast or faster, leading to less equity. Exclusive dependence on market income also heightens exposure to unpredictable risks (accidents and sickness) as well as risks that are hard to cope with on an individual basis (aging and disability), all of which can lead to sharp reductions in living standards. Greater equity in the labour market may also be dependent on improved access to education and health, facilitating the accumulation of human capital for all. This is why expanding social incorporation is extremely important for people's well-being.

Social incorporation refers to people securing their well-being independently of their participation in the labour market.[1] It is shaped by different policies and institutions, including pensions, unemployment insurance and the other social transfers discussed in previous chapters of this volume. In this chapter, we focus on public social services, which have different direct and indirect influences on both market and social incorporation but whose impact is difficult to measure.

The main question addressed in this chapter is how the provision of public social services affects income distribution. Economists traditionally explored this relationship by measuring the Gini coefficient before and after service provision (see also Chapter 9 on redistribution in this volume). Although these studies tend to show the importance of social public services – particularly those with universal provision – their results are not methodologically robust and, as we discuss in this chapter, they are also hampered by measurement problems. Additionally, this kind of study downplays the importance of changing social relations and the influence that social programmes can have, for example, on income distribution along gender lines.

Our main contribution is not empirical but analytical. We place this discussion within the framework of market and social incorporation and discuss the different channels through which social public goods can contribute to both. Free education and childcare facilitates market incorporation for adults. These same public goods improve market incorporation for new generations through the accumulation of human capital and can thus reduce wage inequality in the long term. Public social services also expand social incorporation by insuring people against risks independently of their ability to access remunerated work.

Finally, public social services can influence gender social norms and power relations within the household. Women are particularly affected when public social services are not provided as part of an explicit policy towards social incorporation. Female unpaid labour compensates for the lack of these services, preventing women from entering the formal market or forcing recurrent exits from paid work, exacerbating income and gender inequalities. This expansion of unpaid female care has deep class and gender implications, disproportionally affecting poor women. It also increases gender gaps between highly qualified but underutilized female workers and their male counterparts. Generous social public services can thus reduce women's unpaid work, facilitating their access to labour markets and creating a significant number of well-paying jobs.

To illustrate these links between public social services, social and market incorporation and income distribution, we specifically look at three policy domains: healthcare, education, and early childhood education and care (ECEC). Healthcare and education (when not including tertiary education) are the most progressively redistributive components of social policy. Both are also acknowledged to be matters of right by constitutions worldwide. Public provision of ECEC has emerged as a critical concern in the past 20 years given mass incorporation of women in the labour markets and the changing composition of families. A growing number of studies, including a systematic cross-national comparison conducted among 20

OECD countries, have also highlighted the importance of high-quality services for the development of children at a young age (OECD, 2006) as well as for preventing the perpetuation of inequality from one generation to the next (Addati et al., 2000). We do not systematically compare each of these three policy realms, but use them as illustrative examples of the analytical relations between social public goods and income and gender inequality.

In section 11.2 we first discuss some of the empirical studies linking social public social services and income distribution and explore its many limitations. We then propose an analytical framework that explores the causal channels between public social services, market and social incorporation and income distribution. Future research should explore these different relationships with more detail and consider the way they interact over time. Section 11.3 shows how these channels are embedded in social structures and norms that organize practices and expectations along gender lines in labour markets and families. In section 11.4 we argue that the actual effects of public social services on market and social incorporation and, through this, on income inequality, depend on policy architectures: as a policy principle, universal access to all services has the most positive effects on income distribution, even if its actual implementation has proven difficult in many countries (section 11.5). The chapter concludes with policy recommendations and suggestions for further research.

Although our contribution is primarily analytical, we draw on different examples across developed and developing countries. We borrow on our previous research on Latin America, particularly on Costa Rica but also on the Southern Cone (Martínez Franzoni, 2008; Martínez Franzoni and Sánchez-Ancochea, 2012, 2013a). These countries constitute good examples to explore these relationships in the developing world for several reasons. They benefit from higher state capacity than many other developing countries, particularly those in Sub-Saharan Africa and have thus advanced more in the provision of public social services. At the same time, however, social service provision has significant shortcomings, including excessive segmentation. While focusing on some Latin America countries, we also discuss the experience of East Asia as a contrasting case. European countries, particularly the Nordic countries, are an important reference for our analysis because they have gone further than anyone else in the generous provision of public social services with significant positive effects on the reduction of gender and income inequality.

11.2 LINKS BETWEEN PUBLIC SOCIAL SERVICES AND INCOME DISTRIBUTION

Much of the literature on redistribution focuses on how taxes and social spending change the primary distribution of income, similar to the analysis undertaken in Chapter 9 in this volume. Redistribution is calculated by subtracting the taxes paid by each decile on their market income and adding any transfers received from pensions, unemployment insurance and other monetary benefits. Yet studies that tackle the role of services are few and face significant problems (Esping-Andersen and Myles, 2009). In the last ten years, scholars have sometimes allocated service spending on a per capita basis (Smeeding and Rainwater, 2002), which fails to consider asymmetric uses across income groups. The Organisation for Economic Co-operation and Development (OECD) produced one of the few studies considering these different uses (Marical et al., 2006, cited in Esping-Andersen et al., 2009; Vaalavuo, 2011, see below).

Available data demonstrate that health and education are two sectors particularly capable of redistributing resources. For the OECD, Verbist et al. (2012, p. 52) estimate the changes that available healthcare, education and ECEC (along with social housing and elder care) introduce to disposable income and income inequality. Taken together, their data show public social services reduce income inequality by at least one-fifth (Figure 11.1).

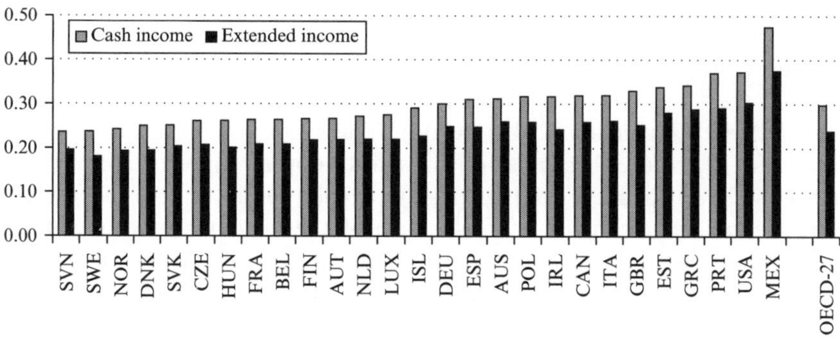

Note: Countries are ranked in increasing order of Gini of cash income. The Gini coefficient ranges from 0 (when everyone has an identical income) to 1 (when all income goes to only one person).

Source: Verbist et al. (2012) based on OECD Secretariat's computations from OECD/EU database on the distributional impact of in-kind services and national survey data for non-EU countries.

Figure 11.1 Gini coefficient before and after all types of public services

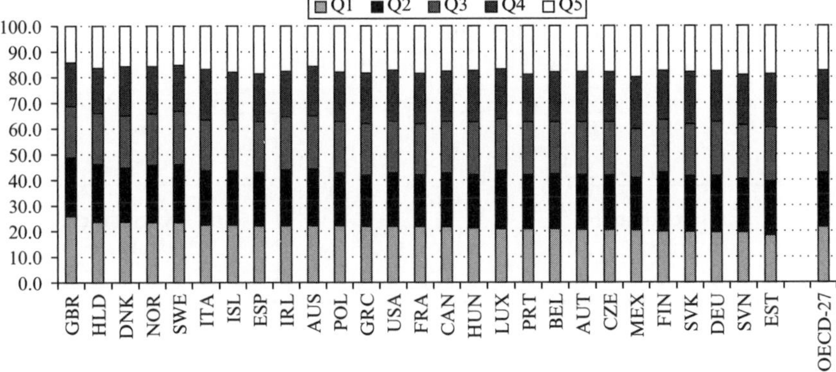

Source: Verbist et al. (2012).

Figure 11.2 Distribution of value of total public services over quintiles, 2007

These data also shed light on the distribution of social public goods across income groups. First, services are more oriented towards the lower-income population but their presence cuts across the social structure (see Figure 11.2) (ibid., p. 35). This means that access extends to people in the middle- and upper-middle-income groups, which in general entails more generosity and a higher quality of services.

Second, their data show that in the OECD, public services increase disposable income as much as 29 percent, compared to 23 percent in the case of transfers.[2] The highest income-increasing effect of services takes place in the Scandinavian countries and Hungary (35 percent or more) and is the lowest in Australia and Greece (around 20 percent). The most important components are healthcare and education, with healthcare having a greater income-increasing effect. Early childhood education and childcare, which is provided for fewer years, has a lower effect (ibid., p. 34).

Still, the methodology used by these studies is problematic because aggregate data do not allow addressing the allocation of services across income groups. Those studies that do consider the asymmetric use of services have to make many complicated and questionable assumptions. Moreover, comparative projects aimed at evaluating the monetary contribution of services to people's lives have only been recently launched and there are limited data available in countries beyond the OECD.

Given the limited data available and the significant methodological shortcomings of this kind of study, we propose a different analytical approach. We argue that the impact of public social services on income distribution takes place through changes in market and social incorporation.

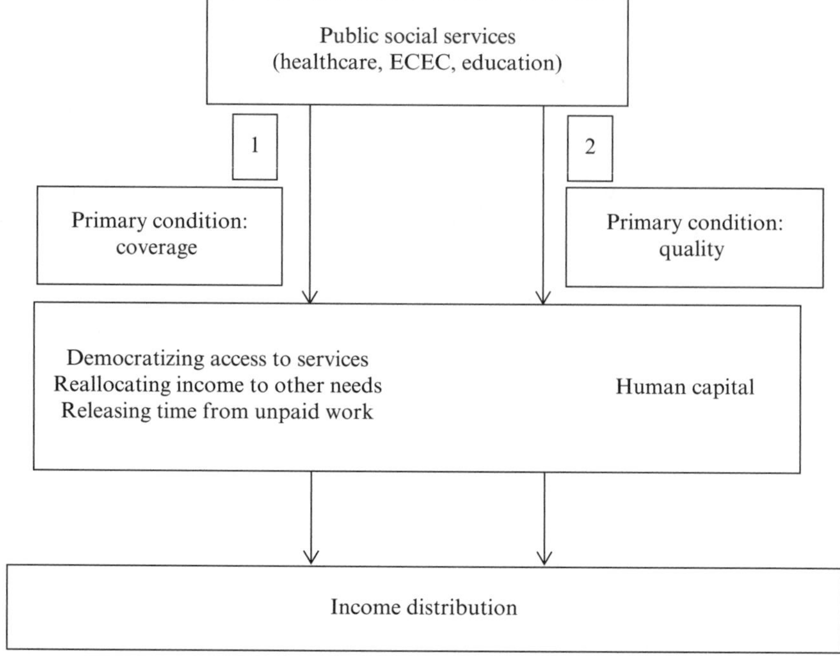

Source: Own elaboration.

Figure 11.3 Channels linking public social services and income inequality

Based on the existing theoretical literature and previous work on social policy in Latin America (Martínez Franzoni and Sánchez-Ancochea, 2012, 2013a, 2013b), we highlight the role of public social services in: (1) providing services that are not sufficiently available in the market or that are supplied at a higher cost; (2) releasing time from unpaid work; and (3) expanding human capital (Figure 11.3).

Channel 1

Public social services may focus on services that markets either do not provide or provide at a higher cost. It includes healthcare education and care services for children, the elderly and people with special needs. These services shape income inequality in at least three ways: (1) democratizing services people would not otherwise consume (e.g., secondary education, complex healthcare procedures); (2) increasing non-primary income and expanding the private income available to cope with other needs; and (3) releasing female time to access labour markets or to work longer hours.

The literature on the care economy (e.g., Elson, 1991; Folbre, 2001; Razavi and Hassim, 2006) has stressed that as long as unpaid work continues to be the backbone of social protection, women will continue to have serious constraints to devote enough time to paid work (Addati, 2009; ECLAC, 2012b). The public provision of childcare has the potential to promote more equitable access to quality care and this either increases female labour participation or their access to formal, regulated and well-paying work (ILO/UNDP, 2009). By reducing the demand on unpaid female work and facilitating access to formal jobs during longer hours, public social services increase income opportunities for women while also reducing poverty and decreasing inequality (Verbist et al., 2012).

Data on how public care services change female labour participation is still limited. Available evidence demonstrates that the presence of public services leads to the substitution of informal care for more formal options, increasing the number of hours women devote to paid work (Chioda, 2011). A recent study conducted among Brazilians suggests that access to free daycare induces women to enter the labour force. Chioda draws on a randomized experiment by Carvalho et al. (2010) to analyze the relationship between Rio de Janeiro's subsidized childcare programme and female labour participation. These services involved 244 properly managed and well-equipped daycare centers for children up to three years of age living in low-income areas. Services opened in March 2008, using a lottery to allocate places among families. A survey was carried out shortly afterwards among beneficiaries and non-beneficiaries. Labour participation upon the launching of the care programme was 17 percent, compared to just 9 percent in the control group – which lacked care services (Chioda, 2011, pp. 129–30).

For public social services to have positive effects on income inequality they ought to reach the broadest coverage possible in terms of the population served with most comprehensive services available. These terms have not been secured in the case of pre-school care where affordable services for children aged up to three years remain minimally available worldwide. Pre-school education has limited coverage, inconvenient locations for commuting parents and insufficient hours – none of which meet the needs of working parents. Among school-age children, education services are usually available yet part-time arrangements and a lack of affordable and adequate out-of-school care services hours indicate that services are not comprehensive enough (Addati et al., 2000).

Channel 2

Many public social services have an effect on the accumulation of human capital needed to access labour markets. This is clearly the case in the areas of nutrition, healthcare and education, but should also be a major consideration when providing early childhood education and care services. Quality is of utmost importance in these services if they are to result in the accumulation of human capital.

The economic literature frequently highlights the positive impacts that education and more recently, early childhood education and care (OECD, 2006; Mos, 2007) have on labour productivity and future income streams. According to the 2013 *World Development Report*:

> [T]here is robust evidence from around the world that each additional year of schooling raises labor earnings substantially, and that this earnings premium reflects the higher productivity of more educated workers. Together, nutrition, health, and education form skills and abilities that have been clearly linked to productivity growth and poverty reduction in the medium to longer run. Better health also brings, directly, higher labor productivity. (World Bank, 2013, p. 296)

Changes in Latin America during the last ten years are particularly illustrative. Authors like Cornia (2010) and López-Calva and Lustig (2010) argue that this 'human capital effect' may explain much of the reduction in income inequality across Latin America in the last decade. In Mexico, for example, the ratio of skilled to unskilled wages increased from less than 2 percent in 1985 to 3 percent in 1997 but has decreased by 10 percent since then. In Brazil, 'the decrease in the labour earnings differentials by education level has been, unquestionably, one of the factors contributing to the recent decline in inequality' (ibid., p. 156).

Yet the transformation of education into human capital and better job prospects is by no means automatic.[3] At least two intervening factors are involved: the quality of the service and the existence of a labour market capable of creating enough well-paying, skilled jobs. In recent years, many developing countries have witnessed significant improvements in enrollment rates: by 2010, primary school completion all over the developing world was at 68 percent and gross lower secondary school enrollment exceeded 50 percent. However, the OECD Programme for International Student Assessment (PISA) in 2009 showed that at least 20 percent of 15-year-old students in Indonesia, Kyrgyztan, Panama, Peru, Qatar, Tunisia, and two Indian states were functionally illiterate. In Indonesia, Panama and Peru, the percentage was above 60 percent. In Gambia around 50 percent of all children in second grade were unable to read at all; in Mali more than 80 percent of the children were in the same situation (World Bank, 2013, pp. 296–7). Similar problems may exist in the case of ECEC (Mos, 2007), even if measurements are not yet as standardized as they are for primary and secondary education. The benefits that care services bring to children, both in the short and longer runs, are conditioned on quality: if quality is low, the effects of early child education and care may even be detrimental (OECD, 2012). International comparisons indicate factors conducive to quality are staff–children ratios; a qualified workforce; duration of the programme; and starting age (Mahon, 2011; OECD, 2012). By the same token, attending medical check-ups and accessing very basic healthcare services is different from cumulative development of good health conditions, let alone reducing income inequality.

The interaction between the provision of public services and income distribution is also mediated by the production regime. Income inequality may decrease because the number of skilled jobs created by the public and private sectors is lower than the growth in the supply of skilled labour. This combination of an improved income distribution with stagnant competitiveness and high emigration – characterizing recent trends in countries like El Salvador (Gasparini et al., 2011; Gindling and Trejos, 2014) – is not desirable. The ideal situation is one in which the demand for skilled labour is growing at the same pace as the supply and a relatively homogeneous distribution of skills (plus well-established regulations regarding minimum and average salaries) and maintains low variances in wage distribution.

11.3 SOCIAL NORMS AND GENDER POWER RELATIONS MATTER

In the previous section, we imply that rational individuals, *independent* from one another, respond equally and immediately to policy changes. This follows much of the work in economics and political science. An expansion of education, for example, increases the number of young people accumulating human capital and should facilitate the access of men and women to the labour market. Yet in reality public social services intervene in social structures made of *interdependent* individuals. Interdependency is twofold: economic and care-related. Social norms addressing how people might handle economic and care interdependency are heavily gendered, reflecting distinct expectations of how to fulfill economic and care obligations for women and men.

During the second half of the 20th century both social structures and social norms radically changed. As discussed by Gammage (Chapter 12 in this volume), women worldwide have entered the labour market in unprecedented numbers. Dual breadwinning families have continued to grow and women's work lives have changed away from the male breadwinner norm. In Latin America, dual breadwinning families have already surpassed the number of male breadwinning families (28.3 and 20.9 percent

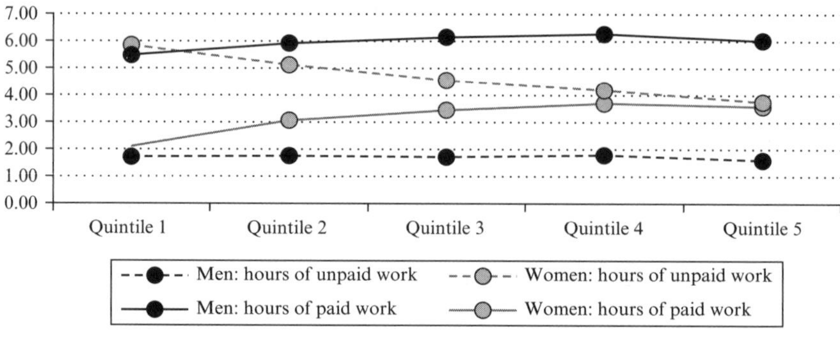

Source: ECLAC (2009, p. 45).

Figure 11.4 Uruguay: time spent performing paid and unpaid work by sex and income quintile, 2007 (hours)

respectively, in 2005) (ILO/UNDP, 2009). Despite these advances, there are still significant shortcomings in gender equality resulting from class differences coupled with social norms of gendered roles.

Women's access to the labour market in many parts of the world is uneven across class lines. Among women with children under six years of age, labour market participation in the poorest quintile is just 40 percent, compared with 70 percent in the richest. These differences – that are likely to perpetuate inequality within and between families – to a large degree result from differential access to childcare. Only 15 percent of all Latin American families devote income to care services for children under five. It rises to 32 percent among the wealthiest quintile and drops to 7.6 percent among the poorest quintile. In absolute terms the wealthiest quintile devotes four times more resources to care than families in the lowest quintile (US$191 and US$40, respectively) (ECLAC, 2012b). Figure 11.4 illustrates the matter based on data for Uruguay: women at the lower end of the income distribution spend twice as much time in paid than in unpaid work, whereas women at the higher income end divide their paid and unpaid work equally.

Drawing on time use surveys for various regions of the world, Gammage (Chapter 12) also shows that across income groups, men continue to undertake the greater proportion of total paid work while women undertake the greater proportion of total unpaid work (80 percent of the total time devoted to this type of work). Figure 11.4 illustrates the point at the country level, using the example of Uruguay. First, women continue to be the primary caregivers. Women in the highest quintile devote the same amount of time to unpaid work than to paid work. Men's dedication to unpaid work, on the other hand, remains very low across income levels. In the absence of social policy, women may still enter labour markets yet under more informal arrangements.[4] The stratified presence of a second, female and full-time income in the household exacerbates income inequality. For this reason income and gender inequality cannot be decoupled.

In short, access to labour markets reflects gender norms that are in turn reinforced by the lack of free public services or resources to buy private services. Gender norms are, however, malleable, and public social services can help in their transformation. Indeed, while the presence of these services has not completely overcome gender inequality, it certainly makes a considerable contribution. Across countries, time devoted to childcare drops considerably when children enter primary school. Time devoted to childcare also drops when there are publicly available care services for young children (European Commission, 2004). Under regulated to a large degree markets where informal, private care services are not available, and where there are expanded social services, full-time female labour participation in formal jobs has grown significantly.[5]

Women have entered highly segregated to labour markets whereby female jobs concentrate in the public sector and in the social services, and are under-represented in top positions (Chioda, 2011). As a result, income inequality does not take place randomly but along gender lines. Because gender relations are embedded in social structures and social norms, the interaction between social services and income inequality is also embedded in such practices and norms. Governments need to consider the interactions between gender and class when establishing spending priorities for the provision of public social services. Policy-makers and researchers should also be aware of the impact that those services can have in shifting social norms and power structures in the household and in the labour market, directly affecting income inequality.

11.4 THE IMPORTANCE OF UNIVERSALISM FOR IMPROVING INCOME DISTRIBUTION

Which policy architectures show the greatest effect on income distribution, that is, have the best performance concerning the channels previously identified? All market economies operate with some amount of non-market production of public social services and these channels are at work to some extent worldwide. However, income inequality varies greatly depending upon how countries manage coverage as well as quality of services.

Below we turn our attention to policy architectures. Architectures involve two primary criteria: principles regarding who is entitled to what (i.e., eligibility criteria), and instruments defining how governments honor the policy principles (Hall, 1993). Universalism as an eligibility criterion contrasts sharply with need as used in liberal, Anglo-Saxon countries (Esping-Andersen, 1990). The former pursues maximum autonomy between market power and access to social services; the latter does so only in the face of market failures. The former is best illustrated by Sweden, the latter by the USA. Under universal services, public social services replace a good deal of unpaid familial care, while providing women with employment. Under the liberal model, many public social services – particularly in childcare and healthcare – are directed at the poor. Women may also enter the labour force in large numbers but services partially replacing mothers' care are private rather than public (Orloff, 1996) and are highly stratified along class lines.

A large body of literature argues that the delivery of basic social services and social protection should follow universal principles to maximize its positive effect on social incorporation and inequality. Universalism is defined in this case as high coverage, assuring that everyone benefits from high-quality and generous income transfers and services (as understood in that particular context), under unified, nation-wide systems (Korpi, 1983; Esping-Andersen, 1990; Huber and Stephens, 2001). The argument is that only universal policies will incorporate the population at large and will fully separate access to services from labour market participation, resulting in consistent reductions in income inequality.

The reason is threefold. First, whether it is schooling or healthcare, individuals from all income levels and personal characteristics enjoy similar treatment based on their condition as citizens. Second, the middle class is more likely to support services that they benefit from – and the social spending associated with these services – whether these services are tailored for specific groups (school children or the elderly – categorical universalism) or the population at large (healthcare). When the middle-class supports universal policies, their mobilization capacity benefits low-income groups as well – a point successfully illustrated for developed countries by Korpi and Palmer (1998).

Third, this cross-class alliance is not only helpful in creating broad access to public services but also guarantees good quality. The resulting expansion of transfers and services in health and education has had a substantial redistributive effect, creating a virtuous circle for social incorporation (Huber, 2002; Mkandawire, 2006a). In Mkandawire's words (2006b, p. 13), 'institutions of welfare also act as intervening variables, shaping the political coalitions that eventually determine the size and redistributive nature of the national budget'.

Societal support could extend beyond the middle class to include the business community. Mandates for employer-provided services are difficult to enforce and often face resistance. As Addati et al. (2000) explain, 'despite the potential benefits of public support for workplace initiatives ... workplace initiatives measures requiring employers to provide childcare support can have negative consequences for workers and employers' (p. 45). Yet there are examples of existing services such as education and primary healthcare that are supported by business. Something similar could happen to early child education and care.

The positive effects of universal approaches to social provision are most clearly reflected in the experience of the Nordic countries. Traditionally, the public sector directly produced a large range of services, including 'healthcare ... day care, elder care, job training programs, temporary employment programs in the public services, and after school programs ... along with improvement of maternal and parental leave' (Stephens, 2002, p. 310). In the Nordic countries, the direct provision of childcare, education and healthcare constitutes a larger share of welfare spending than in Continental Europe and in Anglo-Saxon countries. In absolute terms, both transfers and services are more generous in the Nordic countries and reach a larger share of the population.

Having a robust public sector providing universal social services to all citizens has benefitted income distribution in the Scandinavian countries in several ways. Affordable and quality childcare under integrated systems with unified curriculum and learning standards (OECD, 2012), permitted Denmark, Finland, Norway and Sweden to achieve the highest labour force participation rates in the world for both sexes. It also facilitated access of women into the Denmark, Finland, Norway and Sweden market, particularly benefitting low-income families who lack the resources to pay for private provision of childcare services. Publicly provided social services contributed to securing high-quality, specialized skills, which are in high demand by the private sector (Mares, 2003). Other patterns of service provision such as the 'laissez-faire approach, characterized by the co-existence of several systems, partially age-related, with auspice often proprietary or voluntary, typical of the Anglo-American countries' and the 'the dual system, based on an age break (crèches for infants and toddlers, preschools for those 3 years old to school-age), typified by France and Italy' (Mahon, 2011, p. 2) have poorer results in both human capital accumulation and income distribution.

The Nordic accent on universal public social services extends to education. In 2009 Nordic countries devoted an average of 6.8 percent of GDP to public spending compared with 5.5 percent in Continental SMEs and 5.3 percent in Anglo-Saxon countries. In addition, countries like Sweden emphasize the importance of comprehensive knowledge for all children and give less weight to the type of vocational programmes dominant in Germany and other Continental European countries (Pontusson, 2005).

In the Nordic countries higher public spending has played a key role in equalizing opportunities and reducing gaps in educational attainment. Pontusson (2005) offers some evidence based on test results from the International Adult Literacy Survey implemented between 1994 and 1998. The literacy test results of the best students (those in the 95th percentile) in Northern Europe are 1.76 times better than those of the worst students (those in the 5th percentile). Both in Continental SMEs (2.00 times more) and in the Anglo-Saxon world (2.49) the differences are significantly higher.[6] This is an indication of a more egalitarian formation of human capital, which, in the long run, should also result in improved access to labour markets. Thus, in the Nordic countries, public social services serve to strengthen Channel 2 by improving human capital and thus the ability to secure work in the labour market (what is often referred to as equality of opportunity) as well as Channel 1 by democratizing access to services, releasing time that would otherwise be dedicated to unpaid work as well as helping to equalize incomes.

11.5 CHALLENGES TO BUILDING UNIVERSAL PROVISION

By simultaneously achieving better quality and coverage of people and benefits, universal public social services are capable of reducing income inequality. However, arguing in favor of universalism as the optimum way to build a positive relationship between public social services and inequality can sound naive. In this section, we draw on the difficulties experienced by Latin America and East Asia to discuss some of the complexities involved in building universalism. We focus on these two regions because compared to other parts of the developing world they have made more progress in the provision of social services (Haggard and Kaufman, 2008). In the second part of the section, we briefly account for some factors that may contribute to universalism through the exceptional case of Costa Rica.

Primary Challenges to Building Universalism in Developing Countries

Examining education in Latin America, universalism *in theory* corresponds with significant exclusions *in practice*. Contrary to healthcare – where these problems were the result of high levels of informality and restricted social insurance – deficiencies in education resulted from a shortage of school supplies in many regions and poor quality of services overall. Latin American elites traditionally constrained access to primary and secondary education and focused public investment on tertiary education since independence in the 19th century (World Bank, 2003). Despite growing investment in education during the 20th century – partly as a result of the needs of industrialization – great differences in access and quality still remain. According to Reimers' excellent review of the long-term development of education in Latin America:

> [D]espite more than a century of intermittent progressive policy rhetoric, schools in Latin America still marginalize the children of indigenous groups, of rural populations, and of the poor. This paradox of a resilient conservative school practice and progressive education policy rhetoric is explained by conflict among policy elites, first on the priority of educating the children of the poor at high levels more generally and second on the purposes of schooling. (Reimers, 2006, p. 427)

The recent policy of conditional cash transfers (CCTs) has expanded incorporation to schools, but unfortunately has fallen short of improving quality. Around 100 million previously marginalized poor people now have access to primary education partly thanks to an increasing supply of services associated to CCTs, which have thus become a valuable opportunity for governments to reduce the gross inequalities created by markets and families. At the same time, the fact that overall services are very basic and quality is usually low has undermined the ultimate effect of coverage on improved human capital. In addition, the fact that stratification between private and public schools remains untouched weakens the effects that the formation of human capital could have on income inequality. Last but not least, CCTs have explicitly acknowledged the valuable role of women as mothers but have downplayed the role of women as workers (Molyneux, 2007). Cash transfers are mostly transferred to children via their mothers, who are also made accountable for children's medical check-ups and school attendance. However, programmes are lacking in terms of training and care services as two key requirements to reducing income inequality.

East Asian countries such as the Republic of Korea and Taiwan (China) were more successful in providing universal access to high-quality primary and secondary education than Latin America, thus maximizing the second channel in Figure 11.3. Szekely and Montes (2006) develop a comprehensive comparison of educational attainment and its impact on income distribution in East Asia and Latin America. They compare years of education of people born in different cohorts in almost all Latin American countries, the Republic of Korea and Taiwan (China) and show that Latin

Americans born in every cohort between 1930 and 1970 have on average fewer years of education than Koreans and Taiwanese. Moreover, the gap between both regions increased over time.

As these numbers indicate, East Asian countries such as the Republic of Korea and Taiwan(China) have generally succeeded in providing universal access to public primary and secondary education – which in turn has contributed to lower levels of inequality than found in Latin America, even in the face of rapid economic growth and an increasingly complex and diversified occupational structure. More significantly, the quality of education was better than in Latin America, thus maximizing the positive impact of services on human capital and on labour market outcomes identified in Figure 11.3 (De Gregorio and Lee, 2003).

The provision of other public social services had severe weaknesses in both Latin America and East Asia. In the best-performing Latin American countries, public social spending was high, but services were often stratified and of uneven quality – in the rest of Latin America performance was even worse. Argentina, Uruguay and Chile were among the largest welfare states in terms of spending in the developing world. Between 1973 and 2000, social spending was above 14 percent of GDP, compared to just 5.7 percent in Singapore and 4.3 percent in the Republic of Korea (Segura-Ubiergo, 2007). By the 1970s, more than two-thirds of the population in all three countries were reached by social security systems and almost all children were vaccinated against tuberculosis in their first year, attending primary school by the age of six (Filgueira, 2005). Yet, the outcome of this type of access was stratification rather than decreased inequality. Public servants, professionals and formal, urban employers were incorporated first to social security, benefitting from the more generous provision. Self-employed and informal workers entered into the system later if at all (ibid.). In Argentina, social insurance programmes 'for less influential and organized groups, particularly rural and domestic workers, were largely ineffective in enrolling affiliates and the benefits they offered were usually minimal' (Lewis and Lloyd-Sherlock, 2009, p. 116).[7] Informal workers relied on low-quality public services or depended upon their income and family strategies to confront disease risks and other hazards, negatively impacting human capital.

The performance in the provision of other public social services in East Asia has been contradictory, with insufficient public spending in many areas. Taiwan (China) and the Republic of Korea's attention to basic health during the 1960s and 1970s was certainly impressive and contributed to sharp reductions in infant mortality. Their effort was particularly strong in rural areas: health centres were created in the 1950s (Taiwan) and 1960s (Republic of Korea) and expanded rapidly in the 1970s

(McGuire, 2010). Yet the low quality and high stratification of non-basic health services was more problematic for income inequality, as it was the lacking provision of other public social services. According to Haggard and Kaufman (2008, p. 140): 'health insurance coverage in East Asia . . . was low, and health spending during the 1973–1980 period was low by comparison to Latin America'. Health spending was also unequally distributed: in 1995 – before the introduction of a national health insurance programmes – 40 percent of Taiwanese did not have access to social insurance; private sources contributed to 50 percent of spending in healthcare. In the Republic of Korea, health spending was low and concentrated in the private sector: in 1975, residents of the country consumed more in cigarettes than in health (McGuire, 2010). Childcare services were also of little concern in highly familiaristic societies. Despite the Republic of Korea's expansion of resources for childcare since the 1990s, only 0.39 percent of total government expenditures went to such services in the early 2000s (UNRISD, 2010). In Taiwan (China), social spending in childcare continues to be even lower.

Potential Policy Lessons from the Few Successful Cases: Costa Rica and Beyond

Given the deep-seated obstacles that Latin America and East Asia (the two regions in the developing world with the most robust public policy and social services) have faced to develop universalism, does it make sense to promote it as a policy goal? Can universalism be successfully implemented in countries with weak states, high inequality and lacking political support?

To explore answers to these questions, it is useful to consider the few successful cases of universalism in the South. The state of Kerala in India, Mauritius and Costa Rica are probably the three best known (Heller, 1999; Ghai, 2003; Filgueira, 2007; Sandbrook et al., 2007). All three cases built universalism from scratch in the absence of strong public and private stakeholders. In recent times other developing countries have taken steps towards universalism, the Republic of Korea and Chile as leading examples. Yet these countries embarked on a universal trajectory in terms of healthcare services in the presence of and drawing on robust private services.

Among these five countries, Costa Rica stands out. Particularly in the area of healthcare, it has achieved as much coverage and generosity as Mauritius, but with lower levels of stratification. On the other end, Chile has not performed as well due to stratification and uneven generosity. Kerala and the Republic of Korea have done well in terms of coverage but generosity has been either medium/low (Kerala) or low (the Republic of Korea) and hand in hand with high copayments, stratification is, at present, high in both.

Within the sea of market pressures that threaten universal social services across the globe, Costa Rica has thus been seen as an exceptional case, indeed 'the closest case of a universalistic, egalitarian social state' in much of the developing world (Filgueira, 2007, p. 144).[8] The case also stands out as valuable in light of contemporary debates on the formation of universal social policy. Unlike Mauritius or Kerala, Costa Rica established universal transfers and services based on social insurance and payroll taxes rather than around general revenues. The social-insurance-based incremental building of universalism in Costa Rica speaks to global policy instruments such as the International Labour Organization's (ILO, 2009) 'social protection floor'. The latter proposes to expand monetary transfers and basic healthcare services for everyone, based on a combination of social insurance and social assistance mechanisms. To this purpose, Costa Rica may provide valuable insights concerning specific features of social insurance as well as ways to link social insurance and social assistance. Moreover, it provides valuable policy lessons for the many developing countries where expanding direct taxes has proven hard.

The creation of this exceptional case within Latin America took place in three stages. In the 1940s, Costa Rica created a unified system of social insurance built upward from low-income groups. Social protection targeted the working class first, slowly expanding coverage by successive increases in wage ceilings (Rosenberg, 1983). During the 1950s and 1960s, there was a gradual expansion of social programmes, including healthcare and pensions, as well as education at all levels. The system was completed during the 1970s with the creation of preventive and primary healthcare measures along with an ambitious, cutting-edge social assistance programmes enabling social incorporation among the very poor.

Costa Rica's success was the result of several interlinked factors. First, the fact that the country benefitted from relatively democratic institutions since the mid-20th century has been considered by much scholarly work as the primary driver of its success (Segura-Ubiergo, 2007; Lehoucq, 2010). Yet democracy was by no means a sufficient condition: Uruguay shows that a long-term democracy – in place until the early 1970s – could lead to massive but stratified social services, which may have limited effects on income distribution. By the same token, Mauritius managed to establish a fairly universal non-contributory old-age pension yet failed to achieve equal health services for all, despite a similar macro-political scenario marked by democracy and a prominent role of progressive parties.

In the case of Costa Rica, still at the macro-political level, the role of an emerging elite of small and medium producers and urban professionals was fundamental in driving the expansion of universal social services (Martínez Franzoni and Sánchez-Ancochea, 2013a). Clustered around the National Liberation Party and after winning a Civil War in 1949 the new elite directly benefitted from the formation of human capital and a democratized access to health, education and other social services. Such an expansion helped them broaden the number of good public jobs for their own constituency (for instance, by expanding schools and institutions like the Costa Rican Social Insurance board created prior to the civil war), cope with conflict and secure social peace.

Yet the way social insurance for healthcare provision was designed from the very beginning was even more important as it shaped the type of spending the new elite undertook (Martínez Franzoni and Sánchez-Ancochea, 2014). Costa Rica's social insurance had two unique features. First, the programme was built bottom-up, meaning that initially all salaried workers under a wage ceiling had mandatory social insurance. Consequently, the system was never hijacked by upper-income groups already enjoying generous benefits. From early on, Costa Rican workers, including non-waged workers, had incentives to support further benefit expansion to higher-income groups bringing larger tax contributions to the system. By the time the wage ceiling was eliminated, non-waged workers were incorporated, first on a voluntary basis and later in a mandatory fashion, as were domestic workers.

Second, the provision of the same high-quality healthcare benefits for all insured (salaried and non-salaried workers or their dependent family) created incentives for outsiders to join. Even if coverage took decades to become universal, these two components of the initial architecture ultimately resulted in equality of treatment and broad-based solidarity. Costa Rica's success in promoting formal employment and minimizing the number of non-waged workers during the 1960s and 1970s also facilitated the expansion of the social security system (Martínez Franzoni and Sánchez-Ancochea, 2013b).

While acknowledging Costa Rica's unique features (including its small size and homogeneous population and the characteristics of the elite), the two aforementioned lessons regarding architecture seem to us valuable for other developing countries in which universal social services are on the policy agenda.

11.6 WRAPPING UP: THE ROAD AHEAD TO ENHANCE THE IMPACT OF SOCIAL SERVICES ON PROGRESSIVE INCOME (RE)DISTRIBUTION

The labour market institutions and public transfers discussed in other parts of this book play a central role in the reduction of income inequality. Yet success in this important goal will only be possible if governments commit to expanding the provision of social services. Healthcare, education and ECEC have significant direct and indirect impacts on equity by providing free (or affordable) services, facilitating access to the formal labour market and helping to expand human capital. In this chapter we have proposed an analytical framework to consider the diverse impact that these public social services have on inequality through different channels that affect participation in labour markets, access to fundamental services at a reduced cost and social norms.

We have also followed a growing literature for both developed countries (Huber and Stephens, 2001; Pontusson, 2005) and developing ones (UNRISD, 2010; ECLAC, 2012a and 2012b) in highlighting the importance that universal provision of these services can have for guaranteeing social rights and improving income distribution. Yet, even if universalism is the most promising policy architecture for improving income distribution, is it actually doable? We argue that the challenge is to identify which policy instruments and policy processes promote these services under various national contexts, eyeing how and whether services reorganize paid and unpaid work. The Nordic model has been particularly successful but it is by no means the only way to secure universalism. In fact, universalism can be the outcome of various policy instruments that governments can use, from general services to social insurance and social assistance.

First and foremost, universalism need not be financed solely through general taxation as Costa Rica´s healthcare system clearly shows (Martínez Franzoni and Sánchez-Ancochea, 2012). There, between 1950 and 1980, payroll taxes expanded together with the growth of healthcare, education and technical training. Payroll taxes funded unified social insurance systems but also non-contributory, social assistance programmes.

Second, in many instances the expansion of universal policies is not enough to guarantee access by low-income groups. Those most vulnerable may require affirmative action to ensure their effective incorporation to services available to the rest of the population. For instance, children from low-income families may need uniforms, transport and complementary nutrition to fully benefit from free and high-quality schools (Garnier et al., 1991). Selective affirmative action measures are not contradictory with universalism: as a policy principle the latter can be implemented with a combination of targeted and non-targeted instruments that help reach the entire population.

How can countries move towards universal public social services that reach a large proportion of the population with generosity and good quality? And what are the lessons for other countries and regions? Although this could be the subject of a different chapter, a few comments are in order. Rather than aiming to build universalism overnight, governments should see it as a gradual process that is highly influenced by the policy architecture of public social services. Such gradual processes are important not just for technical, but for political reasons as well – i.e. for building support and effectively dealing with vetoes.

Another well-established lesson from the Nordic countries and the few available examples of social democracy in the developing world is that the middle-income groups must benefit from public social services (Baldwin, 1992; Huber and Stephens, 2001; Sandbrook et al., 2007). Architectures play a decisive role in whether middle class vested interests feed into universal or stratified provision. Beyond the formal adoption of universalism, what matters is whether the middle class actually relies on or exits public services. For example, in education, the universalism of social public services has been declared more often that it has been achieved.

Although building universalism from scratch is a long and painstaking process, a number of developing countries are now taking it more seriously than ever before. Drawing on recommendations from international institutions (ILO, 2009, 2011; UNRISD, 2010), several Latin American countries have created new healthcare programmes for all. Education reform has also expanded coverage and some countries are even introducing new childcare programmes. The main challenge will now be to expand the generosity and quality of services – something that will only be secured if new social coalitions between the poor and the middle class emerge and expand.

NOTES

* We are thankful to Janine Berg and Laura Addati for their valuable comments to earlier drafts of this chapter.

1. Ours is a normative definition for both market and social incorporation. We do not mean just any participation in labour markets or any access to social services; participation in the informal labour market with an unstable, poorly paid job will always be problematic. Instead we are interested in a very specific kind of participation, one that succeeds in providing a 'floor' of cash, labour and social protection and services for most.

2. The value of cash transfers compared to disposable income is higher than that of services only in Austria, Germany and Poland.
3. In fact, the expansion of educational attainment worldwide in recent decades has not been accompanied by significant improvements in income distribution (Castelló-Climent and Doménech Valariño, 2012).
4. Women also may be forced to postpone motherhood as illustrated in Spain, Italy and Latin America. Middle- and middle-high-income women, confronted with the choice between motherhood without social support and professional demands, choose to postpone childbirth (Filgueira and Peri, 2004). The socioeconomic stratification of this pattern shows in the ratio between children under 15 years of age and formal adult workers. In Latin America, these were, on average, more than ten among the lowest income decile and less than one in the highest decile of the population in 2009 (ECLAC, 2009).
5. Unfortunately, skilled jobs continue to view the 'ideal worker' as someone without care responsibilities (ILO/UNDP, 2009) and as a result, men have failed to significantly increase their contribution to unpaid work. In the future, social policy may need to be driven towards turning more men into caregivers – something that has yet to happen in most countries.
6. See similar evidence in Estevez-Abe et al. (2001).
7. In less developed Latin American countries, universal principles translated almost exclusively into practice as very few formal workers secured access to social insurance (Filgueira, 2007). Problems in securing provision of public social services remain (Martínez Franzoni, 2008).
8. In the last two decades, Costa Rica has struggled to protect universal social policy as a result of fiscal and management problems together with growing private sector involvement in health and education. Nevertheless, Costa Rica's social policy outcomes are still impressive when compared to most other developing countries (Martínez Franzoni and Sánchez-Ancochea, 2013a).

REFERENCES

Addati, L. (2009), 'New approaches to social protection and gender equality at work: the effect of childcare on the quality of working life for low-income women in Chile and Mexico', paper presented to the ILO's 1st Conference on Regulating for Decent Work: Innovative Labour Regulation in a Turbulent World (RDW), 7–8 July, Geneva.

Addati, L., C. Hein and N. Cassirer (2000), *Workplace Solutions for Childcare*, Geneva: International Labour Office.

Baldwin, P. (1992), *The Politics of Social Solidarity: Class Bases of the European Welfare State, 1875–1975*, Cambridge, UK and New York: Cambridge University Press.

Paes de Barros, R., P. Olinto and M. de Carvalho et al. (2010), 'Impact of free childcare on women's labor market behavior: evidence from low income neighborhoods in Rio de Janeiro', GAP Workshop 14 June, World Bank Regional Study on Gender Issues in LAC: Washington, DC: World Bank.

Castelló-Climent, A. and R. Doménech Valariño (2012), 'Human capital and income inequality: some facts and puzzles', *BBVA Working Papers, No. 28/12*, November: Bilbao: Banco Bilbao Vizcaya Argentaria Research.

Chioda, L. (2011), *Work & Family: Latin America and Caribbean Women in Search of New Balance*, Washington, DC: International Bank for Reconstruction and Development.

Cornia, A. (2010), 'Income distribution under Latin America's new left regimes', *Journal of Human Development and Capabilities*, **11**(1), 85–114.
De Gregorio, J. and J.W. Lee (2003), 'Growth and adjustment in East Asia and Latin America', *Working Paper No. 245 of the Central Bank of Chile*, December, Santiago: Central Bank of Chile.
ECLAC (2009), *Social Panorama of Latin America: Briefing Report*, Santiago: Economic Commission for Latin America and the Caribbean.
ECLAC (2012a), *Eslabones de la desigualdad: Heterogeneidad estructural, empleo y protección social* [Links of Inequality: Structural Heterogeneity, Employment and Social Protection], Santiago: Economic Commission for Latin America and the Caribbean.
ECLAC (2012b), *Social Panorama of Latin America: Briefing Report*, Santiago: Economic Commission for Latin America and the Caribbean.
Elson, D. (ed.) (1991), *Male Bias in the Development Process: Contemporary Issues in Development Studies*, Manchester, UK: Manchester University Press.
Esping-Andersen, G. (1990), *The Three Worlds of Welfare Capitalism*, Princeton, NJ: Princeton University Press.
Esping-Andersen, G. and J. Myles (2009), 'Economic inequality and the welfare state', in W. Salverda, B. Nolan and T. Smeeding (eds), *The Oxford Handbook of Economic Inequality*, Oxford: Oxford University Press, pp. 639–64.
Estevez-Abe, M., T. Iversen and D. Soskice (2001), 'Social protection and the formation of skills: a reinterpretation of the welfare state', in P. Hall and D. Soskice (eds), *Varieties of Capitalism: The Institutional Foundations of Competitiveness*, Cambridge, UK: Cambridge University Press, pp. 145–83.
European Commission (2004), 'How Europeans spend their time? Everyday life of women and men; data 1998–2002', *Eurostat, Theme 3, Population and Social Conditions*, Luxembourg: Office for Official Publications of the European Community.
Filgueira, F. (2005), 'Welfare and democracy in Latin America: the development, crises and aftermath of universal, dual and exclusionary social states', Geneva: United Nations Research Institute for Social Development.
Filgueira, F. (2007), 'The Latin American social states: critical juncture and critical choices', in Y. Bangura (ed.), *Democracy and Social Policy*, New York/Geneva: Palgrave/United Nations Research Institute for Social Development, pp. 136–63.
Filgueira, C. and A. Peri (2004), 'América Latina: los rostros de la pobreza y sus causas determinantes' [Latin America: the faces of poverty and its determinants], *Serie Población y Desarrollo No. 54*, Santiago: United Nations Commission for Latin America and the Caribbean.
Folbre, N. (2001), *The Invisible Heart: Economics and Family Values*, New York: New York Press.
Garnier, L., R. Hidalgo and G. Monge et al. (1991), *Costa Rica: entre la ilusión y la desesperanza* [Costa Rica: Between Hope and Despair], San José: Ediciones Guayacán.
Gasparini, L., S. Galiani and G. Cruces et al. (2011), 'Educational upgrading and returns to skills in Latin America: evidence from a supply–demand framework, 1990–2010', *IZA Discussion Paper No. 6244*, Bonn: Institut zur Zukunft der Arbeit (IZA).
Ghai, D. (2003), 'Social security: learning from global experience to reach the

poor', *Journal of Human Development: A Multi-Disciplinary Journal for People-centered Development*, **4**(1), 125–50.

Gindling, T. and J.D. Trejos (2014), 'Income distribution in Central America', in D. Sánchez-Ancochea and S. Marti (eds), *Handbook of Central American Governance*, London: Routledge.

Haggard, S. and R. Kaufman (2008), *Development, Democracy, and Welfare States: Latin America, East Asia, and Eastern Europe*, Princeton, NJ: Princeton University Press.

Hall, P. (1993), 'Policy paradigms, social learning and the state', *Comparative Politics*, **25**(3), 275–96.

Heller, P. (1999), *The Labor of Development: Workers and the Transformation of Capitalism in Kerala, India*, Ithaca, NY: Cornell University Press.

Huber, E. (ed.) (2002), *Models of Capitalism. Lessons for Latin America*, Philadelphia, PA: The Penn State University Press.

Huber, E. and J. Stephens (2001), *Development and Crisis of the Welfare State: Parties and Policies in Global Markets*, Chicago, IL: University of Chicago Press.

ILO (2009), 'The UN social protection floor initiative', factsheet, accessed 30 August 2014 at http://www.ilo.org/gimi/gess/ShowRessource.action?ressource.ressourceId=14603.

ILO (2011), International Labour Conference, Meeting Number 100a Reunión, 2012. *Report IV. Social Protection Floors for Social Justice and Equitable Globalization*, ILC.101/IV/1, 1st edition, Geneva: International Labour Office.

ILO/UNDP (2009), *Decent Work in Latin America and the Caribbean. Work and Family: Towards New Forms of Reconciliation with Social Co-responsibility*, Santiago: International Labour Organization/United Nations Development Programme.

Korpi, W. (1983), *The Democratic Class Struggle*, London: Routledge and Kegan Paul.

Korpi, W. and J. Palmer (1998), 'The paradox of redistribution and strategies of equality: welfare state institutions, inequality, and poverty in the western countries', *American Sociological Review*, **63**(5), 661–87.

Lehoucq, F. (2010), 'Political competition, constitutional arrangements, and the quality of public policies in Costa Rica', *Latin American Politics and Society*, **52**(4), 53–77.

Lewis, C. and P. Lloyd-Sherlock (2009), 'Social policy and economic development in South America: an historical approach to social insurance', *Economy & Society*, **38**(1), 109–31.

López-Calva, L.F. and N. Lustig (2010), *Declining Inequality in Latin America. A Decade of Progress?*, Washington, DC: Brookings Institution and United Nations Development Programme.

Mahon, R. (2011), 'Childcare policy: a comparative perspective', *Encyclopedia on Early Childhood Development*, accessed 2 February 2013 at http://www.child-encyclopedia.com/pages/PDF/child_care.pdf.

Mares, I. (2003), *The Politics of Social Risk: Business and Welfare State Development*, Cambridge, UK: Cambridge University Press.

Marical, F., M. Mira and M. Vaalavuo et al. (2006), 'Publicly provided services and distribution of resources', *OECD Social, Employment and Migration Working Paper No. 45*, Paris: Organisation for Economic Co-operation and Development.

Martínez Franzoni, J. (2008), *Domesticar la incertidumbre en América Latina: mercados laborales, política social y familias* [Taming Uncertainty in Latin America: Labor Markets, Social Policy and Family], San José: Editorial Universidad de Costa Rica)

Martínez Franzoni, J. and D. Sánchez-Ancochea (2012), 'The road to universal social protection: how Costa Rica informs theory', *Kellogg Institute Working Paper No. 283*, March, accessed 30 August 2014 at https://kellogg.nd.edu/publications/workingpapers/WPS/383.pdf.

Martínez Franzoni, J. and D. Sánchez-Ancochea (2013a), *Good Jobs and Social Services: How Costa Rica Achieved the Elusive Double Incorporation*, Basingstoke, UK/Geneva: Palgrave Macmillan/United Nations Research Institute for Social Development.

Martínez Franzoni, J. and D. Sánchez-Ancochea (2013b), 'Can Latin American production regimes complement universalistic welfare regimes? Implications from the Costa Rican case', *Latin American Research Review*, **48**(2), 148–73.

Martínez Franzoni, J. and D. Sánchez-Ancochea (2014), 'Filling in the missing link between universalism and democracy: the case of Costa Rica', *Latin American Politics and Society*, **55**(4), forthcoming.

McGuire, J. (2010), *Wealth, Health and Democracy in East Asia and Latin America*, Cambridge, UK: Cambridge University Press.

Mkandawire, T. (2006a), 'Targeting and universalism in poverty reduction', *Social Policy and Development Programme Paper No. 23*, Geneva: United Nations Research Institute for Social Development.

Mkandawire, T. (ed.) (2006b), 'Social policy in a development context', *Social Policy and Development Programme Paper No.* 7, Geneva: United Nations Research Institute for Social Development.

Molyneux, M. (2007), 'Change and continuity in social protection in Latin America: mothers at the service of the state?', *Programme on Gender and Development, Paper No. 1*, Geneva: United Nations Research Institute for Social Development.

Mos, P. (2007), 'Starting strong: an exercise in international learning', *International Journal of Childcare and Education Policy, Korea Institute of Childcare and Education*, **1**(1), 11–21.

OECD (2006), *Starting Strong II: Early Childhood Education and Care*, Paris: Organisation for Economic Co-operation and Development.

OECD (2012), *Starting Strong III: A Quality Toolbox for Early Childhood Education and Care*, Paris: Organisation for Economic Co-operation and Development.

OECD (2013), *World Development Report 2013: Jobs*, Paris: Organisation for Economic Co-operation and Development.

Orloff, A. (1996), 'Gender in the welfare state', *Annual Review of Sociology*, **22**, 51–78.

Pontusson, J. (2005), *Inequality and Prosperity: Social Europe vs. Liberal America*, Ithaca, NY: Cornell University Press.

Razavi, S. and S. Hassim (2006), *Gender and Social Policy in a Global Context: Uncovering the Gendered Structure of the Social*, Basingstoke, UK: Palgrave Macmillan.

Reimers, F. (2006), 'Education and social policy', in V. Bulmer-Thomas, J. Coatsworth and R. Cortes (eds), *The Cambridge Economic History of Latin*

America. Vol. II. The Long Twentieth Century, Cambridge, UK: Cambridge University Press.

Rosenberg, M. (1983), *Las luchas por el seguro social en Costa Rica* [Struggles for Social Security in Costa Rica], San José: Editorial Costa Rica.

Sandbrook, R., M. Edelman and P. Heller et al. (2007), *Social Democracy in the Periphery: Origins, Challenges, Prospects*, Cambridge, UK: Cambridge University Press.

Segura-Ubiergo, A. (2007), *The Political Economy of the Welfare State in Latin America: Globalization, Democracy and Development*, Cambridge, UK: Cambridge University Press.

Smeeding, T. and L. Rainwater (2002), 'Comparing living standards across nations: real incomes at the top, the bottom and the middle', *SPRC Discussion Paper No. 120*, Sydney: Social Policy Research Centre.

Stephens, J. (2002), 'European welfare state regimes: configurations, outcomes, transformations', in E. Huber (ed.), *Models of Capitalism: Lessons for Latin America*, Philadelphia, PA: Penn State University Press, pp. 303–38.

Szekely, M. and A. Montes (2006), 'Poverty and inequality', in V. Bulmer-Thomas, J. Coatsworth and R. Cortes (eds), *The Cambridge Economic History of Latin America. Vol. II. The Long Twentieth Century*, Cambridge, UK: Cambridge University Press, pp. 585–647.

UNRISD (2010), *Combating Poverty and Inequality: Structural Change, Social Policy and Politics*, New York: United Nations Research Institute for Social Development/UN Publications.

Vaalavuo, M. (2011), 'Towards an improved measure of income inequality. The impact of public services on income distribution: an international comparison', PhD thesis, Florence: European University Institute.

Verbist, G., M. Förster and M. Vaalavuo (2012), 'The impact of publicly provided services on the distribution of resources: review of new results and methods', *OECD Social, Employment and Migration Working Papers No. 130*, Paris: Organisation for Economic Co-operation and Development.

World Bank (2003), *Inequality and Poverty in Latin America: Breaking with History?*, Washington, DC: The World Bank.

World Bank (2013), *World Development Report 2013*, Washington, DC: World Bank.

PART IV

The impact of labour market institutions on different groups

12. Labour market institutions and gender equality

Sarah Gammage

12.1 INTRODUCTION

This chapter focuses on the role of labour market institutions in promoting greater gender equality and securing better outcomes for women in the labour market. It begins with a theoretical framework for analysing women's labour market participation, which focuses on the household and the combination or reconciliation of household and employment responsibilities. The premise that underpins this chapter is that the sexual division of labour within the household weakens the position of women in the labour market and contributes to their segregation, often into precarious, low-productivity and underpaid segments of the labour market. At the same time, this weakened position in the labour market contributes to reinforcing the sexual division of labour in the household, thereby increasing women's economic dependence upon the income of others, or upon social transfers. As a result, it is not possible to understand sex-based inequalities in the labour market without addressing unremunerated work in the household sphere.

The chapter provides some salient stylized facts about women's labour market participation in light of these observed gender differences in women's and men's domestic responsibilities, drawing from time use and labour force participation data across different regions and levels of development. Subsequently, it explores some key labour market institutions (LMIs) that have had the greatest impact on promoting gender equality, both in the labour market and in terms of the gender division of labour within the household. The chapter considers three LMIs and describes their theoretical impact on women's labour market participation or the terms and conditions of their employment and illustrates each with examples. These include minimum wages, unions and collective bargaining, and the organization of jobs within the firm. The objective is to explore the impact of such policies and institutions both on the terms and conditions of employment in the market as well as on the gender division of labour within the household, as this affects women's ability to participate in labour markets, informs their reservation wages and is likely to determine the type of employment they seek. The chapter concludes that these three LMIs have positively affected the terms and conditions of employment for women and as a result have significant potential to reduce gender inequalities in the labour market. Yet these LMIs alone will not ensure that greater gender equity prevails within the household, particularly in terms of the allocation of caring responsibilities and domestic work. There is a critical role for the state in actively encouraging men to take on more domestic responsibilities and enjoy both the rights and responsibilities of caring – legislating parental benefits and leave, pursuing gender equity laws, enacting non-discrimination laws and contributing to social change that shifts gender roles over time.

12.2 ACCESSING PAID WORK

Throughout the world, significant gender gaps exist in women's and men's participation rates, with women typically reporting lower levels of participation in paid employment (ILO, 2011a). Moreover, sex segmentation is prevalent in many labour markets, with women clustering in a narrower range of lower-paying occupations. Nearly one-fourth of women globally are defined as unpaid contributing family workers, meaning they receive no direct pay for their efforts, and there is a pronounced segregation of women into lower-paying sectors and informal employment (ILO, 2010). Globally, the gender pay gap is estimated to be 22.9 per cent, which means that on average women earn 77.1 per cent of what men earn (ILO, 2011b).[1] Furthermore, the returns to potential experience (years since leaving full-time education) are lower for women than men and the pay gap for women who are married with children is generally larger (Waldfogel, 1997; Blau and Kahn, 2003; ILO, 2010).

The theoretical framework through which we analyse the impact of labour market institutions on gender equality is one that incorporates the household and unremunerated work. To understand the unequal position of women in the labour market we must also consider their role in unremunerated work and the fixed costs of replacing unremunerated work if women are to participate more equally and on more equal terms in market activities. Even as women are entering the labour market in unprecedented numbers worldwide, their participation rates lag behind those of men; they tend to concentrate in feminized occupations, clustering disproportionately in part-time or informal employment, as a result of which marked gender differences in wages, hours and access to statutory benefits can be observed.

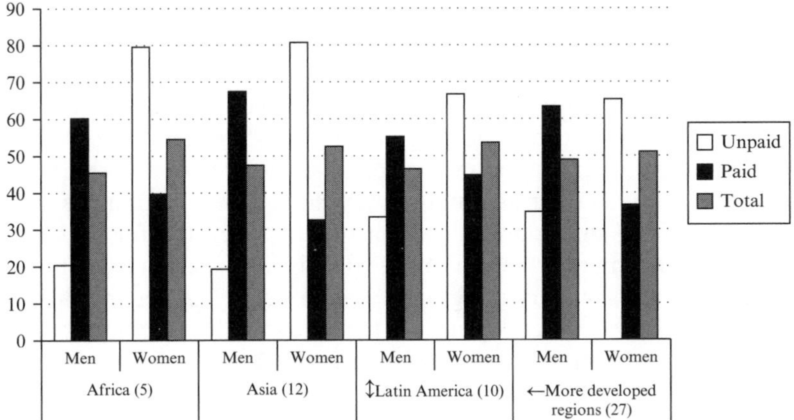

Sources: WISTAT *The World's Women 2010: Trends and Statistics* based on country-level data from Statistics Sweden, United Nations Economic Commission for Europe (UNECE); Gammage (2010) and Mires and Toro (2011); other data from Latin America are from the CEPAL (United Nations Commission for Latin America and the Caribbean) Gender observatory available on line at www.cepal.org/oig; last accessed 3 September 2014.

Figure 12.1 Percentage of total time men and women dedicate to paid and unpaid work

Time Use and Labour Market Participation

The pronounced gender differences in women's and men's engagement in paid and unpaid work are more easily understood when we examine time use data. Figure 12.1 provides data on time use for 54 developed and developing countries. Time use is divided broadly into time dedicated to paid and unpaid work. The figure demonstrates that men undertake the greater proportion of total paid work while women undertake the greater proportion of total unpaid work in the household. In Africa and Asia, women are responsible for approximately 80 per cent of the total time dedicated to unpaid work in the household. Although total time burdens vary, women appear to work longer hours in the sum of paid and unpaid work, with the greatest difference between men and women in Africa and Latin America.

Much of the unpaid household work is devoted to caring for household members and household provisioning such as cooking, cleaning, washing, mending and making clothes. Caring work takes up a significant amount of time in many countries, especially in those countries where infrastructure is poor and publicly provided caring services are limited, or where accessing healthcare and treatment for illnesses requires that family members act as intermediaries, caring for patients in hospitals or in their homes (Floro, 1995a, 1995b).

The gender differences observed in Figure 12.1 in the division of labour within and beyond the household and the differences in men's and women's time devoted to paid and unpaid work are reproduced worldwide. Moreover, decreases in men's time allocated to paid work does not necessarily result in their assuming more unpaid work within the household – suggesting an important role for public policy and for the modification of labour market institutions. Typically, a reduction in men's paid work results in their consuming more leisure time. The best predictor of the hours men apportion to leisure are the hours they must commit to paid work (Bittman, 2004). For women, however, the best predictor of the time they spend in paid work is how much time they spend in childcare and other domestic responsibilities (ibid).

The incremental rise in women's participation in the labour market globally is likely to require replacing reproductive services within the household. Women from social strata with higher incomes have the greatest possibility to replace their unremunerated work in the household since they can commodify and outsource their household labour more easily. Employing a domestic worker in the household, acquiring household appliances, as well as purchasing services directly – such as food prepared outside the household – can reduce the hours of unremunerated work. Indeed, multiple strategies can be used to reduce domestic household labour if the household has sufficient income to do so (ibid.). In contrast, women from poorer income groups may not have the resources to replace their reproductive labour and either add to their total time burdens, by assuming both productive and reproductive work, or use informal networks and redistribute reproductive responsibilities among other, typically female, household members. Assuming both productive and reproductive responsibilities may lead to time poverty, greatly inhibiting individual well-being and potentially reducing welfare for other household members (Vickery, 1977; Gammage, 2010; Zacharias, 2011). For example, where children are pulled out of school to assume reproductive labour responsibilities and provide caring labour, the inter-generational cycle of time and income poverty can be perpetuated. Furthermore, some households may not be able to meet their household production requirements because they devote too much time to employment (relative to the time required for household production). In this case, the well-being of all household members may be compromised.

Time poverty can be understood in terms of the lack of adequate time to sleep and rest. As Bardasi and Wodon (2006) highlight, and in direct contrast to consumption or income measures of well-being, where economists assume that 'more is better', time is a limited resource – both across the life of an individual and in a given day. The greater the time dedicated to remunerated or unremunerated work, the less time is available for other activities such as rest and recreation. Consequently, a person who lacks adequate time to sleep and rest lives and works in a state of 'time poverty'. Individual capabilities can be greatly affected by time poverty. If an individual is time poor this affects not only their contemporaneous capabilities but their future capabilities – it limits their ability to rest, to enjoy leisure and recreation, and to invest in expanded capabilities and opportunities to acquire new or more abilities such as formal education. Moreover, experiencing time poverty can compromise an individual's health and well-being.

The majority of research on replacing unremunerated household work has been undertaken in higher-income countries and underscores that opportunities to participate in the labour market and to replace reproductive labour are greater in higher-income groups. For example, Cohen (1998) uses the US Consumer Expenditure Survey from 1993 to explore the pattern of expenditures on domestic services and food prepared outside the household. Cohen finds that households with women with more income and higher occupational status consume more household cleaning services and childcare services and spend more on food prepared outside the household. Similarly, Van der Lippe et al. (2004) analyse expenditure patterns and the propensity to 'outsource' social reproduction among higher-income households in the Netherlands. These authors conclude that there are many strategies that a household can employ to reduce unremunerated work, among which the purchase of appliances and domestic services features significantly.

Without doubt, replacing or reducing the number of unremunerated hours worked in the household is an important strategy for women who work in the labour market and their labour market participation may be greatly affected by the opportunity to do so. Despite a vast empirical and theoretical literature on women's participation rates (see, for example, Heckman and Willis, 1977; Heckman and Macurdy, 1980; Killingsworth and Heckman, 1986; Goldin, 1990; Del Boca et al., 2000; Blau and Kahn, 2005), many studies largely ignore the time and financial costs of participating in the labour market particularly from a gender perspective. Since the majority of the unremunerated work in the household is undertaken by women, the fixed costs of participating in the labour market and substituting for one's own reproductive labour are likely to account for a significant portion of the reservation wage, particularly for women. The existence of fixed costs of participating in the labour market implies that many individuals are not able to work for less than a given quantity of hours, called reservation hours; these hours can be used to derive a reservation wage that would include the cost of replacing part or all of one's own unremunerated household labour.

If prevailing wages do not compensate for the fixed costs of replacing all or part of one's own unremunerated labour, it is not surprising that some women will choose not to enter the labour market or to remain at home caring for children during their early years. It is likely that such a calculus underpins the significantly different participation rates that we observe between high- and low-income women in many settings. We explore this graphically using available data for Latin America, Asia and Africa. Figure 12.2 graphs the percentage difference in participation rates between

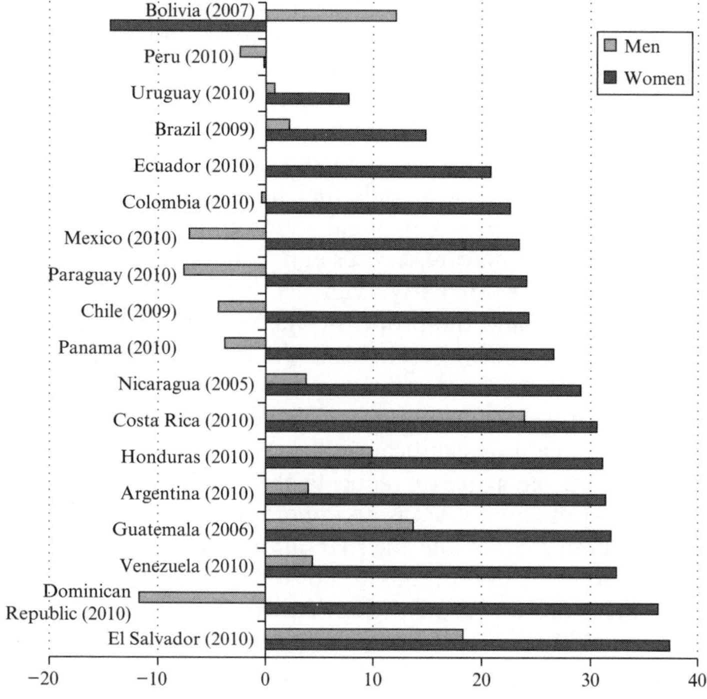

Note: Data for Argentina are for Buenos Aires for 2010.

Source: Household survey data, CEPALSTAT, Table 6: Regional Report – Latin America.

Figure 12.2 The percentage difference in participation rates for men and women in the fifth and first income quintiles in selected countries in Latin America (Q5–Q1)

women in the first and fifth income quintile against those for men in Latin America. Participation rates are significantly higher for all women in the fifth income quintile with the exception of Bolivia and Peru. In contrast, men's participation rates vary surprisingly little by income quintile with the exception of Bolivia, Costa Rica, El Salvador and Guatemala.

Figure 12.3 provides a similar analysis by poverty status for Asia and Africa, comparing differences in participation rates for men and women between the non-poor and the extremely poor using consumption data from household surveys. These graphs offer a distinct picture of female participation rates, where women from extremely poor households often have higher participation rates than women in wealthier households. The differences in participation rates for women are negative for six out of the eight countries analysed in Asia and 15 of the 19 countries analysed in Africa. It is most likely that these households resolve their caring and reproductive responsibilities either by increasing total time burdens and falling into time poverty, or by having other household members, typically women and girls, undertake these duties or using informal networks. Similarly, men from extremely poor households also appear to have higher particpation rates than the non-poor, underscoring that prevailing wages are insufficient to lift households out of poverty and that exigencies of poverty require higher participation rates. It is important to note here that labour force participation rates may not capture all productive work that women and men engage in – particularly in rural settings and contexts with high levels of informal employment. Additionally, it is clear from comparing the three regions that in some contexts women enter the labour market even when prevailing wages do not compensate for the fixed costs of replacing their unremunerated labour. This is because they may be forced into the 'distress sale' of labour by poverty. Indeed, factors that constrain or enable labour market participation of women in low-income countries, especially in agrarian economies or those with high levels of informality, may be different and the institutional responses required to reduce poverty, support their employment and improve gender equality are also likely to be different (see Chapter 10 in this volume).

Comparing these three figures and the time use data, it is obvious that there is more female engagement in total market work in Latin America than in Asia and that women undertake the greatest proportion of unpaid work in Africa and Asia. Considering strategies to replace or outsource reproductive labour, Latin America appears to exhibit similar patterns to many developed nations in that the calculus for numerous women in this region is whether prevailing wages are high enough to substitute market services for reduced family care. It is most likely that if public goods and informal care provision are not sufficiently available to at least partially

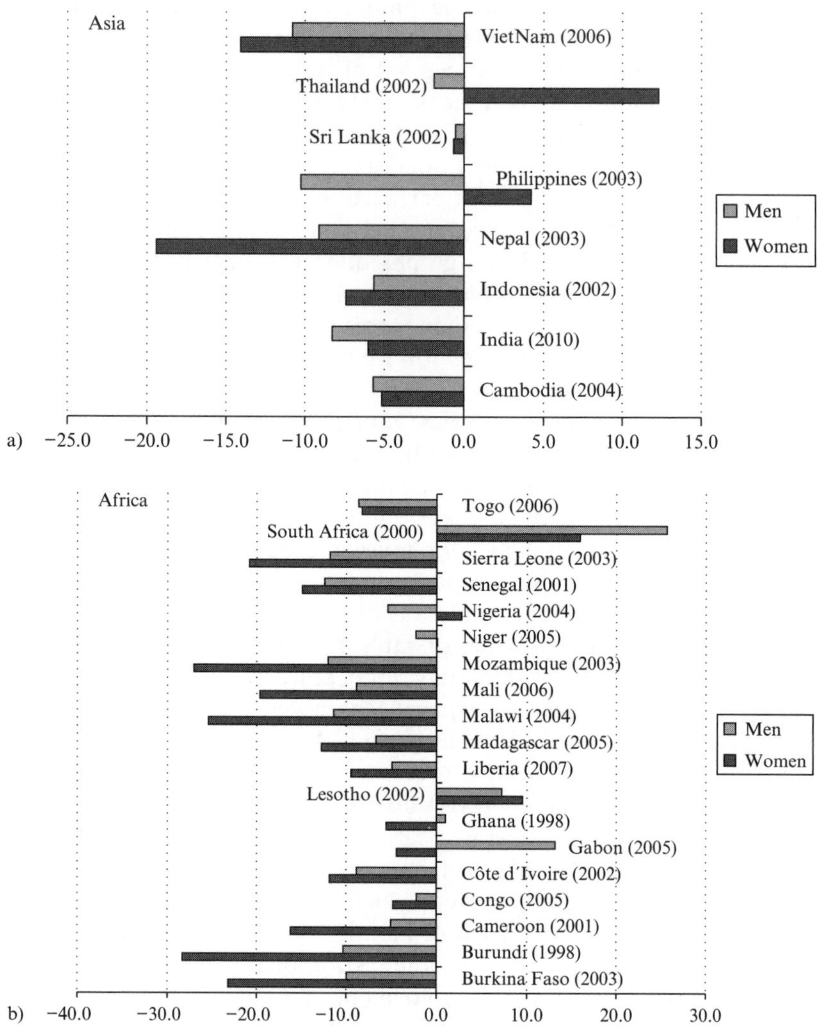

Note: The participation rates express the economically active population as a ratio of the working-age population.

Source: Author's analysis of household survey data for Latin America from CEPALSTAT and for Asia and Africa from KILM (Key Indicators of the Labour Market). India (2004/05): Desai et al. (2010); Philippines (2002): from Orbeta (2005).

Figure 12.3a,b The percentage difference in particiation rates for non-poor and extremely poor households in Asia and Africa (non-poor – extremely poor)

substitute for reductions in individual time allocated to caring work in the household, then women in lower-income groups in Latin America elect not to work in the market. In Africa and Asia, it may be that informal networks, and the expectation that other household members will substitute for caring work, combined with the exigencies of poverty, foster the greater participation of lower-income women in the labour market.

Caring Responsibilities and Access to Care Services

The different labour market outcomes for poor women in Asia, Africa and Latin America may also reflect the extent of the informal economy. In economies where there is more informal employment, women may combine market work and household responsibilities more frequently. This supposition is reinforced by findings from a comparative analysis of women's work, childcare, and the earnings of mothers in the slums of Guatemala City and Accra (Quisumbing et al., 2007). Similar factors affect women's decisions to work and to use formal daycare in both countries, but the use of formal childcare varies greatly with formal employment in each country. In Guatemala, where formal sector work is arguably more widely available than in Ghana, the use of formal daycare services is more widespread. The authors conclude that access to formal daycare services may be more important to mothers' decisions to work in cities where formal sector work is more widely available.

The cost of formal childcare may also affect a mother's decision to work, even in developed counties. A 2011 report by the OECD called *Doing Better for Families* underscores that the net cost of childcare is significant for many households and that the cost of replacing or outsourcing caring responsibilities for children may affect the decision to work, particularly for women from low-income households (OECD, 2011). This report calculated the net cost of childcare, taking into account the direct cost of paying for childcare but also the indirect cost in additional taxes, or the loss of benefits and tax concessions, from having children in formal care. The net average cost of childcare was calculated at about 18 per cent of the average wage for a single earner and around 12 per cent of the families' net income for dual-earner couples with earnings between 150 and 200 per cent of the average wage. Across the OECD, the net cost of childcare is higher for low-income households. As a result, the financial incentives to work for second earners with small children, usually mothers, are weaker relative to the additional earnings of the family; this is particularly true for lower-income families when compared with higher-income families.

Another characteristic of the marked gender differences in men's and women's labour market insertion, which is related to women's disproportionate caring responsibilities, is that transition rates to employment from unemployment are also very different for men and women. As Manning (2003, p. 197) notes in his analysis of gender discrimination in American and British labour markets: 'The most striking differences in earnings in both the United States and the United Kingdom are the premium for being married for men and the penalty for having children for women'. These differences manifest in marked inequalities in transition rates from unemployment and into unemployment for men and women. Certainly, across the developing world women typically exhibit higher unemployment rates and longer periods out of the labour force when compared to men (ILO, 2010).[2]

Differences in labour market transition rates will result in a gender pay gap even if individual employers do not actively discriminate against women. If women enter and leave employment with greater frequency, to have and care for children, or to care for other family members, their job tenure will be lower than that of men. In a world where job tenure means greater experience and the returns to experience are rewarded with greater pay, gender pay gaps are likely to prevail even if equal pay legislation exists. A more equitable gender division of labour within the household and more equitable caring responsibilities are necessary to ameliorate these gender gaps.

The UK British Household Panel Survey asks respondents questions about whether domestic responsibilities limit their job search and mobility. Manning (2003, p. 201) reports that the constraints on job search are much greater for married women with children than for either men or single women. For example, only 4.0 per cent of married men with children report that domestic constraints have prevented job change compared to 13.2 per cent of married women with children. Similarly, only 2.2 per cent of married men with children report that domestic responsibilities prevented them from searching for a job as compared to 12.3 per cent of married women with children.

An additional feature of the constraints that domestic responsibilities may impose upon women is manifest in how far they can travel to work. If women are constrained by domestic responsibilities, then the fixed time and money costs of getting to work are likely to influence the choice of labour markets and type of work – whether that be full- or part-time work. If women with dependents or caring responsibilities are restricted to more local labour markets they are likely to be more prone to discriminatory hiring practices and monopsonistic employers (Manning, 2003).

Taylor and Mauch (1996) report in their analysis of gender, race and travel behaviour using 1990 data from the San Francisco Bay Area that women's travel patterns appear to be a function of both socialization and the sexual division of household responsibilities. These authors find that journey-to-work travel times are about equal for men and women living alone but are significantly lower for women in households with two or more adults when children are present. Moreover, working women with children often combine more transport-related trips with child-chauffeuring and undertake more household-serving activities that require transportation than men. Similarly, Preston and McLafferty (1993) in their analysis of commuting time in suburban and central locations in New York and Toronto, find that women reduce their commuting time by restricting their search for work to jobs available locally. In contexts where cities and suburbs are residentially and racially segregated this has particularly negative consequences for women from poorer communities with fewer employment opportunities available to them (Dickerson, 2002). As Preston and McLafferty (1993) highlight, in urban contexts in New York and Toronto, well-paid professionals, both men and women, tend to live in close proximity to their places of employment and take advantage of dense transit networks. In suburban contexts in New York and Toronto, the spatial separation of jobs and residences contributes greatly to the spatial and gender segregation observed in the labour market, with women clustering in lower-income, more feminized occupations.

Implications for Public Policy

Public policies can be designed to promote women's employment as well as address caring responsibilities and gendered time constraints. India's 2005 Mahatma Gandhi National Rural Employment Guarantee Act (NREGA) created an employment guarantee scheme that provides 100 days of guaranteed wage employment in public works per year for every rural household whose adult members volunteer to do unskilled manual work at the mandated minimum wage. The programme is decentralized and demand driven: people opt into the programme voluntarily on the basis of need. A particular emphasis has been placed on ensuring that rural women have access to the programme, modifying the selection criteria, the types of public works and small infrastructure to be built, and providing assistance with childcare (Ashok and Tankha, 2009). Quotas are in operation to ensure that at least one-third of beneficiaries are women. Moreover, the programme ensures wage parity for men and women to correct for discriminatory hiring and employment practices in the rural labour market that typically undervalue women's work.

In order to increase women's involvement, the programme accommodates their caring responsibilities and attempts to reduce the distance from their home to the place of employment. NREGA provides crèches for children aged between one and five years – that is, for those children who are not yet eligible for public education. Additionally, the scheme provides work within a radius of 5 km from the house to make the jobs more accessible. Work can be undertaken in the absence of direct supervision and women have greater flexibility to choose the period and number of months of employment that are better suited to reconciling their work and family responsibilities. In general, the programme has exceeded the quota for women, with more than 40 per cent of women workers in its ranks. This figure rose to 48 per cent in 2008–09 (Ashok and Tankha, 2009). Despite reports that wages were not initially equal for men and women, there has been a gradual convergence over time as more women become aware of this stipulation in the programme's mandate.

Yet most public policies and labour market institutions have evolved without attention to their impact on family life, time and task allocation or the possibility that they may impose significant constraints or burdens on certain members of the household (Bittman and Folbre, 2004). As Susan Himmelweit (2002, p. 53) notes, '[p]olicies that increase the output of one sector by diminishing that of another may not succeed in meeting their aims, unless compensatory provision is made for the specific outputs lost'. This is particularly relevant when we consider unpaid work and the importance of reproductive and caring labour for individual and household well-being. For example, the more generous provision of childcare and paid family leave for both parents can clearly increase choice and improve opportunities for women as well as men struggling to balance the demands of household and market work (England and Folbre, 2002; Anxo et al., 2011; Gálvez-Muñoz et al., 2011). Such policies can also foster greater gender equality within the household and in the labour market (see Martínez Franzoni and Sánchez-Ancochea, Chapter 11 in this volume).

The analytical framework laid out in this introduction emphasizes the importance of the care economy and time spent in reproductive activities for women's labour market participation. As a result, analysing how labour market institutions affect outcomes in the labour market and can impinge upon the distribution of unpaid work in the household may shed more light on the impediments to achieving greater gender equity, both in the world of work and in the household.

12.3 MINIMUM WAGES AND LABOUR MARKET OUTCOMES

Minimum wages can be an effective tool for promoting greater gender equality by increasing women's wages and their participation in the labour market. Increases may be associated with greater gender equality if women's wages rise more than men's and thus gender wage and poverty gaps narrow. Minimum wages are likely to affect the incentives for job search – with increments being associated with increased labour supply at the lower end of the income distribution, an effect that may also make seeking employment more attractive for women with higher reservation wages. Furthermore, minimum wages can affect the entire wage distribution, reducing inequality and increasing wage compression (see Chapter 5 by Belser and Rani in this volume and Lee, 1999), which has the potential to be gender equalizing.

Minimum wages and centralized wage setting can correct for inefficiencies in the labour market that set differential wages for work of equal or equivalent value (Schettkat, 2002; Rubery and Grimshaw, 2009). This is particularly the case if women concentrate in sectors where rents are low or in sectors where monopsony power acts to limit the sharing of rents where they are sizeable. Indeed, as Plantenga and Fransen observe in their review of the extent and origin of the gender pay gap in Europe that 'Centralised systems of wage-setting . . . tend to reduce inter-firm and inter-industry wage variation thereby potentially lowering the gender pay gap' (2010, p. 418).

Mainstream economic theory argues that higher minimum wages can lead to employment losses, since higher wages reduce the quantity of labour demanded. Substantial empirical evidence exists to the contrary (Card and Krueger, 1994; Manning, 2003; Freeman, 2005, 2007; Belser and Rani, Chapter 5 in this volume), suggesting that minimum wages have negligible effects, or may even have positive effects on employment because of signalling and screening benefits that change the composition of applicants in conjunction with productivity benefits operating through efficiency-wage-type gains. What is more, minimum wage increments may also affect other informal sectors not officially covered by minimum wages through a 'lighthouse effect' whereby they become a reference wage for other sectors and for informal employees. What is clear from reading the recent literature on minimum wages is that the range over which the minimum wage 'bites', and its relationship to the median and mean wage levels, suggests that there is significant policy space for the use of minimum wages in shoring up the wages of those at the lowest end of the income distribution, regardless of whether that minimum applies to the occupation in question.

Women and minority workers tend to be over-represented among the minimum wage workforce or among those who earn close to the minimum wage in most labour markets. As a result, increments in minimum wages are most likely to affect their remuneration and take-home pay. For instance, Rubery and Grimshaw (2009) find in their analysis of gender pay gaps at the lowest decile for full-time workers in OECD countries that the gender pay gap is highest among those countries with neither strong collective bargaining coverage nor a high-value statutory minimum wage. These authors note that although minimum wages do not offer a panacea for gender pay inequity they 'constitute an essential element of any comprehensive policy to tackle the persistent gender gap' (Rubery and Grimshaw, 2009, p. 248). Where minimum wages compress wage distributions and raise wages for those at the lower end of the income distribution they are also likely to facilitate the labour market participation of lower-income women who need to earn sufficient wages to cover the fixed costs of going to work.

Certainly, the experience of Latin America over the last decade highlights the role of labour market institutions in securing both greater income and gender equality. Keifman and Maurizio (2012) conclude that labour market institutions have played a significant role in reducing income inequality in Latin America during the 2000s. Inequality fell more dramatically in countries where formality rose faster and real minimum wages increased more significantly. Braunstein and Seguino (2012, p. 33) also conclude in their analysis of income and gender equality in Latin America that 'three variables stand out as having consistent gender equalising effects in the labor market – social spending, minimum wages, and public investment'.

Dinkelman and Ranchhod (2012) look at the specific case of South Africa where a significant change in the legislation introduced a high and legally binding minimum wage for domestic workers in 2002. What was so striking about this law, was that it set an extremely high minimum wage (fixed at the 70th percentile of the pre-law wage distribution) with no effective penalties and an infinitesimally small probability of being audited. Despite the lack of effective sanctions, employers still chose to respond to the law. Dinkelman and Ranchhod document a large and partial adjustment of wages upwards in the wake of the law and find no evidence that hours increased significantly or that labour supply changed in response to the introduction of the law. Moreover, these authors observed 'dramatic increases in the fraction of domestic workers who have a formal contract of employment, unemployment insurance coverage and employer-provided pension contributions after the law' (ibid., p. 28). Since domestic work absorbs 18 per cent of the total female labour force in South Africa and more than 80 per cent of all domestic workers are female, a significant revision of wages upward in this sector has the potential to reduce gender wage gaps in the overall wage distribution with potential spillovers to other sectors, whether they are covered by minimum wage legislation or not.

Berg (2011) documents a similar effect of the increase in real minimum wages in Brazil. Real minimum wages have risen in Brazil from 1997 onwards, with the exception of a small decline between 2004 and 2005. Poverty rates for men and women also have declined consistently over the same period, as have poverty rates for black and white workers. Moreover, there is evidence of spillovers to other sectors that are not necessarily covered by minimum wage guarantees indicative of lighthouse effects (ibid.). A little over twice the proportion of women receive minimum wages than men. As a result, raising the minimum wage disproportionately benefitted women and contributed to closing the gender wage gap (Vasconcelos et al., 2010).

12.4 UNIONS AND COLLECTIVE BARGAINING

Other important labour market institutions include unions and collective bargaining mechanisms. Unions and collective bargaining have the potential to greatly increase gender pay equity (see Hayter, Chapter 4 in this volume and Hayter and Weinberg, 2010). Blau and Kahn (2003) analyse micro-data for 22 countries from 1985 to 1994 and conclude that collective bargaining is associated with more compressed wage structures and lower gender pay gaps. They also conclude that collective bargaining exerts a greater impact on wage compression than the minimum wage. A similar study by Kim (1993) for the Republic of Korea also finds that the gender pay gap is lower in the union sector than the non-union sector. Moreover, an increase in union density or an expansion of the number and types of contracts covered by collective bargaining may also raise the wages of non-union workers and those not covered by collective bargaining. Manning (2003) uses data from 110 US cities from 1990 to 2000 to explore the impact of union density on the log of average non-union private sector wages. He finds that there are significant positive effects for union density on non-union wages and that this effect is much larger for low-education groups. Similar to the lighthouse effect, such spillovers have the potential to benefit men and women in other jobs not necessarily covered by collective bargaining mechanisms.

In general, reflecting both sectoral and occupational segregation by sex and the erosion of union density over time, union membership is lower for women and women are less frequently covered by collective bargaining mechanisms. Women's membership of trade unions increases dramatically in the public sector – but even in developed countries and in the public sector there is seldom equality in union membership between men and women. Britwum et al. (2012) observe in their analysis of gender and unions, that where negotiations explicitly include gender equality concerns such as paid parental leave, breastfeeding support, childcare concerns and work–life balance issues, these issues are frequently considered to be subordinate to other concerns about pay and benefits that reflect the disproportionate role that men, and male negotiators, play in collective bargaining fora. These authors noted in an early report that: 'There is much evidence that collective bargaining has been slow to respond to women's issues, and indeed in some countries the legislative framework has been ahead of trade unions – especially in the EU which has a strong framework of equal rights' (Britwum et al., 2011, p. 1111). In their analysis of the Philippines, these authors also observed that women's priorities were among the top six items that were most likely to be traded away for other bargaining proposals. Moreover, employers were highly likely to resist agreeing to provisions that they saw as costs, beyond those that were already stipulated by law. As a result, it was frequently in management's interest to resist or at least not to encourage women onto bargaining teams – thereby compounding their exclusion from bargaining mechanisms and further relegating gender equality concerns in bargaining proposals.[3]

Heery (2006) explores the incidence of bargaining on equal pay in the United Kingdom. He also examines the role of the place of negotiation on equal pay within the system of collective bargaining, and the characteristics of the union officers engaged in equality bargaining and the reasons for getting involved in equality bargaining. The author draws a number of conclusions from the findings; the paper suggests that equality bargaining depends on women's voice within unions, the characteristics and preferences of bargainers at the negotiating table, and the public policy environment within which the bargaining takes place. One of the most prominent conclusions of his research is that bargaining on equal pay is also more likely to take place in centralized bargaining systems where the negotiations cover multiple employers.

There are, however, some very notable examples of the role that unions have played in promoting national legislation that expands gender rights and gender equality. Beginning in the mid-1990s, countries in Latin America began to form tripartite gender commissions to address women's issues. In Chile, the Tripartite Commission for Equality of Opportunities for Women at Work was installed in 1995, and in Brazil a Working Group for the Elimination of Discrimination in Employment and Occupation was established in 1996. Similar tripartite commissions were put in place in Uruguay (1997), in Argentina and Paraguay (1998) and in 2010 in Bolivia, Costa Rica and the Dominican Republic. These commissions also include representatives from the Ministries of Labour, the Women's Ministries and representatives of trade unions and employers' associations (Briskin and Muller, 2011). The Tripartite Commission in Uruguay has contributed greatly to legislative initiatives, including drafting the 2006 Law on Domestic Workers and the 2009 Law on Sexual Harassment (Espino and Pedetti, 2010).

It is clear, however, that collective bargaining is more likely to reflect gender equity concerns in contexts where the legal framework incorporates strong equity legislation (Cook et al., 1992). A major project on equal opportunities and collective bargaining in the European Union that was sponsored by the European Foundation for the Improvement in Living and Working Conditions concluded that: 'The pursuit of equal opportunities through collective bargaining is likely to be aided if legislation enacts positive measures to promote equality, requires specific action by the social partners – procedural or substantive – and provides for the monitoring of results and effective sanctions' (Bleijenbergh et al., 2001, p. 11).

One example of such an initiative is in Australia, where under the Equal Opportunity for Women in the Workplace (EOWW) Act of 1999 (now replaced by the Workplace Gender Equality Act, 2012), all companies employing at least 100 employees have to develop and implement specific programmes to promote equal opportunities for women in the workplace. The employers must submit an annual report using the detailed guidelines prepared by the Equal Opportunity for Women in the Workplace Agency (EOWWA), recently renamed the Workplace Gender Equality Agency (WGEA).[4] If an employer fails to respect this statutory requirement they may face sanctions, including possible exclusion from tenders for public contracts. Furthermore, the Federal Government publishes a report to 'name and shame' non-compliant enterprises.

In contrast to trends in many countries, women's union membership actually rose in Australia by 6.7 per cent between 2006 and 2009. Furthermore, using the legislative space created by the EOWW Act, a landmark equal pay case was brought before Federal courts by the Australian Council of Trade Unions disputing pay in the social and community services sector.[5] On 1 February 2012, a historic decision was made when a Fair Work Australia[6] ruling gave social and community sector workers pay increases of between 23 per cent and 45 per cent over eight years, beginning on 1 December 2012. Fair Work laws have restored a number of key benefits that foster better work–life balance, including extra unpaid parental leave after the birth of a child (from 12 to 24 months) if requested by a parent; rights for parents to request flexible working hours or part-time work until their children are in school; the corresponding obligation for employers to consider such requests; access to family emergency leave for all employees including casual labour; and personal/carer's leave as a minimum standard of employment to apply to all employees.

12.5 THE ORGANIZATION OF WORK

It is clear that the organization of work within a company or firm can greatly affect women's ability to work and, as a result, gender equality with their peers in the labour market. Additionally, flexible workplace practices can also improve the work–life balance in a way that is also consistent with enterprise needs while at the same time reducing time burdens and time constraints that emerge from the challenge of mediating reproductive and productive needs. Workplace practices are often governed by collective agreements or informal employer rules, particularly in smaller enterprises. Consequently, many countries have set statutory entitlements on flexibility in working hours. Regular part-time work is the most commonly used form of work-time flexibility that can accommodate caring and household responsibilities, particularly in developed countries, although increasingly we observe more part-time work and more women clustering in part-time work in developing countries.

The majority of high-income countries have flexible working statutes that protect the rights of workers with dependents to negotiate with their employers to reduce or increase working hours, preserve part-time parity in access to benefits, grant parental leave on a part-time basis for a gradual return to work, allow for the more flexible scheduling of hours including 'flextime' and the location of work through options such as telecommuting. Additionally, these statutes often permit the right to refuse overtime or shift patterns that are incompatible with caring responsibilities and almost all protect time for breastfeeding in line with existing ILO Conventions.[7] In Sweden, for example, a parent has the right to work part-time (75 per cent) until a child is eight years of age. In Belgium a parent can take a one-year paid sabbatical (which can also be taken over five years working four days a week). In the United Kingdom a worker has the right to request a change in hours, which includes the amount, the timing and where these hours are worked. In Austria, both parents may reduce their hours or change their scheduling of hours until the child is seven years old. In Norway, parents may ask for reduced hours until the child is ten years old.

In Spain, parents caring for children under eight years old are entitled to reduce work hours by between 20 and 50 per cent.

As Hegewisch and Gornick (2007) note in their review of statutory routes to workplace flexibility, the explicit inclusion of family care-giving responsibilities for adult relatives is not as widespread as rights in relation to parenthood or adoption, but it is rising. In Belgium an employee may take up to 12 months leave full-time or 24 months part-time to look after a seriously ill family member. In Spain, such leave is also available for up to two years. In the United Kingdom, statutes were amended in 2007 to provide adult caregivers with the same rights as parents – primarily because surveys revealed that these employees were much less successful in getting a voluntary agreement from their employer.

In all countries, statutes that regulate alternative work arrangements also include provisions that are intended to protect employers from excessive hardship or escalating costs. First, leaves that temporarily reduce working hours are combined with the right to employ at least a partial wage replacement. In most cases the wage replacement is financed through social insurance or other taxes ensuring that the cost is widely shared (Hegewisch and Gornick, 2007). Second, statutes explicitly grant employers the rights to refuse requests for alternative work arrangements on business grounds – although the definition of business grounds for refusal can be quite strict in many OECD countries. Third, the statutes require substantial notification periods to ensure that employers can plan for the alternative schedules that they are going to accommodate. Small employers are exempt in some OECD countries – but not all – with the definitions of small employers ranging from ten to 20 employees.

Flexible working arrangements have multiple potential benefits and spillovers (see Messenger and Ray, Chapter 7 in this volume). They can contribute to increasing the quality of part-time work, particularly for women who often work below their skill levels because of a lack of reduced hours available in professional work. They can also foster greater gender equality by allowing men to adjust their working hours as well to better distribute caring rights and responsibilities within households. The Dutch statutes that protect flexible working rights explicitly include reference to promoting greater gender equality with the goal of switching from a distribution of working hours where men worked full-time and women worked part-time, to one where both parents have the option to work three-quarters time. Flexible work hours also facilitate the return to work for carers and parents and, as a result, reduce the costs associated with being out of the labour force to undertake these caring responsibilities. Moreover, these arrangements can also accommodate different needs over the life-cycle that can foster lifelong learning or gradual retirement.

There is also the potential for these arrangements to redistribute work and reduce unemployment. Additionally, they can create more churning in the labour market and provide workers and new labour market entrants with critical experience in the labour market that subsequently enable them to find full-time employment.

12.6 CONCLUSIONS

Labour market institutions have a significant role to play in fostering greater gender equity in labour markets and in the gender division of labour within the household. Where women enter and work in the labour market on more equal terms with men, labour markets are less likely to be segregated by sex and gender wage gaps are more likely to be eroded. As a result, achieving greater gender equity in the labour market is also consistent with achieving greater income equality between men and women and in the economy as a whole.

The design of labour market institutions should take account of the gender division of labour within the household and seek to redistribute caring responsibilities more equally between men and women and between the household and the state.

In the absence of strong union representation or a broad coverage of collective bargaining mechanisms, minimum wages have a particularly important role to play in supporting the wages of the most vulnerable – which frequently include women, single household heads, migrants and part-time workers. A judicious combination of minimum wages and tax concessions as well as dependent care benefits can also be used to ensure that compensation is sufficient for second earners to enter the labour market and that the tax penalties and fixed costs of doing so are not greater than the potential returns to work.

Unions and collective bargaining provide important opportunities for achieving greater gender equity in the workplace and in the terms and conditions of employment. This requires, however, that gender equity concerns are on the negotiating agenda and are actively sought as part of bargaining agreements. The evidence appears to uphold the view that this is more likely in contexts where there is strong gender equity legislation and where gender equity standards and conventions are upheld.

Finally, the work-time flexibility measures and the more family-friendly organization of work within enterprises have a vast potential to contribute to greater gender equity within the workplace and in the household. These same measures also have the potential to contribute to greater labour market efficiency by reducing total unemployment and lowering the fixed costs of working. They are also likely to increase tax receipts and social insurance contributions as more parents and carers remain in the workforce. Measures that reduce the labour market costs of having children or caring for dependents are also likely to produce efficiency gains by reducing sex segmentation in the labour market. Consequently, fostering greater gender equity in the labour market and the household makes both economic sense and good policy.

Yet, all three labour market institutions alone will not ensure that greater gender equity prevails within the household and in terms of the allocation of caring responsibilities and domestic work. And if the gender division of labour within the household is not eventually changed, then the underlying causes of inequality in market work will not have been addressed. There is a role for the state in actively encouraging men to take on more domestic responsibilities and enjoy both the rights and responsibilities of caring – legislating parental benefits and leave, pursuing gender equity laws, enacting non-discrimination laws and contributing to social change that shifts gender roles over time. These gender roles are not immutable and we have evidence of change across the world in different contexts and environments, but this change must be part of an emerging social contract between men and women and between households and the state that is clearly located in achieving greater gender equality in the market and the household.

NOTES

1. This is the raw gap without controlling for hours worked and education or skill levels. The pattern in most countries is that the gender pay gap widens as one moves up the skill or education hierarchy (Rubery and Grimshaw, 2009).
2. There are exceptions to this observation in particular regions and countries and at particular moments in time. For example, in the wake of the recent crisis regional unemployment rates were higher for men in the developed economies, in Central and South Eastern Europe (non-EU) and in the Commonwealth of Independent States (CIS) and East Asia (ILO, 2013).
3. Britwum et al. (2012) found that women comprised only 20 per cent of bargaining teams in the Philippines and that there was no union policy about women's participation in bargaining teams among 70 per cent of unions surveyed.
4. The WGEA publishes annual reports on gender equity in the workplace and highlights how companies have sought to implement changes after undertaking their reviews. See https://www.wgea.gov.au/.
5. See http://www.actu.org.au/Campaigns/EqualPay/default.aspx; last accessed 2 September 2014.
6. Fair Work Australia is the national workplace relations tribunal. It is an independent body with power to carry out a range of functions relating to: the safety net of minimum wages and employment conditions; enterprise bargaining; industrial action; dispute resolution; termination of employment; and other workplace matters. It has since

been renamed the Fair Work Commission. See http://www.fwc.gov.au/; last accessed 2 September 2014.

7. Specifically, the Maternity Protection Convention, 1919 (No. 3), the Maternity Protection Convention (Revised), 1952 (No. 103) and Maternity Protection Convention, 2000 (No. 183).

REFERENCES

Anxo, D., L. Mencarini and A. Pailhé et al. (2011), 'Gender differences in time use over the life course in France, Italy, Sweden and the US', *Feminist Economics*, **17**(3), 159–95.

Ashok, P. and R. Tankha (2009), *Women's Empowerment Through Guaranteed Employment: A Case Study of NREGA Implementation in Bihar, Jharkhand, Rajasthan, and Himachal Pradesh*, New Delhi: Institute For Human Development.

Bardasi, E. and Q. Wodon (2006), 'Measuring time poverty and analyzing its determinants: concept and application to Guinea', in M. Blackden and Q. Wodon (eds), 'Gender, time use and poverty in Sub-Saharan Africa', *World Bank Working Paper No. 73*, Washington, DC: World Bank, pp. 75–95.

Berg, J. (2011), 'Laws or luck? Understanding rising formality in Brazil in the 2000s', in S. Lee and D. McCann (eds), *Regulating for Decent Work: New Directions in Labour Market Regulations*, Basingstoke, UK/Geneva: Palgrave Macmillan/International Labour Office.

Bittman, M. (2004), 'Parenthood without penalty, time-use and public policy in Australia and Finland', in N. Folbre and M. Bittman (eds), *Family Time, the Social Organization of Care*, London/New York: Routledge/Taylor and Francis Group, pp. 224–39.

Bittman, M. and N. Folbre (2004), 'Introduction', in N. Folbre and M. Bittman (eds), *Family Time: The Social Organization of Care*, London/New York: Routledge/Taylor and Francis Group.

Blau, F. and L. Kahn (2003), 'Understanding international differences in the gender pay gap', *Journal of Labor Economics*, **21**(1), 106–44.

Blau, F. and L. Kahn (2005), 'Changes in the labor supply behavior of married women 1980–2000', *NBER Working Paper No. 11230*, Cambridge, MA: National Bureau of Economic Research.

Bleijenbergh, I., J. de Brunjn and L. Dickens (2001), *Strengthening and Mainstreaming Equal Opportunities Through Collective Bargaining*, Dublin: European Foundation for the Improvement in Living and Working Conditions.

Braunstein, E. and S. Seguino (2012), *The Impact of Economic Policy and Structural Change on Gender Inequality in Economic Opportunity in Latin America, 1990–2010*, Santiago: International Labour Organization.

Briskin, L. and A. Muller (2011), 'Promoting gender equality through social dialogue: global trends and persistent obstacles', *DIALOGUE Working Paper No. 34*, Geneva: International Labour Office.

Britwum, A., K. Douglas and S. Ledwith (2011), *Gender and Trade Unions*, a research report by the Global Labour University alumni, Oxford: Ruskin College.

Britwum, A., K. Douglas and S. Ledwith (2012), 'Women, gender and power in trade unions', in S. Mosoetsa and M. Williams (eds), *Labour in the Global South: Challenges and Alternatives for Workers*, Geneva: International Labour Office.

Card, D. and A.B. Krueger (1994), 'Minimum wages and employment: a case study of the fast food industry in New Jersey and Pennsylvania: reply', *American Economic Review*, **84**(4), 772–93.

Cohen, P. (1998), 'Replacing housework in the service economy', *Gender and Society*, **12**(2), 219–31.

Cook, A., V. Lorwin and A. Daniels (1992), *The Most Difficult Revolution: Women and Trade Unions*, Ithaca, NY: Cornell University Press.

Del Boca, D., M. Locatelli and S. Pasqua (2000), 'Employment decisions of married women: evidence and explanations', *Labour*, **14**(1), 35–52.

Desai, S., A. Dubey and B. Joshi et al. (2010), *Human Development in India: Challenges for a Society in Transition*, New York: Oxford University Press.

Dickerson, N.T. (2002), 'Is racial exclusion gendered? The role of residential segregation in the employment status of black women and men', *Feminist Economics*, **8**(2), 199–208.

Dinkelman, T. and V. Ranchhod (2012), 'Evidence on the impact of minimum wage laws in an informal sector: domestic workers in South Africa', *Journal of Development Economics*, **99**(1), 27–45.

England, P. and N. Folbre (2002), 'Reforming the social contract', in L.C. Lansdale and G. Duncan (eds), *For Better or Worse: Welfare Reform and the Well-being of Children and Families*, New York: Russell Sage Foundation.

Espino, A. and G. Pedetti (2010), 'Diálogo social e igualdad de género en Uruguay' [Social dialogue and gender equality in Uruguay], *DIALOGUE Working Paper No. 15*, Geneva: International Labour Office.

Floro, M. (1995a), 'Economic restructuring, gender and the allocation of time', *World Development*, **23**(11), 1913–29.

Floro, M. (1995b), 'Women's well-being, poverty and work intensity', *Feminist Economics*, **1**(3), 1–25.

Freeman, R. (2005), 'Labor market institutions around the world', *NBER Working Paper No. 13242*, Cambridge, MA: National Bureau of Economic Research.

Freeman, R. (2007), 'Labour market institutions without blinders: the debate over flexibility and labour market performance', *NBER Working Paper No. 11286*, Cambridge, MA: National Bureau of Economic Research.

Gálvez-Muñoz, L., P. Rodríguez-Modroño and M. Domínguez-Serrano (2011), 'Work and time use by gender: a new clustering of European welfare systems', *Feminist Economics*, **17**(4), 125–57.

Gammage, S. (2010), 'Time pressed and time poor: unpaid household work in Guatemala', *Feminist Economics*, **16**(3), 79–112.

Goldin, C. (1990), *Understanding the Gender Gap: An Economic History of American Women*, New York: Oxford University Press.

Hayter, S. and B. Weinberg (2010), 'Mind the gap: collective bargaining and wage inequality', in S. Hayter (ed.), *The Role of Collective Bargaining in the Global Economy*, Cheltenham, UK and Northampton, MA/Geneva: Edward Elgar Publishing/International Labour Office, pp. 136–87.

Heckman, J. and T. Macurdy (1980), 'A life-cycle model of female labour supply', *Review of Economic Studies*, **47**(1), 47–74.

Heckman, J and R. Willis (1977), 'A beta-logistic model for the analysis of sequential labor force participation by married women', *Journal of Political Economy*, **85**(1), 27–58.

Heery, E. (2006), 'Equality bargaining: where, who and why?', *Gender, Work and Organization*, **13**(6), 522–42.

Hegewisch, A. and J.C. Gornick (2007), *Statutory Routes to Workplace Flexibility in Cross-national Perspective*, Washington, DC: Institute for Women's Policy Research.

Himmelweit, S. (2002), 'Making visible the hidden economy: the case for gender-impact analysis of economic policy', *Feminist Economics*, **8**(1), 49–70.

ILO (2010), *Women in Labour Markets: Measuring Progress and Identifying the Challenges*, Geneva: International Labour Office.

ILO (2011a), *Equality at Work: The Continuing Challenge*, Report of the Director-General, Global Report under the Follow-up to the ILO Declaration on Fundamental Principles and Rights at Work, International Labour Conference, 100th Session 2011, Report I(B), Geneva: International Labour Organization.

ILO (2011b), *A New Era of Social Justice*, Report of the Director-General, Report I(A), International Labour Conference, 100th Session, Geneva: International Labour Office.

ILO (2013), *Global Employment Trends 2013: Recovering from a Second Jobs Dip*, Geneva: International Labour Office.

Keifman, S.N. and R. Maurizio (2012), 'Changes in labour market conditions and policies, their impact on wage inequality during the last decade', *UNU-WIDER Working Paper No. 2012/14*, Buenos Aires: UN University World Institute for Development Economics Research.

Killingsworth, M and J. Heckman (1986), 'Female labor supply: a survey', in O. Ashenfelter and R. Layard (eds), *Handbook of Labor Economics, Vol. 1*, Amsterdam: North-Holland, pp. 103–204.

Kim, H. (1993), 'The Korean union movement in transition', in S. Frenkel (ed.), *Organized Labor in the Asia-Pacific Region*, Ithaca, NY: ILR Press, pp. 133–61.

Lee, D.S. (1999), 'Wage inequality in the United States during the 1980s: rising dispersion or falling minimum wages?', *Quarterly Journal of Economics*, **114**(3), 977–1023.

Manning, A. (2003), *Monopsony in Motion, Imperfect Competition in Labor Markets*, Princeton, NJ: Princeton University Press.

Mires, L. and E. Toro (2011), *Insumos para el análisis de políticas de protección social en Chile* [Inputs for the Analysis of Social Protection Policies in Chile], Santiago: International Labour Organization.

OECD (2011), *Doing Better for Families*, Paris: Organisation for Economic Co-operation and Development.

Orbeta, A.C. (2005), 'Children and the labour force participation and earnings of parents in the Philippines', *Philippine Journal of Development*, **59**(1), 19–52.

Plantenga, J. and E. Fransen (2010), 'The extent and origin of the gender pay gap in Europe', in S. Chant (ed.), *The International Handbook of Gender and Poverty: Concepts, Research, Policy*, Cheltenham, UK and Northampton, MA, USA: Edward Elgar Publishing.

Preston, V. and S. McLafferty (1993), 'Income disparities and employment and occupational changes in New York', in *Regional Studies, Vol. 27*, New York: Taylor and Francis, pp. 223–35.

Quisumbing, A., K. Hallman and M.T. Ruel (2007), 'Maquiladoras and market

mamas: women's work and childcare in Guatemala City and Accra', *Journal of Development Studies*, **43**(3), 420–55.
Rubery, J. and D. Grimshaw (2009), 'Gender and the minimum wage', paper prepared for the ILO Conference 'Regulating for Decent Work', July 2009, Geneva: International Labour Office.
Schettkat, R. (2002), 'Institutions in the economic fitness landscape: what impact do welfare state institutions have on economic performance?', *WZB Discussion Paper No. FS I 02-210*, Berlin: Leibniz-Informationszentrum Wirtschaft.
Taylor, B.D. and M. Mauch (1996), 'Gender, race and travel behavior: analysis of household-serving travel and commuting in the San Francisco bay area', *Proceedings from the Second National Conference, Women's Travel Issues*, October 1996, Baltimore.
Van der Lippe, T., K. Tijdens and E. de Ruijter (2004), 'Out-sourcing of domestic tasks and time-saving effects', *Journal of Family Issues*, **25**(2), 216–40.
Vasconcelos, M., J. Berg and L. Pinheiro et al. (2010), 'Crise económica internacional e o impacto sobre as mulheres: respostas e desafíos no Brasil' [International economic crisis and the impact on women: responses and challenges], *Revista do Observatorio Brasil da Igualdade de Genero, Tema Trabalho e Genero*, December.
Vickery, C. (1977), 'The time-poor: a new look at poverty', *The Journal of Human Resources*, **12**(1), 27–48.
Waldfogel, J. (1997), 'The effect of children on women's wages', *American Sociological Review*, **62**(2), 209–17.
Zacharias, A. (2011), *The Measurement of Time and Income Poverty*, New York: Levy Economics Institute of Bard College.

13. Inequalities and the impact of labour market institutions on migrant workers

Christiane Kuptsch

13.1 INTRODUCTION

Contemporary global migration is linked intrinsically to the world of work. People move in search of employment; family members accompany workers to foreign countries and may enter the labour market themselves; training and educational opportunities abroad lead to employment; and changed patterns of labour force participation and social reproduction in one place set off migration flows in from another place. The International Labour Office (ILO) estimates that approximately half of the estimated 214 million international migrants globally are economically active (ILO, 2010, p. 2). The identity of the migrant in employment cannot be separated from his or her status as a worker and consequently, labour market institutions have a potentially important effect on migrant workers' working conditions as well as their inequality vis-à-vis non-migrant workers.

The focus of this chapter is on international migration as opposed to internal migration, although in terms of economic theory there is no difference between the two. Differences stem from legal issues that arise when someone wishes to cross a border to take up employment in a foreign country or when an employer reaches across the border to recruit a non-national. These issues will be discussed in this chapter. The focus of the chapter is on the more vulnerable groups of migrant workers, namely those who hold jobs that require low or mid-level skills. These migrants have a harder time than highly skilled professionals to defend their interests and their rights, making protection via labour market institutions essential for them. Highly skilled migrants, on the other hand, currently benefit from worldwide demand for their skills, with many countries wishing to attract them because of real or perceived labour market shortages, or simply based on the assumption that human capital rather than natural resource endowments is the key to economic development. Indeed, competition for the highly skilled has altered the power dynamics between workers and employers in the highly qualified segment of the labour market in favour of the workers.[1]

This chapter argues that migrant workers are best protected from exploitation when they are covered – in law and in practice – by labour market institutions, on an equal footing with local workers. This principle has guided international conventions to protect migrant workers as well as the policy work done by the ILO. We begin this chapter with a discussion of the drivers of international migration, including the role of global and national inequalities. We then turn to an analysis of how specific labour market institutions – collective bargaining, minimum wages, social security and employment protection – can help to protect migrant workers. Yet, as the discussion in the sections reveals, in practice migrant workers face many difficulties in realizing these rights.

13.2 INEQUALITIES AND INTERNATIONAL LABOUR MIGRATION

Inequalities, in particular economic differences within and between countries, are the most common 'pull' factor driving international migration. The world's almost 200 nation-states have per capita incomes that range from less than US$250 per person per year to more than US$50 000[2] – a difference that provides a significant incentive to migrate over borders for higher wages and better opportunities. Moreover, over the past several decades these differences have widened. In 1975, per capita incomes in the high-income countries were on average 41 times greater than in low-income countries; in 2000 they were 66 times higher. In 2008, the 30 richest countries of the world accounted for 70 per cent of global GDP, but represented less than 15 per cent of the world's population. One hundred and seventy poorer countries had over 85 per cent of the world population, but less than 30 per cent of world GDP and average incomes of US$2800 per person – a mere one-fourteenth of average earnings in wealthy countries. Moreover, as Milanovic (2011) points out, of the global Gini of 65.4 points, 85 per cent (56.2 points) is due to differences in mean country incomes, and only 15 per cent (9.2 Gini points) is due to 'class' differences within countries. This contrasts sharply with the mid-1850s, when real incomes of workers in most countries were at approximately the same subsistence level, differing by about two to one. In 1850, the global Gini coefficient is estimated to have been 53 points with equal proportions of between-country and within-country differences (ibid.).

Demographic differences in population and labour force growth

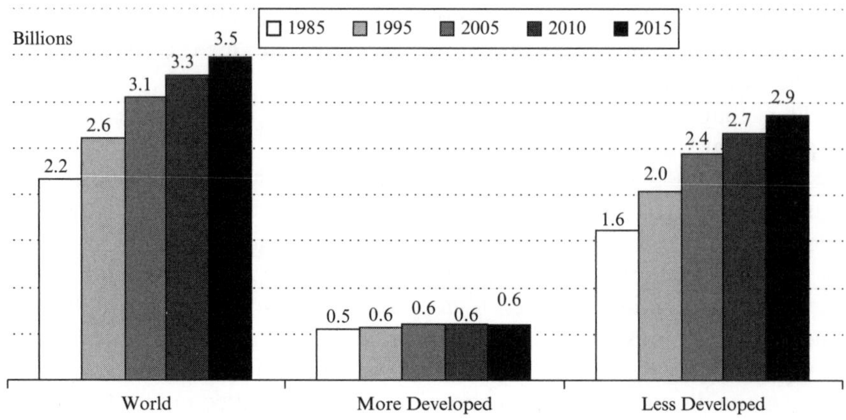

Source: ILO, LABORSTA Database (http://laborsta.ilo.org); last accessed 2 September 2014.

Figure 13.1 Economically active population (EAP), 1985–2015

between more developed and less developed countries also help to fuel more economically motivated international migration. As Figure 13.1 illustrates, the economically active population in less developed countries of the world increased continually between 1985 and 2010 and is projected to reach 2.9 billion by 2015. In the high-income countries, by contrast, the labour force has remained relatively stable since 1990 at just over 600 million workers, a level at which it is expected to remain.

Historical linkages between countries, such as colonial ties, can also fuel cross-border migration. In many instances, migrant networks develop with 'anchor migrants' informing relatives and friends back home about (job) opportunities abroad and making it easier for them to install themselves in a particular destination.[3] A 'culture of migration' may develop in certain regions, with social expectations including a migration experience of at least one family member, or where migration may become a rite of passage. Caribbean islands and West African countries are occasionally cited as cases in point (e.g., Thomas-Hope, 1998). In addition, the sheer existence of recruiters and their business interests may shape and foster migration flows. For example, Connell and Stilwell (2006) argue that international recruiters of healthcare workers 'do not merely satisfy demand but, through their advertisements and promotion, actively *create a desire* for further migration' (p. 243).

In addition, the financial and social costs of migration have fallen with transport and communication 'revolutions'. In the 19th century many

European migrants could not pay their one-way transport to the Americas and had, as their only recourse, to indenture themselves, by promising to work for four to five years in order to repay the transport costs. Today, people may still indebt themselves to be able to migrate but, even when they use smugglers, the costs are not as high. For example, it is estimated that close to 90 per cent of Mexican nationals crossing illegally into the United States used smugglers at an average cost of about US$1800 per person (Roberts et al., 2010). Communication is also much easier so that the emotional costs of leaving family and friends behind are not comparable to the 19th century when it took between four and six weeks before a letter from the Americas reached its European destination. Learning about opportunities has also become easier. Internet and cell phones mean that rural Mexicans may learn of a job in the USA before local residents do. Theoretically, costs for migrant workers should also decline when there are more established migration corridors because of a reduced need for using recruiters and other intermediaries for the cross-border job matching, as current migrants can refer friends and relatives to their employers (Abella, 2004). However, government policies such as sponsorship systems (see below) and recruitment cartels can keep recruitment fees high for decades. And rent-seeking recruiters may set up businesses in corridors hitherto dominated by direct relationships between employers and employees, causing employers to pay more and workers to gain less, as is the case with recruitment of care workers from Poland working in Germany.[4]

Inequalities *within* countries also lead to migration, both internal and international. There are about 3.5 internal migrants for each international migrant; many international migrants begin as national migrants, while others migrate abroad directly from rural areas. This is particularly true of agricultural farmers and workers, some of whom have faced decreasing revenues as a result of international competition. For example, in the two decades following the passage of the North American Free Trade Agreement (NAFTA) in 1994, employment in Mexican agriculture fell by half from 27 per cent to 13 per cent of employment, amidst falling corn prices.[5] As former small landholders and agricultural workers have to make large cultural transitions when they move to urban areas, moving abroad may thus make no difference to them, prompting them to migrate when the infrastructure is there (recruiters, travel agencies, visa facilities, etc.) to take them across the border (Martin et al., 2006, p. 10). As agricultural workers are used to physically demanding work, they represent 'ideal' employees in 3-D jobs (dirty, dangerous and demeaning) that workers in wealthier countries are no longer willing to occupy, at least not for the prevailing remuneration.

Though much international migration is supply driven, it is also true that there has been increased demand for migrants, particularly in the health and domestic services sectors. Much of the literature on the new global division of labour and on global value chains focuses on the dispersion of production between lead and supplier firms in the apparel, electronics and food sectors. But global labour migration chains have also emerged, focusing on moving service workers over borders, in response to increasing demand. With ageing populations in North America and Europe, there has been a need for more healthcare professionals and domestic workers to provide elder care. There is something of a hierarchy in global healthcare labour migration, with the United States among the most attractive destinations, so that some Filipino nurses migrate first to Canada to improve their chances of eventually moving to the USA. Efforts to replace healthcare workers who emigrate can lead to follow-on migration. For example, Bermuda in 2004 expressed concern about the loss of nurses to the United States, and soon Jamaica was worried about recruitment of its nurses by Bermuda (Connell and Stilwell, 2006). The United Kingdom recruits doctors and nurses in South Africa, and South Africa imports healthcare workers from Cuba. These developments have the potential to contribute to global inequalities as they intensify the lack of essential services in developing countries.

In countries with insufficient public care services, double-income families have sought domestic workers to help balance work and family responsibilities (see discussion in Chapters 11 and 12).[6] Thus, global labour migration chains have developed in response to demand for childcare and elder care, domestic help and other forms of personal care services. The 'global care chains' literature identifies transnational routes for domestic workers, such as from Albania and Bulgaria to Greece; the Dominican Republic, Peru and Morocco to Spain; Sri Lanka to Singapore, Saudi Arabia, Kuwait and Canada; and Mexico, Central America and the Caribbean to the USA. Well over 600 000 Filipinas served in foreign households in 2001, from Hong Kong (China) and Singapore to Italy and Spain and the Middle East (Yeates, 2005).

13.3 LABOUR MARKET INSTITUTIONS AND MIGRANT WORKERS

As explained in the introductory chapter, labour laws and policies exist to protect workers, who are recognized as being on an unequal footing when negotiating with employers. To not extend the same protections to migrant workers would be to expose them to unfair treatment. It is for this reason that equality principles are the basis for the protection of migrant workers.

The ILO was created with a view to eliminating competition between states based on dire and unjust labour conditions that had the potential of producing widespread unrest and endangering world peace. The ILO's constitution, dating from its founding in 1919, lists in its Preamble the 'protection of the interests of workers when employed in countries other than their own' as one of the means to improve conditions. In principle, all ILO standards apply to all persons in their working environment irrespective of nationality and immigration status, in the same way that international human rights instruments apply to all persons. But the ILO, in reference to its constitutional mandate, has also elaborated two international labour standards specifically designed to protect migrant workers that underline the importance of equal treatment with local workers, namely the Migration for Employment Convention (Revised), 1949 (No. 97), and the Migrant Workers (Supplementary Provisions) Convention, 1975 (No. 143). Convention No. 97, adopted in 1949, in a context of (anticipated) migration flows in the aftermath of World War II is about migration management while protecting workers crossing borders. It aims to ensure equal treatment for them by encouraging countries to sign bilateral agreements. Convention No. 143 was enacted after oil price hikes led to recessions in European countries that had been importing large numbers of guest workers and recruitment stopped as a response to the economic downturn. Convention No. 143 deals with clandestine migration (to be expected with legal channels being closed) on the one hand (Part I) and with the integration of settled migrants on the other (Part II). Part I represents the first attempt at the international level to secure certain rights for so-called illegal or undocumented workers and to combat clandestine migration and employment (Böhning, 1988). It states clearly that migrants in irregular situations are not stripped of all rights; in particular, migrant workers shall enjoy equality of treatment in respect of rights arising out of past employment as regards remuneration, social security and other benefits. Part II, directed at migrants in regular situations, moves beyond equality of treatment and also provides for equality of opportunity.

Despite these protections, and other instruments that have been elaborated by the United Nations,[7] in practice migrant workers often have difficulty in exercising their rights. Irregular workers fear denouncing employers when their rights are being abused, and regular workers may have limits imposed on them as a result of their contract type. In what follows, we discuss these issues with regard to four labour market institutions that are particularly important for reducing the inequalities that migrant workers face.

Collective Bargaining

Migrant workers' rights to freedom of association and inclusion in collective bargaining are paramount for their protection, precisely to allow for their equal treatment and avoid inequalities. The relevant ILO standards also cover migrant workers, including those in irregular situations, a fact stressed by the ILO's Committee on Freedom of Association when it had to rule on a new law on foreigners adopted in Spain in 2000. The General Union of Workers of Spain (UGT) alleged that this law restricted foreigners' trade union rights by making their exercise dependent on authorization of the foreigner's presence or residence in Spain. The government argued that the purpose of the law had been to make a clear distinction between so-called 'legal' foreigners, who would enjoy trade union rights on an equal footing with nationals, and 'irregular' foreigners, to control migratory flows and combat the mafias who traffic in human beings. The Committee upheld the UGT, pointing to Article 2 of the Freedom of Association and Protection of the Right to Organise Convention, No. 87 (1948), according to which workers, without distinction whatsoever, have the right to join organizations of their own choosing. The Committee also added that 'unions must have the right to represent and assist workers covered by the Convention with the aim of furthering and defending their interests'[8] – in this case the interests of irregular migrants.

Indeed, one can assume that inequalities between local and migrant workers will be most pronounced where migrants are in irregular situations in countries with weak industrial relation systems. Where industrial relations are strong and the social partners are interested in keeping them strong, there would be peer control among employers to avoid unfair competition and trade unions will denounce lesser payments or worse treatment of any workers, including migrant workers whether in regular or irregular situations. Efforts would be made to avoid the creation or growth of a shadow economy and subsequent market for illegal labour. Theoretical and empirical studies suggest that irregular migration is a function of job opportunities and of the existence of irregular employment as such (Tapinos, 2000; Hjarno, 2003; Passel and Cohn, 2009; Sumption and Somerville, 2009). Some observers point to the Scandinavian countries with strong collective bargaining where the incidence of irregular employment is much lower than elsewhere in Europe (Hjarno, 2003).

In practice, however, it is not always easy for migrant workers to exercise their freedom of association and collective bargaining rights. Some migration takes place to destinations where there are no strong institutions at this level. A case in point is migration from Asia to the Gulf States. Gulf Corporation Council members today deplore that their private sector is largely dominated by non-national workers. For example, in Saudi Arabia, foreigners make up 70 per cent of the labour force of 10 million; and while the Kuwaiti government vowed after the 1990–91 Gulf War to never become dependent on foreign workers again, ten years later some 40 per cent of the country's residents and a majority of its workers came from abroad (Martin et al., 2006, p. 40). Voices, such as heard in Bahrain, which claim that granting freedom of association would also provide incentives for nationals to join the private sector, are still rare in the region.

Under certain temporary foreign worker schemes, migrants are tied to their employers who may not allow trade unionists onto their premises. Such instances are reported from North Carolina in the United States, concerning migrant workers who entered the country under the H-2A programme, which allows agricultural employers who anticipate a shortage of local workers to bring non-immigrant foreign workers to the USA to perform agricultural labour or services of a temporary or seasonal nature. As Human Rights Watch (2000) points out, H-2A workers come to the United States openly and legally and are covered by wage laws, workers' compensation, and other standards. However, valid papers are not enough to guarantee H-2A migrant workers' freedom of association. As agricultural workers, they are not covered by the US National Labor Relations Act's anti-discrimination provision meant to protect the right to organize. If they try to form and join a union, the grower for whom they work can revoke their employment contract, thereby placing them in an irregular status, liable to deportation. For Human Rights Watch, 'H-2A workers are caught in the antithesis of a free labor system, unable to exercise rights of association but also unable to move to another employer to seek better terms' (ibid., p. 202).

Moreover, in the past, trade unions were occasionally reticent to include migrant workers among their ranks as they saw it as their role to protect local workers from foreign competition. With increasingly integrated and globalized labour markets, this thinking has gradually disappeared. Instead, one can now observe examples of cross-border cooperation among trade unions. A case in point is the creation of the Union Network International (UNI) Passport. The Global Union Federation UNI organizes crafts' and services' workers (postal, tourism, electricity, telecom, social security commerce, finance, media, cleaning and security) and launched its passport scheme in 2000. The passport allows a unionized migrant to be 'hosted' by an UNI-affiliated union in the destination country. With the passport comes a considerable list of benefits: from information on working conditions, the banking system, tax regulations, opportunities to participate in local union activities and training courses, to advice on labour issues and legal support. Especially in Europe, but also elsewhere (for example, between India and Nepal or in the Caribbean), trade unions have become an important player in the defence and protection of migrant workers (Schmidt, 2006; see also ILO, 2012).

Minimum Wages

In principle, minimum wages are protective labour market institutions for migrant workers. Where they exist, they offer a benchmark for a minimum remuneration equal to that of local workers. As underlined in Article 6 of the ILO Migration for Employment Convention (Revised), 1949 (No. 97) ratifying states undertake to:

> apply, without discrimination . . . to immigrants lawfully within its territory, treatment no less favourable than that which it applies to its own nationals in respect of the following matters: (a) in so far as such matters are regulated by law or regulations, or are subject to the control of administrative authorities – (i) remuneration, including family allowances where these form part of remuneration.

Even where states have not ratified Convention No. 97, international law generally applies and protects migrant workers, as well as the constitutional principle of equal pay for work of equal value. The ILO Committee of Experts, in its General Survey on minimum wage systems presented to the 2014 International Labour Conference, stressed once more the need to comply with this latter principle, including with regard to migrant workers.[9]

However, in practice many migrant workers are paid below levels of national workers in many countries. Certain temporary labour migration programmes set contract rates and can deviate from national law. For example, the Canadian Federal Government acknowledged that there had been problems with the hiring of temporary foreign workers in British Columbia and passed laws to end the practice of paying such workers 15 per cent less than Canadian workers.[10]

A further source of inequality can be the exclusion of particular segments of the labour market from minimum wage legislation. In a few countries, such as the Marshall Islands and Oman, minimum wages do not apply to foreign workers. The exclusion of migrant workers may also be indirect, through the exclusion of domestic workers, most of whom are migrants, from the scope of minimum wage legislation. Countries where domestic workers are not covered by minimum wage legislation include Bangladesh, Egypt, Honduras and the Republic of Korea.

What is more, there are instances where this protective labour market institution is used to further inequalities. For example, with effect from 1 February 2012, Jordan issued a new minimum wage decree that set a lower rate for migrant workers by stating that the new minimum wage in the Kingdom of 190 dinars per month 'shall not apply to non-Jordanian workers, who shall come under the minimum wage stipulated in the previous decision of 16 November 2008'.[11] Apparently, this decision was taken following pressure by the garment industry, with employers expressing concern that raising the minimum wage from JD150 to JD190 would increase their operational expenses by 15–20 per cent and damage the sector's competitiveness. The sector employs around 16000 Jordanians and 27000 guest workers.[12] In Hong Kong (China), the statutory minimum wage introduced in 2011 is not applicable to live-in domestic workers and a separate, reduced, minimum wage applies to foreign domestic workers.[13] In the Seychelles, foreign workers in the tourism and construction sectors are no longer excluded from the national minimum wage. However, the general increase in wages decided in 2010 sets a reduced rate of increase for non-nationals.

Protective minimum wages can also have unintended adverse consequences, as can be illustrated by the Philippines' 'Supermaid' programme. The Philippines, a major emigration country with a large body of protective legislation in favour of migrants and strong institutions in this area, required from early 2007 that Filipina domestic helpers abroad be paid at least US$400 a month. The number of Filipinas deployed as domestic helpers fell sharply from 91000 newly hired household service workers in 2006 to 40000 in 2007. The Philippines Overseas Employment Administration (POEA) suspects that some began to leave as gardeners or other types of workers not covered by the US$400 monthly minimum wage. In other words, establishing a minimum wage for one type of worker, domestic helper, may have led to migrants going abroad to fill jobs not covered by the minimum wage, such as gardeners, and perhaps therefore facing much harder working conditions besides the lesser wages, even if the process stemmed from simple collusion with the foreign employer for de facto contract substitution.

The fact that many migrants are employed in countries that offer relatively low wages and few rights suggests a high degree of migrant self-exploitation. Making a decision to go abroad as a gardener for US$200 a month knowing that the job is domestic helper and should pay US$400 a month may not be in the migrant's best interest, as defined by the migrants' government. However, one should not underestimate the migrants' agency, their capacity to make independent decisions, or their need. Migrants will often forego their rights because they see no better options for themselves (Kuptsch and Martin, 2011, p. 48).

Social Security, Migrants and Welfare States

Migrant workers, when compared with workers who spend their whole working life in only one country, are often disadvantaged with respect to social security coverage and entitlement to benefits.[14] As Hirose (2011) points out, many of these problems have their roots in inherent features of national legislations. The 'principle of territoriality', according to which the scope of application of social security legislation, as of any national legislation, is confined to the territory of the country has as a consequence that migrant workers run the double risk of losing coverage under the national social security system in their country of origin, and of having limited or no coverage in their country of employment. More difficulties stem from the 'principle of nationality'. While some countries recognize the equality of treatment between national and non-national workers in their social security legislations, others discriminate against migrant workers through national legislation that excludes specific categories of migrants, or in more extreme cases, all non-nationals from coverage or entitlement to social security benefits, or applies less favourable treatment to such groups on the basis of this principle. As for the payment of benefits abroad, Hirose (ibid., p. 3) summarizes the situation as follows:

> [M]any countries suspend the payment of benefits to migrant workers who reside abroad, even though they export benefits to their own nationals residing abroad. Some countries completely prohibit the payment of benefits abroad, while others make the export of benefits conditional on the conclusion of reciprocal social security agreements with the countries of residence. Still others may only offer a lump-sum benefit in place of a pension if the insured person leaves the country. Such limitations may be due to monetary restrictions or to administrative problems (e.g., benefits in kind such as medical services cannot be provided directly by the competent social security institution outside of its area of competence), but may also be based on the underlying conception that a State is only responsible for those persons living within its own borders.

The lack of social security coordination leads to further disadvantages for migrant workers. Earned rights to benefits may not be portable from one country to another and migrants thus run the risk of financial loss when leaving their host or home country. The portability of social security rights is the 'ability to preserve, maintain and transfer vested social security rights or rights in the process of being vested, independent of nationality and country of residence' (ISSA, 2011, p. 2). Under most social security systems, the payment of benefits (other than work-accident related benefits) is possible only after a qualifying period of contributions, employment, or residence. Some of these periods can be quite long, 15 years or more, in particular where long-term benefits such as old-age pensions are concerned. Because of these waiting periods, migrant workers may fail to qualify for benefits in any of their respective countries of employment. Social security coordination can remedy these bottlenecks by signing bilateral and multilateral social security agreements[15] that help to ensure that periods of employment in other signatory countries are taken into account.

The International Labour Conference has adopted specific instruments on the social security rights of migrant workers and their family members. These conventions establish five basic principles that form the backbone of all bilateral and multilateral agreements on social security: equality of treatment; determination of the applicable legislation; maintenance of acquired rights and provision of benefits abroad; maintenance of rights in course of acquisition; and reciprocity.[16]

Bilateral social security agreements usually include provisions on non-discrimination between nationals and migrant workers as well as rules of cooperation between the social security bodies of the signatory countries. Such agreements coordinate the aggregation of the periods of contributions that accrue to migrant workers in the two countries and regulate the transfer and payment of acquired social security entitlements. Most agreements refer to long-term benefits. Agreements among high-income countries are widespread, and a few developing and emerging countries such as Algeria, Morocco and Turkey have successfully managed to protect a fair number of their migrants in this manner. However, a majority of developing countries and major migrant origin countries (Bangladesh, China, India, Mexico and Ukraine) have concluded very few bilateral social security arrangements. Multilateral social security agreements currently exist in the European Union (EU), CARICOM (Caribbean Community), the Gulf Cooperation Council (GCC), and in MERCOSUR (El Mercado Común del Sur). An Ibero-American Social Security Convention is being negotiated; further social security coordination is sought under the Euro-Mediterranean Partnership (EMP); and the 2007 Cebu Declaration on the Protection and Promotion of the Rights of Migrant Workers made by ASEAN (Association of Southeast Asian Nations) includes social security provisions. There are three main reasons for less developed nations not to engage more in bilateral or multilateral social security negotiations: the weak domestic development of social security provisions, low coverage levels of the domestic population, and a lack of national administrative capacity (ISSA, 2011, pp. 2, 3).

Some destination countries are afraid that they may become 'welfare magnets', that is, that immigrants will come to exploit their social protection system and extract more from the host country in public services and welfare payments than they contribute either in terms of economic output, taxes or social security contributions. Some studies in the United States have found that while immigrants make more use of public assistance and free medical care than natives, this is mainly because immigrants are on average poorer than natives. In fact, looking specifically at low-income families, further studies have concluded that low-income immigrants are less likely to claim welfare than low-income natives (Fix and Passel, 1999, cited in ILO, 2010, p. 68). As regards irregular migrants, they are often so preoccupied with concealing their existence that they are unlikely to claim benefits, in which case they are making a net contribution. For example, employers who treat them as legal immigrants on the basis of fake social security cards will be paying social security contributions to the government; and in numerous countries undocumented migrants pay taxes through automatic deductions (ILO, 2010, p. 68). Although there are variations from one country to another, the overall fiscal impact of immigration appears to be neutral.[17]

Some analysts have also looked into the links between welfare state retrenchment and migration flows. Misra et al. (2006) highlight how welfare state restructuring in more affluent countries has led to a 'pull for care' as poor women with children are encouraged to work for wages and it pays for households to replace better educated women's care work with low-wage domestic help. By relying on female migrants, social reproduction is ensured despite insufficient public care services (see Chapter 11 on public social services in this volume). Indeed, countries with thinner social safety nets tend to have more immigrant domestic workers (Salazar Parreñas, 2001 and Milkman et al., 1998 cited in Misra et al., 2006).[18] On the other hand, economic difficulties in many developing nations have contributed to a 'push to care' as more and more women have to look for new income-generating strategies and realize they can earn higher wages abroad.

Employment Protection Legislation

Employment protection legislation is defined broadly as regulations that place limits on the hiring and firing abilities of enterprises, independent of whether these regulations originate in law, collective bargaining or court rulings. Thus, provisions that determine the use of temporary or fixed-term contracts and that impose training requirements on the firm will influence hiring decisions, while mandatory pre-notification periods and severance payment scales will affect firing, to name but a few elements.

In practice, migrant workers typically benefit to a lesser degree from employment protection legislation than local workers because they happen to work in sectors not covered by the national employment protection legislation of their host countries. Worldwide, migrant workers are concentrated in construction, manufacturing, agriculture, the hotel and catering sector, health and care work, and domestic services. Often agricultural work and work in private households do not fall under national employment legislation.

In addition, one has to distinguish between migrant workers admitted in a destination country on a permanent basis and those who come under specific temporary foreign worker programmes. Recent years have seen a 'mushrooming' of a range of temporary labour migration schemes. These are usually designed to fill jobs in destination countries that require mid-level or few skills. The programmes typically place more stringent and less favourable conditions of admission and stay on less skilled workers relative to better-skilled workers, and feature strong return control mechanisms, sometimes without regard to actual labour market needs (ILO, 2012). As their name indicates, temporary labour migration programmes are designed to add workers temporarily to the labour force, not settlers to the population: workers are admitted with the understanding that they will leave after a determined period. Therefore, not all employment protection legislation will apply to them.

The increase in temporary labour migration schemes has occurred in parallel with the growth of atypical forms of employment and secondary labour markets. Migration may feed into existing processes of labour market segmentation in the sense of dual labour markets (migrants often wind up in the secondary labour market even if they do not come in under temporary programmes) and in the sense that certain activities will be perceived as 'migrant jobs' shunned by local populations. The Gulf States are an extreme example of labour market segmentation, with the public sector being in the hands of nationals with high wages, good working conditions, employment stability, chances of advancement, while the private sector is largely dominated by migrants, and all 3-D jobs are done by migrants. At the same time, the Gulf States are also an extreme example of enforcement of temporariness in migration programmes.

While the increase of temporary foreign worker programmes may lead to the growth of a less protected workforce in the destination countries as well as contribute to labour market segmentation, the advantages usually put forward are the following. (1) Destination countries seek to meet acute labour demand while avoiding potential economic and societal problems connected with the integration of migrants on a long-term basis. (2) Countries of origin hope to address 'brain drain', promote the transfer of know-how, and gain from the transfer of remittances. And (3) migrant workers and their families may prefer a temporary migration experience over permanent emigration. In addition, this phenomenon has to be seen against the backdrop of states' sovereign right to determine who enters their country, under what conditions and for how long. The human right of leaving one's own country is not matched by a human right to immigrate anywhere.

Temporary migrant workers also have their own, albeit limited 'international employment protection legislation'. According to Article 8 of ILO Convention No. 143 a migrant worker in a regular situation has the right to equal treatment in respect of job security, the provision of alternative employment, relief work and retraining. For example, migrant workers should not be subject to discrimination if the work force has to be reduced for reasons of redundancy. The Model Agreement on Temporary and Permanent Migration in the annex of the Migration for Employment Recommendation (Revised) 1949 (No. 86) also has an article (Article 24) on employment stability. This stipulates that if migrant workers become redundant before the end of their contract, the competent authority shall facilitate a new placement of the migrants in accordance with national laws or regulations. This Model Agreement has been widely used since its adoption in 1949 to guide the negotiations of bilateral agreements because it covers the full migration process, from the organization of recruitment, contracts of employment, supervision of living and working conditions, to the return journey, to name but a few subjects. Recent examples include the conclusion by the Republic of Korea of Memoranda of Understanding with Sri Lanka (2004), Nepal (2009) and the Philippines (2011).

Labour migration programmes that tie migrants to a particular employer, so-called sponsorship systems, are problematic for the migrants and de facto strip them of their employment protection rights. The inability of migrant workers to switch jobs once they are in the host country contributes to weakened bargaining power and worse wages and working conditions for the migrants. Frequently cited in this respect is the Kafala system under which low-skilled workers must have an in-country sponsor, usually their employer, who is responsible for their visa and legal status. The Kafala system is used throughout the Arab States of the Persian Gulf, with the exception of Bahrain. In Bahrain, a 2009 law provided that migrants are now sponsored by the Labour Market Regulation Authority and may switch employers, subject to three months notice.

Enforcement

The difficulties in ensuring protection for migrant workers are intrinsically linked to their status as migrants. Migration policy, even if called labour migration policy, is not always, and perhaps even rarely, the result of labour market concerns. On the one hand, this is because of a heightened concern with security in the aftermath of 9/11, but it is also due to the preponderance of neoliberal thought and its influence in economic and social policy-making over the past several decades.[19] Central to this ideology is the belief that there are 'high politics' and 'low politics', with sovereignty and security issues figuring at the high end, in contrast to economic, labour and social policy at the low end.[20] At most the state should be in charge of 'high politics' but preferably not interfere in other issues that are best dealt with by market forces.

The policy space for ILO's constituents – ministries of labour, workers' and employers' organizations – in migration policy-making has been limited. In Europe, for example, at EU level, the Directorate-General (DG) Home (responsible for internal affairs) and to some extent the DG External Relations, drive much of the migration policy-making, with little scope for the Directorate on Employment, Social Affairs and Inclusion (which would correspond to the labour ministry at the national level). In 2007, France created a new Ministry for Immigration, Integration, National Identity and Co-development, shifting responsibility from the Labour Ministry, where it had been previously. Since 2012, migration issues are the responsibility of the Interior Ministry. Similarly, in the United Kingdom the Home Office is responsible for migration policy, with the UK Border Agency publishing approved shortage occupation lists.

While ILO member States have the sovereign prerogative to determine the conditions of admission and residence of foreigners, all workers, irrespective of status, should enjoy their fundamental rights. The ILO therefore recommends a 'firewall' between labour law and immigration enforcement, and urges governments to allow anonymous representation of undocumented migrant workers by trade unions before labour tribunals. However, a continuing challenge is the role of labour inspectors vis-à-vis migrant workers in an irregular situation. The ILO Committee of Experts has emphasized that the primary duty of labour inspectors under the ILO Labour Inspection Convention, 1947 (No. 81), is to protect workers.[21] Yet some countries require labour inspectors to report undocumented migrant workers to immigration authorities, which can result in deportation.[22] This is problematic given that migrant workers are often concentrated in sectors where labour law violations are more frequent, including agriculture, construction and fisheries.

13.4 CONCLUSIONS

Migrant workers are best protected from exploitation where they enjoy inclusion in and coverage by labour market institutions on an equal footing with local workers. In practice, however, this is not always the case. Migrant workers face particular barriers in joining trade unions and benefitting from collective bargaining; in some instances, special minimum wages exist for migrant workers; their employment in more than one country over their working life may prevent them from collecting social security benefits despite having made contributions; they are often employed in economic sectors excluded from national employment protection legislation; and numerous migrants are recruited to work in countries with weak labour market institutions.

There is recognition that migration may further inequalities by feeding into labour market segmentation, prompting efforts to include migrant workers. Trade unions have begun to increasingly accept migrant workers as members and work towards cross-border membership. Moreover, making social security benefits portable is high on the agenda of the international community. The rights of domestic workers – an occupation of many migrant workers – have also been strengthened with the adoption by the International Labour Conference of the Domestic Workers Convention, 2011 (No. 189).

However, there is still a long way to go, and the interlinkages between the area of labour migration and questions of equality will remain complex. Labour migration is fuelled by differences within and across countries. If income opportunities and other conditions were the same everywhere, there would presumably be little migration. For migrants not to become a source of cheap and unprotected labour, strong and inclusive labour market institutions are important. For the ILO, this means that its intervention strategy will have to continue to be two-fold. The employment and labour market side of migration warrants attention as well as the protection of migrant workers and equality of treatment, with a focus on those economic sectors (e.g., agriculture, construction, domestic work) or individual characteristics (e.g., sex, age, ethnicity) that expose migrant workers to higher risks.

NOTES

1. For a detailed analysis of the competition for global talent, please refer to Kuptsch and Pang (2006).
2. In PPP terms the differences are even starker, with national income ranging from US$350

PPP to US$72 650 PPP in 2011. Data from World Development Indicators, http://data.worldbank.org/indicator/NY.GDP.PCAP.PP.KD/countries/1W?display=default; last accessed 2 September 2014.

3. Many networks are tied to specific occupations as well as geographical spaces, such as Puerto Rican doormen in New York City and Bangladeshi restaurant workers in London.
4. For a more comprehensive analysis of the actors and factors driving international labour migration, including recruiters, please see Kuptsch and Martin (2010).
5. See Wise (2010).
6. Although in some instances the demand is due to families' desire to maintain lifestyle and social status, as is often the case in the Middle East.
7. See in particular the International Convention on the Protection of the Rights of all Migrant Workers and Members of Their Families adopted in 1990 within the UN.
8. For details cf: *Reports of the Committee on Freedom of Association, Spain (Case No. 2121), The General Union of Workers of Spain (UGT), 23 March 2001, Denial of the right to organize and strike, freedom of assembly and association, the right to demonstrate and collective bargaining rights to 'irregular' foreign workers, Report No. 327* (Vol. LXXXV, 2002, Series B, No. 1).
9. See ILO: *Minimum Wage Systems, General Survey of the Reports on the Minimum Wage Fixing Convention, 1970 (No. 131) and the Minimum Wage Fixing Recommendation, 1970 (No. 135), Report of the Committee of Experts on the Application of Conventions and Recommendations, Report III (Part 1B)*, International Labour Conference, 103d session, Geneva, 2014, paras. 189–193, 199 and 396.
10. See Carman (2014).
11. 'Minimum wage decision', *Official Gazette* 31 Dec. 2011, p. 5616 of Issue No. 5134; issued under Article 52 of Labour Law 8/1996 and its amendments; translated and cited by Fair Wage Network, http://www.fair-wage.com/en/fair-wage-observatory/new-legal-provisions/109-the-minimum-wage-increase-in-jordan-from-1st-of-february-2012.html; last accessed 2 September 2014.
12. See Hazaimeh (2012).
13. The statutory minimum wage rate was set at HK$30 per hour in May 2013. The 'minimum allowable wage' for foreign domestic helpers is HK$4010 per month since October 2013.
14. The ILO defines social security as 'protection which society provides for its members through a series of public measures'. The definition covers: (i) social insurance (i.e., contributory systems); (ii) social assistance (i.e., tax-financed benefits for those on low incomes); and (iii) universal benefits (i.e., tax-financed benefits paid regardless of income and need). This is a broader definition than in many countries where social security is equalized with social insurance and distinguished from poverty alleviation measures, notably social assistance (ILO, 2000, p. 29).
15. For a discussion of bilateral vs multilateral agreements, principles and practices of social security agreements and their implementation see Hirose et al. (2011).
16. For details on these standards, the context of their adoption and their ratification, see Hirose (2011, pp. 5–13).
17. For a more detailed discussion see Chapter 2.4.6 in ILO (2010); and for a discussion on the methodological difficulties of measuring the net fiscal impact of immigration see World Bank (2006).
18. See also Martínez Franzoni and Sánchez-Ancochea, Chapter 11 in this volume, on the related issue of social incorporation; inter alia, they point out that women are particularly affected when public social goods are not provided as part of an explicit policy towards social incorporation.
19. For a discussion on neoliberal thought and ensuing perceptions of the state, see, for example, Chang (2002) and Glivanos (2008).
20. These concepts come out of the realist school of thought in international relations theory. For a criticism of this dichotomy, see, for example, Ripsman (2004).

21. ILO: *Labour Inspection, General Survey, Report III (Part 1B)*, International Labour Conference, 95th Session, Geneva, 2006, para. 78.
22. The risk of deportation causes workers to fear reporting employers who do not comply with workplace regulations. In 2013, Jamaican guest workers working in the hotel industry in the state of Florida on H2-B visas went on strike to protest sub-minimum and unpaid wages. The cleaning company that employed them threatened the workers with deportation if they did not return to work (Gordon, 2013).

REFERENCES

Abella, M. (2004), 'The recruiter's share in labour migration', in M. Douglas and E. Taylor (eds), *International Migration. Prospects and Policies in a Global Market*, Oxford: Oxford University Press, pp. 201–11.

Böhning, R. (1988), 'The protection of migrant workers and international labour standards', *International Migration*, **26**(2), 133–46.

Carman, T. (2014), 'Spread of temporary foreign workers in B.C. spurs controversy over hiring practices', *Vancouver Sun*, 10 March 2014.

Chang, H. (2002), 'Breaking the mould: an institutionalist political economy alternative to the neoliberal theory of the market and the state', *Cambridge Journal of Economics*, **26**(5), 539–59.

Connell, J. and B. Stilwell (2006), 'Merchants of medical care: recruiting agencies in the global healthcare chain', in C. Kuptsch (ed.), *Merchants of Labour*, Geneva: International Institute of Labour Studies/International Labour Office, pp. 239–53.

Fix, M. and J. Passel (1999), *Trends in Noncitizens' and Citizens' Use of Public Benefits Following Welfare Reform: 1994–97*, Washington, DC: Urban Institute.

Glivanos, I. (2008), 'Neoliberal law: unintended consequences of market-friendly law reforms', *Third World Quarterly*, **29**(6), 1087–99.

Gordon, J. (2013), 'Subcontractor servitude', *The New York Times*, Opinion Pages, 1 September 2013.

Hazaimeh, H. (2012), 'Garment employers warn of harm to sector if minimum wage rises', *Jordan Times*, 1 January 2012, accessed 17 December 2012 at http://jordantimes.com/garment-employers-warn-of-harm-to-sector-if-minimum-wage-rises-611.

Hirose, K. (2011), 'Protecting the social security rights of migrant workers – an international standards approach', in Hirose et al. (eds), *Social Security for Migrant Workers – A Rights-based Approach*, Geneva: ILO Decent Work Technical Support Team and Country Office for Central and Eastern Europe, pp. 1–18.

Hirose, K., M. Nikac and E. Tamagno (2011), *Social Security for Migrant Workers – A Rights-based Approach*, Geneva: ILO Decent Work Technical Support Team and Country Office for Central and Eastern Europe, International Labour Organization.

Hjarno, J. (2003), *Illegal Immigrants and Developments in Employment in the Labour Markets of the EU*, Aldershot, UK: Ashgate.

Human Rights Watch (2000), *Unfair Advantage: Workers' Freedom of Association in the United States under International Human Rights Standards*, New York/Washington/London/Brussels: Human Rights Watch.

ILO (2000), *World Labour Report 2000: Income Security and Social Protection in a Changing World*, Geneva: International Labour Office.

ILO (2010), *International Labour Migration – A Rights-based Approach*, Geneva: International Labour Office.

ILO (2012), *Labour Migration*, Governing Body 316th Session, Geneva, 1–16 November 2012, GB 316/POL/1, Geneva: International Labour Office, accessed 2 September 2014 at http://www.ilo.org/gb/GBSessions/GB316/pol/WCMS_191013/lang--en/index.htm.

ISSA (2011), 'Social security and migrants: policy challenges and responses', *Social Policy Highlight No. 17*, Geneva: International Social Security Association.

Kuptsch, C. and P. Martin (2010), 'Actors and factors in the internationalization of labour markets', in C. Kuptsch (ed.), *The Internationalization of Labour Markets*, Geneva: International Institute for Labour Studies/International Labour Office, pp. 115–33.

Kuptsch, C. and P. Martin (2011), 'Low-skilled labour migration', in A. Betts (ed.), *Global Migration Governance*, Oxford: Oxford University Press, pp. 34–59.

Kuptsch, C. and E.F. Pang (eds) (2006), *Competing for Global Talent*, Geneva: International Institute for Labour Studies/International Labour Office.

Martin, P., M. Abella and C. Kuptsch (2006), *Managing Labor Migration in the Twenty-first Century*, New Haven, CT and London: Yale University Press.

Milanovic, B. (2011), 'Global inequality: from class to location, from proletarians to migrants', *World Bank Policy Research Working Paper No. 5820*, Washington, DC: World Bank.

Milkman, R., E. Reese and B. Roth (1998), 'The Macrosociology of Paid Domestic Labor', *Work and Occupations* 25(4): 483–510.

Misra, J., J. Woodring and S.N. Merz (2006), 'The globalization of care work: neoliberal economic restructuring and migration policy', *Globalizations*, **3**(3), 317–32.

Passel, J. and D. Cohn (2009), *Mexican Immigrants: How Many Come? How Many Leave?*, Washington, DC: Pew Hispanic Center.

Ripsman, N. (2004), 'False dichotomy: when low politics is high politics', paper presented at the annual meeting of the International Studies Association, Montreal, Quebec, Canada, 17 March, accessed 2 September 2014 at http://www.allacademic.com/meta/p73388_index.html.

Roberts, B., G. Hanson and D. Cornwell et al. (2010), 'An analysis of migrant smuggling costs across the Southwest Border', Department of Homeland Security, Office of Immigration Statistics, Working Paper, November.

Salazar Parreñas, R. (2001), *Servants of Globalization – Women, Migration, and Domestic Work*, Stanford University Press.

Schmidt, V. (2006), 'Temporary migration workers: organizing and protection strategies', in C. Kuptsch (ed.), *Merchants of Labour*, Geneva: International Institute of Labour Studies/International Labour Office, pp. 191–206.

Sumption, M. and W. Somerville (2009), *The UK's New Europeans. Progress and Challenges Five Years After Accession*, Equality and Human Rights Commission, Migration Policy Institute.

Tapinos, G. (2000), 'Irregular migration: economic and political issues', in OECD (ed.), *Combating the Illegal Employment of Foreign Workers*, Paris: Organisation for Economic Co-operation and Development.

Thomas-Hope, E. (1998), 'Globalization and the development of a Caribbean migration culture', in M. Chamberlain (ed.), *Caribbean Migration: Globalised Identities*, London: Routledge, pp. 188–200.

Yeates, N. (2005), 'Global care chains: a critical introduction', *Global Migration Perspectives No. 44*, Geneva: Global Commission on International Migration.

Wise, T. (2010), 'Agricultural dumping under NAFTA: estimating the costs of U.S. agricultural policies to Mexican producers', *Mexican Rural Development Research Report No. 7*, Washington, DC: Woodrow Wilson International Center for Scholars.

World Bank (2006), *Global Economic Prospects: Economic Implications of Remittances and Migration*, Washington, DC: World Bank.

14. Labour market inequality between youth and adults: a special case?

Gerhard Reinecke and Damian Grimshaw*

14.1 INTRODUCTION

Inequality between youth (defined here as persons aged 15 to 24 years old) and adults is a key characteristic of labour markets worldwide. In almost all countries, the youth unemployment rate is more than twice the adult rate, the risk of precarious conditions of employment tends to be higher and wages tend to be lower. Moreover, during economic crises, young workers are disproportionately affected because of their precarious labour market integration. In the absence of effective policy intervention and decent labour market opportunities, the difficulties faced by young people are likely to mushroom into wider problems for economy and society, with several countries during the current economic crisis warning of a lost generation, undermining countries' growth potential and routes out of poverty (Scarpetta et al., 2010; ILO, 2013). Nevertheless, unlike other types of inequality analysed in this book, inequality between youth and adults is not necessarily undesirable per se: for example, higher unemployment rates might reflect an unavoidable process of 'job shopping' as part of the transition between the educational system and the labour market, at least in countries with a significant formal labour segment. Moreover, lower wages may be a seemingly fair reflection of young people's relatively limited work experience and on-the-job training. At stake, therefore, is the question of what level and forms of labour market inequality ought to be tolerated and what types of institutional interventions are most appropriate in the particular country context.

The recent economic crisis in many countries has exacerbated many of the undesirable aspects of youth–adult inequalities, including intractably high youth unemployment rates, a worsening of conditions in formal and informal sectors and a rewriting of countries' social settlements, or social models (involving social security and tax contributions and entitlements to decent pensions, education and healthcare), which often disadvantage younger generations. A key challenge, therefore, is to identify where the real problems begin: who are the youth at most risk of failing their transition from education to employment? Are young people more likely than older people to be locked out of the benefits associated with formal employment? Is inequality among young people perhaps more significant than that between younger and older people in the labour market? To what extent do labour market inequalities between youth and adults, as well as among youth, hinder efforts to diminish inequalities in society as a whole? What labour market institutions and policies can diminish these types of inequalities and provide young people entering the labour market with stable, fulfilling work and decent pay prospects?

This chapter addresses these questions in the context of regions and labour markets of different levels of socio-economic development. The character and extent of labour market risks faced by youth differ between developed and developing economies. Low levels of education, poverty, limited opportunities of formal employment and high shares of own-account and family-based working characterize young people's experiences in many developing country labour markets, while in wealthier economies young people are experiencing a transformation in traditional employment forms towards casualized contracts, reduced entry-level wages and social security and pension provisions despite bringing higher levels of education to the labour market. To reflect these different issues this chapter draws in particular on detailed findings for two contrasting regions that reflect the authors' expertise, namely Europe and Latin America, but also because Latin America is the developing region with the best coverage of periodical household surveys. The chapter also provides supplementary data on other countries wherever possible.

The chapter is organised as follows. Section 14.2 assesses three basic features of inequality in the labour market facing young people – namely unemployment, pay and access to the formal sector. Section 14.3 focuses on key features of vulnerability experienced by young people with a concern to understand the differential experiences among young people by economic class (household income) and gender. Section 14.4 asks what role labour market institutions can play in mitigating youth inequality and considers specific examples of education and training policy, employment protection, employer subsidies to hire youth and statutory minimum wages. Section 14.5 concludes with a summary of the issues and policy lessons.

14.2 BASIC FEATURES OF YOUTH–ADULT INEQUALITY: UNEMPLOYMENT, PAY AND INFORMAL SECTOR EMPLOYMENT

While inequality between youth and adults as such is not necessarily a problem, the labour market situation for young people is likely to reach a tipping point, potentially leading to social and political unrest, where high inequality between youth and adults combines with a critical overall labour market situation. Such is the case of Spain and Greece, where youth unemployment in 2012 reached 55 per cent and 58 per cent respectively, and young people accounted for more than 40 per cent of the total unemployed. On the other hand, other European countries, such as Germany (8 per cent), Austria (9 per cent) and the Netherlands (10 per cent) have not experienced excessively high youth unemployment as a result of the crisis, both because overall unemployment has remained relatively low and because of favourable labour market institutions.[1]

A key issue in assessing the degree of inequality faced by youth in unemployment relates to their risk of experiencing unemployment compared to adults. Around the world, this risk varies enormously, from a ratio of youth to adult unemployment rates of between 2.0 and 2.5 in developed economies and Sub-Saharan Africa to a ratio of more than 5 in the South-East Asia and Pacific region (Figure 14.1). The extent to which such a risk factor is likely to drive policy action depends on other conditions. First, where overall unemployment rates are high for adults and youth, this ratchets up unemployment on the policy agenda regardless of the relative risk; such is the case in the Middle East region and Southern European countries at present.

Second, given the long-standing general decline in young people's labour market participation (Blanchflower and Freeman, 1999; Grimshaw, 2012), the significance of young people's higher rate of unemployment needs to be balanced against their share of total unemployment. In North Africa and South Asia, the youth–adult inequality of unemployment experience is significantly heightened by the fact that at a regional level young people constitute a majority of the unemployed (52 per cent and 53 per cent respectively),[2] far higher than the youth share of the working-age population in these regions. Comparing country experiences, we find a majority of youth among the unemployed in ten countries across a variety of regions in the world – highest in Zambia, Paraguay and Sri Lanka (Figure 14.2).

And third, policy attention to young people's unequal experience also needs to be responsive to the scale of the problem among the wider population of young people. In regions where participation in non-compulsory post-16 education is low, the rate of youth unemployment has a far greater

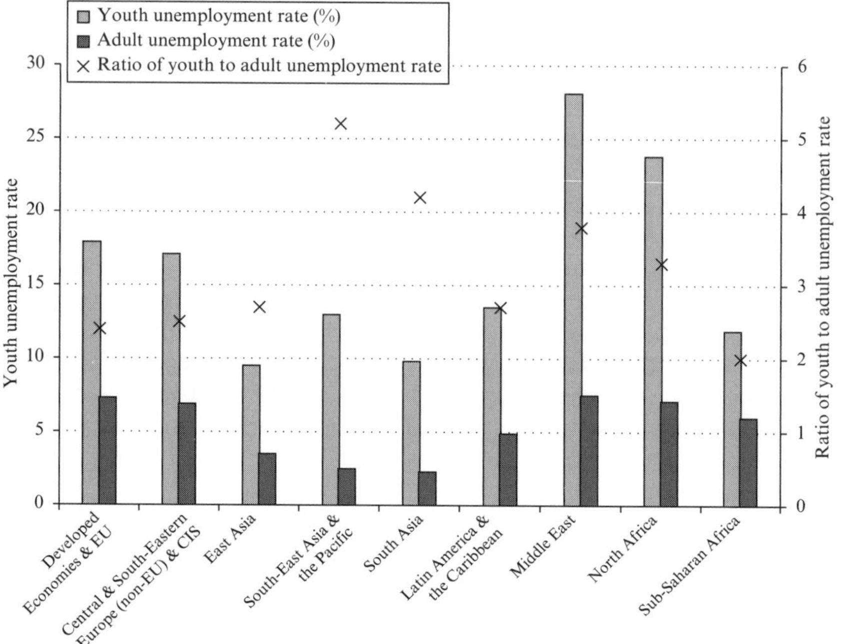

Source: ILO Key Indicators of the Labour Market (KILM) database, 7th edition, own compilation.

Figure 14.1 Youth and adult unemployment rates in the main regions of the world, 2012

significance because of young people's higher dependence on the labour market. Consequently, in Sub-Saharan Africa, a region with an apparently modest level of youth unemployment and a relatively low risk compared to adults (Figure 14.1), we find the highest share of the total youth population in unemployment (one in ten) coupled with the highest shares of child labour in the world, the lowest years of average schooling, and among the highest population growth rates and levels of poverty (albeit with variation within the region) (Guarcello et al., 2005).

A second basic feature of inequality between youth and adults relates to wages. While one might anticipate a wage differential given conventions of rewarding age, experience and expertise in a job, there is considerable variation in what the literature refers to as the youth 'wage discount' among countries, suggesting that differences in labour market institutions and age norms play a role. Within the OECD region, earnings data for the mid-2000s suggest that young workers (aged 15–24) earned on average around

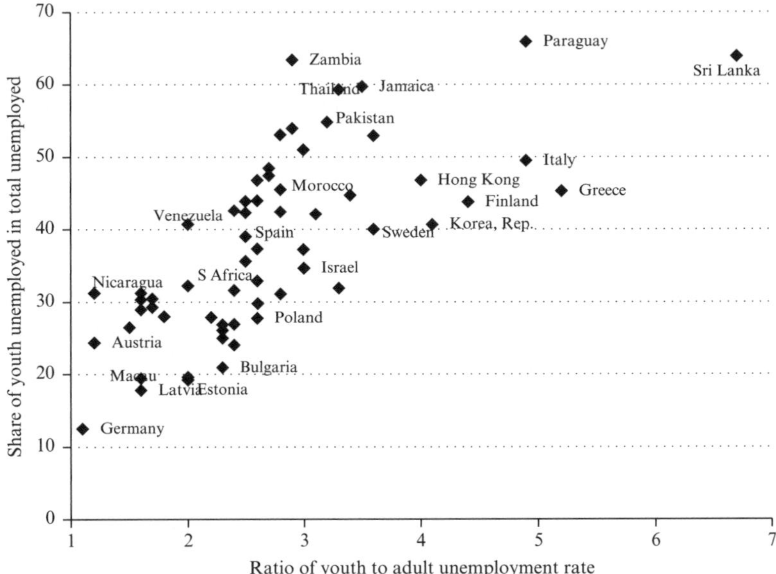

Source: ILO KILM database, 7th edition, own compilation.

Figure 14.2 Indicators of youth unemployment: youth rate relative to adult rate and youth share of total unemployed

three-fifths (62 per cent) of the wages of older workers:[3] the largest wage discount for age is found in the United States where young people earned just 55 per cent of that of adult workers and the smallest in Norway at 73 per cent. Using alternative definitions, ILO data for 2010 indicate that in South Africa youth earned around 75 per cent of the median wage of all workers and in Mexico youth earned 77 per cent of the average earnings of all workers (Grimshaw, 2012, p. 3) Furthermore, huge youth–adult wage gaps prevail in the cities of several West African countries: for example, in Niamey, the capital of Niger, young men and women aged 15–19 earned just 24 per cent and 28 per cent, respectively, of that of adult workers, and the older cohort, 20–24 years old, earned 44 per cent and 48 per cent, respectively (DIAL, 2007, Table 9a).

A focus on developing countries sheds light on a third crucial source of labour market inequality experienced by young people, that of access to the formal economy and the various protections that go with it. Many studies highlight the greater risk of vulnerable employment experienced by young people, with especially high shares employed as contributing family workers with meagre and sometimes zero remuneration (Huynh and Kapsos, 2013); moreover, exposure to family work is especially high among young people from poor households – estimated at around 60 per cent of youth employment in Cambodia and 40 per cent in Indonesia (ibid., Figure 15). Here we draw on special tabulations of labour force surveys from countries in Latin America for 2011.[4] While informality and the corresponding access to social security is still a pressing problem for workers of all ages in Latin America (despite some recent progress, especially in Argentina), the situation for youth is especially worrying (Figure 14.3). The share of youth employment in jobs that make contributions to pension schemes is lower than the share of adult employment in all countries and is less than half the adult rate in Paraguay and Peru. Also, the share of private sector salaried workers with a written employment contract is significantly lower among young workers than among adult workers. Although labour legislation in some countries such as Paraguay does not oblige employers to issue a written contract, previous research (ILO, 1998; Valenzuela and Reinecke, 2000) shows that the absence of a contract is systematically linked to limited access to a raft of employment rights. Interestingly, Brazil and Panama, the countries with the highest coverage of written employment contracts among adults, are characterized by a small gap between youth and adults.

A further indicator of young people's limited access to some of the better conditions and employment rights often associated with the formal sector of the economy concerns their protection by trade unions. Pedersini's (2010) summary of EU developments is that young people 'seem to be almost invariably the most problematic group to organise'. In France, for example, only 3 per cent of young people aged less than 30 years old are union members compared to 8 per cent for all workers (Rehfeldt, 2010). Also, in four Latin American countries where union membership data are available by age group (Costa Rica, Mexico, Paraguay and Uruguay), youth are systematically less likely than adult workers to be affiliated to a trade union, by a factor of more than three in Paraguay and Uruguay. Explanations for their lower union membership point to the greater incidence of precarious employment status among young workers, their lower average tenure in the workplace, and union failings in mobilizing among young people. Available data by age group indicate that the share of fixed-term employment is higher among youth (15 to 24 years) than among prime age workers in all OECD countries except Australia (5.7 per cent vs 5.8 per cent). In some countries, such as Austria (35.6 per cent vs 5.0 per cent) and Switzerland (52.5 per cent vs 6.2 per cent), the incidence among youth is more than seven times higher and in nine out of 30 OECD countries more than half of young salaried workers are in temporary employment (OECD, 2013); see Cazes and de Laiglesia (Chapter 6, this

a. Coverage of social security contributions (percentage share of total employment): contribution to a pension scheme by age group

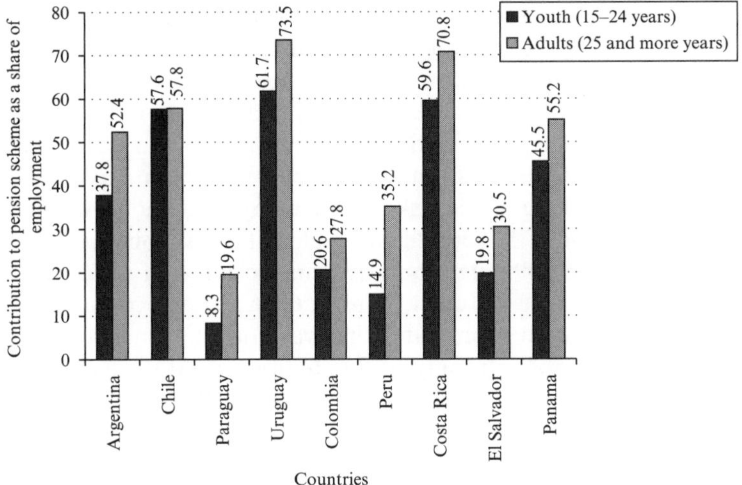

b. Written employment contracts (percentage share of private sector wage employment): availability of a written work contract by age group among private sector salaried workers

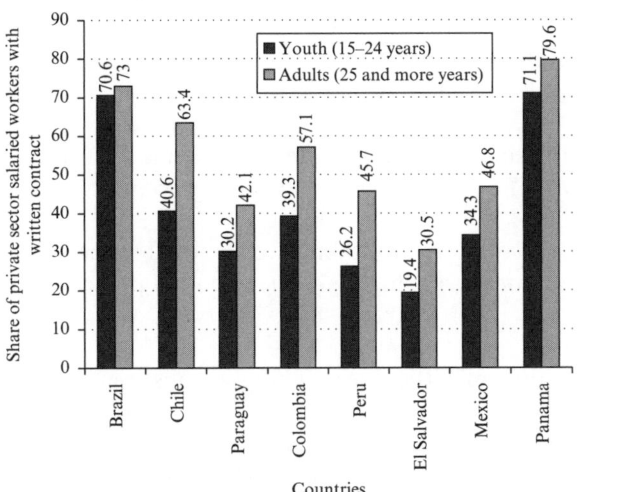

Source: ILO and ECLAC (2012, Table A-3). Own compilation.

Figure 14.3a,b Indicators of youth and adult access to formal sector employment benefits, selected Latin American countries, 2011

volume) for a detailed analysis of the interaction between fixed-term contracts and inequality.

Finally, many studies show that young people's weaker integration into formal, or standardized, employment makes them more vulnerable to the downturns of the economic cycle. As such, youth–adult inequality is heightened during economic crises. This vulnerability combines with other productivity-related characteristics of young people – in particular their relatively low tenure and less enterprise-specific human capital (OECD, 2006) – to generate heightened risks of unemployment and flows into inactivity. For this reason, the term 'super cyclicality' was coined in the 1980s to describe youth employment and used in more recent research (Ryan, 2001). Moreover, a recent study of four Latin American countries (Brazil, Chile, Mexico, Peru) demonstrates that variation in youth employment rates is correlated more strongly to fluctuations in GDP than is the case for adults (ILO, 2007).

14.3 INEQUALITY AMONG YOUTH

Comparison of the gaps between the average labour market experiences of young people and adults obscures some of the more extreme patterns of vulnerability faced by many youth. This section considers evidence of inequality among youth in order to shed further light on the labour market integration problems discussed above:

- Data for Latin America disaggregated by income quintile and by gender illustrate the different nature of labour market entry problems for youth.
- While a 'wage discount' for youth may to some extent be justifiable, cross-country comparisons highlight the need for policy-makers to monitor both the youth share of low-wage work and exit rates to higher wage jobs.
- Youth face a range of difficulties making a transition from unemployment or inactivity into paid employment and suffer significant and long-lasting scarring effects, highlighting the need to improve opportunities for education and training to access better jobs.

Youth Labour Market Status in Latin America by Economic Class and Gender

As a first illustration of inequality among youth, Table 14.1 presents the key indicators of youth labour market status for the region of Latin

Table 14.1 Indicators of youth labour market status by household income quintiles, 2011

	Persons Between 15 and 24 Years									25 Years and Older		
	I			V			TOTAL					
	Men	Women	Total	Men	Women	Total	Men	Women	Total	Men	Women	Total
Latin America												
Unemployment rate[a]	20.9	35.9	26.7	7.1	9.0	7.9	11.6	17.3	13.8	3.8	6.1	4.7
Does not study or work[a]	20.3	40.6	31.1	6.7	11.7	9.0	12.4	28.5	20.4	18.1	46.8	33.2
Of which: household tasks[a]	13.7	70.2	52.9	18.8	62.3	45.4	14.5	69.5	52.7	23.4	77.3	63.4
With written employment contract[b]	25.5	15.8	22.1	62.9	67.1	64.6	48.0	52.0	49.5	63.0	58.4	61.2
Contributes to health insurance[c]	12.9	10.8	12.3	57.1	59.7	58.2	39.4	44.0	41.2	48.7	48.8	48.7
Contributes to pension system[d]	13.5	10.2	12.4	59.3	61.5	60.3	42.7	46.1	44.0	56.4	53.1	55.0

Notes:
a. Includes Argentina, Brazil, Colombia, Costa Rica, Ecuador, El Salvador, Mexico, Panama, Paraguay, Peru, Uruguay and Venezuela.
b. Includes Brazil, Colombia, El Salvador, Mexico, Panama, Paraguay and Peru.
c. Includes Argentina, Brazil, Colombia, Costa Rica, Ecuador, El Salvador, Mexico, Panama, Paraguay, Peru and Uruguay.
d. Includes Argentina, Brazil, Colombia, Costa Rica, El Salvador, Panama, Paraguay, Peru and Uruguay.

Source: ILO on the basis of household survey data from the respective countries.

America, disaggregated by income quintile and gender. Overall, the results show that for all five main indicators, the gap between poor youth and rich youth is more important than the average gap between youth and adults.

The youth unemployment rate for Latin American countries with available data in 2011 was 27 per cent among youth from the poorest income quintile, but only 8 per cent in the fifth quintile. Also, while women face a higher unemployment rate in all age groups and among poorest and richest households, the penalty is especially high among the poorest women, for whom the rate of unemployment was 36 per cent in 2011. The share of youth with NEET status (not in employment, education or training) was 31 per cent in the poorest quintile but only 9 per cent in the fifth quintile. Once again, the difference between men and women for this indicator is especially strong in the poorest income quintile, with a large number of young women who have withdrawn from the labour force and education due to household obligations (see below). Finally, in the poorest income quintile, only a very small minority of salaried workers have written employment contracts and access to social protection, while in the richest quintile, these indicators for employment are similar or even superior to those for the average of adult workers, for both men and women.

The structural problem of NEET status affects the employment prospects of a large proportion of young people, especially women, largely because of a high incidence of unpaid employment undertaking 'household tasks' (such as childcare or care for other family members). The results in Table 14.2 show that two in three young women with NEET status are in fact responsible for a bundle of household tasks, compared to one in ten young men with NEET status. Strikingly, the proportion is almost identical among very young women, aged 15 to 17 (65 per cent) and those aged 18 to 24 (66 per cent).

Among young people with NEET status in Latin America, therefore, two very different situations emerge. On the one hand, the high percentage of young women devoted to household tasks points to a problem that is not just a matter of young people's job prospects, but has more to do with work, gender relations and family, and in particular with the unequal distribution of tasks among male and female household members (see Chapter 12 on gender equality). In this context, the availability of services, especially of childcare facilities, has an important role to play, as has been demonstrated for the Brazilian case (Chioda, 2011). Nevertheless, the availability of such services seems to impact more on the number of hours worked and the formality of employment than on labour market participation as such (Martínez Franzoni and Sánchez-Ancochea, 2013). On the other hand, a significant percentage of young men (and young women too, to a lesser degree) do not work, study or perform household tasks;[5] some

Table 14.2 The proportion of youth with NEET status undertaking household tasks by age group, Latin America (12 countries), 2011

Categories of Study or Work		15 to 17 Years		18 to 24 Years		15 to 24 Years	
		Youth not in education or employment (as a share of working-age population)	Household tasks (as a share of youth not in education or training)[a]	Youth not in education or employment (as a share of working-age population)	Household tasks (as a share of youth not in education or training)[a]	Youth not in education or employment (as a share of working-age population)	Household tasks (as a share of youth not in education or training)[a]
Latin America	Men	9.9	18.3	13.3	8.0	12.1	10.7
	Women	16.7	65.2	34.0	66.2	28.5	66.0
	Total	13.2	47.4	23.7	50.0	20.3	49.4

Note: a. Calculation does not include Brazil.

Source: ILO on the basis of household survey data from the respective countries.

of them are looking for work, but others are not engaged in any of these activities. Although many young people find themselves temporarily in this situation, as part of a transition between different employment or educational activities, there is a core group of young people who are excluded from the labour market. This calls for a public policy response for the sake of both young people's own life prospects and social cohesion.

Low-wage Work Among Youth

Given the size of the youth wage discount (section 14.2 above), it is likely that young people in work face a considerably higher risk of being employed in a low-wage job than adult workers.[6] Indeed for some countries, the bulk of low-wage jobs are in fact occupied by young people, which has a considerable influence on policy debates about the role of low-wage jobs either as stepping stones towards more stable better paid jobs or as low-wage traps.

Drawing on early 2000s data, the OECD *Employment Outlook* (2006) reported a higher incidence of low-wage work among youth than adult workers – at least twice the size – in all OECD countries for which data were available (2006, p. 175). More recent data for five European countries and the USA reveal that young women and young men are between 2.5 and 5.8 times as likely to be in low-wage employment as the overall average for the country (Mason and Salverda, 2010, Table 2.2). In terms of the absolute incidence of low-wage employment, a majority of young male and female workers are in low-wage employment in all six countries (with the one exception of young men in the UK for whom the low-wage incidence is 44 per cent) (Figure 14.4). The gender divide is mixed, with two out of six countries (UK, USA) recording a significantly higher incidence of low-wage employment among young women, two recording similar incidences (France, Netherlands) and two a higher rate among young men (Denmark, Germany). This contrasts markedly with the clear penalty experienced by female older workers among whom the risk of lower pay is consistently greater than among male older workers.

Because young workers experience a greater risk of low pay than older workers, they account for a disproportionate share of all low-wage workers, up to 62 per cent in Denmark, compared to a far lower share in France, just 30 per cent, explained by the lower relative risk in France than in Denmark (Figure 14.4). In Danish policy circles, therefore, low-wage employment is considered to be almost entirely a problem of young people and framed as a temporary problem associated with a 'transitional workforce' (Esbjerg et al., 2008). This is certainly not the case in other countries, however, where policy evaluations emphasize the fact that low-wage

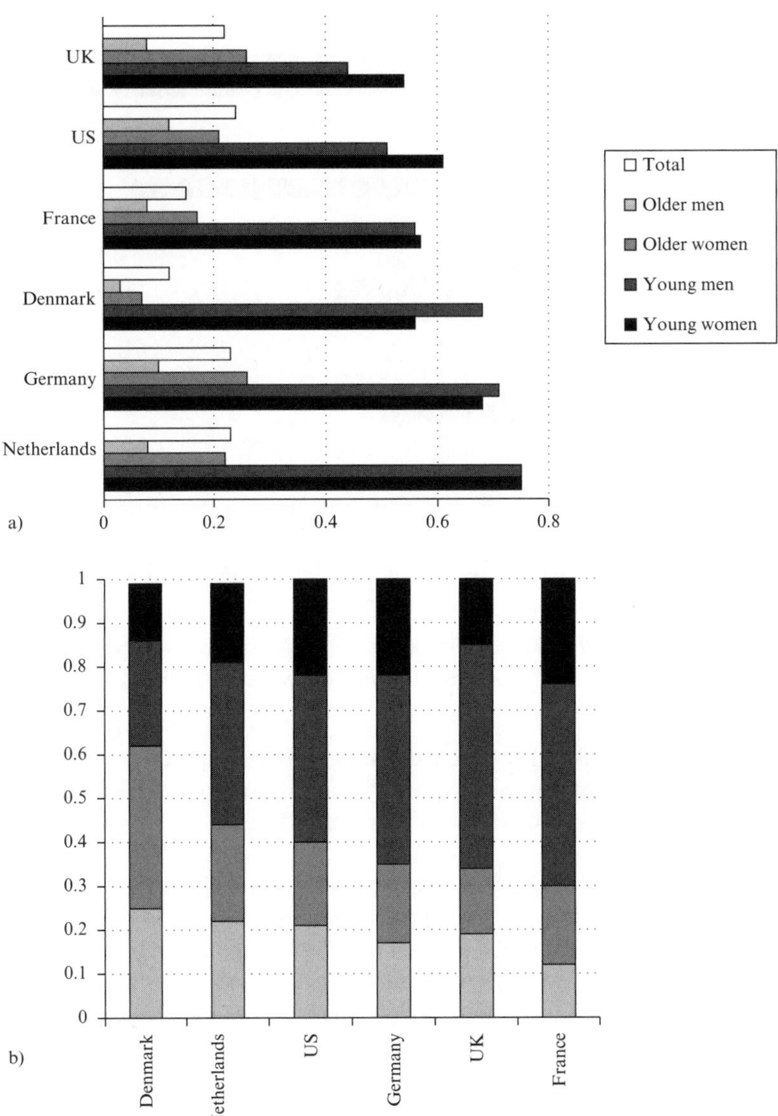

Note: Low-wage employment defined as earnings less than two-thirds of the median for all employees.

Source: Adapted from Mason and Salverda (2010, Table 2.2).

Figure 14.4a,b The incidence and composition of low-wage employment among young/older males/females, Europe and the USA

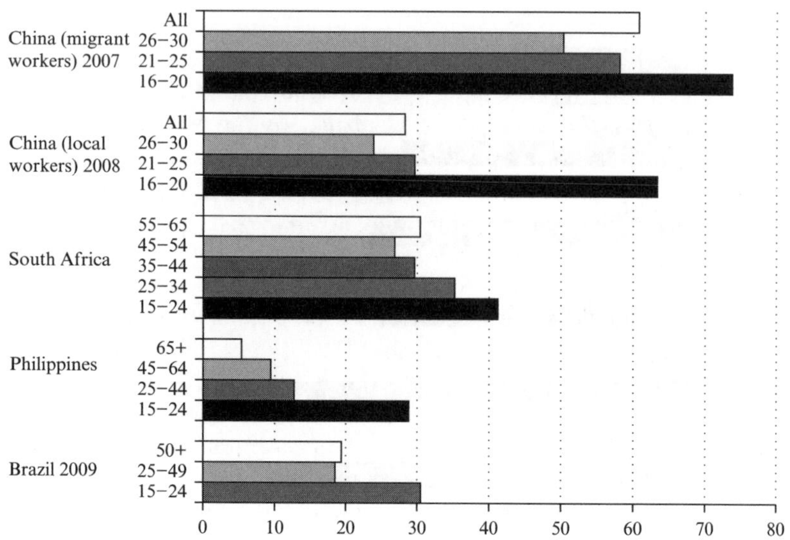

Source: ILO *Global Wage Report* (2010b, Figure 23), own compilation.

Figure 14.5 The incidence of low-wage employment by age group in China, South Africa, the Philippines and Brazil

work is more a problem for the core-age workforce, especially women, and not the result of employers paying low wages to a young, inexperienced, more transient workforce (see, for example, Boushey et al., 2007 for the United States).

Country data collected by the ILO for its *Global Wage Report 2010/11* (ILO, 2010b) also show a consistently higher risk of low-wage employment among young workers than older workers (Figure 14.5). The risk is particularly high among young migrant workers in China where the data records a low-pay incidence of 74 per cent among 16–20-year-olds and 58 per cent among 21–25-year-olds, compared with an incidence of 28 per cent for all local workers.

While they experience a greater risk of low pay than older workers, young people generally enjoy a stronger chance of exiting low-wage work into higher paid employment. As Solow argues in a review of comparative data for Europe and the United States, 'there are substantial differences among the countries, although mobility is fairly substantial everywhere, if only because younger workers eventually propel themselves into better jobs' (2008, p. 6). Quintini and Martin (2006) show that only a very small share of young people in low-wage employment remained trapped over a five-year period in their examination of 13 European countries and the United States. Exit rates nevertheless vary significantly across countries. The share of young people trapped in low-wage employment over a five-year continuous period varies from zero in Denmark to more than 10 per cent in the UK, USA and Greece, leading Solow (2008, p. 6) to conclude, 'the self-image [of the USA] of an extremely mobile society is not valid, at least not in this respect'.

Trap or Transition and the Scarring Effects of Unemployment

A key issue for youth labour market policy is to smooth transitions into paid employment both to improve the productive capabilities of the economy and to minimize the long-lasting scarring effects of youth unemployment and time spent in a poor-quality job. Transition analyses show that country policies may be able to effectively target those obstacles that cause certain short-term transition problems as youth move from the educational system into the labour market, or from unemployment into paid work, but face major challenges of institutional design in addressing fundamental impediments that cause long-lasting failures to enter paid employment (see section 14.5). However, analyses of youth transitions are complicated for several reasons, including the lengthening of the transition period as education is extended and students combine education and casual employment, the difficulties of defining an end point when young people alternate between jobs, unemployment and inactivity and how to assess the many states of employment in developing countries where casual jobs, family work, household chores and self-employment are widespread (Guarcello et al., 2005; Matsumoto and Elder, 2010).

For Latin America, this literature is still scarce but some relevant studies exist. Cunningham and Bustos (2011), in their study based on household panel data from Argentina, Brazil and Mexico, present many results that appear to strengthen the 'normal transition' view, given the relatively high incidence of transition among youth from informal employment and unemployment into formal employment. However, the study also finds that workers from the poorest income quintile have less likelihood of moving from informal to formal employment than others, reflecting the relative lack of social mobility in these societies and contributing to overall labour market inequality. Not surprisingly, youth from poor households are more frequently trapped in bad-quality jobs than those from other income quintiles.

Paz (2012) and Maurizio (2011), based on household survey data from Argentina for the 2003–11 and 1995–2003 periods respectively, find that transition rates from unemployment into employment are lower for youth than for adults. This finding is consistent with the earlier study by Lépore and Schleser (2007), which uses a panel based on household survey data from 1998 to 2000, although the difference between youth and adult transition rates from unemployment to employment is relatively modest. The study by Maurizio (2011) established that job rotation among youth is higher than among adults, even controlling for other variables that have an impact on rotation patterns. This study also highlights the heterogeneity of professional careers. For instance, seven years after initial labour market entry, 50 per cent of those who abandoned secondary education are in jobs with less than one year of tenure, whereas for those with university education, this share is only 26 per cent. Chacaltana (2005), in his study on Peru, confirms the generally high job rotation of youths. Rotation among youth was found to be linked on average to wage increases, that is, transitions to better-quality jobs. However, the study also found that the cost of job search was excessively high, especially in a context of high rotation.

The complexity of transition analyses is illustrated in Guarcello et al., (2005) study of 13 Sub-Saharan African countries. The study finds that the character of transition of young people who had attended school is strongly influenced by urban/rural residency and gender. Transitions are especially prolonged among young women in urban areas who in several countries enter the labour market at a later age despite quitting education earlier than young men (ibid., Figure 10). An initial period of unemployment is 'not unusual' among these young people and 'extends well beyond what could plausibly be considered "wait" unemployment' (ibid., p. 24).

The problem with poor transitions is that they not only have adverse immediate effects on a young person's income and perceptions of social inclusion, but also have long-lasting scarring effects on labour market prospects. High rates of unemployment experienced in many countries as a result of the economic crisis and a failure (at the time of writing) of active labour market policy make matters worse. While it is too early to examine the medium-term effects of the post-2008 crisis, past studies provide a good indication of the adverse effects. Scarpetta et al.'s (2010) analysis finds that a 1 percentage point increase in the unemployment rate at the point a young person enters the labour market reduces annual earnings by up to 8 per cent in the UK in the first year and, remarkably, still registers a 2 per cent penalty ten years on. In other countries, the initial effect is smaller but, in the case of France and Spain, it is longer-lasting – a scarring effect for up to 15 years after labour market entry (ibid.). In Japan, scarring is associated with the more limited opportunities for young people to enter stable, full-time employment and the need instead to accept non-regular, unstable employment forms. Genda et al.'s study (2010, p. 182) shows that entering the labour market during a recession 'has a persistent negative effect on earnings for young Japanese men'. Moreover, the results suggest that entry during a recession not only lowers annual earnings but also, for lower-educated persons, increases the risk of non-employment and the acceptance of part-time employment; indeed, a substantial portion of the decline in earnings is attributed to the lower likelihood of regular, stable employment (ibid.).

For the UK, Gregg and Tominey (2004) find that youth unemployment imposes a substantial scar on subsequent earnings and the wage scar increases in size for individuals with a worse experience of unemployment when young. The results are striking (ibid., pp. 13–15). In terms of the raw wage gap, an individual with a history of 13 or more months of unemployment when they were young experiences an average reduction in earnings compared to an individual with no youth unemployment of: 30 per cent (male) and 34 per cent (female) at age 23; 42 per cent (male) and 35 per cent (female) at age 33; and 32 per cent (male) and 25 per cent (female) at age 42 (ibid., pp. 13–19). Education differences among groups affected by youth unemployment reduce some of this raw effect on wages, shrinking the actual scarring effect. However, the study also shows just why the rise of long-term unemployment among young people during the present crisis is so damaging. For both men and women, a period of unemployment for more than six months when young carries a scar on wages at age 42 of 6–10 per cent (ibid., p. 19). The authors conclude that 'interventions to reduce the exposure of young adults to substantive periods of unemployment could if successful have substantial returns in terms of the individual's lifetime earnings and could represent a good investment' (ibid., p. 24).

In sum, transitions from unemployment and inactivity are more difficult for youth than for adults and the resulting jobs are often unstable, informal and precarious. The research demonstrates that these risks are especially acute for youth from low incomes and with incomplete secondary education. Given the well-known scarring effects of poor transitions for young people it is imperative for policy-makers to recognize the need for labour market interventions in areas of education and training, job search, employment rights and career development and design policy in response to heterogeneous patterns of labour market transitions among youth in developed and developing countries.

14.4 LABOUR MARKET INSTITUTIONS TO ADDRESS THE INEQUALITY BETWEEN YOUTH AND ADULTS

In some recent studies by the World Bank and the OECD, labour market policies are presented as possible culprits of persistent problems of inequality faced by young people in a renewed argument pitched against labour market regulation, this time in the discursive framework of insiders and outsiders. In an argument reminiscent of the overly simplistic neoclassical economics thesis of the 1970s/1980s that the union wage premium destroyed jobs by sustaining wages above the market clearing level, OECD and World Bank reports now routinely argue that institutions that bolster employment protection, a high minimum wage and equal rights for part-time and temporary workers benefit incumbent workers at the cost of 'outsider' groups such as young workers. Our review of international experience of various labour market policies suggests this view is flawed – that young people's disadvantaged labour market position is not determined by the advantages associated with older workers' 'insider' status, that there is a great deal of fluidity and variability in labour market conditions and that better employment conditions through a strengthening and widening of labour market regulations can act as an effective incentive (as well as compensation) for transitions out of inactivity, unemployment and informal or unprotected work (for a gender critique, see Rubery, 2011). Instead, well-designed labour market institutions can diminish many of the disadvantages experienced by young people (see Table 14.3 for a summary of issues). In this section, we review examples of country policies that have improved the conditions for labour market integration of youth and diminished the gap in labour market indicators between adults and youth.

Education and Training Policy

The type of skill formation system and route from schooling into paid employment is one of the most important institutional features of a country that can facilitate young people's integration into the labour market and their entry into stable and fulfilling work with decent pay prospects. There is no consensus of policy approach however, with a range of country approaches reflecting reliance on 'market-led solutions' at one extreme (where decisions about training programmes for young people are largely made by individual employers) and incorporating collective solutions on the other (where decisions and policy are formulated by collective associations of employers and trade unions, as well as the state), as well as differences between an emphasis on general skills and skills specific to a firm or industry (Crouch et al., 1999; Rubery and Grimshaw, 2003; Whitley, 2007). Moreover, levels of economic development matter enormously in shaping levels of school attendance, such that education policy in many countries in the world is obliged to focus on initiatives to incentivize participation of young people in education in an effort to improve literacy rates.

Table 14.3 The potential positive and negative effects of institutions on youth labour market conditions

Relevant Institutional Feature	Potential Effects on Youth Labour Market Conditions	
	Positive effects	Negative effects
Education & training policy		
Quality of compulsory schooling Conditional cash transfers Infrastructure for vocational training Reputation and quality of skill credentials Employer willingness to provide training Balance of investment in industry and firm-specific skills/general skills	Raised school attendance improves conditions for labour market integration Good basic schooling boosts pay prospects and raises efficiency of firms' training investment Strong emphasis on industry and firm-specific skills generates demand for vocational skill and raises pay relative to youth with higher education	Stratification of good/bad schooling reduces participation in further education and widens pay differential among youth Weak employer commitment to vocational training diminishes pay prospects of young school-leavers Privatized higher education drives up wage premiums to pay off private debt, increasing wage differentials among youth
Employment protection rules for part-time and temporary workers		
Incidence of part-time and temporary contracts Legal rules to protect equal status of part-time and temporary contracts Part-time and temporary jobs as peripheral or core to employment practices	Opportunities for transitions to standard employment forms Access to equivalent pay and benefits (e.g., health cover, unemployment compensation, pension, unfair dismissal, etc.)	Weak rules risk high proportion of youth becoming trapped in part-time and temporary jobs Risk of low status part-time and temporary jobs in segmented labour markets

Table 14.3 (continued)

Relevant Institutional Feature	Potential Effects on Youth Labour Market Conditions	
	Positive effects	Negative effects
Youth wage subsidies		
Targeted subsidies to encourage employers to hire young unemployed people Or subsidies targeted at youth from low-income households, low education, low-skill, etc.	Reduce cumulative risk of unemployment among youth Equip youth with work experience and access to decent work Provide employers a less costly means of assessing youth performance on the job	Substitution of younger for older workers Destructive job churning caused by opportunistic employers who continually hire and fire to maximize subsidies Where integrated into welfare benefits may eliminate employment rights
Youth minimum wage		
Special sub-minimum for youth or standard minimum wage extended to cover youth Single or multiple youth rates High or low level relative to adult rate Limit application of sub-minimum rate to workers with short work experience Specific provisions for training or apprenticeship Policies to improve compliance	Coverage under adult minimum wage avoids risk of age discrimination Use of sub-minimum encourages better response to high youth unemployment Provisions for experience avoid problems of rewarding age more than experience and on-the-job skills Provisions for apprentice positions reduce training disincentives	Sub-minimum wage conflicts with principle of equal pay for work of equal value Use of multiple sub-minima increases the risk of age-substitution effects Very low youth sub-minimum wage risks exploitative pay

In developing economies, much of the literature focuses on the effectiveness of labour market interventions designed to raise rates of literacy and levels of school enrolment, as well as to improve the conditions for youth labour market integration. An important policy initiative is that of the conditional cash transfer scheme, which stipulates the attendance of children and adolescents in educational institutions as a condition for receiving welfare benefits. Several studies have evaluated the effectiveness of such schemes in Latin America, where conditional-cash-transfer schemes have been designed to assist youth labour market integration by extending education and improving young people's skills profile. Impact evaluation studies in Brazil and Mexico found that conditional-cash-transfer programmes significantly raised school attendance in rural areas, while the results in urban areas have been positive but rather modest (Attanasio et al, 2008; Schaffland, 2012). A strengthening of conditional cash transfers can also be used to avoid high dropout rates from education during the economic crisis and help to improve conditions for labour market integration once the crisis is over, as can be illustrated with the case of Costa Rica. The programme, ¡Avancemos!, first implemented prior to the 2009 crisis, contains an incentive to remain in the educational system that increases with the educational level of adolescents in the household. The coverage of this programme was extended during the crisis (Marinakis, 2009). However, a key challenge of conditional-cash-transfer schemes is to ensure adequate provision of services, as some countries are unable to deliver sufficient school places mandated under the programmes (see discussion in Chapter 10). Moreover, incentives for school attendance are not by themselves sufficient to improve academic performance given that the quality of educational institutions is a limiting factor in many Latin American countries.

In developed economies, research has compared and contrasted the overall approaches of states, employers and trade unions to the regulation and management of skill formation systems for young people, including the variety of efforts to standardize the skill formation system (ranging from low in countries such as the UK and the USA to high in the inclusive state systems of Germany and Sweden) (Whitley, 2007, pp. 45–6). These differing approaches bring different kinds of benefits and limitations. States that operate at arm's length may enjoy responsiveness to market demands (providing employers can be trusted to commit to the needed investment) but may suffer problems of market signals for skills because of poorly defined systems of skills accreditation that lack acceptance and recognition among the employer community. By contrast, inclusive states enjoy the advantage of being able to coordinate the introduction of new skill standards by virtue of the active participation and cooperation

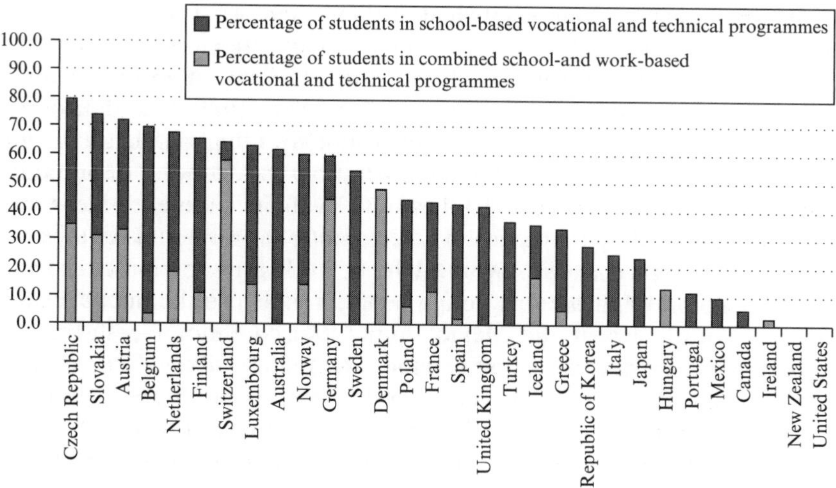

Source: OECD (2008, Table C1. 1). Own compilation.

Figure 14.6 The share of students engaged in vocational education and training, OECD (2008)

among social partners, yet may suffer problems of lagged responsiveness to market demands. Figure 14.6 provides data on the importance of vocational education and training (VET) for OECD countries, with more than half of students in some form of dual or school-based VET in Germany, the Netherlands and Sweden, for example, and less than half in Canada, France, Japan, the Republic of Korea and the UK.

In Latin America, evaluations of training policy interventions point to the need for a more targeted, longer-term investment strategy. A recent impact evaluation of different training programmes in Chile (targeted at both youth and adults) did not identify a positive impact of the majority of them; positive findings were related to longer-term interventions, such as the Programa Especial de Jóvenes (Ministerio de Trabajo y Previsión Social, 2011). Also, in Peru, while an impact evaluation study (Chacaltana, 2005) confirmed the positive impact of the training programmes on income and employment variables, its main insight was to open the 'black box' of training provision to discern whether or not participants had concluded the practical and theoretical components of the programme. The study concludes that only trainees who completed both theoretical and practical components benefitted positively.

As well as enskilling youth and facilitating labour market entry, comparative analysis of countries' skill formation systems finds a strong association with the wage structure, with implications for relative earnings of young people stratified by level and type of education. Comparative analysis of developed economies suggests that in inclusive corporatist countries, such as Germany, the high share of young school leavers in apprenticeship training, coupled with the strong reputation of high-quality vocational training programmes among employers, generates high demand. In the UK and USA, by contrast, a reliance on the market to produce general skills generates a high risk that school leavers do not acquire valued skills and, as Estevez-Abe et al. put it, 'end up as low-paid unskilled workers for most or all of their working lives' (2001, p. 177). The result is a higher differential between the pay of highly qualified young workers and low-qualified young workers in countries with a market-led skill formation system. This result finds support in the comparative statistical analysis of Bassanini and Ok (2003, Table 3) who show that in countries with more compressed wage structures, less educated workers receive more training.[7] This also fits with an institutional approach that recognizes wage differentials in market-led systems, such as the UK and USA, also reflect pressures for higher premiums for education to enable graduates to pay off student debt in privatized higher education systems.

Employment Protection Rules and Contractual Status

During the 1980s and 1990s a series of studies sought to demonstrate that employment protection legislation had a negative impact on employment, leading to the recommendations of the 1994 OECD *Job Strategy*. However, subsequent studies found mixed results and evidence against such a clear-cut impact. Part of the debate has shifted to the relative impact of employment protection for different groups in the labour market, with special emphasis on the possible negative impact for youth and women.

According to recent OECD studies, countries with more stringent employment protection legislation tend to have lower youth employment rates than countries with looser employment protection, although the estimated magnitude of its impact depends on the specification. However, the impact on unemployment according to the same studies is less clear-cut (OECD, 2006) and some other studies reject the link between employment protection legislation and low youth employment rates or high youth unemployment altogether (Noelke, 2011). A 2007 study on Chile (Pagés and Montenegro, 2007) found a statistically significant negative link between employment protection legislation and salaried youth employment, though there was an absence of a statistically significant link between employment protection legislation and overall employment.

The impact of different country rules of employment protection on youth inequalities (Table 14.3) depends to a great extent on their integration into paid employment via part-time and temporary contracts of work. Relative to adult workers (aged 25–59 years), OECD data show that young workers are almost always more likely to experience a higher incidence of flexible forms of employment. Even prior to the crisis, young people across the OECD were approximately twice as likely to be employed in part-time work as older workers and three times as likely to be employed in temporary work (Grimshaw, 2013, Figure 3.4 – 2006 data). Detailed country studies provide further information. In Japan, the proportion of young workers in part-time jobs is in fact relatively low: just 2 per cent for young men and 11 per cent for young women (Asao, 2011). Instead, temporary work is far more commonly experienced among young people as part of the school-to-work transition – 19 per cent of young male workers and 21 per cent of young female workers compared to 7 per cent and 9 per cent of all male and all female workers respectively. While some Japanese youth may be content with the match of job type with other obligations (such as education, for example) a substantial minority express dissatisfaction – around one in four youth in part-time jobs say they accepted the work because of a lack of regular employment type and this rises to more than a third of young men in temporary jobs and almost half of young women in temporary jobs (ibid., Table 2). Temporary employment is also very common among young workers in Latin America, with approximately 37 per cent of young salaried workers on these contracts in 2008 (weighted average of 14 countries) (ILO, 2010a, p. 190). However, the interpretation of these data is complicated by the fact that, as reported in Table 14.1 above, in Latin America most young salaried workers do not have written contracts at all, which in many cases makes it difficult to distinguish temporary from permanent labour market insertions. In the Netherlands, where part-time has almost become a standard employment form, young people are over-represented in part-time employment and are also the age group who most wish to increase their hours. Keizer (2011) finds between 11 per cent and 18 per cent of male and female young workers in part-time jobs (aged 15–20 and 20–25) would prefer more hours of work compared to 4–11 per cent of core age workers.

Finally, risk of weak integration of young people also depends on their length of tenure in low status part-time and temporary contracts. The OECD (2010, pp. 66–8) provides a valuable analysis through a focus on a group of young people it refers to as 'poorly integrated new entrants'

– those in a temporary job with little chance of moving into a permanent job. Drawing on EU Statistics on Income and Living Conditions (EU-SILC) data for 2005–07, the analysis suggests around 7 per cent of youth aged 15–29 who left education and found a temporary job were not in a stable job 24 months later. Spain had the highest share of 'poorly integrated' youth with 22 per cent (reflecting its high overall use of temporary employment contracts) and the UK the lowest (2 per cent).

Youth Wage Subsidies for Labour Market Entry

In many countries, wage subsidies have been designed and applied to encourage employers to hire young unemployed people. Given the high levels of unemployment faced by young people, together with a belief among some employers that they do not have sufficiently reliable market signals relating to the potential work performance of young labour market entrants, many governments implement youth wage subsidies in one form or another in order to equip young people with work experience and to provide employers with a less costly means of assessing their performance on the job (Table 14.3). While it is recognized that these programmes generally do not have a significant net impact on overall employment, several of them have been successful in helping the most vulnerable youth 'to jump the queue' and thus diminish inequality between youth and adults or at least between the most vulnerable and other youth.

One form of youth wage subsidy applies to the hiring of all young people within a certain age range and regardless of labour market status (that is, they may be in unemployment, just out of education or moving from one job to another). An example is the youth wage subsidy introduced in South Africa in 2013, which raises issues that are to some extent generic to all countries. The policy covers newly recruited 18–29 year-old workers earning below a low wage threshold; the subsidy amounts to 50% of earnings up to R2000, a fixed payment of R1000 for earnings between R2000 and R4000 and a declining amount thereafter (by comparison the monthly minimum wage agreed for the retail sector was a little over R3000 in 2014[8]). It is too early to evaluate the relative merits of the policy. Anticipated positive effects include a reduction in cumulative risk of unemployment among young people, improvement of young people's access to good jobs and improved prospects of finding a job once the period of wage subsidy expires. Unintended consequences, highlighted by South African trade unions prior to its introduction, include substitution of younger for older workers and 'destructive churning' caused by opportunistic employers who continually hire and fire young people to maximize wage subsidies (ibid., pp. 33–5). The former problem was addressed by excluding claims for subsidies where the newly recruited young person replaces another older employee.

A quite different example is illustrated by a raft of new wage subsidy policies in the UK, which in fact substitute for the payment of minimum wages. Implemented in 2011, the policies target the unemployed.[9] Both policies grant job search organizations (involving both public sector job centres and private sector contractors) the right to oblige an unemployed person to take up voluntary work for a fixed duration at a designated workplace on the understanding that they receive no wage payment but continue to receive unemployment benefits (as well as a contribution towards travel and childcare expenses) (DWP, 2011). The policies are controversial. While the government defends the work experience policy as an appropriate method to provide young unemployed people with work experience, it has come under fire both because of the harsh sanctions imposed on individuals who refuse voluntary work (leading to benefits sanctions of 13 or 26 weeks) and the use of voluntary placements in many of the leading high-profit firms. The schemes introduce a new segment of youth workers into the UK labour market, outside of national minimum wage legislation that covers workers.

Youth Minimum Wages: Regulating Decent Pay for Youth

The practice of setting a youth minimum wage at a lower level than the standard, or adult, minimum wage raises many issues for youth inequalities. Where countries have not adopted a youth minimum wage or have moved to reduce the starting age for the adult rate it is often motivated by a concern to avoid problems of age discrimination or to encourage the matching of pay with competency; moreover, as we described above, alternative policies may be in place such as wage subsidies that encourage employers to hire young people. By contrast, the persistence of youth minimum rates is usually justified by arguments about the lower productivity of young workers, the need to compensate employers for the costs of training investments, the dangers of pricing out participation in post-compulsory education and the need to respond to high youth unemployment (Table 14.3).

From an ILO perspective, the setting of sub-minimum youth rates potentially conflicts with its defence of the principle of equal pay for work of equal value as set out in the Equal Remuneration Convention, 1951 (No. 100) and the Discrimination (Employment and Occupation) Convention, 1958 (No. 111). In other words, rather than age, it ought to be the value of work performed that carries greater weight in determining the wage. The ILO Minimum Wage-Fixing Convention, 1970 (No. 131) therefore does not provide for the setting of different minimum wages on the basis of age. Nor, however, does it prohibit them, as Ghellab (1998, pp. 47–8) points out, since the convention allows for the exclusion of certain groups of workers on agreement with social partners, although subject to periodic examination in light of the principle of equal remuneration.

In their wide-ranging and detailed international review of minimum wage systems, Eyraud and Saget (2005, p. 48) demonstrate that the world is divided on the policy measure of youth minimum wages. They report that slightly less than half of the countries examined (45 out of 101) have a specific minimum wage for young workers set at a level lower than the adult rate. Among those countries with a youth minimum wage, the age distinguishing young workers from older workers varies between 18 (the most common) and 23 (the Netherlands). Most countries set one or two youth rates, typically for the 16–17 age group, although there are up to eight in the Netherlands. There are potential risks with the use of multiple youth rates. As young employees age, employers face a significant annual increase in labour costs and may be tempted, or pressured, depending on the context of labour and product market conditions, to substitute them with even younger workers. Wider age bands with smaller differentials between minimum wages lessen the problem of annual cost increases.

An important source of inter-country differentiation, and one that impacts upon debates about fairness and employment effects, is the level of youth minimum rates relative to the adult rate. Estimates of the average youth rate (a simple average of multiple rates where these are present) relative to the adult minimum wage range from lower levels of 53 per cent in the Netherlands and 59 per cent in the USA to upper levels of 85 per cent in France and Tunisia; note that the youth sub-minimum in the USA only applies for the first 90 consecutive days of employment. However, this averaging of youth rates obscures some of the very low relative levels set in certain countries for particular age groups (Figure 14.7). The lowest is found in the Netherlands, where 15-year-olds are entitled to a minimum wage set at a fixed 30 per cent of the adult minimum, and Australia where the newly established Minimum Wage Panel recently set a minimum wage for workers younger than 16 years old at 37 per cent of the adult rate.

An indication of the relevance of the youth minimum wage for young workers can be demonstrated by evidence of the proportion paid at this level (Table 14.4). In all countries shown, young people are far more likely to be paid at (or below) the statutory minimum wage than older workers. Indeed, non-compliance with the minimum wage is a concern in many countries, particularly for rural migrant workers in China.

The appropriateness of youth minimum wages remains a controversial

Table 14.4 Share of young workers paid the minimum wage in selected countries

Country	Source	Age Group	% Paid the Age-related Minimum Wage	% of all Minimum Wage Earners
Croatia	Nestić (2010)	<25	6.3	–
		25–34	3.2	
		35–44	3.6	
		45+	2.1	
		Total	3.2	
France	Schmid and Schulten (2006)	<26	–	31.7
		Total		100.0
Hungary	Köllő (2010)	15–20	31.2	0.4
		20–24	13.2	6.9
		25–64	10.8	15.1
		Total 15–64	9.6	49.8
Netherlands	Salverda (2010)	15–19	16.8	23
		20–24	10.5	25
		25–64	2.4	51
		Total 15–64	4.0	100
UK	Low Pay Commission (2011)	16–17	5.7	–
		18–20	7.3	
		Total	4.2	

Country	Source	Age Group		% Paid at or Below the Minimum Wage	
Argentina	Kristensen and Cunningham (2006)	12–17		70.0	
		18–24		20.3	
		25–64		12.4	
		65+		31.7	
Brazil	Kristensen and Cunningham (2006)	12–17		16.5	
		18–24		9.9	
		25–64		5.6	
		65+		6.4	
China	Du and Pan (2009, Table 5), reference to hourly minimum wage 2005 data	*Local workers:*		*Migrant workers:*	
		16–20	68.4	16–20	89.6
		21–30	46.5	21–30	74.2
		31–40	59.6	31–40	78.8
		41–50	59.6	41–50	83.4
		50+	47.4	50+	91.5
Mexico	Kristensen and Cunningham (2006)	12–17		25.6	
		18–24		6.5	
		25–64		6.0	
		65+		24.4	
Ireland	Nolan (2009)	<19		64	
		19–25		13	
		26+		2	

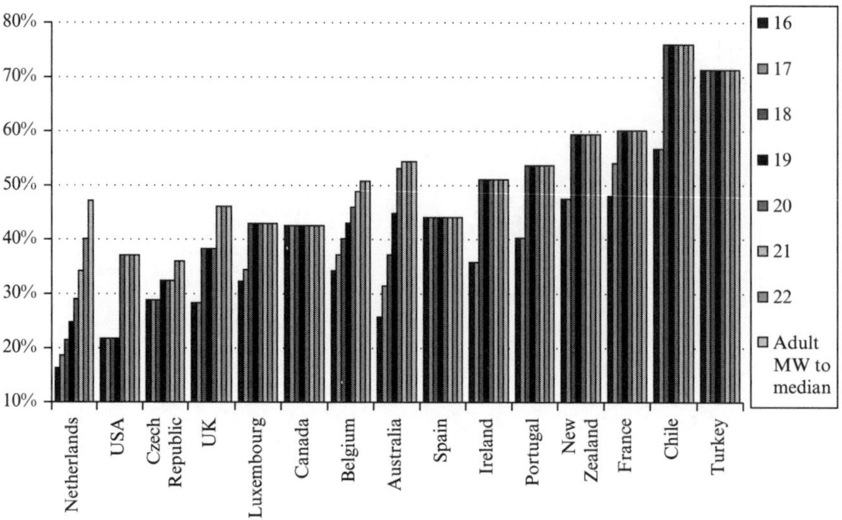

Note: Country selection on the basis of data availability. Youth minimum wage data are for October 2010. Minimum wage to median earnings are 2009 data. The sub-minimum in the USA only applies for the first 90 consecutive days of employment.

Sources: OECD minimum wage database and Grimshaw (2012: Table 4.1) for country details of minimum wage rules.

Figure 14.7 Youth minimum wages relative to median earnings of all employees, 2009

policy issue. Youth minimum wage policy raises several questions. Do higher minimum rates price young people out of the labour market? Do lower minimum wage rates for youth increase their employment chances? Does the use of a standard minimum wage encourage employers to substitute older for younger workers? Does a youth minimum wage pitched too high discourage participation in further education?

Numerous empirical studies investigate these questions, including the potential disemployment effects, substitution effects, gender effects and interaction effects between formal and informal sectors. The US literature is substantial (for reviews, see Ghellab, 1998; Neumark and Wascher, 2008; Allegretto et al., 2011). Also interesting is a smaller batch of country studies that were designed explicitly to interrogate the impact of minimum wage policy reforms on the labour market situation of youth. In Spain, for example, several studies sought to understand the impact of a reform that abolished sub-minimum wages for young workers; a single rate applied for 16–17-year-olds during 1990–95[10] and was converted to the adult minimum wage over a three-year period ending in 1998. Empirical studies point to mixed results. On the one hand, Antón and Muñoz de Bustillo (2011) find a significant negative impact on young workers aged 16–17 years old between 1995 and 1998. On the other hand, Blázquez et al. (2011) find no significant youth employment effects during the period 2000–08 (with controls for labour market context [including regional differences in wage structures and seasonal fluctuations in wages] and integrating a lag effect), and Cebrián et al. (2010) similarly find no evidence that the employment rate is affected, largely due they argue to the low level of the statutory minimum wage in Spain coupled with its low workforce coverage. With a similar policy goal of creating a more cohesive minimum wage policy, New Zealand reduced the starting age for the adult minimum wage from 20 to 18 years old and raised the relative level of the youth minimum wage for 16–17-year-olds from 60 per cent to 80 per cent of the adult rate (in two stages in 2001 and 2002). In their analysis of the effects, Stillman and Hyslop (2007) analyse household data for three groups of youth – 16–17, 18–19, 20–25-year-olds – for the 1997–2003 period. They report a statistically significant positive effect for hours worked by 16–17-year-olds (by 2.2 hours per week or 10–15 per cent), but also identify a significant drop of 3–4 per cent in hours of education, a significant rise in unemployment and in inactivity.

As with other studies (see Ghellab's 1998 review), the results of alternative analyses of policy reforms are somewhat conflicting. Reducing the starting age for the adult minimum wage is associated with the full range of employment effects (from a positive to a negative effect), but generally negative effects on unemployment and some evidence of substitution of older for younger workers. There is some evidence of reduced enrolments in education although other factors act as far stronger determinants of young people's education/employment decisions, such as the level of qualifications at age 16 and opportunities to enter trainee positions with government support. Raising the relative level of the minimum wage affecting young workers can have at worst no significant employment effect and at best a small positive effect, albeit with some evidence of negative effects for unemployment and inactivity.

14.5 CONCLUSIONS

In the public policy debate on youth employment, there are basically two positions. While some view the situation of youth unemployment and precariousness as serious and argue for measures to be taken urgently, others reckon that the youth unemployment problem is mainly transitional and goes away with age. Still, even in this second view, action can be taken to smooth the transition to work and to help the most vulnerable youth.

While labour market inequality between youth and adult workers is a robust finding in all countries, aggregate data hide very different realities among youth with regard to access to employment that can provide basic employment rights and a decent level of pay. While for many young workers, especially the better-educated ones, problems with labour market integration mainly reflect poor transitions that for the most part are resolved in the short to medium term, others are trapped between precarious jobs in the formal and informal sectors, unemployment and inactivity with limited long-term prospects. Evidence for Latin America presented in this chapter demonstrates that youth in the poorest income quintile face a high likelihood of being trapped in bad jobs, whereas those from wealthier households are far more likely to complete a successful transition into decent work. More generally, taking this longitudinal perspective, the concern with inequality between youth and adults is closely linked to inequality among youth and to overall inequality. Each young person who is trapped in a succession of bad jobs from youth through to adulthood represents a lost opportunity for the policy goals of reducing inequalities and maximizing human potential and capabilities over the lifecycle. There are also marked gender differences among youth who neither work nor study, with sex-disaggregated data for Latin America revealing that the share of NEETs is markedly higher for young women (29 per cent) than for young men (12 per cent) and among women in this situation, household tasks are the declared reason. As we know from other studies of developing countries, much of the problem relates to unequal access to education with low educational enrolments among children from low-income households, especially in rural areas and especially among girls (Huynh and Kapsos, 2013).

This chapter has also shown that young workers face a considerably larger risk of low pay than older workers. On the one hand, upwards mobility can often be high among young workers, as we saw in the case of Denmark where we find rising numbers of students in transitional low-wage jobs. On the other hand, young people may be concentrated in low-wage, dead-end jobs where casualized and informal employment, such as zero-hour contracts and family-based working, offer bleak prospects for skill development and employment stability in both developed and developing countries. An issue that deserves further consideration is the possibility that new models of work organization in knowledge-based, formal sectors of the economy may increase the openness of competition for jobs (e.g., through the per-task pay structure of 'crowd work' or unpaid internships) and thereby inject pay and employment uncertainty over longer periods in young people's early career stages (Marsden, 2007; Kittur et al., 2013).

Country variation in youth–adult inequalities, as well as in the form and degree of inequalities among youth, suggest labour market institutions are influencing factors. One of the problems lies in the abundance of short-term policy interventions and the relative scarcity of integrated, long-term policies. The success of youth employment policies depends to a large extent on the effectiveness of the wider architecture of institutions for employment. In countries where the main policy challenge is how to tackle obstacles to youth transitions, our analysis supports the need for further research into country experiences in the functioning of public employment (including training, careers and job search) services, with the aim of shortening transition periods and reducing the damaging scarring effects of unemployment and time spent in casualized and low-wage jobs. In countries where large numbers of youth are concentrated in low-wage jobs and upward mobility is low, then lessons need to be learned from international experiences of minimum wage policy. Key insights from our brief analysis include: acknowledging a wide variety of youth minimum wage rules, the potential for intersections with targeted youth wage subsidies, and the need to invest in resources to ensure high rates of compliance. Finally, the application of the deregulation debate to the youth employment challenge, in the form of the renewed insider–outsider discussion, generates a strong risk of both distracting from the main structural problems and obtaining spurious short-term gains in youth employment rates at the cost of longer-lasting precarious employment conditions and uncertain prospects for the future.

NOTES

* The authors would like to thank Bolívar Pino of OIT-SIALC and Jacobo Velasco for providing data, and two anonymous referees and Janine Berg, Sarah Gammage, Roxana Maurizio and Marzia Fontana for helpful comments on the chapter.

1. Unemployment data from Eurostat.
2. Data sourced from 'KILM 10, Youth unemployment: Figure 10c' (*Key Indicators of the Labour Market*, 7th edition).
3. OECD *Distribution of Gross Earnings of Full-time Workers* database, 2006; own compilation. Notes on data source at http://www.oecd.org/employment/emp/onlineoecdemploymentdatabase.htm; last accessed 4 September 2014.
4. These data have also been analysed in ECLAC and ILO (2012). The countries are Argentina, Brazil, Chile, Colombia, Costa Rica, Ecuador, El Salvador, Mexico, Panama, Paraguay, Peru, Uruguay and Venezuela. Data for Paraguay are for 2010 instead of 2011; Chile and Costa Rica present series breaks (methodological changes) that require their exclusion from some comparisons over time.
5. The proportion of women devoted to household tasks in the Latin American region has nevertheless fallen markedly in recent decades.

6. Low-wage work is defined as earnings that are less than two-thirds of the median wage for all employees.
7. This is not to say that all features of the German skill formation system work towards a relatively equitable distribution. The PISA 2000 survey results revealed large socio-economic disparities in education outcomes between schools due to streaming of children into a highly segmented secondary schooling system in a manner that was biased against children from a less privileged socioeconomic background; policy reforms have subsequently sought to remedy this bias (OECD, 2011, p. 18).
8. Minimum wage data sourced from Cosatu data, available at http://www.cosatu.org.za/docs/misc/2014/neilcoleman_llcnmw.pdf.
9. One policy covers all unemployed claimants regardless of age ('mandatory work activity') and another targets youth (16–24) specifically (four-week 'work experience' placements).
10. Prior to 1990 two youth minimum wages were set for 16- and 17-year-olds separately at the levels of 38 per cent and 61 per cent of the standard minimum wage (Antón and Muñoz de Bustillo, 2011).

REFERENCES

Allegretto, S., A. Dube and M. Reich (2011), 'Do minimum wages really reduce teen employment? Accounting for heterogeneity and selectivity in state panel data', *Industrial Relations*, **50**(2), 404–28.

Antón, J.-I. and R.M. de Bustillo (2011), 'The impact of the minimum wage on Spanish youth: evidence from a natural experiment', mimeo, Salamanca: University of Salamanca.

Asao, Y. (2011), 'Overview of non-regular employment in Japan', *JILPT Report No. 10*, Tokyo, The Japan Institute for Labour Policy and Training.

Attanasio, O.P., C. Meghir and A. Santiago et al. (2008), 'Better coating for the silver bullet: improving conditional cash transfers in Urban Mexico', mimeo, London/Washington, DC: University College of London/Institute for Fiscal Studies and Inter-American Development Bank.

Bassanini, A. and W. Ok (2003), *How Do Firms' and Individuals' Incentives to Invest in Human Capital Vary Across Groups?*, Paris: Organisation for Economic Co-operation and Development, accessed 3 September 2014 at www.oecd.org/dataoecd/4/8/34932892.pdf.

Blanchflower, D.G. and R.B. Freeman (1999), 'The declining economic status of young workers in OECD countries', mimeo, Hanover, NH: Dartmouth College, accessed 2 September 2014 at www.dartmouth.edu/~blnchflr/papers/DecliningYouth.pdf.

Blázquez Cuesta, M., R. Llorente Heras and J. Moral Carcedo (2011), 'Minimum wage and youth employment rates, 2000–2008', *Revista de Economía Aplicada*, **56**, 35–57.

Boushey, H., S. Fremstad and R. Gragg et al. (2007), 'Understanding low-wage work in the United States', *Mobility Agenda Paper*, Washington, DC: Inclusion and Center for Economic Policy and Research, accessed 2 September at http://www.inclusionist.org/files/lowwagework.pdf.

Cebrián, I., J. Pitarch and C. Rodriguez et al. (2010), 'Análisis de los efectos del aumento del salario mínimo sobre el empleo de la economía española' [Analysis of the effects of the minimum wage increase on employment in the Spanish economy], *Revista de Economia Laboral*, **7**, 1–37.

Chacaltana, J. (2005), 'Programas de empleo en el Perú: Racionalidad e impacto' [Employment programs in Peru: rationale and impact], *Diagnósticos y Propuestas Series No. 19*, Lima: CEDEP/CIES.

Chioda, L. (2011), *Work & Family: Latin America and Caribbean Women in Search of New Balance*, Washington, DC: International Bank for Reconstruction and Development.

Crouch, C., D. Finegold and M. Sako (eds) (1999), *Are Skills the Answer? The Political Economy of Skill Creation in Advanced Industrial Economies*, Oxford: Oxford University Press.

Croucher, R. and G. White (2011), *The Impact of Minimum Wages on the Youth Labour Market: An International Literature Review for the Low Pay Commission*, Greenwich/Middlesex, UK: University of Greenwich/University of Middlesex.

Cunningham, W. and J. Bustos (2011), 'Youth employment transitions in Latin America', *Policy Research Working Paper No. 5521*, Washington, DC: World Bank.

DWP (2011), *Could you Offer Work Experience?*, London: Department for Work and Pensions.

DIAL (2007), 'Youth and labour markets in Africa: a critical review of literature', *Document de travail DIAL No. DT/2007/02*, Paris: Développement, Institutions & Analyses de Long Terme.

Du, Y. and W. Pan (2009), 'Minimum wage regulation in China and its applications to migrant workers in the urban labor market', *China and World Economy*, **17**(2), 79–93.

ECLAC and ILO (2012), 'Youth employment: crisis and recovery', in *The Employment Situation in Latin America and the Caribbean No. 8*, December, Santiago: Economic Commission for Latin America and the Caribbean/International Labour Organization.

Esbjerg, L., K.G. Grunert and N. Buck (2008), 'Job satisfaction in a low-wage, low-status industry: the case of Danish food retailing', paper presented at the 60th annual meeting of the Labor and Employment Relations Association, New Orleans.

Estevez-Abe, M., T. Iversen and D. Soskice (2001), 'Social protection and the formation of skills: a reinterpretation of the welfare state', in P.A. Hall and D. Soskice (eds), *Varieties of Capitalism*, Oxford: Oxford University Press.

Eyraud, F. and C. Saget (2005), *The Fundamentals of Minimum Wage Fixing*, Geneva: International Labour Organization.

Genda, Y., A. Kondo and S. Ohta (2010), 'Long-term effects of a recession at labour market entry in Japan and the United States', *Journal of Human Resources*, **45**(1), 157–96.

Ghellab, Y. (1998), 'Minimum wages and youth unemployment', paper prepared for the Action Programme on Youth Unemployment, Employment and Training Department, Geneva: International Labour Office.

Gregg, P. and E. Tominey (2004), 'The wage scar from youth unemployment', *CMPO Working Paper Series No. 04/097*, Bristol: University of Bristol.

Grimshaw, D. (2012), *Decent Pay and Minimum Wages for Young People in Work: An International Review of Issues, Evidence and Policy*, report prepared for the ILO Youth and Employment Programme and the Conditions of Work and Employment Branch, Manchester, UK: University of Manchester.

Guarcello, L., M. Manacorda and F. Rosati (2005), 'School-to-work transitions

in Sub-Saharan Africa: an overview', paper for the Understanding Children's Work project funded by the ILO, the World Bank and UNICEF.
Huynh, P. and S. Kapsos (2013), 'Economic class and labour market inclusion: poor and middle class workers in developing Asia and the Pacific', *ILO Asia-Pacific Working Paper Series*: Bangkok: ILO Regional Office for Asia and the Pacific.
ILO (1998), *Chile: Crecimiento, empleo y el desafío de la justicia social. Un informe de las Naciones Unidas en Chile* [Chile: Growth, Employment and the Challenge of Social Justice. A Report by the United Nations in Chile], Santiago: International Labour Organization.
ILO (2007), *Decent Work and Youth in Latin America 2007*, Lima: ILO Regional Office for Latin America and the Caribbean.
ILO (2010a), *Trabajo decente y juventud en América Latina 2010* [Decent Work and Youth in Latin America], Lima: ILO Regional Office for Latin America and the Caribbean.
ILO (2010b), *Global Wage Report 2010/11: Wage Policies in Times of Crisis*, Geneva: International Labour Office.
ILO (2013), *Global Employment Trends for Youth 2013: A Generation at Risk*, Geneva: International Labour Office.
Keizer, A. (2011), 'Non-regular employment in the Netherlands', *JILPT Report No. 10*, Tokyo: The Japan Institute for Labour Policy and Training.
Kittur, A., J.V. Nickerson and M. Bernstein et al. (2013.),'The future of crowd work', in *Proceedings of the 2013 Conference on Computer Supported Cooperative Work*, pp. 1301–18, accessed 3 September 2014 at acm.org/citation.cfm?id=2441923.
Köllő, J. (2009), 'Hungary: the consequences of doubling the minimum wage', in D. Vaughan-Whitehead (ed.), *The Minimum Wage Revisited in the Enlarged EU*, Cheltenham, UK and Northampton, MA, USA/Geneva: Edward Elgar Publishing/International Labour Office.
Kristensen, N. and W. Cunningham (2006), 'Do minimum wages in Latin America and the Caribbean matter? Evidence from 19 countries', *World Bank Policy Research Working Paper No. 3870*, Washington, DC: World Bank.
Lépore, E. and D. Schleser (200), *Diagnóstico del desempleo juvenil* [Diagnosis of Youth Unemployment], Buenos Aires: Ministerio de Trabajo, Empleo y Seguridad Social.
Low Pay Commission (2011), *National Minimum Wage: Low Pay Commission Report*, London: Low Pay Commission.
Marinakis, A. (2009), *Costa Rica: Transferencias condicionadas a la educación secundaria. Notas OIT sobre la crisis* [Costa Rica: Transfers Conditional on Secondary Education. ILO Notes on the Crisis], Santiago: International Labour Organization.
Marsden, D. (2007), 'The growth of extended "entry tournaments" in the labour markets of knowledge intensive sectors in Britain since 1975', *CEP Discussion Paper No. 989*, London: Centre for Economic Performance.
Martínez Franzoni, J. and D. Sánchez-Ancochea (2013), *Good Jobs and Social Services: How Costa Rica Achieved the Elusive Double Incorporation*, London: Palgrave Macmillan.
Mason, G. and W. Salverda (2010), 'Low pay, working conditions and living standards', in J. Gautié and J. Schmitt (eds), *Low-wage Work in the Wealthy World*, New York: Russell Sage Foundation.

Matsumoto, M. and S. Elder (2010), 'Characterizing the school-to-work transitions of young men and women: evidence from the ILO school-to-work transition surveys', *Employment Working Paper No. 51*, Geneva: International Labour Office.

Maurizio, R. (2011), 'Trayectorias laborales de los jóvenes en Argentina: ¿Dificultades en el mercado de trabajo o carrera laboral ascendente?' [Career paths of young people in Argentina: difficulties in the labor market or upward career?], *Serie Macroeconomía del Desarrollo No. 109*, Santiago: United Nations Commission for Latin America and the Caribbean.

Ministerio de Trabajo y Previsión Social (2011), *Informe Final de la Comisión Revisora del Sistema de Capacitación e Intermediación Laboral* [Final Review of the Commission Training System and Labor Intermediation Report], Santiago: Ministerio de Trabajo y Previsión Social.

Nestić, D. (2010), 'Croatia: moving towards a more active minimum wage policy', in D. Vaughan-Whitehead (ed.), *The Minimum Wage Revisited in the Enlarged EU*, Cheltenham, UK and Northampton, MA, USA/Geneva: Edward Elgar Publishing/International Labour Office.

Neumark, D. and W.L. Wascher (2008), *Minimum Wages*, Cambridge, MA: MIT Press.

Noelke, C. (2011), *The Consequences of Employment Protection Legislation for the Youth Labour Market*: Mannheim: Mannheimer Zentrum für Europäische Sozialforschung.

Nolan, B. (2009), 'Ireland: a successful minimum wage implementation?', in D. Vaughan-Whitehead (ed.), *The Minimum Wage Revisited in the Enlarged EU*, Cheltenham, UK and Northampton, MA, USA/Geneva: Edward Elgar Publishing/International Labour Office.

OECD (1994), *The OECD Jobs Strategy*, Paris: Organisation for Economic Co-operation and Development.

OECD (2006), *Employment Outlook*, Paris: Organisation for Economic Co-operation and Development.

OECD (2008), *Education at a Glance 2008: OECD Indicators*: Paris: Organisation for Economic Co-operation and Development.

OECD (2010), *Off to a Good Start? Jobs for Youth*, Paris: Organisation for Economic Co-operation and Development.

OECD (2011), *Education at a Glance 2011: OECD Indicators*, Paris: Organisation for Economic Co-operation and Development.

OECD (2013), *Employment Outlook*, Paris: Organisation for Economic Co-operation and Development.

Pagés, C. and C. Montenegro (2007), 'Job security and the age-composition of employment: evidence from Chile', *Estudios de Economía*, **34**(2), 109–39.

Paz, J. (2012), 'El desempleo juvenil en la Argentina durante la recuperación económica' [Youth unemployment in Argentina during the economic recovery], *Documento de Trabajo*, Salta: Instituto de Estudios Laborales y del Desarrollo Económico.

Pedersini, R. (2010), *Trade Union Strategies to Recruit New Groups of Workers*: Dublin: European Foundation for the Improvement of Living and Working Conditions, accessed 2 September 2014 at www.eurofound.europa.eu/eiro/studies/tn0901028S/tn0901028s.htm.

Quintini, G. and S. Martin (2006), 'Starting well or losing their way? The position of youth in the labour market in OECD countries', *OECD Social, Employment and Migration Working Papers No. 39*, Paris: Organisation for Economic Co-operation and Development.

Rehfeldt, U. (2010), *Trade Union Strategies to Recruit New Groups of Workers – France*, Dublin: European Foundation for the Improvement of Living and Working Conditions, accessed 2 September 2014 at www.eurofound.europa.eu/eiro/studies/tn0901028S/fr0901029q.htm.

Rubery, J. (2011), 'Towards a gendering of the labour market regulation debate', *Cambridge Journal of Economics*, **35**(6), 1103–26.

Rubery, J. and D. Grimshaw (2003), *The Organisation of Employment: An International Perspective*, London: Palgrave.

Ryan, P. (2001), 'The school-to-work transition: a cross-national perspective', *Journal of Economic Literature*, **39**(1), 34–92.

Salverda, W. (2010), 'The Netherlands: minimum wage fall shifts focus to part-time jobs', in D. Vaughan-Whitehead (ed.), *The Minimum Wage Revisited in the Enlarged EU*, Cheltenham, UK and Northampton, MA, USA/Geneva: Edward Elgar Publishing/International Labour Office.

Scarpetta, S., G. Quintini and T. Manfredi (2010), 'A scarred generation: leaving school when recession hits', *OECD Social, Employment and Migration Working Paper*, Paris: Organisation for Economic Co-operation and Development.

Schaffland, E. (2012), 'Treatment evaluation of the "Bolsa Família" program on education', *Discussion Paper* (revised version), Göttingen: Georg-August-University.

Schmid, B. and T. Schulten (2006), 'The French minimum wage (SMIC)', in T. Schulten, R. Bispinck and C. Schafer (eds), *Minimum Wages in Europe*, Brussels: European Trade Union Institute.

Solow, R. (2008), 'Introduction: the UK story', in C. Lloyd, G. Mason and K. Mayhew (eds), *Low-wage Work in the UK*, New York: Russell Sage Foundation.

South Africa National Treasury (2011), 'Confronting youth unemployment: policy options for South Africa', *National Treasury Discussion Paper*, accessed 3 September 2014 at http://www.treasury.gov.za/documents/national%20budget/2011/Confronting%20youth%20unemployment%20-%20Policy%20options.pdf.

Stillman, S. and D. Hyslop (2007), 'Youth minimum wage reform and the labour market in New Zealand', *Labour Economics*, **14**(2), 201–30.

Valenzuela, M.E. and G. Reinecke (eds) (2000), *¿Más y mejores empleos para las mujeres? La experiencia de los países del Mercosur y Chile* [The Need for More and Better Jobs for Women? The Experience of the Countries of Mercosur and Chile], Santiago: International Labour Organization.

Whitley, R. (2007), *Business Systems and Organizational Capabilities: The Institutional Structuring of Competitive Competencies*, Oxford: Oxford University Press.

Index